Literature and the Scottish Reformation

In memory of
Professor David F. Wright, 1937–2008

Literature and the Scottish Reformation

Edited by

CRAWFORD GRIBBEN
Trinity College Dublin, Ireland

and

DAVID GEORGE MULLAN
Cape Breton University, Canada

ASHGATE

Published by
Ashgate Publishing Limited
Wey Court East
Union Road
Farnham
Surrey, GU9 7PT
England

Ashgate Publishing Company
Suite 420
101 Cherry Street
Burlington
VT 05401–4405
USA

www.ashgate.com

British Library Cataloguing in Publication Data
Literature and the Scottish Reformation.
      – (St Andrews studies in Reformation history)
      1. Christian literature, English – History and criticism 2. English literature
      – Early modern, 1500–1700 – History and criticism 3. English literature
      – Scottish authors – History and criticism 4. Scottish literature – To 1700 –
      History and criticism 5. Religion and literature – Scotland – History – 16th
      century 6. Reformation – Scotland
      I. Gribben, Crawford II. Mullan, David George
      820.9'382'09031

Library of Congress Cataloging-in-Publication Data
Literature and the Scottish Reformation / [edited by] Crawford Gribben and
      David George Mullan.
          p. cm. – (St. Andrews studies in Reformation history)
      Includes index.
      ISBN 978–0–7546–6715–5 (alk. paper)
      1. Reformation – Scotland. 2. Scottish literature – To 1700 – History and
      criticism.
      I. Gribben, Crawford. II. Mullan, David George.

      BR385.L58 2008
      274.11'06–dc22

                                                                2008035800

ISBN 978–07546–6715–5

Mixed Sources
Product group from well-managed
forests and other controlled sources
www.fsc.org Cert no. SA-COC-1565
© 1996 Forest Stewardship Council
FSC

Printed and bound in Great Britain by
MPG Books Ltd, Bodmin, Cornwall.

Contents

Contributors

David Allan is Reader in History at the University of St Andrews and the author of numerous studies of the intellectual history of early modern Scotland, including *Philosophy and Politics in Later Stuart Scotland: Neo-Stoicism, Culture and Ideology in an Age of Crisis, 1540–1690*.

Rudolph P. Almasy is Professor of English at Eberly College of Arts and Sciences, West Virginia University. He is the author of a number of studies on the literature of the English and Scottish reformations.

Marina Dossena is Professor of English Language at the University of Bergamo. She is the author of *Scotticisms in Grammar and Vocabulary* and is editor of the Online Bibliography of Scots and Scottish English.

Martin Holt Dotterweich earned his PhD at New College, Edinburgh, where he wrote a thesis on 'The emergence of evangelical theology in Scotland to 1550'. He is Associate Professor of History at King College, Bristol, Tennessee.

Kenneth D. Farrow is the author of *John Knox: Reformation Rhetoric and the Traditions of Scots Prose, 1490–1570*, and is currently in receipt of a larger research grant from the British Academy, to work on the writings of Alexander Scott.

Crawford Gribben is Long Room Hub Senior Lecturer in Early Modern Print Culture at Trinity College Dublin. He is the author of *God's Irishmen: Theological Debates in Cromwellian Ireland* and a number of other studies of literature and theology in early modern Scotland and Ireland.

David George Mullan is Professor of History and Religious Studies at Cape Breton University in Nova Scotia. He is the author or editor of five books on early-modern Scotland, and is currently completing a study of religious narrative in the period.

Amanda J. Piesse is a Senior Lecturer in early modern literature at Trinity College, Dublin, and a Fellow of the College. She is editor of *Sixteenth-century identities* and is author of various articles of early modern and children's literature.

David Reid recently retired from the Department of English Studies, University of Stirling. He has edited David Hume of Godscroft's *History of the House of Douglas* and *History of the House of Angus* for the Scottish Text Society.

Adrienne Scullion works in the Department of Theatre, Film and Television Studies at the University of Glasgow where her research and teaching interests focus on Scottish theatre and drama from the eighteenth century to the post-devolution period.

Deirdre Serjeantson is the Munby Fellow in Bibliography at the University Library, Cambridge, and a Fellow of Darwin College. She is currently engaged in a study of the religious and political aspects of early-modern petrarchism.

Astrid Stilma has taught English literature at the Vrije Universiteit Amsterdam, the University of Amsterdam and the University of Groningen and is now Senior Lecturer in Renaissance Studies at Canterbury Christ Church University. She is finalizing a monograph on the writings of King James VI & I and their reception in Protestant Europe (primarily the Netherlands) in the wake of his English accession in 1603.

Mark S. Sweetnam is a Government of Ireland Scholar at Trinity College Dublin, where he has completed his PhD on religious authority in the sermons of John Donne. His recent work includes a study of the significance of the Reformation of the Eucharist in *Hamlet*, in *Literature and Theology*, and of African missionary writing, in *Journal of Ecclesiastical History*.

Abbreviations

ODNB   *Oxford Dictionary of National Biography*
RES   *Review of English Studies*
RSCHS   *Records of the Scottish Church History Society*
SHR   *Scottish Historical Review*
SHS   *Scottish History Society*
SLJ   *Scottish Literary Journal*
SSL   *Studies in Scottish Literature*
SSR   *Scottish Studies Review*
STS   *Scottish Text Society*

Introduction[1]

Crawford Gribben

In 1692, 'Jacob Curate' attacked the literary conventions of the erstwhile Kirk party in his critique of *The Scotch Presbyterian Eloquence*: 'when they speak of Christ, they represent him as a Gallant, Courting, and kissing, by their Fulsome, Amorous Discourses on the mysterious Parables of the Canticles ... they have quite debased Divinity, and debauched the Morals of the People'.[2] Curate's analysis, loaded with the ecumenical hostilities of the 1690s, set the pattern for the subsequent reception of early modern Scottish theology. From the late seventeenth century to the present day, as critics have moved from satirizing the Kirk's licentiousness to complaining of its censoriousness, the theological literature of early modern Scotland has continued to fascinate and repel its readers. Modern critical orthodoxy has followed Curate's example in dismissing the theological literature of the period as almost uniformly unworthy of serious scholarly attention, imagining those interested in Calvinism as a vocal but unrepresentative minority; historical scholars, meanwhile, increasingly assert that Calvinism was a true 'religion of the people', and that even the bishops of the church to which 'Jacob Curate' apparently adhered shared the Presbyterians' basic Reformed consensus.[3] Early modern Scottish theology was much more universally Calvinist than has been imagined. Nevertheless, since the seventeenth century, the Scottish literary canon has been forged in a climate deliberately opposed to the theological ideas – especially the Calvinist ideas – that repeatedly appear at its heart. As Sarah Dunnigan has noted, while 'Scottish literary history ... still ignores, or misunderstands, the late sixteenth and seventeenth centuries', arguments for 'reforging the canon' must

---

[1] This introduction is developed from my essay, 'The literary cultures of the Scottish reformation', *RES* 57:228 (2006), pp. 64–82.

[2] Jacob Curate, *The Scotch Presbyterian Eloquence; Or, the Foolishness of their Teaching discovered from their Books, Sermons and Prayers* (London, 1692), p. 23. On earlier responses to the literary style of English puritans, see Larzer Ziff, 'The literary consequences of Puritanism', *English Literary History*, 30 (1963), pp. 293–305.

[3] Margo Todd, *The Culture of Protestantism in early modern Scotland* (New Haven: Yale UP, 2002), p. 83; David Mullan illustrates this throughout *Scottish Puritanism, 1590–1638* (Oxford: OUP, 2000). 'The danger', Mullan argues, 'is to be lured into the covenanters' view of things' (p. 1).

continue to be a canonical plea.[4] This is nowhere more necessary than in the scholarly reception of the literary cultures of the Scottish reformation.[5]

This scholarly misunderstanding – fostered by a canon-shaping rejection of Scottish Calvinism – has not merely been to the detriment of theological texts. As R.D.S. Jack has recently shown, the rejection of Calvinism's material cultures is part of a very self-conscious attempt by some literary scholars to construct the criteria of an 'essential' literary Scottishness.[6] Jack has noted how scholars constructing the criteria of canon have emphasized the importance of the Scots vernacular, unpretentious writing, patriotic themes, and a democratic viewpoint. Only those texts that exemplify these traits are identified as sufficiently 'Scottish'.[7] This myth of essentialism creates 'author-heroes' and 'author-villains', Jack complains, and, inevitably, 'makes it more difficult for some authors – for example, those who write manneristically in English on universal themes from a right-wing viewpoint – to enter the introductory curriculum'.[8] The multiple languages of early modern Scotland defy attempts to create a single or bi-vernacular canon, and, perhaps unavoidably, occlude the merits of many writers who represent important elements of the early modern national imagination. But scholarly pressure for linguistic and thematic conformity continues to overlook the merits of the neo-Latinists, like George Buchanan (1506–82), who took a respected place in international letters;[9] Gaelic traditionalists,

---

[4]   Sarah Dunnigan, review of Theo van Heijnsbergen and Nicola Royan (eds), *Literature, Letters and the Canonical in early modern Scotland* (East Linton: Tuckwell, 2002), in *SSR* 4:2 (2003), p. 143. Thus R.D.S. Jack attempts to 'redefine the accepted canon', in 'Where stands Scottish literature now?', in R.D.S. Jack and P.A.T. Rozendaal (eds), *The Mercat Anthology of Early Scottish Literature, 1375–1707* (Edinburgh: Mercat Press, 1997; revised, 2000), p. vii; and R.J. Lyall notes that 'even the best-established canonical judgements serve ideological purposes'; "A new maid channoun?': Redefining the canonical in medieval and Renaissance Scottish literature', *SSL* 26 (1991), p. 1.

[5]   The literary cultures of European reformations are surveyed in Brian Cummings, *The Literary Culture of the Reformation: Grace and Grammar* (Oxford: OUP, 2002). On the recent scholarship of early modern Scotland, see A.I. Macinnes, 'Early modern Scotland: The current state of play', *SHR* 73 (1994), pp. 30–46.

[6]   Jack, 'Where stands Scottish literature now?', p. xi.

[7]   On the eclipse of Scots vernacular, see Amy J. Devitt, *Standardizing Written English: Diffusion in the Case of Scotland, 1520–1659* (Cambridge: CUP, 1989).

[8]   Jack, 'Where stands Scottish literature now?', p. xi.

[9]   This culture is illustrated in Christopher A. Upton, 'National internationalism: Scottish literature and the European audience in the seventeenth century', *SSL* 26 (1991), pp. 218–25; David Allan, *Philosophy and Politics in Later Stuart Scotland: Neo-Stoicism, Culture and Ideology in an Age of Crisis, 1540–1690* (East Linton: Tuckwell, 2000); and Tom Hubbard, 'Early Scottish internationalism through translation: Landmark records in the Bibliography of Scottish Literature in Translation (BOSLIT)', *Scottish Language*, 22 (2003), pp. 36–45.

such as Niall MacMhuirich (1637–1726);[10] and Anglo-centric writers
like William Drummond of Hawthornden (1585–1649), whose writing
continues to be more widely celebrated (or at least anthologized) outside
Scotland than inside it.[11] It inverts contemporary values, elevating to
the 'Scottish literary tradition' the unrepresentative prose of Sir Thomas
Urquhart (1611–60), which, David Reid complains, 'is a freak compound
of all that Scottish prose after Knox is not'.[12] And, because of its anxiety to
measure Scottish culture by the genres popular in the south, it finds space
for the drama of Sir David Lindsay, and elevates its importance far beyond
that recognized by Lindsay's contemporaries.[13]

But traditional critical orthodoxy presses on regardless, listing
Drummond with James VI and John Knox as the three arch-villains of
the Scottish literary establishment, an unholy trinity who presided over
vernacular writing as it slipped ever closer to the abyss of standard
English.[14] Combine Knox's linguistic opportunism, and its undermining
of the Scots language, with his Calvinism, and its repression of traditional
Scottish culture, and early modern religious writing starts at a serious
disadvantage in the race for canonical status.[15] But Calvinist writers have
not merely been disadvantaged; their elevation to canonical status has
been explicitly forbidden. When opposition to Calvinism is itself identified
as part of the criteria of Scottish essentialism, those writers concerned to
articulate their voice within religious parameters discover that there is no
room for them at the canonical inn. But, at the very least, there ought to
be room for them in the writing of Scottish literary history.

In this respect, therefore, the challenge to accepted historical narratives
issued by Edwin Muir and Hugh MacDiarmid during the twentieth-

---

[10] Derick Thomson, 'The Poetry of Niall MacMhuirich', *Transactions of the Gaelic
Society of Inverness*, 46 (1970), pp. 281–307.

[11] Jack, 'Where stands Scottish literature now?', p. ix.

[12] David Reid, 'Prose after Knox', in R.D.S. Jack (ed.), *The History of Scottish
Literature: Origins to 1660 (Medieval and Renaissance)* (Aberdeen: Aberdeen University
Press, 1988), p. 195.

[13] On Lindsay, see David Reid, 'Rule and Misrule in Lindsay's *Thrie Estaits* and
Pitcairne's *Assembly*', *SLJ* 11 (1984), pp. 5–24; Greg Walker, 'Sir David Lindsay's *Ane
Satire of the Thrie Estaitis* and the politics of Reformation', *SLJ* 16 (1989), pp. 5–17; Carol
Edington, *Court and Culture in Renaissance Scotland: Sir David Lindsay of the Mount* (East
Linton: Tuckwell, 1995); and the essay by Amanda Piesse in this volume.

[14] Jack, 'Where stands Scottish literature now?', pp. vii–ix.

[15] The relationship between the Scots language and the reformation has been examined
in Mairi Robinson, 'Language choice in the Reformation: The Scots Confession of 1560',
in J. Derrick McClure (ed.), *Scotland and the Lowland Tongue: Studies in the language
and literature of Lowland Scotland in honour of David D. Murison* (Aberdeen: Aberdeen
University Press, 1983), pp. 59–78.

century 'Scottish Literary Renaissance' has achieved its worst success.[16] Muir's *John Knox: Portrait of a Calvinist* (1929) presented a searing critique of the cultural implications of the Scottish reformation, identifying the Protestant theological cultures of the late-sixteenth and seventeenth centuries as factors leading to the decimation of a rich medieval tradition: 1560 became 'year zero' in a Scottish cultural revolution.[17] In *John Knox*, Muir wanted to conceal his 'concluding generalities' to the 'comparative obscurity of an appendix', but the ideas he articulated have enjoyed immense influence:

> What did Calvinist Scotland produce during [the century after Knox's death]? In politics a long and wearisome series of civil conflicts; in theology 'The Causes of the Lord's Wrath,' 'The Poor Man's Cup of Cold Water ministered to the Saints and Sufferers for Christ in Scotland,' and 'Lex, Rex'; in literature the charming diary of James Melville, the letters of Samuel Rutherford with their queer mixture of religious feeling and Freudian symbolism, and the Scottish version of the psalms; in philosophy, profane poetry, the drama, music, painting, architecture, nothing. Whatever was done in literature during this time came from the opponents of Calvinism or from men out of sympathy with it ... Looking down on the island of Great Britain in the century which followed Knox's death, the Almighty, it seemed, had rejected Shakespeare, Spenser, and Donne, and chosen Andrew Melville, Donald Cargill and Sandy Peden.[18]

Throughout the next few decades, Muir elaborated on the theme. 'Scotland 1941' contrasted the 'simple' and 'rustic' medieval with the 'blighted' and 'starving' reformation, and rooted the parsimony of the modern in the dislocation of the past: 'Out of that desolation we were born.'[19] Hugh MacDiarmid went further, projecting a literary-theological antithesis upon the entire canon of Scottish writing. In 1940, introducing his *Golden Treasury* anthology, he claimed that 'our poets and our clergy have always been at variance', and the entire canon of Scottish poetry demonstrates 'that mock-serious poetic gibing at the Puritan regime which characterizes

[16]   For recent work on the religious contexts at work in the twentieth-century Scottish Renaissance, see Liam McIlvanney, 'The Scottish Renaissance and the Irish invasion: Literary attitudes to Irishness in inter-war Scotland', *SSR* 2 (2001), pp. 77–89; and Hanne Tange, 'Cooking and Calvinism: History in the *Voice of Scotland* books', *SSR* 3 (2002), pp. 72–85.

[17]   On Calvinism and the arts more generally, see Abraham Kuyper, *Calvinism: Six Stone Foundation Lectures* (Grand Rapids: Eerdmans, 1943), pp. 142–70, and Paul Corby Finney, *Seeing Beyond the Word: Visual Arts and the Calvinist Tradition* (Grand Rapids: Eerdmans, 1997). Significantly, Finney's book provides no discussion of Scottish Calvinism.

[18]   Edwin Muir, *John Knox: Portrait of a Calvinist* (London: Jonathan Cape, 1929), pp. 303, 307–8.

[19]   'Scotland 1941', vol. 2, pp. 5, 10–12, in *The Complete Poems of Edwin Muir*, ed. Peter Butter (Aberdeen: The Association for Scottish Literary Studies, 1991), pp. 100–101.

so many of Scotland's best poems (no matter in what tongue) throughout the whole range of our literary history'.[20] Whatever may be said about MacDiarmid's 'essential' Scottishness, his identification of a consistent 'Puritanism' throughout the entire history of Scottish Christianity seems, at best, reductive. Muir and MacDiarmid were reconstructing history along with the literary tradition.

Despite the evident weaknesses of their approach, the reading of the reformation developed by Muir and MacDiarmid has exercised immense influence on twentieth-century criticism. Tom Scott introduced his *Penguin Book of Scottish Verse* (1970) by noting that the seventeenth century was a 'poetic wasteland', in which 'few birds' were 'heard to sing, although the jackdaw clacked loudly enough in the pulpit'.[21] Here, the influence of Muir is obvious, extending even to the images of cultural wasteland and clerical jackdaws that Scott appears to have lifted directly from 'Scotland 1941'. Less obviously derivative, but equally assertive, are the opinions of Marshall Walker's *Scottish Literature Since 1707* (1996). Walker describes Calvinism's belief in election as 'absurd'; Calvinism itself is 'toxic'.[22] Substitute 'Calvinism' with 'Catholicism' and we find ourselves back at the same kind of sectarianism that called forth the Muir-MacDiarmid revisionism in the first place. This kind of analysis should not now be acceptable simply because the target of its hostility has changed. The bigotry of this new literary orthodoxy, like that of the old theological orthodoxy, survives only because it has been largely untested. As Walker's comments demonstrate, the new orthodoxy lacks nothing in confidence: if it has not the coercive powers of the old, it has lost none of its rhetorical barb.

Despite these strident tones, the Muir-MacDiarmid thesis does appear to have undermined its own purpose. The heirs of the Renaissance revisionists have become the victims of their thesis' success. With the elevation of their thesis to the status of a new orthodoxy, Knox's place in the modern Scottish imagination seems ironically assured. Critical vituperation has not displaced Knox from the national imagination, but has provided the theological literature he encouraged with a contemporary status it would not otherwise enjoy – Knox is now a very necessary 'other'. Simultaneously, there are also signs that the anti-theological bias of this critical hegemony may be moving into eclipse. A number of recent publications suggest that

---

[20]   Hugh MacDiarmid, 'Introduction', *A Golden Treasury of Scottish Poetry* (1940; London: Macmillan, 1946), pp. xiv–xv.

[21]   Tom Scott, 'Introduction', in Tom Scott (ed.), *The Penguin Book of Scottish Verse* (London: Penguin, 1970), p. 42.

[22]   Marshall Walker, *Scottish Literature since 1707* (London: Longman, 1996), pp. 99, 173.

scholars are moving towards a more balanced analysis of the period. David Allan has described how eighteenth-century 'North Britons' emphasized the barbarity of pre-Union Scotland and linked the intellectual flowering of the Enlightenment with the civility and sophistication provided by closer contacts with the South. Their means to this end was to exaggerate the claustrophobia and myopia of sixteenth- and seventeenth-century Presbyterianism.[23] Thus Samuel Johnson, for example, complained of 'the waste of reformation', the 'tumultuous violence of Knox', the 'ancient rigour of Puritanism', and 'malignant' Calvinism; but he also confessed that the Renaissance 'soon ... found its way to Scotland, and from the middle of the sixteenth century, almost to the middle of the seventeenth, the politer studies were very diligently pursued'.[24] The Muir-MacDiarmid thesis, however, lacked the subtlety of Johnson's ambivalence. Despite its nationalist claims, the revisionist thesis presupposed the accuracy of a long tradition of anti-nationalist propaganda, and provides yet another example of Scots colluding in the marginalization of their own culture. More recently, Robert Crawford has challenged the idea of 1560 as a cultural 'year zero' by illustrating the literary and theoretical potential of the iconoclastic temper at the heart of Scottish Reformed thought.[25] Patrick Collinson has likewise argued that 'the Reformation was awash with words', and that in Scotland these words contributed an 'immense creative as well as disruptive influence'.[26] The effect of his argument is a denial of the 'ignorant if understandable proposition' that 'protestant art' is virtually an oxymoron'.[27] A pattern of re-revision does seem to be emerging.[28] Scottish critics, following the lead of non-Scottish peers, seem, at last, to be coming to terms with their reformation past.

Although these developments have made some impact in historical studies, it remains to be seen how these changing theoretical perspectives will impact the study of Scottish literature. Some elements of a new

---

[23]   David Allan, Virtue, *Learning and the Scottish Enlightenment: Ideas of Scholarship in Early Modern History* (Edinburgh: EUP, 1993), p. 29.

[24]   Samuel Johnson and James Boswell, *A Journey to the Western Islands of Scotland and The Journal of a Tour to the Hebrides*, ed. Peter Levi (London: Penguin, 1984), pp. 48–9, 108, 79, 51.

[25]   Robert Crawford, 'Presbyterianism and the imagination in modern Scotland', in T.M. Devine (ed.), *Scotland's Shame? Bigotry and Sectarianism in Modern Scotland* (Edinburgh: Mainstream, 2000), pp. 187–96.

[26]   Patrick Collinson, *The Reformation* (London: Weidenfeld and Nicolson, 2003), pp. 27, 87.

[27]   Ibid., p. 155.

[28]   One signal of this change is the inclusion of a chapter on 'Theological literature, 1560–1707', in Ian Brown, Susan Manning, Thomas Clancy and Murray Pittock (eds), *Edinburgh History of Scottish Literature*, 3 vols (Edinburgh: EUP, 2006), vol. 1, pp. 231–7.

approach already seem to be in place. Knox's prose has been considered by R.D.S. Jack and Kenneth D. Farrow; Roger A. Mason's *On Rebellion* (1994) provided a much-needed critical edition of Knox's political writings; and the essays in *John Knox and the British Reformations* (1998) indicate the rapid recent growth of Knox studies.[29] It is unfortunate, however, that interest in Knox is still largely restricted to historians and political theorists, especially when, as Farrow claims, 'it is perhaps the literary critics who can lay fair claim to the largest part of Knox's canon'.[30]

The situation is worse in the study of prose of the seventeenth century. The Aberdeen *History of Scottish Literature* (1988) included an essay by David Reid on 'Prose after Knox'.[31] Reid noted that only three writers during the period developed 'elaborately mannered prose' – Drummond, Urquhart and Rutherford.[32] Despite its strong advocacy of the merits of some of the texts, however, Reid's essay did not provoke a wider renaissance of interest in these writers. Rutherford, in particular, has still to find his literary champion.[33] Other Covenanters have been more fortunate. David W. Atkinson has published pioneering work in the study of Zachary Boyd.[34] His enthusiasm for his subject has not prevented him from describing some of Boyd's poetry as 'exceedingly dull', although, he admits, the corpus of his poetry is 'not uniformly bad'; instead, Boyd 'must be considered one of the most accomplished seventeenth-century

---

[29] Ronald D.S. Jack, 'The prose of John Knox: A reassessment', *Prose Studies*, 4 (1981), pp. 239–51; Kenneth D. Farrow, 'Humour, logic, imagery and sources in the prose writings of John Knox', *SSL*, 25 (1990), pp. 154–75; Kenneth D. Farrow, 'The literary value of John Knox's *Historie of the Reformatioun*', *SSL* 26 (1991), pp. 456–69. Roger A. Mason (ed.), *John Knox and the British Reformations* (Aldershot and Burlington: Ashgate, 1998), pp. 6–7, contains a recent bibliography of historical studies of Knox, to which should be added Farrow's recent monograph, *John Knox: Reformation rhetoric and the traditions of Scots prose, 1490–1570* (Oxford: Peter Lang, 2004).

[30] Farrow, 'Humour, logic, imagery and sources', p. 158.

[31] Reid, 'Prose after Knox', pp. 183–97.

[32] Ibid., p. 186.

[33] John Coffey has provided a definitive intellectual biography in *Politics, Religion and the British Revolutions: The mind of Samuel Rutherford* (Cambridge: CUP, 1997). See, more recently, Alison Searle, 'The Biblical and imaginative interiority of Samuel Rutherford', *Dalhousie Review*, 85 (2005), pp. 307–20.

[34] D.W. Atkinson, 'Zachary Boyd and the *Ars Moriendi* tradition', *SLJ* 4 (1977), pp. 5–16; David W. Atkinson, 'Zachary Boyd: A Reassessment', in Roderick J. Lyall and Felicity Riddy (eds), *Proceedings of the Third International Conference on Scottish Language and Literature* (Stirling/Glasgow: University of Glasgow, 1981), pp. 438–56; *Selected Sermons of Zachary Boyd*, ed. David W. Atkinson (Aberdeen: STS, Aberdeen University Press, 1989); David W. Atkinson, 'Zachary Boyd as minister of the Barony Parish: A commentator on the late Reformation Church', *RSCHS* 24 (1990), pp. 19–32.

Scots writers' of English prose.[35] R.D.S. Jack has discussed the writing of Boyd's fellow Covenanter, Sir William Mure;[36] Crawford Gribben has examined the sermons of George Gillespie;[37] Gribben and Allan have each considered the intellectual world of Robert Leighton.[38] These micro-studies, though uneven in their literary interests, are important because of the lack of solid intellectual biographies of early modern Scottish writers and theologians. F.N. McCoy and John Coffey have each made important forays into the field,[39] but no other Scot between George Buchanan in the sixteenth century and Andrew Fletcher at the end of the seventeenth has been the subject of sustained modern biographical study.[40]

Despite this lack of interest in the religious writing of early modern Scotland, a discernable canon of theological literature has emerged. Over the last century, three major studies have surveyed the literature to vindicate their authors' often competing theological presuppositions. James Walker's *The Theology and Theologians of Scotland* (1872), John Macleod's *Scottish Theology* (1943) and Thomas F. Torrance's *Scottish Theology* (1996) have identified their subject as a battleground of competing ideologies. Whatever their merits, they are limited by their concentration on the Reformed tradition, and should not be used uncritically. Neither should readers allow themselves to be restricted by the 'canon-forming' interests of those publishers whose valuable work has ensured that early modern Scottish theological writing now has a larger readership than ever before. While a number of definitive critical editions have appeared, most republications of early modern Scottish theological texts, addressing a popular or clerical market, lack conventional scholarly apparatus. Readers would be missing a great deal if they allowed the essentialism of canon-makers, the rival concerns of historical theologians, or the commercial or ideological interests of publishers to limit the possibilities of their research. The literary cultures of the Scottish reformation were far broader than these competing canons suggest.

---

[35] Atkinson, 'Zachary Boyd as minister', pp. 21–2.

[36] R.D.S. Jack, 'Sir William Mure and the Covenant', *RSCHS* 17 (1969), pp. 1–14.

[37] Crawford Gribben, *The Puritan Millennium: Literature and Theology, 1550–1682* (Dublin: Four Courts, 2000), pp. 101–26.

[38] David Allan, 'Reconciliation and retirement in the Restoration Scottish Church: The neo-Stoicism of Robert Leighton', *Journal of Ecclesiastical History*, 50 (1999), pp. 251–78; and Allan, *Philosophy and Politics*, pp. 176–85; Crawford Gribben, 'Robert Leighton, Edinburgh theology and the collapse of the Presbyterian consensus', in Elizabethanne Boran and Crawford Gribben (eds), *Enforcing Reformation in Ireland and Scotland, 1550–1700* (Aldershot, Hants, and Burlington, VT: Ashgate, 2006), pp. 159–83.

[39] F.N. McCoy, *Robert Baillie and the Second Scots Reformation* (Berkeley, CA: University of California Press, 1974); Coffey, *Politics, Religion and the British Revolutions*.

[40] Coffey, *Politics, Religion and the British Revolutions*, p. 25.

The variety of the 'theological'

'Protestantism', Margo Todd has recently argued, 'is above all a religion of the book ... Particularly in the Calvinist version of the faith, the word – read, preached, sung, remembered and recited back at catechetical exercise or family sermon repetition – became the hallmark of communal worship and individual piety'.[41] Thus, as Brian Cummings has recently noted, a broad spectrum of aesthetic activity can be usefully classified as 'theological'. There is significant value, Cummings has argued, in juxtaposing sermons and poems: 'Without reference to religion', he claims, 'the study of early modern writing is incomprehensible ... Without reference to writing, the study of early modern religion is incomprehensible.'[42]

It becomes evident, therefore, that theological projects in early modern Scotland had vast ambitions. Refusing to restrict their interests to the world to come, they sought to control and even define the Scottish nation, allowing writers to develop a variety of genres through which they might realize that goal. Whether by the private circulation of manuscripts or by formal publication, the writing of early modern Scottish theology paralleled the writing of the nation, its politics, its economy, its church, its families and individuals.[43] The nation state was being defined by its formal theological convictions: proficiency in catechism, for example, was required in all those seeking marriage in the state church, and the beliefs of public servants were restricted by the state's confessional boundaries. But the success of the project to fashion Scotland as a 'puritan nation', so usefully described in Margo Todd's *The culture of Protestantism in early modern Scotland* (2002), is indicative of the extent to which varieties of early modern Scottish theology were embraced by and often internalized in the nation's range of languages, cultures, literary interests and religious preferences.

It now seems clear that Muir and MacDiarmid overstated the social hegemony of the Reformed church. While it is certainly the case that Reformed orthodoxy sought and often wielded immense cultural authority, and commanded the support of divines across the Protestant ecclesiological spectrum, it never managed to eradicate competing systems of belief: it existed in tension with an increasingly confident and well-organized Roman Catholicism; in the 1670s it responded to the sudden fashionability of Bourignianism; and some of its basic structures seemed

---

[41] Todd, *Culture of Protestantism*, p. 24.

[42] Cummings, *Literary Culture*, p. 6.

[43] Mullan has noted the close family connectedness of the 'community of saints', and notes the importance of manuscript circulation among this coterie. Publication was this group addressing a wider audience; Mullan, *Scottish Puritanism*, pp. 13–15.

questioned by the programme of the Scottish-born ecumenical pioneer John Dury (1596–1680). But the established church itself existed in flux. In the 1650s it split into two competing factions, each with their own General Assembly, and each claiming to exist as the nation's true kirk.

This kind of competition did not fundamentally challenge the idea of Scotland existing as a Protestant nation.[44] The construction of nationhood took place in the writing of histories, largely under the influence of Knox (c.1514–72), David Calderwood (1575–1650) and Robert Lindsay (c.1532–c.1580), Scotland's first vernacular prose historian. But while Protestants were attempting to fashion the nation in their own image, they were also defining themselves in opposition to the state. Scottish theologians used their political theology to develop a position of radical dissent. The 'two kingdoms' theory of Andrew Melville (1545–1622) was allied with the resistance theories pioneered by Knox, George Buchanan (1506–82), Christopher Goodman (1519–1603), Samuel Rutherford (1600–61), and Alexander Shields (1660–1700). The sheer ambiguity of this literary activity – affirming, controlling and even rejecting the identity of Scotland – challenges the reductionism of the Muir-MacDiarmid thesis.

These tensions permeate the writing of early modern Scottish theology, where theological flux merged with cultural flux in several important areas. The Muir-MacDiarmid orthodoxy, for example, has consistently pointed to the reformation's collusion in the Anglicization of Scotland. But the Reformed movement was not inherently Anglophone. James Kirkwood (c.1650–c.1709) and the Gaelic publications he sponsored illustrate the extent to which Reformed ideas could penetrate and dominate the largely oral cultures of the north and west.[45] Despite the educational ambitions of the Books of Discipline, neither English orality nor Gaelic literacy was required for the successful consolidation of the reformation movement in the Highlands and Islands.

The drive towards English was more evident in the south, where linguistic grievances were driven by sectarian tension. The Catholic apologist Ninian Winzet (c.1518–92) criticized Knox's Anglicized style as part of a wider project to strip the Reformed movement of its patriotic credentials, and the Catholic party in general 'made a point of writing

---

[44]   The following discussion of literary production is heavily indebted to relevant entries in Nigel M. de S. Cameron (gen. ed.), *Dictionary of Scottish Church History and Theology* (Edinburgh: T&T Clark, 1993). No attempt has been made to document individual references.

[45]   Jane Dawson describes the evolution of a 'distinctively Gaelic form of Calvinism' (p. 232), which survived 'with little help from the printing press and without a popular literate culture based on the printed word' (p. 253); 'Calvinism and the Gaidhealtachd in Scotland', in Andrew Pettegree *et al* (eds), *Calvinism in Europe, 1540–1620* (Cambridge: CUP, 1994), pp. 231–53.

staunchly conservative Scots'.[46] In the Lowlands, however, the evidence of surviving manuscripts suggests that although most sermons were published in English, they were often originally preached in Scots.[47] In fact, evidence seems to suggest that for many Lowland Presbyterians, the most serious threat to the culture of Presbyterian Scotland came not from the south, but from the west: ministers returning from the Ulster plantations were frequently charged with introducing innovations in worship, such as the omission of the doxology, and were soon charged with adopting an ungodly sermonic style. An English traveller had, in 1617, described Scottish sermons as 'nothing but railing'.[48] Surveying notes taken by sermon auditors, however, Todd argues that Presbyterian sermons were an 'interactive oral medium' that combined 'rather dry exposition of texts ... with intensely emotional and evocative language in exhortation'.[49] Robert Baillie (1599–1662) lamented their new and increasingly fashionable style of preaching, and accused Hugh Binning (1627–53), Andrew Gray (1633–56) and Robert Leighton (1611–84) of popularizing it more widely.[50]

Despite Baillie's consternation, the success of the Scottish reformation meant that God's word – in sermon and in Scripture – was widely disseminated in Scotland. At times it appeared that God and the Kirk spoke in different tongues. While preaching continued in Scots, sermons were explanations, more often than not, of an English Bible. Although Murdoch Nisbet (*fl.*1545) had translated the Wycliffe New Testament into Scots around 1520, his version remained in manuscript until its publication by the Scottish Text Society (1901–1905). The first Bible published in Scotland was a printing of an edition of the Geneva Bible published in England in 1562.[51] The sales of this 'Bassandyne Bible' (1579) were assured

---

[46] Reid, 'Prose after Knox', p. 185.

[47] Robinson, 'Language choice in the Reformation', suggests that this opposition may be overstated. The published sermons of Robert Bruce of Kinnaird are in Scots; *Sermons by the Rev. Robert Bruce with Collections for his Life by Robert Wodrow*, ed. William Cunningham (Edinburgh: Wodrow Society, 1843). *Cf.* John MacLeod, *Scottish Theology in Relation to Church History since the Reformation* (Edinburgh: Publications Committee of the Free Church of Scotland, 1943), p. 56.

[48] Todd, *Culture of Protestantism*, p. 52.

[49] Ibid., pp. 54, 50.

[50] Robert Baillie, letter to William Spang, 19 July 1654, in Robert Baillie, *The Letters and Journals of Robert Baillie*, 3 vols, ed. David Laing (Edinburgh: Bannatyne Club, 1841–42), vol. 3, pp. 244, 258.

[51] T.H. Darlow and H.F. Moule, *Historical Catalogue of the Printed Editions of Holy Scripture in the Library of the British and Foreign Bible Society* (London: British and Foreign Bible Society, 1903), p. 89; A.S. Herbert, *Historical Catalogue of Printed Editions of the English Bible, 1525–1961: Revised and Expanded from the edition of T.H. Darlow and H.F. Moule, 1903* (London: British and Foreign Bible Society, 1968), pp. 88–9.

by a law that stipulated that every substantial household should possess a copy. The next printing of the Bible came in 1610, when Andrew Hart, the Edinburgh printer, published a new edition, again in folio, with a revised New Testament and more radical notes on Revelation.[52] The third Scottish Bible was published in 1633, as an octavo edition of the new Authorized Version.[53] Only three complete Bibles had been published in Scotland in the ninety years since Parliament had authorized the reading of vernacular translations of Scripture.[54]

But the Bassandyne Bible was more than just a translation of Scripture. Designed to educate its readers in the technique of proper interpretation, it came supplied with some 300,000 words of marginal commentary that discussed manuscript variations as well as the doctrinal and practical implications of the text. The annotations were notoriously opposed to the 'divine right' theories of the Stuart monarchy, and, after his accession to the English throne, James moved to have the Geneva translations – including the Bassandyne Bible – replaced. When the new 'authorized' translation appeared in 1611, Scots were generally slow to abandon the old text with its useful interpretive apparatus. George Gillespie was unusually swift in transferring his loyalty to the new version. This may have been partly due to supply: the 'authorized' New Testament was first printed in Scotland in 1628, and the complete Bible, as we noted, appeared in 1633. But the supply of the Bassandyne Bible dried up after the last English-published edition of the Genevan translation appeared in 1644, and Scottish Protestants were left with a translation whose language and theological terminology was designed to foster Anglican (if not Anglophone) uniformity in James's three-kingdom ecclesiastical project.

If the voice of God was ubiquitous, projects to control the meaning of his words were almost as pervasive. Concerned by the unspiritual tenor of the land, the Kirk set about an ambitious programme of catechism to instruct the population in the rudiments of the Reformed faith. An indication of its early internationalism, the Kirk initially adopted the catechism prepared by Calvin. Liturgical innovations, on the other hand, were generated by domestic concerns. Perhaps the nation's most obvious evidence of

---

[52]   Darlow and Moule, *Historical Catalogue*, pp. 130–31; Herbert, *Historical Catalogue*, pp. 128–9. For a discussion of the various editions of the Geneva Bible, see Crawford Gribben, 'Deconstructing the Geneva Bible: The search for a puritan poetic', *Literature and Theology*, 14 (2000), pp. 1–16. The 1610 edition was a printing of the Geneva-Thomson-Junius edition.

[53]   Darlow and Moule, *Historical Catalogue*, pp. 170–72; Herbert, *Historical Catalogue*, pp. 167–8.

[54]   David F. Wright, '"The Commoun Buke of the Kirke": The Bible in the Scottish reformation', in idem (ed.), *The Bible in Scottish Life and Literature* (Edinburgh: The Saint Andrew Press, 1988), pp. 155–6.

reformation, the *Book of Common Order* (1564) dominated Scottish
church life until it was replaced by the Westminster Assembly's *Directory
for Public Worship* (1645). The symbolic importance of liturgical order is
illustrated by the fact that a Gaelic edition of the *Book of Common Order*,
translated by John Carswell (d. *c*.1572), was the first Gaelic book ever
printed in Scotland or Ireland, appearing in 1567. Translators were slower
to provide Gaelic worshippers with materials for song. Thomas Wood (*fl.*
1560–92) compiled the St Andrews Psalter (1562–66), the first metrical
psalter of the Scottish Reformed church. Paraphrases of other Scripture
passages were added in 1575. Popular hymnody – which was never allowed
in contexts of formal worship during this period – was provided by the *Gude
and Godlie Balletis* (1565), a Lutheran-influenced collection of sometimes
ribald verse that was republished in 1567, 1578, 1600 and 1621. Interest
in translating the psalms was not uniquely Calvinist. The Covenanter Sir
William Mure (1594–1657), for example, shared an interest in translating
the psalms with his Catholic uncle Alexander Montgomerie (*c*.1545–98)
and Drummond of Hawthornden.[55] Psalmody, nevertheless, was linked
to a wider puritan agenda during the wars of the three kingdoms, when
a psalter was prepared by the Westminster Assembly as a text designed
to promote the unity of the Reformed churches in England, Scotland and
Ireland. Its first draft had been prepared by Francis Rous – a Cornishman
– but Scottish participation was made certain by the fact that the General
Assembly looked at six revisions of his text before adopting it on behalf
of the Scottish church in May 1650.[56] The changes were so significant,
however, that Rous denied that the text was any longer his own.[57] Robert
Baillie defended their caution, arguing that 'all possible diligence' should
be invested in lines that 'are likely to go up to God from millions of
tongues for many generations'.[58] Subsequently known as the *Scottish
Metrical Psalter*, its versification of the psalms has exercised immense
influence on succeeding generations of writers.[59] When the Reformed
churches eventually turned their attention to providing Gaelic worshippers
with new materials for praise, those interested in the project were not

[55]   Millar Patrick, *Four Centuries of Scottish Psalmody* (London: OUP, 1949), p. 83.

[56]   Michael Chibbett, 'Sung Psalms in Scottish worship', in Wright, *Bible in Scottish Life
and Literature*, p. 145; Michael Bushell, *Songs of Zion: A Contemporary Case for Exclusive
Psalmody* (1977; Pittsburgh: Crown and Covenant Publications, 1980), p. 191.

[57]   Patrick, *Four Centuries of Scottish Psalmody*, p. 94.

[58]   Quoted in ibid., p. 93.

[59]   On the history of Scottish psalmody, see also Kenneth Elliott, 'Some Helpes for
Young Schollers: A new source of early Scottish psalmody', in A.A. MacDonald (ed.), *The
Renaissance in Scotland: Studies in Literature, Religion, History and Culture offered to John
Durkan* (Leiden: Brill, 1994), pp. 264–75.

always the most discriminating theologians. Robert Kirk (*c*.1644–92), an Episcopalian minister and Gaelic scholar, published the first complete metrical psalter in Gaelic in 1684, transliterated the Classical Gaelic Bible into Roman type (1688–90), and wrote *The Secret Commonwealth of Elves ... Faunes and Fairies* in 1691 (eventually published in 1815).

If Lowlanders were able to draw upon a wider corpus of Reformed song, they were also well served by developments in exegetical theology. Protestantism's intense focus on the word preached acted as a catalyst in the evolution of Biblical studies. This exegetical theology was assisted by the development of Oriental studies in Scotland. William Simson (*c*.1580–*c*.1625) produced *De Accentibus Hebraicis Breves et Perspicuae Regulae* (1617), the first book on Hebrew produced in Scotland. (The manuscript collection of George Strachan (*c*.1572–*c*.1640) proves that Orientalism was also an interest of Scottish Catholics.) This interest in cultural contexts is remarkably rare in one of the most ambitious publishing projects of the period. David Dickson (*c*.1583–1663), whose teaching of theology at Glasgow and Edinburgh wielded immense influence over a generation of students, pioneered a series of Bible commentaries designed for use by educated parishioners. They included Dickson's own commentaries on Hebrews (1635), Matthew (1647), Psalms (1655) and the Pauline epistles (1659); commentaries on Philippians and Colossians (1656), Galatians and Ephesians (1659), and the letters to the Thessalonians (1674) by James Ferguson (1621–67); commentaries on Revelation (1658) and the Song of Solomon (1668) by James Durham (1622–58); commentaries on the minor prophets (1654), John (1657) and Job (1669) by George Hutchison (1615–74); and commentaries on the Petrine epistles (1658) and Ecclesiastes (1694) by Alexander Nisbet (1623–69). Robert Blair (1593–1666), Robert Douglas (1594–1674) and Samuel Rutherford were also involved in the project, but their works were never published. Robert Leighton's celebrated and stylish commentary on 1 Peter (1693–4) was not part of Dickson's project, but mirrored its air of textual certainty, historical myopia and devotional application.

These commentaries – which were often little more than sermons that ranged throughout the orbit of systematic theology – paralleled the growth of native traditions in dogmatics. It is in developments in systematic theology that the intellectual life of early modern Scotland can best be seen in international perspective. Scotland provided the European academy with many of its most able teachers – John Cameron (*c*.1579–1625), Mark Duncan (*c*.1570–1640) and Robert Menteith (1603–*c*.1660), for example. While a number of Scottish Catholics found congenial homes in Continental colleges, many of the trends in Scottish Reformed theology were central to the intellectual development of the Calvinist international. Scots led the way in elaborating the federal theology that came to dominate

Protestant scholasticism. Robert Rollock (*c*.1555–99) provided federal theologians with many of the basic tropes they would develop as Scottish theologians progressed from the outlines of the 1560 Scots Confession to the more complex structures of the 1647 Westminster Confession of Faith (which, interestingly, was only translated into Gaelic in 1725).[60] But Scots were also active in the more abstruse of the theological disciplines. John Napier, Lord of Merchiston (1550–1617), was using Biblical data and the Sibylline oracles in an attempt to calculate the end of the world when he discovered logarithms; he published the results in his *Plaine Discovery of the Whole Revelation* (1593).

Something of the Bible's saturation of Scottish life and thought can be seen in the allusions and assumptions in texts that might not be considered formally theological. Biblical discourses are inescapable, from poetry by the Catholic Alexander Montgomerie to that of the Presbyterian Lady Grisell Baillie (1665–1746), from the diaries of Archibald Johnston of Wariston (1611–63) to the letters of Samuel Rutherford. While these informal writings lacked the scholastic rigour of a formal treatise, they were often every bit as analytical in their pursuit of the interpretation of Scripture and providence. Scotland may well have been becoming a 'puritan nation', but the sheer variety of this literary and cultural activity qualifies suppositions that the Kirk was ambivalent, if not explicitly hostile, to humane studies.[61] As David Reid has concluded, 'Calvinism … can hardly be blamed for crushing the Renaissance in Scotland.'[62]

Introducing the papers

The chapters in this book sustain these themes. David Mullan's historical overview situates the Scottish reformation within a European context of intellectual ferment. Scottish writers responded in complex ways to the breakdown of the European religious consensus, but, Mullan reminds us, their experience of reformation did not develop along an irreversible teleology. Conversion worked both ways, and some individuals oscillated repeatedly between the competing demands of emerging religious poles. Simultaneously, differences between Protestants were often as important as those that they cited to justify their departure from the Catholic Church. Marina Dossena provides a parallel argument, focusing instead

---

[60] On the theology of the Scots Confession, see W.I.P. Hazlitt, 'The Scots Confession 1560: Context, Complexion and Critique', *Archiv für Reformationsgeschichte*, 78 (1987), pp. 287–320.

[61] Atkinson, 'Zachary Boyd as minister', p. 19.

[62] Reid, 'Prose after Knox', p. 184.

on the evidence of linguistic change. Scotland did experience a process of Anglicization, she argues, but that process was slow, complex, and far from complete at the end of the seventeenth century. David Allan finds more rapid change in the reformation eclipse of neo-Latin culture. While Protestants continued to participate in a trans-national and trans-confessional linguistic exchange, others deliberately disengaged from this aspect of the European scholarly tradition.

The blurring of differences developed in these chapters on context is tested in a series of readings of texts. In her study of drama in the 1550s, Amanda Piesse considers the style of David Lindsay's theatrical writing, and its constructive ambivalence about the allegory that typified one kind of medieval exegesis. In style, if not in content, Lindsay's play moderates the divisions between Catholic and Reformed, even as it challenges the divisions between audience and actors. Acting – on and off the stage – was endemic throughout the reformation world. Rudolph Almasy considers Knox's fashioning of himself, as prophet in exile, in an essay that challenges many of the ways critics tend to read the Reformer's work. But, as Kenneth Farrow reminds us, these individual and national identities emerged from a situation of conflict, and his chapter turns our attention to the place of women in Protestant discourse, reflecting on the break-up of the exile community as its members turned increasingly to national and historical themes and concerns. This interest in pamphlet debates is a useful reminder of the range of literature discussed by the chapters in this book. Reformation Scotland produced a lively textual culture.

The next three chapters focus on that culture's most important nexus. The textual culture of the Scottish court is examined by Astrid Stilma, who considers James as a religious writer, deliberately constructing a solidly Protestant self-image as he gathered together his 'Castalian Band'. Stilma explains the complex relationship of state Protestantism and what is sometimes perceived to be James's Catholic sympathies. Perhaps the ambiguity of that relationship fuelled the religious experience of Alexander Montgomerie, who, as Mark Sweetnam demonstrates, articulated his mature Catholicism in terms that resonated with his Calvinist past. Deirdre Serjeantson develops the point, and demonstrates the evident impact of Scottish religious poetry on English devotional writing, as Jacobean 'Britishness' began to emerge. David Reid's essay, which concludes these textual studies, examines the response to James's Episcopalian movement in the aftermath of the Union of the Crowns and the collapse of a native Scottish court culture. Reid shows Hume of Godscroft returning to the humanism of an earlier period in an essay that anticipates the division of the Protestant church later in the seventeenth century. Two final essays consider the subsequent reception of the literary culture of the Scottish reformation. Adrienne Scullion focuses on the development of the play with which these chapters began, *Ane Satire of the Thrie Estatis*. Fittingly, her chapter describes the symbolism of its revival, and the enduring contest in the reception of much of the literature from this period, the contest between self-conscious heritage value and satirical parody, in Scotland's changing political contexts. Martin Dotterweich's essay on the complexities of establishing a text of Scripture in the Scottish reformation brings the volume to a suitably symbolic conclusion.

Conclusion

As these chapters demonstrate, therefore, the varied and complex theological literature of early modern Scotland generated immense cultural authority. The state struggled to contain the interests of both pro- and anti-reformation readers. Printers were regularly imprisoned, but deviations from the state's theological consensus only rarely met with the ultimate penalty. Scottish Protestantism provided twenty-two martyrs for its cause. John Ogilvie (*c.*1579–1615), later canonized, was Scotland's only Roman Catholic martyr, and Thomas Aikenhead (1678–97) became a martyr for independent thought. He admitted to scorning the Trinity and the incarnation, but his appeals for clemency, based on his youth, went unheeded. He was the only individual ever executed by a Scottish court on a charge of blasphemy.

The authoritative aspiration of the theological cultures of early modern Scotland has provided a rich vein of inspiration for subsequent writers, as Dickson suggests. *The Scotch Presbyterian Eloquence* criticized the Covenanting movement's 'Fulsome, Amorous Discourses';[63] Samuel Rutherford's letters have been seen by some as 'bright with unearthly glory' and by others as 'offending against all sacred proprieties';[64] but this frisson has energized writers from Scott and Hogg to Liz Lochhead and James Robertson. Throughout this tradition, Scottish writers and literary critics have interrogated stereotypes of early modern theological cultures within frameworks provided by contemporary concerns. From the late seventeenth century to the present day, the identification of Scotland with its reformation experience has been systematically deconstructed, yet the influence of its old orthodoxy continues most obviously in those writers who, ironically, resist it. Muir and MacDiarmid constructed a thesis that

---

[63] Curate, *Scotch Presbyterian Eloquence*, p. 23.

[64] James Walker, *The Theology and Theologians of Scotland, Chiefly of the Seventeenth and Eighteenth Centuries. Being the Cunningham Lectures for 1870–71* (Edinburgh, 1872), p. 7.

is turning in upon itself. Early modern Scottish theology is still the denied but interrogated centre of Scotland's contemporary literary imagination.[65]

[65]   I would like to thank Carole Jones and members of the Graduate Research Seminar in the School of English, Trinity College Dublin, for their comments on an earlier version of this paper.

PART I
Contexts

CHAPTER 1

Writing the Scottish Reformation

David George Mullan

Mid sixteenth-century Scottish culture was dominated by a struggle between two versions of Christian faith and practice, the Roman and the Protestant. In this latter case, initial Lutheran influences gave way to Calvinist or Reformed.[1] The impact of Geneva grew after about 1550, and continued to gain strength with Andrew Melville's return in 1574. However, there were those, sometimes few in number, who might accept Calvin's theology but not his conclusions about ecclesiastical polity, and thus the later-divided Protestantism of Scotland would witness conflicting interpretations of events culminating in the Scottish Reformation of 1560. This bifurcation of the spiritual, moral, and political universe deepened over the decades, so that in the revolutionary period of the National Covenant, the same dichotomized view dominated the Protestant mind, even if the primary battles were now being fought between varieties of Protestants. Presbyterians identified Episcopalians and Arminians as Roman Catholics, and Episcopalians, who included all the Arminians, sometimes cast the Presbyterians as Jesuits!

Catholic Scotland made about 22 martyrs from *c.*1527 to 1558.[2] When the tables turned in the late spring and summer of 1560, Protestants lacked the overwhelming force necessary to suppress Catholicism; indeed Catholic benefice holders were granted two-thirds of their incomes for life, while the new Protestant church had to negotiate for a portion of

---

[1] When the word 'Reformed' appears with the upper case initial 'R', it refers to 'Calvinism' and other expressions of the Reformation in Switzerland, Strasbourg, and some south German cities, i.e. non-Lutheran. Likewise, 'Catholic' refers to the Medieval Catholic Church or the Roman Catholic Church; 'catholic' means either universal, or the church of Christian antiquity.

[2] Jane E.A. Dawson, 'The Scottish Reformation and the Theatre of Martyrdom', in *Martyrs and Martyrologies*, ed. Diana Wood (Oxford: Blackwell, 1993), p. 260n; and I have added to this list a Frenchman who had been in Scotland with the Duke of Albany and espoused Protestant ideas, for which he was prosecuted upon his return to France. *Journal d'un Bourgeois de Paris sous le Règne de François Premier (1515–1536)*, ed. Ludovic Lalanne (Paris, 1854), pp. 326–7; E. Haag and E. Haag, *La France Protestante*, 11 vols (Geneva: Slatkine Reprints, 2004), vol. 7, p. 381. The narrative gives the date as 1525, but the item is set squarely amongst other entries for 1527. See also David Hay Fleming, *The Reformation in Scotland: Causes, characteristics, consequences* (London: Hodder and Stoughton, 1910), p. 173, but who has misconstrued the French in writing that the man's servant died from his torments.

the remainder with the crown. Furthermore, at no time did the entire country become Protestant, and a steady flow of Catholic Scots continued to arrive from various Continental locations through the entire period. Noble families were pressured to give up Catholic loyalties, but the landed classes continued to harbour, and to produce new generations of, priests. The Protestant kirk was also subject to a number of internal conflicts. There was constant jockeying between church and state for jurisdiction, and this manifested itself in a division over polity – ultimately between episcopacy and presbytery. By 1610/1612 King James VI (and since 1603, James I of England) had restored the estate of bishops in church and in state (without suppressing Presbyterianism in all its operations), and his successor Charles I found high civil servants amongst the 13 (14 from 1634) bishops. James sought a greater degree of 'congruency'[3] between the Scottish and English churches, and to this end promoted liturgical reform. The most notorious of these Five Articles of Perth (introduced in 1617) was kneeling at communion, which evoked the bugbear of Rome in the fevered minds of Presbyterian non-conformists. James was relatively lax in his enforcement, but his son was not, and his promotion of 'high-church' worship and Arminian divinity led to Presbyterianism's accession to an aristocratic rebellion in 1637.[4] The church's own revolution was effected at the Glasgow General Assembly in November 1638 with the rolling back of all 'innovations' in belief and practice.

Right from 1520, with the papal bull *Exsurge Domine*, the emerging Protestantism under Luther's pre-eminent leadership found itself backed into a corner by a hostile papacy, and the Saxon reformer's hyperbolic reaction drove a wedge deep into western Christianity. As medieval commentators had already done, the Reformers took up the language of the New Testament about the Antichrist and applied it to the papacy. They identified themselves as the faithful ones, the remnant, the righteous prophets who suffered for their obedience to God; the pope was in league with the devil, and now sat on the seven hills as the whore of Babylon, leading the people to perdition and making martyrs of the godly. In fact Protestantism could not exist without this simple dualism – good and evil, light and darkness, papal and Protestant churches – and the next several generations would find themselves captive to this schema, adapting the theology of historical periodization supplied by the author of the Apocalypse.

In those parts of Europe where Protestantism made permanent inroads upon religious culture, a number of features may be identified. First, the

---

[3]   John Morrill (ed.), *The Scottish National Covenant in its British Context 1638–51* (Edinburgh: Edinburgh University Press, 1990), p. 8.

[4]   Laura A.M. Stewart, *Urban Politics and the British Civil Wars: Edinburgh, 1617–53* (Leiden and Boston: Brill, 2006), pp. 185–202.

repudiation of the papacy and its claims to religious hegemony meant the enhancement of local and national elites in an environment where new possibilities of social power were offered by the renunciation of the authority of the old church. There was no longer an international court to which governments and citizenry might appeal in a variety of spheres, though one must state that this limitation had a history which preceded Luther and Henry VIII. Now, titled aristocrats, borough councils, and monarchs were called upon to determine, to lead, and to enforce in ways not seen hitherto. The practice of religion was also challenged and changed. Wherever Protestantism prevailed, vernacular Bibles were printed and distributed, sometimes with results more dynamic than the issuing authorities had intended. Services were likewise conducted in the vernacular, during which the centrepiece was the not the altar but the pulpit, and the ability to preach immediately became the *sine qua non* of the new, frequently married, clergy, sometimes to the discomfiture of the magistrate. New forms of ecclesiastical organization appeared, especially the eldership of Genevan fame. However, the vultures gathered about the corpse of the old church, seizing its financial resources and undermining the ambitions of the reformed bodies. The fabric of the church was re-evaluated. Some church buildings – especially abbeys, priories, convents – were vandalized and destroyed. Others were surplus to requirements and so fell, whether in whole or in part, into desuetude and ruin. And what of freedom? Was the Reformation about an unleashing of the thoughts and passions of everyman (or everywoman?), or was it about liberation from a corrupt parody of the virgin bride of Christ so that one's behaviour might be ordered anew in public and private spheres by social elites exercising new powers of social regulation through an alliance of pulpit and council chamber?

If the early Reformers hoped for one outcome, it soon became apparent that the Reformation itself contained a number of ambiguities. These did not appear in identical form in all places, but nowhere was the Reformation a straightforward affair, and certainly not in Scotland, where the writing of the history of that seismic event would produce, over the succeeding generations, more than a single narrative of achievements and failures.

Conversion and deconversion:[5] The Reformation

Reform was in the air by the time of John Knox's birth in 1514. The medieval Catholic Church had been reforming itself for centuries with the

---

[5]   John D. Barbour, *Versions of Deconversion: Autobiography and the Loss of Faith* (Charlottesville: University Press of Virginia, 1994).

rise of new monastic orders and the mendicants. Erasmus brought to a new height the impact of Christian Humanism in its quest for a more historically-informed appreciation of the Bible, a deepened spirituality which was not dependent upon ecclesiastical ceremonial and institutions, as well as a moral renovation in both the church's hierarchy and society at large. These ideas found keen advocates in Scotland. However, Lutheran notions very quickly began to seep into the country through east-coast ports like Dundee, and in 1528 Patrick Hamilton became the first Lutheran martyr in the country. In the year of Hamilton's burning, Sir David Lindsay of the Mount wrote his *Dreme*,[6] a lengthy poem in which he is taken by Dame Remembrance to the lowest circle of a Dantean Hell where he hears cries of the damned, including popes and emperors. He asks his guide why this fate should be theirs, to which she replies, 'couatyce, luste, and ambysioun' (l. 185).

> Als, they did nocht instruct the Ignorent,
> Prouocand thame to pennence, be precheing,
> Bot seruit wardlie Prencis insolent,
> And war promouit be thare fen eit flecheing,
> Nocht for thare science, wysedome, nor techeing.
> Be Symonie was thare promotioun,
> More for deneris nor for deuotioun.

There follows a condemnation of misspent ecclesiastical wealth and sexual misconduct, to which Protestant voices would add various doctrinal issues. Lindsay, most famous for his *Satyre of the Thrie Estatis* (1540), was tutor[7] to James V who might, had he lived longer, have manifested an interest in reform similar to that of his French father-in-law, Francis I. Lindsay's concerns are reflected in the resolutions of the provincial council held in 1549.[8] Then, in January 1559, Archbishop Hamilton (St Andrews) wrote to Archbishop Beaton (Glasgow) a letter calling another council to be held in the spring, noting that

> Lutheranism, Calvinism, and very many other nefarious heresies are being propagated everywhere in this realm by heretics, heresiarchs … who daily and continually strive with all their care, effort, and industry directly and utterly

---

[6] *The Works of Sir David Lindsay of the Mount, 1490–1555*, ed. Douglas Hamer, 4 vols (Edinburgh and London: STS, 1931–6), vol. 1, pp. 3–38.

[7] Carol Edington, *Court and Culture in Renaissance Scotland: Sir David Lindsay of the Mount* (Amherst: University of Massachusetts Press, 1994).

[8] David Patrick (ed.), *Statutes of the Scottish Church 1225–1559* (Edinburgh: SHS, 1907), pp. 84–134; David George Mullan, *Episcopacy in Scotland: The History of an Idea, 1560–1638* (Edinburgh: John Donald, 1986), pp. 4–6.

to disturb, destroy, and subvert the ecclesiastical liberty, the standing, rights, and privileges of the holy kirk of Scotland; but that by the removal of all errors and obstacles to the contrary whatsoever she may ever remain securely and peacefull as she ought in the unity of the Christian faith..[9]

The priest Ninian Winzet, schoolmaster at Linlithgow and finally abbot in Ratisbon, Germany, was a harsh critic of the faults in the Catholic Church. In his *Certane Tractatis for Reformatioun of Doctryne and Maneris* (Edinburgh, 1562) he asks the leaders of the church in the land: 'Quhat part of the trew religion be zour sleuthful dominion and princelie estait is not corruptit or obscurit?'[10] His view of 'reformation' implicated all the leadership of Scotland in a purgation of the accumulated impurities of the late medieval church, and recognized the role of all these in the latter-day appearance of heresy. But this acknowledgement did not lessen his severity in dealing with Knox and other Protestants.[11]

A modern historiographical survey, though somewhat confused about the chronology of reform in Scotland, notes the complexity and ambiguity of that most famous of Scottish reformers, John Knox. He was 'the greatest of his nation and period, although by no means the most attractive .. the leading figure in the politico-religious victory … [and] its chief contemporary historian … a Calvinist fanatic who never doubted his divine commission, never overlooked the shortcomings of a follower, never had a generous word for his Catholic enemies'.[12] His most recent student, Professor Jane Dawson, sees him in subtler and less peremptory terms and adds significantly to his humanity, describing an emotionally over-wrought man whose vision was dashed in the milieu of Reformation politics.[13]

Those who write about Knox draw attention to his self-image as a latter-day prophet, Isaiah or Jeremiah *redivivus*, though he attempted to moderate these descriptions of himself.[14] Such comment began contemporaneously,[15] and one Catholic writer, John Leslie, Bishop of Ross, alleges that Knox believed 'that him selfe was cum, as Johne the Baptist, Amos, or vtheris of

---

[9]   Patrick, *Statutes*, p. 150.

[10]   Ninian Winzet, *Certain Tractates*, 2 vols, ed. James King Hewison (Edinburgh and London, 1888), vol. 1, p. 5. See the essay by Kenneth Farrow in this volume.

[11]   K. Farrow also surveys the work of Quentin Kennedy.

[12]   A.G. Dickens and John Tonkin, *The Reformation in Historical Thought* (Oxford: Basil Blackwell, 1985), p. 70.

[13]   Jane E.A. Dawson, 'Knox, John (c.1514–1572)', *ODNB*.

[14]   Richard L. Greaves, *Theology and Revolution in the Scottish Reformation: Studies in the Thought of John Knox* (Grand Rapids: Christian University Press, 1980), p. 1. See the essay by Rudy Almasy in this volume.

[15]   John Durkan, 'Smeaton, Thomas (1536–1583)', *ODNB*.

the Prophetes to that office apostolick without signe or takne, and sa fra heuin to be elected'.[16] According to the controversialist Nicol Burne, Knox claimed an extraordinary calling like John the Baptist. Such was the public answer, but privately he said his calling came 'be gunnis, and pistolis'.[17] Presbyterian antiquarians offered effusive praise. John Row, whose father worked alongside Knox, writes that 'God used [him] as a principall mean and instrument ... being a zealous, godlie preacher of God's trueth; yea, I may say a verie extraordinarie prophet of God ... '[18] David Calderwood (1575–1650), the great Presbyterian historian of the Jacobean church, makes extensive use of Knox's *History of the Reformation in Scotland* (1587), and labels him as 'one of the first and chiefe instruments of reformation of religion within this Realme';[19] Robert Baillie, covenanting theologian, upholds the authority of Knox's treatment of predestination, along with the Lambeth and Irish Articles, and the Synod of Dort;[20] Samuel Rutherford cites him in *Lex, Rex* (1644).[21] Otherwise few writers not engaged in creating narratives of the time had much to say about him. An exception is the Presbyterian minister James Fraser of Brae who, when writing a spiritual autobiography in the 1670s, credited Knox, along with Patrick Hamilton and George Wishart *inter alios*, with directing him in a better way: 'I thought I saw another scheme of divinity, much more agreeable to the Scriptures and to my experience than the modern.'[22] John Erskine of Carnock records the death of his godly friend John Knox, in 1684, and writes that he was worthy of the name.[23]

Naturally, in view of his public profile which has long tended to obscure the contributions of his fellows, Knox became the primary target of Roman Catholic artillery. Leslie began to write his *Historie of Scotland* after his

---

[16]   John Leslie, *The Historie of Scotland*, 4 vols (London and Edinburgh, 1895–6), vol. 2, p. 467.

[17]   Nicol Burne, *The Disputation concerning the controversit Headdis of Religion, haldin in the Realme of Scotland, the yeir of God ane thousand, fyve hundreth fourscoir yeiris* (Paris, 1581), sig. 128v.

[18]   John Row, *The History of the Kirk of Scotland, from the Year 1558 to August 1637* (Edinburgh: Wodrow Society, 1842), p. 9.

[19]   [David Calderwood], *A Re-examination of the Five Articles enacted at Perth, anno 1618* (n.p., 1636), p. 1.

[20]   Robert Baillie, *Operis Historici et Chronologici Libri Duo* (Amsterdam, 1663), second order of pagination, p. 148.

[21]   Ian Michael Smart, 'The Political Ideas of the Scottish Covenanters, 1638–88', *History of Political Thought*, 1 (1980), p. 178.

[22]   W.K. Tweedie (ed.), *Select Biographies*, 2 vols (Edinburgh: Wodrow Society, 1845–47), vol. 2, p. 305.

[23]   *Journal of the Hon. John Erskine of Carnock, 1683–1687*, ed. Walter MacLeod (Edinburgh: SHS, 1893), p. 97.

Queen's deposition in 1567. He holds Protestant leaders in contempt: 'Paul Meffen a baxter, Harlau a tailzeour, Johne Douglas ..., ane apostat of a Carmelit, and sum uther proud clattereris unleirnet, to quhome the calvinistis becan [began] to propine [proffer, present], and draw thame to thair bande, and in thair counselis privatlie propyne thair haeresies ... '[24] Leslie refers to Knox as one of Calvin's apes,[25] and a contemporary Scottish Jesuit, John Hamilton, voices the slander that this 'renegat prest' 'was excommunicat for having ado with the mother and the daughter in ane killoggy [the bottom part of a kiln] ...'[26]

First-generation Protestant Reformers in Scotland, as elsewhere, were born into Roman Catholic countries and families, and they had knowingly and willingly abandoned their first experience of the Christian religion.[27] However, some who did convert went back again, and their stories remind us of the instability of religious commitment in the time. As Louis Desgraves writes of early-modern France, the two communities, Catholic and Calvinist, were enclosed within semi-permeable membranes, and there would be a lengthy history of to-ing and fro-ing between the two.[28] The Scottish Reformed émigré Archibald Adair writes of the arrangements made for the public conference with the Protestant du Moulin and the Catholic Cayer as being at the request 'd'une honeste dame, *flotante entre les religions*'.[29] That history would not be so noteworthy in Scotland because of divergent political conditions, but it is never the less to be kept in mind as one examines the religious conflicts and the conflicted religious folk of the time, as one can read in *The Confession and Conversion of ... my Lady Countess of Livingston* (Edinburgh, 1629).

---

[24] Leslie, *Historie*, vol. 2, p. 382. On Harlaw, see Mary Verschuur, *Politics or Religion? The Reformation in Perth, 1540–1570* (Edinburgh: Dunedin Academic Press, 2006), p. 104.

[25] Leslie, *Historie*, vol. 2, p. 464.

[26] John Hamilton, *A Facile Traictise* (Louvain, 1600), p. 60; excerpted in Thomas Graves Law (ed.), *Catholic Tractates of the Sixteenth Century, 1573–1600* (Edinburgh and London, 1901), p. 229. This accusation appears in Alexander Baillie, *A True Information of the Unhallowed ... Scottish-Calvinian Gospel* (Wirtsburgh, 1628), pp. 14, 40, who cites other sources.

[27] Richard Hudleston, *A Short and Plain Way to the Faith and Church* (London, 1844; first published London, Dublin, Edinburgh, 1688), p. 21: 'If any Protestant allege, in behalf of their succession, Waldo, Wickliff, Huss, &c I answer, first, they were all of them originally Roman Catholics ... '

[28] Louis Desgraves, 'Un Aspect des Controverses entre Catholiques et Protestants: les récits de conversion (1598–1628)', in *La Conversion au xviiᵉ Siècle. Actes du xiiᵉ Colloque de Marseille* (January 1982), p. 93.

[29] Archibald Adair, *Le Narré de la Conférence verbale, & par escrit, tenüe entre Monsieur du Moulin & Monsieur Cayer* (n.p., 1602), p. 7, emphasis added.

Even those raised in a Reformed culture were not immune to conversion to Rome. Nicol Burne relates that he had been raised 'from his tender eage in the perversit sect of the Calvinistis', and later became a professor of philosophy at St Leonard's College, St Andrews. He became a Catholic after God had delivered 'me out of the thraldome and bondage of that idolatrous Calvinisme, with the quhilk (alace) manie be ane blind zeal ar fraudfullie deceavit to the lamentabil perdition of thair auin saulis ... '[30] He reduces Calvinism to 'ane collectit mass of auld and condemnit haereseis', and accuses his opponents of treating Calvin as an idol and Beza as an oracle.[31] A brief chapter on predestination has Burne denying its Calvinist-Augustinian presentation, for God 'hes maid man to be man and not to be ane stok or stane', so co-operation is required from that person who would be saved.[32] He alleges corruption in the vernacular, i.e. Geneva (1560), Bible, 'be privat men not having commissione of the kirk nor knaulege of the scriptures, turnit in the inglishe toung, pervertit in infinit places...',[33] and its accessibility to the unlearned has resulted in various abominations. Of course, the Bible was the most vulnerable point on the body of Calvinism, and Burne goes after it:

> And I mervel that ye, quha estemis your self to be learned, considder nocht, that the Luaterianis, Zwinglianis, Calvinistis, and Anabaptistis admittis the wryttin word as onlie judge, and yit ye can nocht aggrie amang your selfis, everie ane of you aledging the wryttin word for his pairt, persuading him self that the wryttin word aggreis with that opinione, quhilk he hes alreddie forgit befoir in his awin brayn, even as gif tua men quha war in controversie about onie mater...[34]

Calvinists were undeterred by such criticism, and they continued to pour out a stream of exegetical works and sermons predicated upon an absolute knowledge of what the Bible meant; and no less were the laity encouraged to read the Bible in private and at the family table. The Jesuit John Hamilton asked in 1600, if the Bible is easily interpreted and should be read in every home, why then does one need ministers? 'War it not sufficient that everie man red his salvation with his wyf and familie in his privat hous, and send thair Ministers to keip scheip ... '[35] Ironically, when

---

[30]   Nicol Burne, *The Disputation concerning the Controversit Headdis of Religion* (Paris, 1581), Epistle.

[31]   Ibid., sigs 8v, 29v.

[32]   Ibid., sig. 6v.

[33]   Ibid., sig. 54v.

[34]   Ibid., sig. 109r.

[35]   Law, *Tractates*, p. 225.

the Jesuit Patrick Anderson was imprisoned in Edinburgh in 1620 and treated less than hospitably, he was refused access to a Bible. He repaid his Protestant hosts with ridicule for their obsession with it.[36]

Another Scottish assault on Protestantism comes from the pen of George Thomson, a somewhat shadowy figure whose footprints John Durkan has located in Ross-shire and in France.[37] The work in question is entitled *De Antiquitate Christianae Religionis apud Scotos* (Rome and Douai, 1594). Most of its three thousand-odd words are a paean to the antiquity, orthodoxy, and fruitfulness of the Scottish church. Apart from the question of Easter's proper dating and the appearance of Pelagianism, there was nothing to allege against the church's orthodoxy until the Bohemian Paul Craw met his condign punishment at the stake in 1433 for his Hussite beliefs. His act of betrayal was more than compensated by the work of famous men, not least among them John Major.

> But since they [Scots] severed themselves from obedience to the Apostolic Chair, they not only appear to have degenerated from their former worth, but those who before were famous and known to the world are now in truth, or seem to be, obscure. All who consider the former condition of the kingdom, and the greatness of the people when the Catholic religion flourished among them, are moved with surprise that in so short a space of time the kingdom could have so sadly degenerated. For although from about the year 1540 some seeds of heresy were sown in the kingdom secretly, and gradually too sprouted forth in the minds of many men, still before 1560 open defection had not broken out. From that time the kingdom was so on fire with civil wars, was so polluted with massacre and bloodshed, that nought else seemed to exist but a perpetual shambles. But God, who is not wont to check His wrath till it reaches its limit, has now after several years opened many men's eyes, and theirs, too, who enjoy almost the chief authority in the kingdom.[38]

He comforts himself with the belief that the pendulum has begun to swing back, with many defections now from Protestantism. James Tyrie's *Refutation* of John Knox (Paris, 1573) attacks reformers, 'heretikis', as devilish instruments designed to mislead people. However, it is by this means that God has seen to the 'correctioun of his kirk'. The heresies have by no means overcome the church, and in fact have caused its truth to

---

[36] David George Mullan, *Scottish Puritanism, 1590–1638* (Oxford: Oxford University Press, 2000), p. 46.

[37] John Durkan, 'The Identity of George Thomson, Catholic Controversialist', *Innes Review*, 31 (1980), pp. 45–6.

[38] George Thomson, *The Antiquity of the Christian Religion among the Scots*, trans. Henry D.G. Law, in *Miscellany of the Scottish History Society ii* (Edinburgh: SHS, 1904), pp. 130–31.

shine more brightly, as demonstrated by numerous conversions and moral improvement.[39]

Stories of persons who changed religion were not confined to the sixteenth century. George Leslie[40] was the son of a laird and grew up in a Protestant household. He was sent to Paris to continue his studies, in the course of which he fell in with the two sons of a French *seigneur*. Over time he was captivated by the Catholicism of his pious friends and underwent an emotional conversion experience – to the dismay of his mother who more or less disowned him. The friends' father stepped in and treated George as his own son, continuing his education and taking him to Italy. George remained in Rome, in the Scots College, in 1608, but soon decided to become a Capuchin friar. In later years he would become a missionary to Scotland, known as Father Archangel.[41] Robert Menteith, 'of Salmonet', studied at Edinburgh and taught at the Huguenot academy at Saumur in the Loire Valley, and came home still a Protestant. Later he was overcome by moral defect:

> Your bosome companion Mr. Menteth having deboshed a prime Lady in his flock, when no secret advertisement could break off that wickednesse, though a child or two were brought forth, the honourable friends of the Knight who was wronged, could keep no longer patience, but did openly crave justice, whereby Menteth was cast out of the Church and Kingdome, and the Adulteresse divorced from her Husband...[42]

He fled back to France, where he published *Histoire des Troubles de la Grand Bretagne* (Paris, 1649), and died a canon of Notre Dame;[43] a Catholic source notes him only as minister in the parish of Duddingston who 'became a Catholic in 1638, and was banished'.[44] William Stuart writes about himself or another Scot (John Walker?) who had grown up amongst Presbyterians but became convinced of Catholic truth and

---

[39]   Thomas Graves Law (ed.), *Catholic Tractates of the Sixteenth Century, 1573–1600* (Edinburgh and London, 1901), p. 21.

[40]   Mark Dilworth, 'Leslie, George [name in religion Archangel] (d. 1637?)', *ODNB*.

[41]   Jean Baptiste Rinuccini, *Le Capuchin Écossois*, trans. from Italian by François Barraut (Paris, 1650). He was apparently related to both Thomas Dempster and George Con. He was cited by the Privy Council in 1629. See William Forbes-Leith, *Memoirs of Scottish Catholics during the xvii^th and xviii^th Centuries*, 2 vols (London: Longmans, Green, 1909), vol. 1, p. 364.

[42]   Robert Baillie, 'The Unloading of Issachar's Burthen', p. 24, in *An Historicall Vindication of the Church of Scotland* (London, 1646).

[43]   Mullan, *Scottish Puritanism*, p. 221.

[44]   Forbes-Leith, *Memoirs*, vol. 1, p. 373.

converted.[45] Patrick Crawfurd left Scotland a Calvinist but fell in with Catholics in France and Italy, soaking up his new religion in a Jesuit college. His *Declaration of Mr. Patrik Crawfurd his returne from poperie to the true religion* (Aberdeen, 1627) was delivered publicly first at Irvine on 26 August 1627. Thomas Abernethy was likewise a cradle (if not completely sheltered) Calvinist, went off to the wars, came home a Jesuit, but turned again and was accepted as a Protestant at the General Assembly in 1638; his sermon on the occasion of his reception was published.[46] A letter from the Jesuit Scottish Mission in 1642 to the head of the order claims that two Calvinist ministers had converted, including a philosophy professor at Aberdeen who was then banished, and a minister with the covenanting army in England, 'where he accidentally fell in with some Catholics, who persuaded him to embrace their faith. He afterwards endured much obloquy and insult from the heretic soldiers, which he bore with patience and piety'.[47] One may reasonably be suspicious of these reports (there is no trace of the Aberdeen professor in *FES*), but it is clear enough that Protestantism was not something so magnetic that *nothing* could ever again escape from its field.

Past and present

Protestants might have taken heart in January 1581 when the King and his household, *inter alios*, signed the King's or Negative Confession. This document was a reaction to a perceived popish threat. It included typical Protestant denunciations of Rome: 'in speciale we detest and refuse the usurped authoritie of that Romane Antichrist upon the scriptures of God, upon the kyrk, the civill magistrate and conscience of men: All his tyrannous lawes made upon indifferent thinges, agaynst our christiane libertie ... ', and on it goes.[48] The interpretation of this text would become a major bone of contention between Presbyterians and Episcopalians, with the king siding with the latter after the Presbyterian high-water mark in 1592, to

---

[45] *The Presbyteries Triall* (Paris, 1657); see also M.V. Hay, *The Blairs Papers (1603–1660)* (London and Edinburgh: Sands & Co., 1929), p. 204.

[46] Thomas Abernethy, *Abjuration of Poperie* (Edinburgh, 1638); Alasdair Roberts, 'Thomas Abernethy, Jesuit and Covenanter', *RSCHS* 24 (1991), pp. 141–60.

[47] Forbes-Leith, *Memoirs*, vol. 1, p. 214.

[48] Likewise the rhetoric of the famous minister of Ayr, John Welsh, in his *A Reply against M. Gilbert Browne, Priest* (Edinburgh, 1602), 'To Maister Gilbert Browne Priest': 'It is a lamentable and pitifull thing, to see the glorious gospell of his deare Sonne our Saviour so obscured and darkned in this Countrey with the smoke of that kingdome of darknesse of yours, that hes ascended & come out of the bottomis pit, to their eternal damnation, who is blinded and deceaved thereby.'

the extent of resuscitating the Scottish episcopate. As Presbyterians noted, episcopacy came first, then came liturgical innovation (especially kneeling at communion) in the Five Articles of Perth, and then finally doctrinal revisionism in the embrace of Arminianism.

One may to some extent observe this process in the persons of some Jacobean bishops. In the *History of the Church of Scotland*, John Spottiswood (1565–1639),[49] Archbishop of Saint Andrews from 1615, embraces the Scottish church from its very beginning. However, his narrative of the Christian past contains some criticisms, as when he refers to Regulus's (fourth century) introduction of some relics of St Andrew: 'for in those times Christians did hold the bones and relics of martyrs in a respectful reverence; which doth in no sort justify the abuses which afterwards crept into the Church, when from the keeping of relics they grew to worship and adore them; yea, and in many places, priests out of their covetousness did use impostures, foisting in the bones of asses and other beasts instead of the relics of martyrs and saints departed'.[50] In this ancient part of the story, Spottiswood also appeals to another Greek churchman Palladius (mid fifth century) whose work as a bishop draws the Archbishop's commendation. In fact nowhere in the *History* is the very notion of episcopacy attacked; quite to the contrary, and criticism is limited to the acts of individuals, while those who attacked the institution itself are depicted as vandals. Spottiswood emphasizes the evangelical labours of his heroic figures from antiquity and their virtuous lives, like Aidan (seventh century) who, at a feast, would eat lightly and depart. He also writes that in the ninth century, King Constantine II called a convention during which steps were taken to reform the church: 'Thus was it not held, in that time, a diminution of ecclesiastical authority for princes to give laws to the clergy, and to punish them if they were found guilty of any offence or crime.'[51] In the succeeding century Kenneth III, having committed murder, was counselled to certain acts of external penance, but he conducted himself 'most piously, not thinking by these outward deeds of penance to make expiation for his sin; for men were not become as yet so grossly ignorant as to believe that by such external works the justice of God is satisfied'.[52] He notes the grasping nature of the papacy and the failure of some attempts at reform; thus he is sympathetic to the rise of reforming movements such as those bearing the names of Wycliffe in England and

[49]   Maurice Lee, Jr., 'Archbishop Spottiswood as Historian (1973)', in idem, *The 'Inevitable' Union and Other Essays on Early Modern Scotland* (East Linton: Tuckwell, 2003), pp. 158–68.

[50]   Spottiswood, *History*, vol. 1, p. 9.

[51]   Ibid., vol. 1, p. 52.

[52]   Ibid., vol. 1, p. 56.

Hus in Bohemia. When listing the Lollard articles he wonders whether they actually held to all the 20 points – Knox, followed by Calderwood, gives 34 – and in any event, 'granting that they held the same, we are not to wonder that in the first breaking up of the light, men saw not the truth in every point, considering the darkness and gross ignorance of preceding times',[53] an apologetic tone found first in Knox and also in Calderwood. So it is clear that Spottiswood affirms the ecclesiastical renewal heralded by the Reformation, and tells at length the stories of some of the martyrs, particularly George Wishart. However, there enters into a summary of late medieval abuses the following comment, that 'ignorance and impiety' abounded, until 'in end the laity putting their hands to the work, made that violent and disordered reformation' which he proceeds to describe in Book III. A Catholic writer refers to the iconoclasm in Scotland as 'that black reformation', blaming it on Knox, 'that sacrilegious serpent and venemous viper'.[54] In his letter of presentation to King Charles I, Spottiswood claims that ignorance of the Scottish church's history 'hath bred in our Church many strange mistakings; for did men understand how things went at our Reformation, and since that time, they would never have been moved to think that episcopacy was against the constitutions of this Church, one of the first things done in it being the placing of Superintendents with episcopal power in the same ... Consistorial Discipline [being] brought from Geneva some sixteen years after the Reformation ... '[55] Elsewhere the Archbishop contends that the King's Confession recognizes only that polity consisting of bishops and superintendents.[56]

Such warmth for the 'historic episcopate' was welcome in places like Aberdeen, but elsewhere fell on deaf Presbyterian ears. Calderwood wrote endlessly against the return of episcopacy. In *The Altar of Damascus*, he states: 'All the errours and heresies in doctrine and matters of faith, which have entered in the Church, could not have brought him [pope, i.e. Antichrist] in, unless errour and corruption in the government had entred in also; for unless this had been he could pretend no claime at all to governe and rule.'[57] In his *History* he includes a controversy between Bishop Cowper and the lay Presbyterian intellectual David Hume of Godscroft where Cowper defends the essentially episcopal nature of the Scottish

---

[53]   Ibid., vol. 1, p. 121.

[54]   Alexander Baillie, *True Information*, pp. 24, 25.

[55]   Spottiswood, *History*, vol. 1, p. cxxxviii.

[56]   David George Mullan (ed.), *Religious Controversy in Scotland, 1625–1639* (Edinburgh: SHS, 1998), p. 139, n.11.

[57]   David Calderwood, *The Altar of Damascus* (n.p., 1621), p. 74. This book was followed in 1623 by a much longer Latin edition, *Altare Damscenum*.

Reformation settlement, and which Hume denies.[58] Another Presbyterian minister John Murray writes of 'thritten [thirteen, the number of bishops in the Church of Scotland at the time] rotten pillars, but painted with ceremonial colours, all of the workmanship of Rome'.[59] Robert Baillie, not immediately so contrary, soon found his place amongst the covenanting leadership and writes in 1638:

> Heere we might close, wer not an obscure rumour that waks in corners of another kynd of bishop then yet we have spoken of, to wit, such a one as was truelie in the auncient church, such a one as is this day oversea and was at the beginning in our church – the superintendents or a bishop with so many caveats as the church pleases to put upon him; a person who hath prioritie of order, no superioritie in degree above his fellow presbyters ... to be removed as the assemblie thinks convenient.[60]

The pastor and historian William Scot writes that, in any event, 'Mr John Knox his ministry did more good then all the superintendents.'[61]

John Row was the son of a first-generation reformer of the same name, and he married the daughter of another early reformer David Fergusson. He writes at the behest of younger ministers who recognized the worth of his knowledge from such sources, and his own reminiscences about events in his own lifetime. He begins his history:

> The Lord God, who works his works merveouslie, wrought this work of the Reformation of Religion in Scotland above men's expectation, consider the work and few instruments whom god used in the same, and the power, authoritie, and multitude of these that were against them; even as it was now of late in anno 1637, 1638, &c., the King, Prelats, Malignants, and all their followers and adherents, opposeing this blessed work.

Here one finds the connection between the National Covenant and the Reformation – to men like Row, it was all one story. The same battle for the truth continued, under newer forms of subversion, but where Catholic

---

[58] Arthur H. Williamson, *Scottish National Consciousness in the Age of James VI: The Apocalypse, the Union and the Shaping of Scotland's Public Culture* (Edinburgh: John Donald, 1979), pp. 91–3; Mullan, *Episcopacy in Scotland*, pp. 116–25, 136–7.

[59] [John Murray], *A Dialogue betwixt Cosmophilus and Theophilus* (n.p., 1620), p. 28.

[60] Robert Baillie, *A Discourse anent Episcopacy. 1638*, in Mullan, *Religious Controversy*, p. 185.

[61] William Scot, *An Apologetical Narration of the State and Government of the Kirk of Scotland since the Reformation* (Edinburgh: Wodrow Society, 1846), p. 11.

wolves were dressing themselves as Protestant sheep. Row condemns the emasculation of Presbyterianism and the imposition of bishops who infected the church with 'antichristian and unnecessare ceremonies and nocent impositions, labouring to make us altogether conforme to the Kirk of England, who themselves wes never well reformed; and to make both us and them more conforme to the sea and seat of Rome'.[62]

Spottiswood was actually something of a moderate. He was guilty of playing games and taking the ferry on the Sabbath, but he was not avid for new ceremonies and revisionist theology. However, he is reported to have said that 'the King is Pope now, and so shall be',[63] meaning that personal conviction must cede to the requirement of obedience to Josiah or Constantine. In other circumstances Spottiswood might have manifested his innate moderation, but now, when necessary, he would follow the King's command and persecute Presbyterians. Needless to say he had no friends among them, but ominously, despite Spottiswood's role in the examination of the Jesuit John Ogilvie (executed in 1615), Ogilvie himself writes in the narrative of his arrest and judgement that 'the Archbishop talks to me in public in the most friendly fashion';[64] he had nothing but scorn for Andrew Knox who made the mistake of matching wits with the priest. In 1628 another Jesuit John Macbreck had kind words for this one of the 'pseudo-bishops': 'he treated me very kindly ... [he] shows great favour to Catholics, and often sent his servant to visit me in prison'.[65] If the Archbishop's moderation might have led to a different outcome, liturgical changes continued under Charles I, including new canons in 1636, a new ordinal, and with greatest impact, a Scottish Book of Common Prayer, introduced to riotous reception in July 1637.[66] One Scottish Jesuit thought that despite its defects, it was 'still in many respects in accord with the orthodox worship',[67] and was heartening for Catholics. However, William Spang, minister of the Scots kirk in Campvere in the Netherlands and moderate in his characterizations, writes boldly in 1638 that

---

[62] Row, *History*, pp. 411–12.

[63] Calderwood, *Altar of Damascus*, p. 7; Scot, *Apologetical Narration*, p. 275.

[64] W.E. Brown and P. McGlynn, *John Ogilvie: An Account of his Life and Death* (London: Burns Oates & Washbourne, 1925), p. 192; James Forbes, *Jean Ogilvie, Écossais, Jésuite* (Paris, 1901), p. 200; William Forbes-Leith, *Narratives of Scottish Catholics under Mary Stuart and James VI* (London, 1889), p. 314.

[65] Forbes-Leith, *Memoirs*, vol. 1, p. 6.

[66] Gordon Donaldson, *The Making of the Scottish Prayer Book of 1637* (Edinburgh: Edinburgh University Press, 1954).

[67] Forbes-Leith, *Memoirs*, vol. 1, p. 197.

though I do not approve the English liturgie, yet I will be loath to go so far as to call that church guilty of idolatry, heresye, and that because of her liturgy. Errours to be in it I confess, but heresie and idolatry as yet I hav fond non. I know some new English popish divins hav given just occasioune to the imputations, but it were unjustic to chairg the church for the errors of privat men, though manteined [and] printed by authority.[68]

In fact, by the 1630s some Scottish bishops had consumed the new churchmanship of England, and their advocacy of more catholic forms led to a breakdown in the Church of Scotland. Consider the views of James Wedderburn, who became Bishop of Dunblane in 1636. Like England's Canterburians or Laudians, with whom he had strong connexions, Wedderburn, along with like-minded English clerics such as Richard Montague and William Laud, could be sharply critical of the Roman church, and in his writings Wedderburn offers a less than stellar defence of the Protestant paladins of the previous century:

Notwithstanding of all this, it had been better ... if our Reformers had not so left the Church of Rome and their obedience to the pope, as they did, but had still communicated with that church in all things, except those which in their conscience they held to be altogether unlawfull, and still yeelded canonicall obedience to the pope, *salvo iure principum suorum*, and prayed for him, as their highest pastor and patriarch, yet professing withall their dislike of such things as were amisse, reprooving them as their calling and place would have permitted, and using all moderate, peaceable courses to have obtained reformation thereof. But you may say: So it might have cost them their lives. I answer: So did it the prophets of God whom Jezabell slew, who, notwithstanding the idols sett up by Jeroboam and the grosser idolatrie erected by Ahab, left not the church of Israel, but reprooved their idolatry, and in things lawfull communicated with them.[69]

So Wedderburn allows that the Reformers were not without justification for their schismatic actions; however, would that they had never introduced this doleful division into the church. One can hardly overstate the outrage such provocations might arouse in Presbyterian hearts and minds. His colleague John Maxwell, Bishop of Ross and later Archbishop of Tuam in Ireland, writes that he was happy to have been 'delivered from the Pope's tyrannie', but he could not approve of 'the manner of proceeding', and 'I dayly heartily bewaile that, that too too much idolized Reformation, in an excessive hatred against Poperie, did run too much to the other extreame ... '[70]

---

[68] Mullan, *Religious Controversy*, p. 122.
[69] Ibid., pp. 80–81.
[70] [John Maxwell], *The Burthen of Issachar* ([London], 1646), p. 28.

Something else separated Spottiswood from the more-or-less enthusiastic supporters of the early Scottish Reformation. Knox, 'whose sayings were by many esteemed as oracles',[71] gained some admiration from the Archbishop – enough for the latter to deny his authorship of the *History* so closely attached to him as not worthy of the man[72] – but thinks that he tended to extremism, and that he may have been responsible for unleashing the destructive tendencies of the masses.[73] He records some words of Willock and Knox from 1559 which were prejudicial to the authority of the idolatrous, i.e. Roman Catholic, magistrate:

> It had been a better and wiser part in these preachers to have excused themselves from giving any opinion in those matters, for they might be sure to have it cast in their teeth, to the scandal of their profession. Neither was the opinion they gave sound in itself, nor had it any warrant in the Word of God. For howbeit the power of the magistrates be limited, and their office prescribed by God, and that they may likewise fall into great offences; yet it is nowhere permitted to subjects to call their princes in question, or to make insurrections against them, God having reserved the punishment of princes to himself.[74]

These, of course, were the opinions of James VI, as expressed in his *The True Law of Free Monarchies* (1598). This critique had begun decades earlier, amongst Catholic writers. Leslie relates the assassination of Cardinal David Beaton in 1546 and how Knox thereafter entered the castle, describing him as 'the chief minister of the Calvinistes, quha thocht the perfectioune of thair Evangel in nathing to consist bot in the slauchter and blode of the Cardinal and Preistes'.[75] In fact Leslie continues to regard heresy as a cloak for sedition, and another Catholic writer, Archibald Hamilton, attacks the Protestant Humanist and royal tutor George Buchanan for his political views, as expressed in *De Jure Regni* (1579) which threatened to subvert the power of the prince while giving the *regnum* into the hands of the people.[76] Buchanan cast a long shadow, and when his countrymen

[71] Spottiswood, *History*, vol. 1, p. 373.

[72] Ibid., vol. 1, pp. 167–8 (and the editorial notes on pp. 375–8); ibid., vol. 2, p. 184; Roger A. Mason, *Kingship and Commonweal* (East Linton: Tuckwell Press, 1998), p. 186.

[73] David McRoberts, 'Material Destruction Caused by the Scottish Reformation', in idem (ed.), *Essays on the Scottish Reformation, 1513–1625* (Glasgow: Burns, 1962), pp. 415–62. But see Ian B. Cowan, *The Scottish Reformation* (London: Weidenfeld and Nicolson, 1982), pp. 189–92.

[74] Spottiswood, *History*, vol. 1, pp. 301–2.

[75] Leslie, *Historie*, vol. 2, p. 291.

[76] Archibald Hamilton, *De Confusione Calvinianae Sectae apud Scotos Ecclesiae nomen ridicule usurpantis, Dialogus* (Paris, 1577), sig. 61r: 'in Scotia denuo repetens, praeclaram suam politiam in *Dialogo de regno* expressit. Ubi mysteria Calvinianae sectae detecta (ut

John Cameron and Gilbert Primrose, then pastors at Bordeaux in France, ran into some political difficulty in 1615–16, a couple of hostile elders in their Huguenot congregation reported that these Scots were 'imbued with the maxims of their country, according to which no distinction was made between absolute authority and tyranny',[77] the ministers' fault being their lack of trust in the honourable intentions of Louis XIII. Just after the disruptive events of 1638, the deposed minister John Corbet writes to the Presbyterian rebels that they are acting alone: 'Howbeit all reformed Churches in Europe are condemning your course.'[78]

In that century some Huguenots called for reconciliation with Rome, though there might also be spirited criticism of such suggestions, as one observes in the experience of the respected Alexandre Dyze of whom *La France Protestante* writes: 'unhappily there came to him in 1676 an idea as inopportune as good and decent'. The nature of that ill-advised idea can be gleaned from the title of his book, *Proposals and Means to Achieve a Reunion of the Two Religions in France* (n.p., 1677), which was suppressed as far as possible.[79] In the furious reaction he was relieved of his faculty duties at the academy at Die, and was even suspended from the Lord's supper until the ensuing provincial synod; the affair ended with his death in 1678. There is not so much of this in Scotland, but William Forbes, first Bishop of Edinburgh (1634),[80] 'the onely father of the most of these who fell away from the doctrine of our kirke',[81] was a leader of the few Scots interested in such a movement. Calderwood alleges that an Edinburgh merchant John Fleming reported that Forbes said 'that we, and the Papists may be easily reconciled in many of the heeds controverted betwixt us and them, but specially in the heed of Justification',[82] anticipating by nearly four hundred years the Lutheran-Roman concord on justification (1999). But Forbes does not affirm the intrinsic worth of good works and

---

aiunt) fronte recludens'. See also Mason, *Kingship and Commonweal*, p. 200n; and Jon Robinson, 'The slippery Truth of George Buchanan's Autobiography', *Sixteenth Century Journal*, 39 (2008), p. 85.

[77]   *The Life of Mr Robert Blair*, ed. T. McCrie (Edinburgh: Wodrow Society, 1848), p. 38n, citing Élie Benoist, *Histoire de l'Édit de Nantes*, 3 vols in 5 (Delft, 1693–95), vol. 2, pp. 188–95 (the quotation is from p. 191). See also John Quick, *Synodicon in Gallia Reformata*, 2 vols (London, 1692), vol. 2, pp. 101–4; 'Life of Cameron', in Robert Wodrow, *Collections upon the Lives of the Reformers*, 2 vols (Glasgow, 1834–45), vol. 2, pt. 1, p. 210.

[78]   John Corbet, *The Ungirding of the Scottish Armour* (Dublin, 1639), p. 56.

[79]   Haag & Haag, *La France Protestante*, vol. 5, p. 1115.

[80]   David George Mullan, 'Forbes, William (1585–1634)', *ODNB*.

[81]   Mullan, *Religious Controversy*, p. 27.

[82]   David Calderwood, *The True History of the Church of Scotland* (n.p., 1678), p. 803.

so his irenicism does not absolve Rome of all doctrinal corruption.[83] The same anonymous historian who blames him for so much of the 'Iliad of troubles' which descended on Scotland in the years before the National Covenant cites Robert Baillie to sum up the accumulated wrongs of the Laudians or Canterburians. They bear the burden of guilt '1. of avouched Arminianisme; 2. of profest affectione toward the pope and poprie in grosse; 3. in joyneing with Rome in his grossest idolatries; 4. in avouchinge there imbraceinge of popish heresies and grossest errors; 5. in there popish superstitions; 6. in there imbraceinge the masse itselfe; and lastly, in there maximes and practises of most barbarous tyranie'.[84] After the Restoration, according to the diarist John Erskine, John Edmondstone, minister of Kilmadock, allegedly pronounced that Protestants and Catholics 'might be easily reconciled'.[85] But on the other side, all the besetting problems for Protestants were linked – bishops, liturgy, theology, politics. Any attempt to bridge the gulf was treason against God, and consistently, one finds in the Presbyterian rhetoric of these years a simple association of Episcopalians with Roman Catholics.

One forceful means of articulating the Presbyterian sense of their own now-failing achievement is found in their language about the superiority, the 'perfection', of the Reformed churches, not least of all in Scotland. This was not something invented in Scotland, and some form of national pride can be located in probably every country west of the Urals (and perhaps beyond!), but even while one does not wish to fall into a trap of taking Presbyterian self-congratulation at face value, it remains that Presbyterian cadres had a view of the country and its recent history which was incompatible with alteration – episcopacy and its rotten fruit undermined Scotland's privileged status in the eyes of a wrathful God.[86] This claim obviously distinguished the Church of Scotland and the half-reformed Church of England, and Presbyterians were concerned that Scotland was to be reconstituted according to the English model through changes in polity and liturgy. David Lindsay, the second Bishop of Edinburgh, insisted, though, that both countries were now emulating an older model which predated popish corruption and which would produce 'harmony and conformitie' amongst the reformed.

A Franciscan priest Patrick Hegarty writes to the Propaganda on 29 August 1646 claiming 'that there was then a greater chance than ever of

---

[83]   William Forbes, *Considerationes Modestae et Pacificae*, 2 vols (Oxford, 1850–6), vol. 1, p. 497.

[84]   Mullan, *Religious Controversy*, p. 29.

[85]   Erskine, *Journal*, p. 153.

[86]   Mullan, *Scottish Puritanism*, pp. 265–79.

winning the Scots over to the faith'.[87] If this strikes the modern reader as groundless optimism, certainly the leadership of the covenanters believed it, or at the very least exploited it. It was probably David Calderwood who wrote 'Motives and Causes of Humiliatioun', *c*.1638.[88] At the outset he states: 'Crying to God with fasting and humiliatioun never more necessarie since the reformatioun of religioun.' What follows is an expression of *Angst* over the advances of Arminianism and popery, the former a widely-used code word for the latter. Baillie later writes in England that so-called Arminianism is 'nothing but masked Popery, but a high path-royall way to Rome'.[89]

Covenants and critics

Those who spoke for the covenanting movement conceived of themselves as continuing the work of the first Reformation (1560) and restoring the kirk to its pristine Protestant glory. However, despite the loyal language of the National Covenant, it was a rebellion, and its enemies were not slow to attack it as such. Henry Leslie, a Scot who was then an Irish bishop, in his *Confutation of the Covenant* (1639) states that the National Covenant serves to identify the covenanters with the Jesuits, indeed justifies the Jesuits in their subversive politics. The next year John Corbet, a recalcitrant Scottish Episcopalian who later died in the Irish rebellion, wrote a satire entitled *The Epistle Congratulatorie of Lysimachus Nicanor*, ostensibly a Jesuit writing favourably to the covenanters. In 1644 Bishop Maxwell wrote *Sacro-Sancta Regum Majestas: or, the Sacred and Royall Prerogative of Christian Kings*, which he devoted to disproving 'the Puritanicall, Jesuiticall, Antimonarchical grounds [of government] ... '[90] In 1658 James Guthrie published a work with respect to the Protester-Resolutioner schism in the Church of Scotland. Its title is *Protesters no Subverters, and Presbyterie no Papacie* (Edinburgh, 1658). Accusations of radical Presbyterians behaving like Jesuits continued during the Restoration.[91]

---

[87]   Cathaldus Giblin, *Irish Franciscan Mission to Scotland, 1619–1646* (Dublin: Assisi Press, 1964), p. xiv.

[88]   Mullan, *Religious Controversy*, pp. 132–6.

[89]   Robert Baillie, *Errours and Induration* (London, 1645), sig. A2v. See also David George Mullan, 'Masked Popery and Pyrrhonian Uncertainty: The Early Scottish Covenanters on Arminianism', *Journal of Religious History*, 21 (1997), pp. 159–77.

[90]   The identification of Puritan and Jesuit is contextualized in Lori Anne Ferrell, *Government by Polemic: James I, the King's Preachers, and the Rhetorics of Conformity, 1603–1625* (Stanford: Stanford University Press, 1998), e.g. pp. 70–72.

[91]   Clare Jackson, *Restoration Scotland, 1660–1690* (Woodbridge: Boydell, 2003), pp. 127–8; *Passages in the Lives of Helen Alexander and James Currie, of Pentland* (Belfast,

In 1690 George Meldrum preached against the ungodliness of the time, asserting that it 'is no less offensive to God than Popery'.[92]

As Independents, Quakers, and then in the 1720s Glassites, would demonstrate, English and Scottish magisterial Protestantism – the primary Reformation heritage – generated longings which could not be satisfied within a Presbyterian church committed to the traditional bonds of church, state, and society; which is to say, in Troeltschian terms, church-type Presbyterianism produced various sect-type species which rejected traditional definitions of those linkages. As a result of Cromwell's victory over and occupation of Scotland in 1650, new manifestations of the Protestant spirit showed themselves in Scotland. The country had had little first-hand experience of Separatists, Brownists, Baptists, and Quakers, though of course based on his experiences in London during the 1640s Robert Baillie had composed some substantial tomes against more radical forms of Protestantism. The Scots at the Westminster Assembly, including Baillie, became hostile to the five Independent divines, and in fact, Independency, in whatever form, never gained the footing in Scotland that it did in England.[93] Wariston was the typical Presbyterian in his evaluation of Independency, and, noting the death by misadventure with a horse in 1656 of Thomas Charteris, Independent minister at East Kilbride, writes that 'God hes blasted the only two gathered congregations in Scotland'.[94]

Some Scots, able men and women among them, did join the Independents and the Quakers, and so became Protestant critics of the magisterial Reformation in their own country. These men tended to be northerners, by residence if not by birth, i.e., north of the Tay, and one might investigate the nature of religious culture in that area both in its preference for an episcopal Protestantism and other varieties to the left of Presbyterianism. Alexander Jaffray had hitherto been 'zealous for presbytery',[95] but after meeting Cromwell and John Owen he came shortly to reject the Covenants (1638 and 1643) and the Presbyterianism which underlay them both. He later described the Covenants as 'the great idols of our invention',[96] and drew a daring conclusion, that theological debates must be conducted 'without passion or bitternes in contending with others, but embracing in

1869), pp. 39–40; see also Erskine, *Journal*, p. 24.

[92] [George Meldrum], *A Sermon preached in the High Church of Edinburgh, 27 April 1690* (Edinburgh, 1690), p. 12.

[93] G.D. Henderson, *Religious Life in Seventeenth-Century Scotland* (Cambridge: Cambridge University Press, 1937), p. 116.

[94] *Diary of Sir Archibald Johnston of Wariston, 1655–1660*, ed. J.D. Ogilvie (Edinburgh: SHS, 1940), p. 35.

[95] Alexander Jaffray, *Diary*, 3rd edn, ed. John Barclay (Aberdeen, 1856), p. 60.

[96] Ibid., p. 142.

love all that are truly gracious, and walk soberly according to the gospel of Christ', cautioning against the persecution which rose from 'men's pride and corruption'.[97] His pilgrimage led him to question baptism of children in a 'national' church, a notion which had lost its credibility in his now Independent eyes.[98]

Jaffray's acquaintance John Row *tertius*, minister in Aberdeen and principal of King's College, wrote in 1652 to inform his brother William, minister of Ceres, Fife, that he, too, had come under the spell of Independency.[99] Row was vexed that people ignorant of the Christian faith should have access to the sacraments: 'Quhat one amongst a hundreth in Scotland is fitt, according to the patterne, to be sett att the Lord's Table?'[100] But by January 1661, Jaffray had begun to consider the rather more radical message of the Quakers: 'Whatever may be of mistake in the way and opinion of the people called Quakers about the light within them, as to the universality and operation of it; after some inquiry thereabout, my resolution is, to wave the debatable part thereof, and, as I may, in the strength of the Lord, to improve and make use of what I find in the thing itself ...'[101] In 1662 he joined the sect, and so entered into another round of religious conflict. He was warned to cease holding meetings, and then in 1668 spent nine months in the Banff Tolbooth. Jaffray writes to Bishop Patrick Scougal that 'this present imprisonment, and the usage I am meeting with, may very warrentably be termed, cruel severity and oppression'.[102]

Jaffray's co-religionist Patrick Livingstone was born in Montrose in 1634. He writes that later, when he was living in and around Edinburgh, he attended Remonstrant, i.e. radical Presbyterian, services. He was, however, dissatisfied and in due course concluded that the ministers he heard were wrong; indeed 'they turned us from the light and brought us into a slight esteem of it, as being dark and dim, and weak and natural, and insufficient to lead us to God'. So Livingstone and his fellow seekers had to follow their own path, and it was during this period of doubt, *c.*1659, that he heard the Quakers, 'and my soul was much affected in hearing of them'.[103] This message set him free from the ministers he had heard hitherto, but he found now that he was despised by all the rest, Presbyterians and other

---

[97] Ibid., pp. 64–5; see also p. 115.

[98] Ibid., p. 98.

[99] Henderson, *Religious Life*, pp. 109–11.

[100] Row, *History*, p. 534.

[101] Jaffray, *Diary*, p. 134.

[102] Ibid., p. 231. See also David George Mullan, 'Scougal, Patrick (1607–1682)', ODNB.

[103] Patrick Livingstone, *Selections from the Writings* (London, 1847), p. 29.

sectarians. Robert Barclay (1648–90), a leading Quaker theologian of the century, wrote the briefest of recollections about his early years. He was raised among 'the strictest sort of Calvinists', but as an adolescent, while studying in Paris amongst Catholics, he fell in with them, to his later regret. 'In both these sects, the reader may easily conceive that I had abundant occasion to receive impressions contrary to this principle of love herein treated of, seeing the straitness of several of their doctrines, as well as their practice of persecution, do abundantly declare how opposite they are to universal love ... '[104] In 1667 he joined the Quakers, and was subsequently imprisoned on several occasions.

Finally, John Glass was a young Presbyterian pastor at Tealing near Dundee who fell out with the Church of Scotland and was dismissed in 1728. What led him to found his own church – the Glassites endured until late in the twentieth century – was his rejection of the magisterial nature of the Reformation and the egregious error of the National Covenant, based on a Roger Williams-like critique of the idea of a new elect nation under the New Testament – ancient, Biblical, Israel has no earthly successor – arguing on the basis of a radical, spiritualizing, typology, borrowed ultimately from the General Baptists.[105]

It is difficult for moderns to evaluate this episode, the Reformation, of such outstanding significance for subsequent history, but also possessed of an essential ambiguity. In his *Traictise* of 1600 John Hamilton writes: 'We crave reformation of religion, and submittis our selfis maist willinglie thairto ... '[106] The general cultural evaluation of the word 'reformation' is positive. One thinks of correcting and purging something good, e.g. an institution, which has now fallen into decay and impurity, restoring it to the condition of some putative 'golden age'. However, it is clear that to these late medieval, Renaissance, and early modern Scots the notion of 'reformation' – and 'Reformation' – was ambiguous. Few thinking people at the time did *not* regard the Latin, Western, Church as being in real, indeed dire, need of renewal, but believing that did not necessarily impel a person into 'heresy', i.e. Protestantism. Loyal Catholics believed that their church, under the pope, was the one true church, and possessed all things necessary to achieve a morally prosperous institution cleansed of certain odoriferous corruptions which arose at least in part from the

---

[104]   Robert Barclay, *Universal Love Considered* (n.p., 1677), pp. 2–3.

[105]   David George Mullan, 'The Royal Law of Liberty: A Reassessment of the Early Career of John Glass', *Journal of the United Reformed Church History Society*, 6 (1999), pp. 233–62; idem, 'Williams, Roger (*ca.* 1603–1683)', in Francis J. Bremer and Tom Webster (eds), *Puritans and Puritanism in Europe and America: A comprehensive Encyclopedia*, 2 vols (Santa Barbara: ABC Clio, 2006), vol. 2, pp. 276–7.

[106]   Law, *Catholic Tractates*, p. 220.

weighty economic burdens then associated with ecclesiastical bureaucracy and even salvation itself. Underneath the layers of cracked and yellowing varnish the teachings of the church were sound, ready to be restored to their pristine beauty. Protestants were the new Vandals, barbarians besieging the City of God, and what *they* regarded as reformation was to men like Hamilton simply deformation. Both sides quickly learned to hate and to fear the other, and the dichotomy wormed its way deep into the western European psyche. As Catholics pointed out, the elevation of the Bible did not solve the problems of the church – in fact, it compounded them, since many different reformers might drink from the same well then scatter in a variety of directions. The Scottish experience would prove the truth of the allegation as, first, Catholics and Protestants, and then, second, Presbyterians and Episcopalians struggled for hegemony over church and, for the former, also over the monarchy, all the while identifying the other as Romish or Jesuit. For Presbyterians in particular the world was defined in the same dichotomized terms, and anyone who tried to bridge the divide was obviously an adherent of the enemy, and ultimately of Antichrist himself. Moderation was no virtue in this climate, and those who would bridge the divide found themselves scorned and isolated and grieving for their broken church. In Scotland each of the religious factions would both exact and pay a high price for its beliefs and practices, and it is all but impossible for the 'impartial' historian – if there can be such a creature – to judge whether that price was too high. For the religious heart has reasons of its own and in some ways these remain beyond our ken at this or indeed any chronological distance. But in our common humanity we might draw didactically upon this history and examine those things for which we think suffering – our own or others' – is warranted.

CHAPTER 2

Language attitudes and choice in the Scottish Reformation

Marina Dossena

Together with the Union of Crowns (1603) and the Union of Parliaments (1707), the Reformation is often seen as one of the key factors which hindered, if not stopped, the development of a fully fledged 'high' register in Scots prose: owing to the adoption of an English Psalter and of English Bibles, the influence of Southern English models proved particularly significant. However, in religious and political controversy, the choice of language could be seen as indexical of allegiance to one side or the other, John Knox himself being accused, for example, of having forgotten 'our auld plane Scottis', as we will later see.

The aim of this chapter is to discuss ways in which Scots and English were perceived in different social circles, and the extent to which these attitudes reinforced the trend towards anglicization that was to characterize educated usage in Scotland in the following centuries. Starting from the writings of propagandists and pamphleteers, I intend to analyse what linguistic comments were made for argumentative purposes and, in turn, whether such comments proved influential in the anglicization process. The time span taken into consideration will encompass the Reformation and the Puritan Revolution; after the final defeat of the Stuart dynasty at Culloden in 1746, an idealization of these older uses and linguistic forms interwove with an idea of antiquity which involved both Scots and Gaelic.

Stages of linguistic awareness in early modern Scotland

Scholars have frequently, and appropriately, stressed that Scots is a highly composite linguistic entity, whose long history in relation to English is equally complex and multi-faceted.[1] The year when James VI became James I of England and Scotland, 1603, is generally assumed to be one of the turning points in Scotland's linguistic history. As a matter of fact,

---

[1] See, for instance J. Derrick McClure, 'English in Scotland', in R. Burchfield (ed.), *The Cambridge History of the English Language* (Cambridge: Cambridge University Press, 1994), vol. 5, pp. 23–93.

language change is a slow, ongoing process, and speakers' attitudes towards specific usage are equally varied at different points in space and time, and in different social contexts. Indeed, recent research has shown that the process of language standardization in Scotland was not uniquely in the direction of anglicization, but there were simultaneous trends of divergence of the two varieties, especially in the second half of the sixteenth century. Meurman-Solin has shown that, among the conditioning factors that determined the density of distinctively Scottish features in prose texts, geographical distribution of the texts themselves, date, sex of the writer, genre and subject matter were crucial.[2] In addition, the author's personal history in terms of education, place of residence, job, and ideological beliefs could and did play a role in the choice between Scottish and English variants. It is therefore important to investigate when linguistic awareness started to develop in relation to the distinctiveness of Scots and English.

The first recorded use of *Scottis* dates back to 1494, but even such strongly patriotic compositions as Blind Harry's *Wallace* used *Inglis* to indicate the poet's language.[3] On the other hand, Gavin Douglas's declaration of intent in the Introduction to his translation of Virgil's *Æneid* (1513) has often been singled out as the epitome of early Scottish linguistic pride: 'I set my bissy pane, as that I couth to mak it braid and plane, kepand na sudron bot our awyn langage, and spekis as I lernyt quhen I was page.' However, Douglas acknowledged his own mixed usage when in search of a satisfactory translation:

> Nor ȝit sa cleyn all sudron I refuß, bot sum word I pronounce as nyghtbouris doys: lyke as in Latyn beyn Grew termys sum, so me behufyt quhilum or than be dum sum bastard Latyn, French or Inglys oyß quhar scant was Scottis – I had nane other choys.

In the advancement of anglicization a crucial role is also commonly attributed to the introduction of printing to Scotland in 1508, though Scots was first 'branded' as a homely language about a century later. Aitken refers to the works of Sir William Alexander, Earl of Stirling, and he quotes the address 'To the Reader' of his *Darius* (1603), in which the author describes the language of the poem as 'mixt of the English and Scottish

---

[2]   Anneli Meurman-Solin, 'Change from Above or Below? Mapping the Loci of Linguistic Change in the History of Scottish English', in Laura Wright (ed.), *The Development of Standard English 1300–1800: Theories, Descriptions, Conflicts* (Cambridge: Cambridge University Press, 2000), pp. 155–70; and 'On the Conditioning of Geographical and Social Distance in Language Variation and Change in Renaissance Scots', in Dieter Kastovsky and Arthur Mettinger (eds), *The History of English in a Social Context: A Contribution to Historical Sociolinguistics* (Berlin: Mouton, 2000), pp. 227–55.

[3]   McClure, 'English in Scotland', p. 32.

Dialects' and then goes on to beg his readers to bear with him, although this mixture 'perhaps may be unpleasant and irksome to some readers of both nations', because he has retained 'peculiar' words 'especially when [...] propre, and significant'.[4] Yet, 'for the more parte [he used] the English phrase, as worthie to be preferred before our owne for the elegance and perfection thereof'.

In fact, sixteenth-century usage still required Latin in many educated contexts, whether scientific, philosophical, or religious. Gilbert Skeyne justified his choice of language in his *Descriptioun of the Pest* (1568) with an interest in being understood by the general public:

> Howbeit it become me rather [...] to had vrytin the samin in Latine, ʒit vnderstanding sic interpryses had bene nothing profitable to the commoun and wulgar people, thocht expedient and neidfull to express the sam in sic langage as the vnlernit may be als weil satisfyit as Masteris of Clargie.[5]

The point of intelligibility was also made by the author of the *Complaynt of Scotland* (1550) when he said he used 'domestic scottis langage, maist intelligibil for the vlgare pepil', and indeed it was a crucial issue at the time of the Reformation. Sir David Lyndsay's 'Exclamatioun to the Reidar, tuitching the writing in vulgare and maternall language' was to become famous as a passionate appeal in favour of translations of religious texts into the people's 'toung maternal':

> Thoch every Commoun may not be a clerk,
> Nor has na leid, except thair toung maternal,
> Quhy suld of God the mervellus hevinly werk
> Be hid from them? I think it not fraternal.
> [...] efter my conceit,
> Had Sanct Herome bene born into Argyle,
> In Irisch toung his buikis he had done compile.[6]

As a matter of fact, Sibbald (1802) reports that during the regency of the Earl of Arran (1542) an Act of Parliament was passed which gave liberty

---

[4]   A.J. Aitken, 'Scottish speech: A historical view with special reference to the Standard English of Scotland', in A.J. Aitken and T. McArthur (eds), *Languages of Scotland* (Edinburgh: Chambers, 1979), p. 89.

[5]   Text in HCOS; see Anneli Meurman-Solin, 'A new tool: The Helsinki Corpus of Older Scots (1450–1700)', *ICAME Journal* 19 (1995), pp. 49–62.

[6]   James Sibbald, *Chronicle of Scottish Poetry; from the 13th c. to the Union of the Crowns: to which is added a Glossary*, 4 vols (Edinburgh, 1802), vol. 3, pp. 13–18.

to the Queen's 'lieges to haif the Halie Writ in the vulgar toung, in Inglis or *Scottis*, of ane gude and true translatioun'. Less than a year later, however, the concession was withdrawn, and 'readers of 'Halie Wrytt' in the vulgar tongue were again threatened with fire and sword'. Sibbald comments on the use of *Scottis* in the Act in the following terms:

> The word *Scottis*, in Arran's first statute, leads one naturally here to enquire whether there was, about this time, any translation of the Old or New Testament different from those of Tyndall and Coverdale. – Keith reports, upon the authority of Sir James Balfour, that the Earl of Arran then entertained in his house a friar Guilliam, or Williams, (born near Elstonford, in East Lothian) who translated the New Testament into the vulgar tongue. [...] Lewis, in his History of Translations, says, nearly under this period, that three editions of the New Testament appeared, without the name of printer or place; and seems to think they were printed in Scotland. They are not, however, mentioned by Ames; nor does Lewis say that they were different from Tyndall's.[7]

As we can see, elements indicating linguistic awareness were not uncommon, though controversy on language choice did not concern English vs Scots, but English vs Latin; one of the points on which such a controversy relied was the greater antiquity of one language as opposed to the other; the counterargument was that Latin was no longer intelligible to everybody.

Language and controversy at the time of the Reformation

The first indications of an opposition between Scots and English, not for stylistic purposes, as in the case of Gavin Douglas, but for argumentative ones, are actually found in late sixteenth-century texts. As the foremost leader of the Scottish Reformation, John Knox is generally regarded as one of the most influential anglicizers of Scots, possibly on account of his intermittent imprisonment and exile in England[8] and on the continent, and of his education. John Major, with whom Knox is supposed to have studied at the University of St Andrews, had stated that English was 'spoken by the English and by the civilised Scots' in his *History of Greater Britain*, and this kind of sociolinguistic consideration was possibly as widespread as the one that stressed the differences existing between the two varieties,

---

[7]   Sibbald, *Chronicle of Scottish Poetry*, vol. 3, p. 18.

[8]   R.D.S. Jack describes a similar case for James I, whose language was inevitably influenced by his imprisonment in England from 1406 to 1424; 'The Language of Literary Materials: Origins to 1700', in Charles Jones (ed.), *The Edinburgh History of the Scots Language* (Edinburgh: Edinburgh University Press, 1997), pp. 214–15.

since these could be made to suit ideological stances.[9] However, McClure reminds us that these remarks should not be overemphasized (since each opponent did, in fact, focus on arguments relating to doctrine, history and politics).[10] Perhaps the two most famous comments on Knox's language come from John Hamilton and Ninian Winzet; the first stated:

> Gif King James the fyft war alyue, quha hering ane of his subjectis knap suddrone, declarit him ane trateur: quhidder wald he declaire you triple traitours, quha not only knappis suddrone in your negative confession, but also hes causit it be imprentit at London in contempt of our native language?

Winzet, instead, ironically supposed that Knox had not answered his doctrinal challenge on account of his bad handwriting:

> It apperis to me, Brother, ʒat ʒe haif sum grete impediment, quhareby ʒe ar stoppit, to keip promise tuecheing ʒour anssuering to yis our tractate, eftir sa lang aduisement. […] gif my hand writt peraduentuir hes nocht bene sa legible, as ʒe wald: pleis resave fra yis beirar, ye samin mater now mair legible.

Or perhaps the problem was more strictly linguistic:

> Gif ʒe throw curiositie of novatiounis, has forʒet our auld plane Scottis, quhilk ʒour mother lerit ʒou: in timis cuming I sall wryte to ʒou my mynd in Latyn: for I am nocht acquyntit with ʒour Southeroun.[11]

Both remarks are obviously sarcastic, but it is interesting to note that both Hamilton and Winzet use *suddrone* as a disparaging label. In fact, Winzet always refers to his translations as 'put in Scottis', and the density of Scots forms in his usage can be observed in the following excerpts from his *First Tractat to the Quenes Maiestie, Pastouris, and Nobililitie* [sic] (1562):

> Efter that we thy graces humill Subditis, Marie maist excellent and gracius Quene, be our small Jugement hes considerit the stait of this thy Realme, at this present, tweching religion (quhair upõ the weilfair thairof is only groundit)

---

[9] J. Derrick McClure, 'Scottis, Inglis, Suddroun: Language labels and language attitudes', in *Proceedings of the Third International Conference on Scottish Language and Literature, Mediaeval and Renaissance, Stirling 1981* (Stirling and Glasgow, 1981), reprinted in J. Derrick McClure, *Scots and its Literature* (Amsterdam: Benjamins, 1995), p. 54.

[10] McClure, 'Scottis, Inglis, Suddroun', p. 53.

[11] Letter to John Knox, written 27 Oct. 1563. McClure, 'Scottis, Inglis, Suddroun', p. 53, reports this comment and Hamilton's; the former is also discussed by Aitken, p. 18.

can esteme it, to na thing mair lyke, thã to ane schip in ane dedely storme, enforsed be contrarius wyndis, betuix maist daingerus sanddy beddis on ye rycht hãd, and terrible roikis presenting deth alrady on the left. [...] ȝit sen the godlye wysedome of thi Maies. hes be ane edict inhibit ony questioun or controuersie to be mouit in this action for a tyme, to the end that seditioun be eschewit: we differ to present our said aduertisment and ressoning to the crabit rewlaris foresadis, quhill thy gracious licence be had thairto: quhilk we hope to obtene, our ressonable desyris being knawin, alrady presēt in wryt, as we for schortnes mycht collect to that effect.[12]

The thrid tractat. [...] Quhen it come to my earis, gentill reidar, of the seditious calking of the buith durris of certane catholiks in Edinburgh at the cõmand of the reularis thairof, on Pasche monũday last passit: And quhow at that nycht at euin the durris of certane Caluinianis wes calkit also with sum notes of dishonour, I wes panceãd, quhou happy ane thing it war, giue euerie man mycht leue according to his vocatiõ, at ane tranquillitie in godliness.[13]

A slightly earlier text, also by a Catholic author, Quintin Kennedy's *Compendius Tractiue* (1558), shows similar linguistic traits. The address to the reader (conventionally) expresses the author's modesty, but no comments are offered on linguistic choices:

I am assurit (benevolent redare) quhē thow dois mark and considder the tytle of our lytle tractiue, thairefter persauis quha is the furthsetter and author of the samyn, thow wyl wounder gretlie and meruell: that I (quha am ane mã void of all Eloquence, rude of ingyne, and iugemēt) durst be sua baulde, as to attempt sua heych ane purpose, specialie in this miserable tyme, quhairinto thair is sua gret diuersitie of opinioun amangis swa mony pregnant men of ingyne.[14]

In the text we then observe a skilful alternation of Scots and English lexical items for stylistic purposes. 'Ask', 'speir', and 'inquire' are employed as synonyms, on an equal footing, in order to avoid repetition, and 'speir', a specifically Scots form, is not highlighted as such:

I wyll aske thame of ane questioun, quhilk is verray easie to answeir to, [...]
Than wyl I speir, geue thair wes ane ordour tane to suppresse the heresyis or nocht: [...]
Than wyll I inqyre, quhat wes the ordoure [...] quhilk wes tane.[15]

---

[12]   Ninian Winzet, *First Tractat to the Quenes Maiestie, Pastouris, and Nobililitie* (Edinburgh, 1562), pp. 3–4.

[13]   Ibid., p. 25.

[14]   Quintin Kennedy, *Compendius Tractiue* (Edinburgh, 1558), pp. 2–3.

[15]   Ibid., p. 17.

As regards the reformers' side of the controversy, in David Fergusson's *Answer to ane Epistle written by Renat Benedict* (written in 1562, and published in 1563) we find a similar display of modesty (lack of eloquence is pleaded by both Kennedy and Fergusson), but fewer Scots forms, both in spelling and morphology:

> I have not interprised (beloued brethrē in Christ Jesus) to answer this Epistle as one more able so to do, then the rest of my fellowes in office: but rather driuen thereunto by the uncessant requeist of some Zealous and godlie persones, [...] I haue thoght good to write sumwhat in this mater: unto the which writting I have added my name, not for vain glorie God knowes, but to this end one lie, that when the Reader shal find the reules of Rethorick transgressed, and ornate Eloquence omitted (no man be blamed but I alone).[16]

The controversy is in fact conducted on issues of antiquity and authority. The Catholic side had stated:

> loke well I pray you how great is this your boldnes, to professe a new doctrine against the antiquitie consent and uniuersalitie of Religion, without any plaine testimonies or auctorities of holy Scripture, or of Christiane Authores, ancient and tryed in learning and godliness.[17]

To which Fergusson replied, first of all demanding more detailed challenges:

> The nixt tyme [...] that ye write let us hear these good mennis names that agreeth not with us, and the sentences of Scripture that be against us (for we can not answer to nameles mē and wordles sentences) and then I truste by the grace of God that ye shalbe answered accordinglie, for preased be God we be readie to giue a reckning of that hope that is in us, to all men that demandeth it.[18]

He also discussed the issue of antiquity stressing the extent to which the Catholic church had introduced rites inexistent in early Christianity:

> Ye boste much of antiquitie, but [...] your moste precious geare & oldest constitutions [...] are in veray deid, [...] beggerly cerimonies inuēted by the foolhardy and rashe conceit of man, without the warrand of Gods worde, or

---

[16] David Fergusson, *Answer to ane Epistle written by Renat Benedict* (Edinburgh, 1563), pp. 1–3.

[17] Ibid., pp. 3–4.

[18] Ibid., pp. 5–6.

any exemple of that first or primatiue Church moste happely planted by the Apostles & reuled by the holy Ghoste.[19]

As we can see, Scots forms are very few, and indeed we can compare this text with a similarly anglicized one issued in 1566 by the same Edinburgh printer, Robert Lekprevik, on behalf of the General Assembly:

> The present troubles being somewhat considderd, but greater feared shortly to follow. It wes thought expedient (dearelie beloued in the Lord Iesus) that the whole faithfull within this Realme, shuld together, and at one tyme prostrat themselues before their God, craving of him pardone and mercy, for the great abuse of his former benefites, and the assistance of his holie Spirite, by whose myghtie operation we may yet conuert to our God, that we prouoke him not to take from vs the lyght of his Euangle, whiche he of his mercie hath caused so clearely of laite dayes to shyne within this Realme.[20]

Given the official status of this source, we may conclude that linguistic issues were not central to Scottish reformers: the point was doctrine, not language. Robinson has shown that early printed texts of the Scots Confession of 1560 did not attribute any considerable importance to language variation, and explains why a similar attitude was taken towards the importation of English Bibles.[21] Tyndale's version had reached Scotland by early 1527 and indeed the first reprint of the Geneva Bible in Scotland, the so-called Bassandyne Bible of 1579, did not present 'the slightest attempt at adaptation in vocabulary or spelling for a Scots readership'.[22] Murdoch Nisbet had transcribed the New Testament into Scots around 1520, but his text only circulated in manuscript and its Wycliffite roots are probably the reason why lexical choices are very close to the Latin Vulgate on which other Lollard versions were based.[23] For instance, the text made available to modern scholars in the *HCOS* [24] reads:

---

[19]   Ibid., p. 9.

[20]   *The Ordour and Doctrine of the Generall Faste, appoynted be the Generall Assemblie of the Kirkes of Scotland. Halden at Edinburgh the 25. day of December. 1565* (Edinburgh, 1566), pp. 1–2.

[21]   Mairi Robinson, 'Language Choice in the Reformation: The Scots Confession of 1560', in J. Derrick McClure (ed), *Scotland and the Lowland Tongue* (Aberdeen: Aberdeen University Press, 1983), pp. 59–78.

[22]   D.F. Wright, '"The Commoun Buke of the Kirke": The Bible in the Scottish Reformation', in idem (ed.), *The Bible in Scottish Life and Literature* (Edinburgh: The Saint Andrew Press, 1988), p. 155.

[23]   On the history of Bible translations in Scotland see also Graham Tulloch, *A History of the Scots Bible* (Aberdeen: Aberdeen University Press, 1989).

[24]   See fn. 5 above. The manuscript was not printed until the very beginning of the twentieth century.

In the begynnyng was the word, and the word was at God, and God was the word. This was in the begynnyng at God. Al thingis war made be him, and without him was made na thing. That thing that was made in him was lijf: and the lijf was the licht of men: And the licht schynes in mirknessis, and mirknessis comprehendit nocht it.

If this is compared with the twentieth-century translation of the New Testament into Scots by W.L. Lorimer,[25] we see a much more conscious attempt to adhere to Scots usage, syntax and spelling in the latter:

In the beginnin o aa things the Wurd wis there ense, an the Wurd bade wi God, an the Wurd wis God. He wis wi God in the beginnin, an aa things cam tae be throu him, an wiout him no ae thing cam tae be. Aathing at hes come tae be, he wis the life in it, an that life wis the licht o man; an ey the licht shines i the mirk, an the mirk downa slocken it nane.

In the case of Nisbet, it would be anachronistic to expect the same degree of linguistic awareness and activism seen in Lorimer's text, as the point was doctrine and access to the Scriptures in the vernacular, as opposed to Latin, not language maintenance or promotion. Indeed, similar usage is observed in the texts 'vsed in the English Churche at Geneua, approued and receiued by the Churche of Scotland', in which Scots forms do not occur very frequently at all; for instance, the Creed included in *The Cathechisme of M. Iohn Caluin* (1571) reads:

I beleue in God the Father almightie, maker of heauen and earth: And in Iesus Christe his onely Sonne our Lord: Who was cōceiued by the holie Ghost, borne of the virgine Marie: Suffered under Pontius Pilate, was crucified, dead, buried and descended into hell: He rose again the thride day from death: he ascended into heauen, and sitteth at the right hand of God the Father almightie: From thence he wil come to iudge the quicke and the dead.

I beleue in the holie Ghost: the holie Churche vniuersall, the communion of Saintes: the forgiuenes of sinnes: the rising againe of the bodies; and life euerlasting.[26]

Scots, however, was not completely excluded from texts of religious controversy on the Protestant side. The introduction to the 1835 reprint of Winzet's *Tractatis* refers to a text 'translatit out of Frenche into Scottis be ane faithfull Brother, printed at Edinburgh in 1565', in which the

---

[25] W.L. Lorimer, *The New Testament in Scots* (London: Penguin, 1983), p. 159.

[26] *The Cathechisme of M. Iohn Caluin* (Geneva, 1571).

translator stated that as 'the tractat is sa proper and parfite an answer to syndrie of the said Winzet's Questionis,' he had therefore 'causit this little buikie be set further *in our Scottis toung to make the treuth knawin to all our countrie men that hes not the knawlege of the uther leid*, and that it may be partely ane answer to Winzets Questiouns quhil the compleit answer be prepared for the rest. Sua that in my judgement, Papis men sal not haif greit occasioun, God willing, to brag thaim self in this behalfe' (p. xvii, emphasis added).

The question of intelligibility re-emerges, but again what is stressed is the importance of understanding the Scriptures, of having direct access to their powerful, universal message, which was a crucial theme in religious controversy. Anglicized forms may indeed have been adopted in official texts, but ordinary usage was still distinctive;[27] for this reason, any attention given to the language used by 'all our countrymen' could only be welcome, because it would help understanding of essential religious concepts, not necessarily because it would reflect social identity in any modern sense.

As numerous studies have shown, the distinctiveness of popular speech could vary considerably in different geographical and social circles, especially after the Union of the Crowns. In addition, it should be borne in mind that in Scotland Gaelic-speakers were still numerous in the Highlands and Islands, though speakers of English or Scots did not see this very favourably at all. In a petition addressed to the Scottish Parliament by William Master of Tullibardin on 6 July 1606 (and granted three days later), the object is the Gaelic name of the area under discussion, which the petitioner asks to change into 'another more proper name' – from *Trewin* to *Earne*:

> quhair it hes pleasit Johne Lord Murray of Tullibardin my father To provyde me to the heretable fee of the haill lands leving and Lordschip of Tullybairdin quhairof the landis and Barony of Trewin ar ane pairt and pertinent and because the name thairof is derivat fra the Erische language and that I intend to big ane hous thairupon quilk will be verie proffitabill in tha pairtis of the cuntrie: In respect quhairof necessary it is to me to have the name of the saidis landis and barony alterit and changeit in ane uther mair proper name: heirfoir

---

[27] On education in the decades under discussion see John Durkan, 'Education in the Century of the Reformation', in David McRoberts (ed.), *Essays on the Scottish Reformation 1513–1625* (Glasgow: Burns, 1962), pp. 145–68; and 'The Cultural Background in Sixteenth-Century Scotland', ibid., pp. 274–331. Uses of the vernacular in popular literature are discussed by Brother Kenneth, 'The Popular Literature of the Scottish Reformation', in ibid., pp. 169–84.

I beseik your Ll. that ye wald change the foirsaid auld name of Trewin in the name of Earne.[28]

In this petition we see a negative attitude to Gaelic that was to find official expression in the Statutes of Iona (1609): a traditional Lowland bias towards speakers of Gaelic linked 'the Irishe language' to 'barbaritie and incivilitie', so the King had a 'special care' that complete anglicization should be achieved:[29]

Forasmekle as, the Kingis Majestie haveing a speciall care and regard that [..] the vulgar Inglishe toung be universallie plantit, and the Irishe language, whilk is one of the chief and principall causis of the continewance of barbaritie and incivilitie amongis the inhabitantis of the Ilis and Heylandis, may be abolisheit and removit.[30]

By the late eighteenth century this trend was reversed: a new approach to antiquity, especially in literature, made of Ossian a paradigmatic case of linguistic re-evaluation. The intervening decades, however, saw further turmoil and dramatic changes, both historically and linguistically.

Usage in mid-seventeenth-century Scotland

It is beyond the remit of this chapter to present an overview of the historical events that affected Scotland at the time of the Puritan Revolution and the Civil War; our concern here is to assess the attitudes that prevailed towards the use of Scots in written texts.[31] To this end, it is important to make a distinction between official documents and those drawn up for

---

[28] The text, 'read to the Society [of Antiquaries of Scotland] 16th January 1835', is in *Archaeologia Scotica*, 4 (1857), p. 405.

[29] This attitude was most famously and even hyperbolically represented in the Flyting of Dunbar and Kennedy, where the former poet attacks the latter on account of his speech.

[30] The text is provided in Manfred Görlach (ed.), *Introduction to Early Modern English* (Cambridge: Cambridge University Press, 1991), p. 384.

[31] Hence the decision to concentrate on letters, diaries and official documents. Although sermons might also be an interesting source of information, we cannot be sure of the extent to which the written text reflects the spoken one. Private documents, such as autobiographies, in addition to letters and diaries, also shed light on social categories that may be underrepresented in official texts, but whose voice is more clearly audible at times of reformation and revolution – see, for instance, David G. Mullan (ed.), *Women's Life Writing in Early Modern Scotland: Writing the Evangelical Self, c.1670–c.1730* (Aldershot and Burlington: Ashgate, 2003).

private circulation, in order to see whether the latter (as may be expected) are indeed more 'conservative' in the use of Scots grammar and lexis.

As our attention focuses on the language of religion, an 'official' document certainly worth investigating is *The Doctrine and Discipline of the Kirke of Scotland* (1641). The text includes the 'Acts of the Generall Assembly for the Cleering and Confirming the said Bookes of Discipline, and against the adversaries thereof', dated 30 July 1562, where we see that Scots lexis is remarkably rare – indeed, if we exclude such specialized vocabulary as 'ministers', 'elders' and 'superintendents', only 'anent' is recognizable as a distinctively Scottish form:

> Because the lives of Ministers ought to bee such, as thereby others may be provoked to godlinesse, It becomes them first to be tried, after the triall of the Superintendents, if any man have whereof to accuse them in life, doctrine, or execution of their office. After the Ministers, must the Elders of every Kirk be tried, &c. *In that whole ordinance anent triall, and in the Constitution following anent the subjection of all sorts of Ministers to the Discipline of the Kirk, there is no mention of Bishops, or any sorts of Prelates, as not acknowledged to have any place in the Ministry of the Reformed Kirke.*[32]

Dispositions elsewhere in the text are equally anglicized in spelling and morphology – see for instance the quotations below:

> Of the priviledges of the Universitie. [...] All other things touching the bookes to be read in ilk classe, and all such like particular affaires we referre to the discretion of the Masters, Principals and Regents, with their well-advised counsel; [...] Ministers and the poore, together with the Schooles, when order shall be taken thereanent, must bee susteined upon the charges of the Kirk.[33]

Such an observation, however, raises the question of what was the case in manuscript (as opposed to printed) texts, possibly issued in a more peripheral area. In order to investigate this we may consider a letter dated 17 October 1656, sent by Robert Blair and James Wood (based in St Andrews) to Robert Douglas, minister in Edinburgh, in relation to a fast about which they had serious doubts:

> Wee doubt not but it is evident to you that for many respects wee cannot intimate [that fast] to our Congregations to be observed; the way and maner of envoying it (what over the civil power were, from which it proceedeth) as it is contrair to the order, and constant practise of this Kirk, even under our

---

[32] *Doctrine and Discipline*, p. 1.
[33] Ibid., pp. 50–51.

former unquestionable Rulers: […]. Besydes, wee beleeve everie intelligent man will easilie perceive in the mater thairof, not a few things positivelie contrair to our sworne engagements and vows, and some things repugnant to the truth of doctrine, beleeved and taught amongst us; particularlie that of tolleration, which, to us, is, ^so^ clearlie held forth in it, as that the contrar is directed to be confessed as sinne. Neverthelesse for preventing, or removeing, (if possible may be) any offence that the power may haply take at our not observing that order, wee conceive it to be expedient and necessare, that both ^to^ the Generall hon by word of mouth, and to My Lord Broghill by letter, it be represented that our refusall is not from contempt or neglect of the power; but upon grounds of conscience.[34]

This letter, encoded by educated authors, appears to be thoroughly anglicized, except for occasional forms (such as *contrair*) and the culturally-specific form *kirk*. In addition, as the letter had two encoders, there may have been cases of mutual correction, in order to imitate formal usage as closely as possible.

If we now turn to private diaries, we find that spelling is much more distinctive.[35] The first instance we may take into consideration is the so-called *Chronicle of Fife* – that is, the Diary of John Lamont of Newton.[36]

1650. Feb. – Ther was sundrie persons in Edenbroughe that had ther eares nayled to the Trone, for bearing false witnes, and one that had his tounge pearced with a hott iyron. About the same tyme, ther was one scourged by the hangman, for having 7 weemen at one tyme with chielde. […]

May 21. – James Grahame (sometyme Earle of Montrosse), was execute at the crosse of Edenbroughe. […]

1654, May. – This month ther was ane act published att the mercat crose of Edenbroughe, entituled Ane Ordidance [sic] of Pardon and Greace to the Peopell of Scotland, wherein severall of the nobilitie of Scotland were forfated, […].

---

[34]   National Library of Scotland, Wodrow MSS, Folio XXVI 1, fo 22.

[35]   The texts under discussion were edited in the early nineteenth century; however, editorial care is stressed in the Advertisement of Lamont (1810): 'The Orthography of the original has been uniformly adhered to; and blanks are left where the Manuscript was defective.' Similarly, Nicoll (1836) is stated to have been 'printed […] from the original Manuscript in the Advocates Library'.

[36]   The Advertisement informs us that 'The Author was John Lamont of Newton, in the Parish of Kennoway; a person of whom little is now known, but he is supposed to have been related to the Family of Lamont of Lamont, in Argyllshire; and, during the period of the transactions recorded in this Work, he was settled in Fifeshire, as Factor to the Family of Lundin of Lundin.'

1670. – One Major Weyer, [...] was brunt at the Gallo-lay, [...] He wold not suffer the ministers to spake or pray for him (nether wold he seike God's mercy;[...]) And Apr. 12, being Tuesday, his sister [...] was hanged at Edb. She confest incest, witchcraft, &c. [...] They dyed both impenitent persons, as was supposed by the standers by.

Another interesting diary is that of John Nicoll,[37] in which the same years are discussed, and in which the density of Scots forms is equally high:

James Grahame, sumtime Erle of Montrois, did give out a lairge prented Declaratioun and paper, quhairwith he chargeth his awin natioun with hatching a rebellioun in this Kingdome, with promoting the lyke in England, and with the sale and murthour of thair awin native King, and robbing his sone of all rycht, and uther horrid crymes. [...] efter reiding of this ansuer of the Kirk and Stait fullie and at lenth, and eftir sounding of four trumpettis on the Croce, the hangman threw that the said James Grahame his Declaratioun in the midst of the fyre, set thair on a scaffold upon the eist side of the Croce, [...] This done 9 Feb., 1650. [...]

22 Julij 1650 being ane Monday, the Inglische airmy under the commandement of Generall Oliver Cromwell, croced the watter of Tweid and marched in to our Scottis bordouris to and about Aytoun; [...]. The enymie also advanced the lenth of Restalrig. [...]

9 Marche 1656. Ane man callit James Fortoun being condempnit for airt and pairt of murthour, committit in the north, he was hangit in the Castelhill of Edinburgh [...] He suffered death with ane invincible curage; and rather beseeming a brydgroome, nor ane going to the gallous.

On the other hand, if we look at other diaries, such as those available in the HCOS, we see that Scots forms occur less frequently in the diary of Andrew Hay of Craignethan (excerpts for the years 1659–60). In the quotation below, for instance, the author reports on services attended; the words of the preacher are as anglicized as those of the author, so we cannot be sure if the diarist reported the forms he actually heard, or his (anglicized) perception:

19, (^The Lords Day^), 7 (^a'cloak^) . – This morning after I was readie I went to Bigger kirk, and heard M=r=. Alex. Lev. lecture on Exod. 33; cap hath 2

[37] John Nicoll, WS, born in Glasgow, 'appears to have resided a considerable portion of his life in Edinburgh'. Part of the text is also in Alexander Peterkin (ed.), *Records of the Kirk of Scotland* (Edinburgh, 1838), pp. 612–17.

parts. Some means for reclaiming that people and Moses familiar dealing with God. (^v.^) 1. OBS. That sinfull practices provock the Almighty to be ashamed of a people. 2=o= That the choise way of consolation in a sad tyme is to act faith on the Cov=t=. (^v.^) 2. OBS. That folk may find reall demonstrations of divine pouer that have not his heart toward them (^v.^) 3. That ther is much mercy in God's acquainting sinners with this contraversie. (^v.^) 4. That its a relevant cause of mourning to mourn for Gods anger. (^v.^) 7. that its a forrunner of sad judgm=t= when God threatens departure and folk lay it not to heart many more. OBS=s= on 2=d= pt of cap, etc. [...] Afternoone he lectured on 2 Pet. 1. 8, etc., consisting of many argts to presse grouth in grace and holines. (^v.^) 8. OBS. That the way to pleas God is to have thes graces abounding in ws. 2=o= The more thes graces abound, the more shall we abound in saving knowledg. (^v.^) 11. That holines is the only way to get ane open dore to heaven. (^v.^) 12. That folk that even know their dutie are very ready to forget it under a temptation. (^v.^) 14. That its a ready way for following dutie, to intertein constant thots of death, etc.

These apparently conflicting witnesses do in fact highlight the complexity of language use in varying contexts. The case of religious debate is a particularly relevant one, as a number of different factors contribute to linguistic choices, that may be more or less self-conscious, more or less indexical of the writer's social background, education, and wish to signal affiliation to one side or the other.

Scots and the search for antiquity: concluding remarks

As we saw in the paragraphs above, the process of anglicization was still far from completed in the second half of the seventeenth century, especially where texts meant for private circulation are considered. However, the pressure to make usage less geographically marked was increasing.

The first occurrence of the notorious term 'Scotticism' is in 1678. In the pamphlet *Ravillac Redivivus* the author asks his reader to 'make remarks upon [his] Letters, and faithfully Admonish [him] of all the Scotticisms, or all the Words, and Phrases that are not current *English* therein'. Bailey has challenged Aitken's idea that this usage was a symptom of early linguistic self-consciousness, as the author was not a Scot, 'but an Anglo-Catholic Englishman, George Hickes (1642–1715), pretending to be a Scot in this anonymous pamphlet written for an English audience'.[38] However, whether the author was Scottish or simply pretended to be Scottish, would not seem to be a crucial issue, since what appears to matter most is the kind of linguistic comment which is provided. Besides, it is hardly likely

---

[38] Richard W. Bailey, 'Scots and Scotticisms: Language and Ideology', *SSL*, 26 (1991), p. 71; Aitken, 'Scottish Speech', pp. 85–118.

that Hickes should have expressed his view in these terms if it had been completely unimaginable for Scottish speakers. As a matter of fact, the text does comment occasionally on certain lexical items; for instance, we are informed that 'Tolbooth' is the Scots word for 'prison' and that the judges are the 'Lords Justitiary'.[39] However, what is also of particular interest in this text is the comment on the link between Saxon and Scots and Northern English:

> I confess I have a great Veneration for our own and the Northern English Language, upon account of the *Anglo-Saxon*, to which they are so nearly ally'd; [...].

In a note in the margin, the author referred to William Lisle's work on Saxon texts, one of the earliest texts in which emphasis was placed on the greater distance of Scots from Norman influence, and therefore its greater proximity to Anglo-Saxon:[40] an issue on which the debate would grow considerably in the eighteenth and nineteenth centuries.[41]

As the eighteenth century progressed, the 'ideology of improvement', with its strenuous attempts to avoid specifically Scottish forms in 'polite' usage, was gradually supplemented with an equally forceful idealization of the past.[42] Especially after the final defeat of the Jacobite cause, a new attitude developed in relation to Gaelic and Scots.[43] While the Ossian controversy was to grow on a continental scale, Scots found an unexpected champion in James Adams, an English Jesuit whose views were not devoid

---

[39]   [George Hickes], *Ravillac Redivivus* (1678), pp. 8, 10.

[40]   William Lisle in the Preface to his *Ancient Monuments of the Saxon Tongue* (1637) had claimed 'that he improved more, in the knowledge of Saxon, by the perusal of Gawain Douglas's Virgil, than by that of all the Old English he could find, poetry, or prose; because it was nearer the Saxon, and further from the Norman' (quoted in George Chalmers, *The Poetical works of Sir David Lyndsay* (London, 1806), p. 146n).

[41]   See Marina Dossena, '"The Cinic Scotomastic"? Johnson, his commentators, Scots, French, and the story of English', *Textus*, 18/2 (July–December 2005), pp. 51–68.

[42]   Charles Jones, *A Language Suppressed: The Pronunciation of the Scots Language in the Eighteenth Century* (Edinburgh: John Donald, 1995); Robert McColl Millar, '"Blind attachment to inveterate customs": Language Use, Language Attitude and the Rhetoric of Improvement in the first Statistical Account', in Marina Dossena and Charles Jones (eds), *Insights into Late Modern English* (Bern: Peter Lang, 2003), pp. 311–30.

[43]   Murray G.H. Pittock, *The Invention of Scotland: The Stuart Myth and the Scottish Identity, 1638 to the Present* (London: Routledge, 1991).

of political overtones.[44] The success of Burns as 'heaven-taught ploughman' could also be set in this framework: the educated establishment looked at a 'distant' language with curious amusement.

Scots thus became associated with poetic expression, or – on a diametrically opposing level – with jocular discourse: nineteenth-century travelogues abound with entertaining anecdotes, the protagonists of which are Scots speakers, and the days of the Reformation were not excluded: in 1828 David Laing read to the Society of Antiquaries of Scotland the following excerpts from the Hawthornden MSS:

> After the Reformation, Nile Ramsay, the Lard [sic] of Dalhowsie, having been at pretching with the Regent Murray, was demanded How he liked of the sermon? Passing well, said he; Purgatorie he hath altogedder tane away: if, the morne, [tomorrow] he will take away Hell, I will give him the half of the lands of Dalhowsie.[45]

Indeed, this attitude would continue for a long time: as late as about a century ago Johnston, describing the famous episode in which Jenny Geddes threw her stool at the bishop, quoted – supposedly verbatim – her exclamation, as an emblem of popular anger: 'Deil colic the wame o' thee'.[46] The (almost proverbial) pithiness of Scots was thus to contribute decisively to its definition as a variety *sui generis*, acceptable as an authenticating device in narration, or as a token of lyrical, sentimental fondness of the past, but inexorably distant from contemporary 'polite' usage: a long-lasting legacy, though certainly an undeserved one for a language with such deep historical roots as Scots.

The widespread use of Scots forms in private documents indicates how much material can still be taken into consideration, in order to contribute further insights into the history of English in Scotland. The letters, diaries and autobiographies of ordinary people, especially at times of heated public debate, allow us to witness language use in which self-monitoring is less strict than in the encoding of official, more public documents. These texts have always been of great interest for historians, but historical linguists have only just begun to stress their importance for the study of

---

[44] Marina Dossena, *Scotticisms in Grammar and Vocabulary* (Edinburgh: John Donald, 2005), pp. 85–90.

[45] David Laing, 'A Brief Account of the Hawthornden Manuscripts in the possession of the Society of the Antiquaries of Scotland; with Extracts, containing several unpublished Letters and Poems of William Drummond of Hawthornden', *Archaeologia Scotica: or, Transactions of the Society of Antiquaries of Scotland*, 4 (1857), pp. 79–81.

[46] J.C. Johnston, *Treasury of the Scottish Covenant* (Edinburgh, 1887), p. 290.

historical varieties of a language. Far from being a linear sequence of successive developments, language history is a complex phenomenon in which the speakers' social networks, their attitude towards (self-imposed) prescriptive norms, and their varying roles in interaction, all contribute to the realization of language use in different contexts. As a result, we may witness greater or lesser density of geographically or socially marked forms, depending on the group of recipients with whom the encoder wished to express solidarity and identification. Nowadays the role of language as a very powerful marker of social identity is a widely recognized principle; the study of earlier stages of the language, especially at times of reformation (and resulting controversy), may prove a very rewarding pursuit for historical sociolinguists. In addition, they may provide ground for more and more fruitful cooperation in interdisciplinary studies across the borders of social, religious and linguistic history.

CHAPTER 3

'The Divine Fury of the Muses': Neo-Latin poetry in early modern Scotland

David Allan

When he visited Marischal College in Aberdeen on 23 August 1773, Samuel Johnson was forcefully struck by one painting in particular that he was shown in the college hall. 'Large and well lighted', this impressive space was marked, as Johnson later recorded, by 'the picture of Arthur Johnston, who was principal of the college, and who holds among the Latin poets of Scotland the next place to the elegant Buchanan'.[1] Like so much else that fell from Johnson's lips during that memorable journey, the remark was neither casual nor uninformed. For he was already an ardent admirer of Johnston's verse, attempting unsuccessfully to buy his own copy of the latter's works while he was in Aberdeen and still searching for one in London as late as February 1777.[2] Moreover, when Johnson and Boswell finally reached Inverness, the long-dead Aberdonian poet was still on the traveller's mind, only this time in his alternative guise as chief promoter and publicist of his countrymen's Latin verse. Johnson, striving now to conjure up a striking contrast between Scotland's longstanding success in the cultural sphere and what he considered its continuing lack of material progress, fell instinctively back upon a famous collection of poetry, edited by none other than Arthur Johnston, that had been published at Amsterdam in 1637: 'from the middle of the sixteenth century', the lexicographer pronounced with audible satisfaction, 'almost to the middle of the seventeenth, the politer studies were very diligently pursued. The Latin poetry of *Deliciae Poetarum Scotorum* would have done honour to any nation…'.[3]

These anecdotes are, of course, a reminder that, for all his subsequent reputation as the tireless compiler of *A Dictionary of the English Language* and magisterial author of the *Lives of the English Poets*, Samuel Johnson's literary and intellectual interests were in reality at least as much classical

---

[1]   Samuel Johnson and James Boswell, *A Journey to the Western Islands of Scotland* and *The Journal of a Tour to the Hebrides*, ed. Peter Levi (Harmondsworth, 1984), p. 43.

[2]   Ibid., pp. 209, 413.

[3]   Ibid., p. 51.

as vernacular, and rested in particular upon a lifelong enthusiasm for Latin composition, especially as it had been practised since the Renaissance.[4] It is in this context that his recognition of Arthur Johnston's labours as poet and editor needs to be seen, and, indeed, in which the contribution of Scots writers in general to the early-modern cultivation of Latin verse is best appreciated. For neo-Latin poetry had been – as aficionados like Johnson fully understood, even if increasing numbers of his sceptical British and European contemporaries no longer did – a cultural tradition of the first importance in the sixteenth and seventeenth centuries, its eminence sustained by the fact that it was not merely genuinely international in extent but had also shown itself capable of considerable brilliance in the manner of its expression and of being both challenging and wide-ranging in what it had to say. As a contribution to a better understanding of this phenomenon, the purpose of the present essay is three-fold: to survey this now largely-forgotten phase in the development of Scottish poetry in particular; to establish its relationship with the wider history of the same period, above all with the Reformation; and finally, but also the specific problem with which we should begin, to explore the peculiar conditions that lay behind its wildly-fluctuating fortunes.

I

Probably the greatest obstacles to modern admiration of Scottish neo-Latin poetry, and so to gaining some insight into the grounds of Johnson's unfeigned passion for the tradition, are the linguistic and cultural hurdles that confront scholars and readers. On the one hand, there is, of course, the catastrophic decline of technical proficiency in Latin among even many professional students of literature, to say nothing of other groups of educated readers, which became especially pronounced in the twentieth century and now seems unlikely ever to be reversed. On the other there is the rather earlier shift, already an important factor during Johnson's lifetime (and which in part may account for the tenacity of this notoriously conservative reader's attachment to it), which has seen Latin progressively marginalized in both literary and scholarly discourse as a variety of vernacular European languages have assumed absolute dominance in print culture. The practical result of these profound long-term trends is that, far more than is the case with Scots poetry, and even perhaps more than with Gaelic, the study of

---

[4]   Useful emphasis upon Johnson's Latin scholarly and literary interests has recently been offered in J.C.D. Clark, *Samuel Johnson: Literature, Religion and English Cultural Politics from the Restoration to Romanticism* (Cambridge, 1994).

Scotland's neo-Latin literary heritage suffers badly today from a simple lack of an audience equipped with the basic tools required for its decipherment, let alone its proper appreciation. This, then, was largely why the poetry of Arthur Johnston, George Buchanan and their colleagues steadily slipped from view from the 1660s onwards. It was neither their contemporary marginality nor their mediocrity that consigned them to near-oblivion. Rather their important place in early-modern literary culture and their frequent excellence in their art failed to save them from a fate that their immersion in Latin composition, a decision that would later come to appear literally incomprehensible to most readers, would turn out almost to have pre-ordained.

A second contributory factor also needs to be borne in mind, however, when seeking to explain the extent of this tradition's subsequent relegation. And this derives less from its Latin means of expression than from its characteristic poetic moods and modes. For the composition of neo-Latin verse was invariably an intensely cerebral activity, driven in most cases by an expectation that its practitioners should display technical excellence and inventiveness and also shaped by an understanding that its subject matter needed to be approached not merely discursively and descriptively but analytically, inquisitively, even argumentatively. The result was a style of poetry that, although at its worst still perfectly capable of plumbing the depths of banality and of cliché, was in its finest moments characteristically rarefied and abstruse, often giving rise to thought-provoking epigrams that were densely packed with classical allusions, with obscure tropes, and with stark contrasts, surprising inversions, and unsolvable paradoxes. These poems therefore typically had something of the air of intellectual difficulty that also surrounded the work of the 'Metaphysical Poets' of early seventeenth-century England who, not coincidentally, with what Grierson identified as their 'more intellectual, less verbal' wit and their 'game of elaborating fantastic conceits and hyperboles', were the exact contemporaries of many of Scotland's finest architects of neo-Latin verse: Buchanan's *De Sphaera* (published posthumously in 1586), an ambitious poem which successfully melds an account of Ptolemaic cosmology with a critique of Habsburg political ambitions, is merely an early and extreme example of this capacity for philosophical seriousness.[5] But just like the metaphysicals, the aesthetic promoted by the work of the neo-Latinists fell substantially out of favour even before that century had ended, to

---

[5]   H.J.C. Grierson, *Metaphysical Lyrics and Poems of the Seventeenth Century* (Oxford, 1921), pp. xv, xx. On the Scots' philosophical poetry, see, for example, my *Philosophy and Politics in Later Stuart Scotland: Neo-Stoicism, Culture and Ideology in an Age of Crisis, 1540–1690* (East Linton, 2000), esp. pp. 46–87. On the contemporaneous English tradition of Latin composition, see J.W. Binns, *Intellectual Culture in Elizabethan and Jacobean England: The Latin Writings of the Age* (Leeds, 1990).

be succeeded by a vernacular poetry which, whether in lyric form or otherwise, generally offered more regular constructions (particularly with the use of rhyming lines) as well as distinctly less challenging themes. A consequent sense that they had been responsible for a deliberately inaccessible – because essentially indigestible – verse, designed not for the enjoyment of wider audiences but for the amusement of themselves and a narrow circle of similarly inclined devotees, helped further accelerate their fall from grace and bring about the later under-estimation of their contribution to the history of Scottish literature as a whole.

As John MacQueen has correctly insisted, however, it is important to remember that this tradition nevertheless comprised, in its own time, 'not merely Latin verse composed by Scotsmen. It was in a real sense *Scottish* poetry, and it holds an important place in any assessment of Scottish literature as a whole'.[6] And the reasons for neo-Latin's emergence as a major force in the first place are in many ways the obverse of the factors that would eventually bring about its historical marginalization. For its Scottish exponents were from the outset subjected to most of the same pressures and responded to many of the same impulses as other neo-Latinists elsewhere in Europe. The most important of these was simply the unchallenged hegemony of Latin itself as the *lingua franca* of Europe's educated elites – something that, crucially, the centrifugal forces unleashed by the Reformation did little during the rest of the sixteenth century and throughout most of the seventeenth to change. As a result, the decision of a Scottish writer at this time to work in Latin was precisely *not* to choose to consign one's efforts to an arcane medium. It was instead to participate consciously in an activity that was intelligible to an extended community of contributors and observers from the Arctic Circle to the Mediterranean and from the Atlantic coastlines to the borders of the Ottoman Empire – and which, moreover, had already sustained a prestigious tradition of observation, argument, and sensibility stretching back the greater part of two thousand years. In short, neo-Latin poetry, when it was written in Buchan (as a significant quantity of it was), just as when it was produced in Bordeaux, Bologna or Breslau, may have made intellectual demands upon its readers; and it was certainly highly-worked and elaborate in form.[7] It was not, however, and never could be, inaccessible. For unlike,

---

6   John MacQueen, 'Scottish Latin Poetry', in Cairns Craig (ed.), *A History of Scottish Literature*, 4 vols (Aberdeen, 1988), vol. 1, p. 213.

7   On the Breslau poets, for example, see the fascinating study by David Halsted, *Poetry and Politics in the Silesian Baroque: Neo-Stoicism in the Work of Christophorus Colerus and His Circle* (Wiesbaden, 1996). French work in the same vein is best approached through G. Castor and T. Cave (eds), *Neo-Latin and the Vernacular in Renaissance France* (Oxford, 1984).

for example, the compositions of other sixteenth-century writers like Francois Rabelais, William Shakespeare, Torquato Tasso or, for that matter, Sir David Lindsay, each of whom elected to work in his immediate national vernacular, it was actually conceived quite deliberately in such a way as to allow it to contribute to the widest possible contemporary literary discourse.[8]

It follows naturally that this enmeshment in a cultural matrix of genuinely European proportions must also be linked in some way with the Scots' celebrated early-modern connections, as travellers, soldiers, merchants, students and professors, with the Continent.[9] Certainly this assumption is strongly supported by the evidence of direct personal ties, as we shall see, between some of the leading Scottish neo-Latin poets and the great European centres of learning and literature: several, including both Johnston and Buchanan, had not only studied but also taught at Continental universities – a circumstance which only increases the temptation to regard their neo-Latin compositions as, at one level, part of a continuing conversation between intimates and acquaintances who were united by common experiences, tastes, and preoccupations and separated only by the inconvenient fact of geographical distance. Yet an unforced cosmopolitanism – again, these writers were anything but parochial in their outlook – was not the only thing shared by its widely-scattered European exponents. All were, of course, greatly affected by the Renaissance admiration for skill in Latin composition of all kinds, which had one focus in (though it was by no means confined to) the veneration of Cicero in particular. All also wrote within an environment in which considerations of patronage, and of the personal relationships between writers and great men, necessarily influenced their art as it also shaped

---

[8] C.A. Upton, 'National Internationalism: Scottish Literature and the European Audience in the Seventeenth Century', *SSL*, 26 (1991), pp. 218–23.

[9] See, for example, from an immense body of literature on the subject, John Durkan, 'The French Connection in the Sixteenth and Early Seventeenth Centuries', in T.C. Smout (ed.), *Scotland and Europe, 1200–1800* (Edinburgh, 1986), pp. 19–44; J.K. Cameron, 'Some Aberdeen Students on the Continent in the Late Sixteenth and Early Seventeenth Centuries', in Paul Dukes (ed.), *The Universities of Aberdeen and Europe* (Aberdeen, 1995), pp. 57–78; George Molland, 'Scottish–Continental Intellectual Relations as Mirrored in the Career of Duncan Liddell (1561–1613)', ibid., pp. 79–101; W. Caird Taylor, 'Scottish Students at Heidelberg, 1386–1662', *SHR*, 5 (1908), pp. 67–75; M.F. Moore, 'The Education of a Scottish Nobleman's Sons in the Seventeenth Century: I. Study in Holland', ibid., 31 (1952), pp. 1–15 and '... II. Study in France', ibid., pp. 101–15; and Elizabeth Bonner, 'Continuing the "Auld Alliance" in the Sixteenth Century: Scots in France and French in Scotland', in Grant G. Simpson (ed.), *The Scottish Soldier Abroad, 1247–1967* (Edinburgh, 1992), pp. 31–46.

their careers.[10] Most in addition utilized satire as the weapon of choice for the analysis of the world – and especially the political realm – that they had set themselves to observe.[11] Many were touched, more specifically, by similar philosophical concerns. Largely associated with the re-emergence of interest in ancient stoicism that swept across Europe from the early sixteenth century onwards, this tendency encouraged poets, as it led other intellectuals, to ponder such questions as the respective merits of virtuous retirement and active involvement in a corrupted and chaotic public sphere; and, with obvious implications for the figurative character of much of the resulting poetry, to juxtapose the moral qualities of the city and the countryside, and the tensions between the court and the country.[12]

This last feature should, of course, remind us of a further contingent factor in the growth of neo-Latin poetic composition that was of particular significance to the experience of its Scottish practitioners. This was the impact – long, complex and ultimately unresolved – of the Reformation, which, if it did not loosen their attachment to the classical languages, certainly affected Scotland's poets in a number of different ways. First, and most obviously, the religious revolution reinforced, though in modified form, the established pattern of direct connections with Europe: the Huguenot academies at Sedan, Saumur, Nîmes and Montauban, the Protestant-tinged University of Bourges, and the universities of the Calvinist northern Netherlands (principally Leiden but also Groningen), rather than the Sorbonne and Italy, now became the preferred destinations for Protestant Scots – though their Catholic compatriots, as we shall see,

---

[10]   Patricia Thomson, 'The Literature of Patronage, 1580–1630', *Essays in Criticism*, 2 (1952), pp. 267–84; Robert Harding, 'Corruption and the Moral Boundaries of Patronage in the Renaissance', in Guy Fitch Lytle and Stephen Orgel (eds), *Patronage in the Renaissance* (Princeton, NJ, 1981), pp. 47–64.

[11]   J. Ijsewijn, 'Neo-Latin Satire: *Sermo* and *Satyra Menippea*', in R.R. Bolgar (ed.), *Classical Influences on European Culture, AD 1500–1700* (Cambridge, 1976), pp. 41–55.

[12]   In recent years the literature on neo-Stoicism has expanded rapidly. See, for example, Herschel Baker, 'Sixteenth-Century Ethics and the Development of Neo-Stoicism', in his *The Dignity of Man: Studies in the Persistence of an Idea* (Cambridge, MA, 1947), pp. 293–312; J.L. Saunders, *Justus Lipsius: The Philosophy of Renaissance Stoicism* (New York, 1955); Robert Hoopes, *Right Reason in the English Renaissance* (Cambridge, MA, 1962); G. Oestreich, *Neostoicism and the Early Modern State* (Cambridge, 1982); Audrey Chew, *Stoicism in Renaissance English Literature* (New York, 1988); William C. Marceau, *Stoicism and St Francis de Sales* (Lewiston, NY, 1990); Mark P.O. Morford, *Stoics and Neostoics: Rubens and the Circle of Lipsius* (Princeton, 1991); R.C. Evans, *Jonson, Lipsius and the Politics of Renaissance Stoicism* (Durango, CO, 1992); and Adriane McCrea, *Constant Minds: The Lipsian Paradigm in England, 1584–1650* (Toronto, 1997).

predictably remained loyal to the older centres.[13] Second, and even more importantly, the resulting ideological and religious crises that convulsed Europe until at least the middle of the seventeenth century had specific consequences for Scotland and thus for its poets. In particular, successive revolutions in church and state in the 1560s, the instability that marked James VI's Scottish reign, and the worsening crisis and ensuing British warfare that obliterated Charles I's regime served to make Scots poets of all denominations peculiarly sensitive to the kinds of question with which the neo-Latin tradition everywhere had come to be concerned.[14] Is earthly power necessarily unstable? What are the essential qualities of a good and successful ruler? Are ambition and avarice the roots of political evil? What is the role of wisdom and philosophy in the public sphere? Can we change, or can we at least learn to accept, what fate apparently has in store for us? And is virtue itself only possible in a private place of seclusion? These would prove questions profound enough and problematical enough to underpin an impressive Scottish contribution to the wider achievements of neo-Latin poetry.

II

The true beginnings of the Scots neo-Latin tradition actually lie not in Scotland but, appropriately enough, in France. For it was there, in the second quarter of the sixteenth century, that one émigré Scots writer in particular, employed during the 1520s at Paris but during the 1540s and 1550s at the Collège du Guyenne in Bordeaux, then at Coimbra in Portugal and finally back in Paris, first seems to have begun to participate actively in the gathering late-Renaissance fascination with the composition of Latin poetry. This was, of course, George Buchanan, the professor, tutor, historian, political theorist, propagandist, and, not least, writer of verse, whom the elder Henri Estienne, humanist scholar-publisher and certainly no mean judge, hailed as 'a poet easily the most eminent of his age'.[15] The precise dating and explanation of Buchanan's poems in relation

---

[13]   Paul Néve, 'Disputations of Scots Students Attending Universities in the Northern Netherlands', in W.M. Gordon and T.D. Fergus (eds), *Legal History in the Making: Proceedings of the 9th British Legal History Conference*, Glasgow, 1989 (London, 1991), pp. 96–108; Marie-Claude Bellot-Tucker, 'Scottish Students and Masters at the University of Bourges in the XVIth and XVIIth Centuries' (Master's dissertation, Université de Clermont II, 1992).

[14]   Allan, *Philosophy and Politics*, passim.

[15]   Philip J. Ford, *George Buchanan: Prince of Poets* (Aberdeen, 1982), p. vii. For biography, see I.D. McFarlane, *Buchanan* (London, 1981), and P. Hume Brown, *George Buchanan: Humanist and Reformer* (Edinburgh, 1890).

to his known career is not helped by the fact of their complicated and partly-posthumous publishing history. It is widely accepted, however, that they first emerged during his brief initial spell back in Scotland between 1536 and 1539, with the *Somnium*, the *Palinodiae*, and in particular in the *Franciscanus* (not published until 1567), ostensibly describing a dream in which St Francis had invited him to join his order of friars but plainly a satirical attack upon the Church's morality that had been written under encouragement from King James V. Thereafter, following his return to the Continent, his interests in Latin composition quickened, initially finding expression at Bordeaux in the translation of two Greek plays by Euripides (the *Alcestis* (published without performance in 1544) and the *Medea* (acted in 1543 and published in 1556)) and the writing of two more Latin prose dramas of his own, *Baptistes* (written and produced in 1542, published in 1577) and *Jepthes* (published in 1554).[16]

There followed a rich and brilliant succession of individual poems, written at various points during Buchanan's French and Portuguese periods, reflecting many of the characteristic concerns of the wider neo-Latin movement.[17] A late example, 'To the Most Invincible King Henri II of France, After the Capture of Calais', probably composed around 1558 and shortly before Buchanan's final return to Scotland, captures many aspects of his poetry at its most controlled and inventive. Indeed, beneath the conventional flattery of a royal addressee, there lies the typical philosophical preoccupation with the actions of destiny or fortune, particularly as they impress themselves upon the lives of the powerful: 'It is not Fate, aware of what is ordained, nor the unstoppable wheel of slippery Fortune, nor the course of the stars', Buchanan argues at one point, asserting a strongly Christian interpretation of events in the public domain, 'but the creator of the universe alone who governs the world'.[18] Overweening ambition and human pride, especially in political figures, are

---

[16] *George Buchanan: Tragedies*, eds P. Sharratt and P.G. Walsh (Edinburgh, 1983).

[17] D. Sabrio, 'George Buchanan and Renaissance Latin Poetry', *Explorations of Renaissance Culture*, 7 (1981), pp. 36–46; idem, 'George Buchanan's Secular Latin Poetry and New Historicism', *SSL*, 26 (1991), pp. 319–27; I.D. McFarlane, 'George Buchanan and French Humanism', in A.H.T. Levi (ed.), *Humanism in France at the End of the Middle Ages and in the Early Renaissance* (Manchester, 1970), pp. 295–319; and R.W. Bushnell, 'George Buchanan, James VI and Neo-Classicism', in Roger A. Mason (ed.), *Scots and Britons: Scottish Political Thought and the Union of 1603* (Cambridge, 1994), pp. 91–111. The political verse has also been presented anew, with useful critical apparatus, in *George Buchanan: The Political Poetry*, eds and trans. Paul J. McGinnis and Arthur H. Williamson (Edinburgh, 1995).

[18] Ford, *Buchanan*, p. 133.

also specific targets. Henri's mortal enemy, the Emperor Charles V, now living in retirement in a Spanish monastery after a career marked by grand ambition and ultimate disappointment, is a warning to all: 'see how he lies broken and in despair who was cherished by Fortune in her bosom, and but recently swept, swollen with pride, through all the nations', observes a coolly judgemental Buchanan. Similar lessons are pressed home in other politically-oriented poems, such as the 'Poem of Thanks to Francois Olivier, Chancellor of France', which belongs apparently to the later 1540s. Here, in addressing a former associate in Bordeaux who had gone on to enjoy high office, Buchanan is able both to emphasize his admiration for his subject's current assiduousness in his public responsibilities and to hint darkly at the great dangers of abandoning it: 'he controls from his lofty height the functions of the French commonwealth, and handles with just authority the reins entrusted to him by the king', Buchanan notes; 'he does not groan when he has to shoulder an unfair load, nor grow arrogant, puffed up by success, being equally unbreakable and upright in mind in both kinds of fortune'.[19]

Intermingling with the political commentary, however, and sometimes even in the same poems, Buchanan was to show himself equally concerned with other aspects of the neo-Latin aesthetic – a thematic variety in such a condensed format that the requirement to display technical virtuosity in composition strongly encouraged. The poem to Olivier, for example, is noteworthy because it manages to illuminate the potential perils of public office by transposing them onto a consideration of the role of art in human existence and a contemplation of the contrasting moral qualities of urban and rustic life. For Olivier, we are told, was himself formed by an earlier attachment to learning and literature that he had shared with the poet: as Buchanan reports, 'once, in his youth, as a companion of the Muses, he was made famous and powerful through them'.[20] As a result, the poet proposes that a continuing relationship – an agreeable accommodation, that is, rather than the expected dichotomy – is possible between Olivier's political activities in distant Paris and his former haunts in the provincial south:

And if, by the banks of the Gascon Garonne, I enjoy leisure granted by you, free from cares and inspired by the divine fury of the Muses, if our Muse, lacking splendid apparel and more suited to the wild woods, shuns the splendour of the court and cities that are quick to learn better poetry than mine, Echo hiding in the chattering crag, the stream surrounded by thick reeds, the pools of water, and the verdant recesses of the woods will celebrate you, Olivier.

---

[19] Ibid., p. 143.
[20] Ibid., p. 145.

In other words, Buchanan's poem imagines the Muse and the natural landscape together singing the praises at least of this particular courtier and statesman. Olivier, it seems, is to be understood as an exception to the rule – a politician, that is, who can safely be embraced by the innocent and virtuous because of his pious commitment to learning and to wisdom.

Buchanan's interest in rusticity and in pastoral themes, another developing convention within the neo-Latin tradition and rooted in particular in admiration of Virgil's *Eclogues* and *Georgics*, was also in evidence in contexts that are less overtly political.[21] 'Silva II: Agrius' is a fine example of this, addressed to Pierre de la Taste, a friend then studying civil law at Poitiers, in which Buchanan uses his subject's absence so as to explore, again in intensely argumentative fashion, the tensions between what is presented as the arid sterility and distractions of the city and the natural fertility and moral innocence of the countryside. As Buchanan asks:

> Still do Garuma's shores offend thine Eye?
> Still must thy native Climes neglected lie?
> Still do Pictonian Prospects please thy taste?
> Her rocky Mountains, and her barren Waste?[22]

Yet, at the end of a comparatively lengthy poem, Buchanan is once again able to conjure up an ingenious resolution, successful at least within the infinitely flexible confines of this imagined situation. De la Taste, evidently beguiled by Poitiers, will remain at his studies; and the woods and fields and shepherds of Guyenne will continue to feel his loss. Ultimately recanting his initial laments, Buchanan therefore invokes the assistance of nature to soothe his fevered brow – 'O ye Winds! ye Zephyrs! send Relief' – and anticipates that they will communicate his fond regrets to his absent friend ('these Petitions bear/To my Tastaeus's unattending Ear').[23]

By no means all of Buchanan's inventiveness, however, found expression in poems that pondered the timeless questions of politics, nature, art and philosophy. He was equally at home and no less masterly in developing a variety of other themes, both sacred and profane. At one extreme – and

---

[21]   See, for example, W.L. Grant, *Neo-Latin Literature and the Pastoral* (Chapel Hill, NC, 1965); Helen Cooper, *Pastoral: Medieval into Renaissance* (Ipswich, 1977); Jasper Griffin, 'Virgil', in Richard Jenkyns (ed.), *The Legacy of Rome: A New Appraisal* (Oxford, 1990), pp. 125–50; Robin Sowerby, *The Classical Legacy in Renaissance Poetry* (London, 1994), esp. pp. 189–249; and Gilbert Highet, *The Classical Tradition: Greek and Roman Influences on Western Literature* (Oxford, 1949), pp. 166–77.

[22]   *Renaissance Latin Poetry*, ed. I.D. McFarlane (Manchester, 1980), p. 211.

[23]   Ibid., p. 219.

a work still much-prized by bibliophiles and scholars in the nineteenth century – was Buchanan's Latin rendering of the Psalms. Apparently first written during his incarceration by the Portuguese Inquisition on charges of heresy between 1549 and 1551, these translations were not published in full until Henri and Robert Estienne's famous edition of 1565/6, the *Psalmorum Davidis paraphrasis poetica*, which was widely regarded, then and long afterwards, as the very greatest of his poetic achievements, and among the most significant literary works of a religious nature – frequently re-printed and endlessly praised by people from all backgrounds – to adorn the Protestant side of the newly established religious divide.[24] At the other extreme, and notwithstanding the subsequent reputation of the Scottish Reformation for outright hostility to the aesthetics of sensuousness, it is worth noting that even the mysteries of carnal passion proved not to be outside Buchanan's extensive poetic province: in fact, influenced in particular by the Roman poet Catullus, he also produced two cycles of erotic lyrics, *Leonora* and *Neaera*, which richly repay modern study.[25] Creativity within the technical constraints of traditional forms and structures; remarkable breadth of imagination in the conception; and, above all, consummate skill in the execution – these were the singular virtues of the very finest neo-Latin composition that Buchanan eventually came to exemplify like no other contemporary Scot and, indeed, like few other Europeans.

III

The formative impact of Buchanan's powerful and wide-ranging contribution to early-modern Scottish poetry as a whole can hardly be gainsaid. Not least, every succeeding Scots practitioner of the craft was only too aware that he was obliged to labour in Buchanan's inescapable shadow, which, as Estienne's famous testimonial recalls, also stretched widely across the European scene. The enigmatic Mark Alexander Boyd was among the first to attempt to do so. Nephew of James Boyd, titular Archbishop of Glasgow, and a student at the University of Bourges where he was taught by the famous humanist and jurist Jacques Cujas, as well

---

[24] I.D. McFarlane, 'Notes on the Composition and Reception of George Buchanan's Psalm Paraphrases', *Forum for Modern Language Studies*, 7 (1971), pp. 319–60. See also Roger Green, 'Davidic Psalm and Horatian Ode: Five Poems of George Buchanan', *Renaissance Studies*, 14 (2000), pp. 91–111; and idem, 'Classical Voices in Buchanan's Hexameter Psalm Paraphrases', in Ceri Davies and John E. Law (eds), *The Renaissance and the Celtic Countries* (Malden, MA, and Oxford, 2005), pp. 55–89.

[25] P.J. Ford, '*Leonora* and *Neaera*: A Consideration of George Buchanan's Erotic Poetry', *Bibliothèque d'Humanisme et Renaissance*, 40 (1978), pp. 513–24.

as at Paris, Orleans and Toulouse, his career, apart from a visit to Italy after 1584 and some active service in the army of Henri III from 1587, is frustratingly obscure.[26] We do know, however, that by the 1580s he was composing both poetry and prose in Latin, which was first published at Bordeaux in 1590 as the *Epistolae quindecim*; a second volume, *Epistolae heroides et hymni*, followed at La Rochelle (though with a bogus Antwerp imprint) two years later. These collections comprise a rich mixture of epigrams (including work dedicated to James VI and to the Dauphin), epitaphs (notably one for his uncle) and other poems, mainly in Latin but also in French and Greek. As with Buchanan's work, moreover, they impress not only with their range but also with their sheer dexterity.

The majority of the Scots neo-Latinists, however, were active in the first forty years of the seventeenth century. Again the existing European tradition, with which education, travel and wide reading had familiarized them, was an important inspiration, and a context without which it is impossible fully to understand and appreciate their art. But the poetry that emerged was also unmistakably Scottish, touching upon the personal concerns of its makers, the divisive consequences of the nation's Reformation, and even sometimes the distinctive local landscapes of Scotland, all presented in beautifully-constructed Latin verse. William Barclay, for example, Catholic physician and author of *Nepenthes, or, The Vertues of Tobacco* (1614), and not to be confused with his older namesake who was principal of the Catholic college at Pont-à-Mousson (which the defender of smoking did, however, attend, along with Louvain and Paris), was a poet who, though by no means prolific, more than made up for this with his rigorous mastery of Latin composition.[27] His 'Apobaterium, or Last Farewell to Aberdeen', for instance, a late piece first published in the *Sylvae tres* (1619), can be read autobiographically, as a reminder of Barclay's then place of residence and of his apparent intention of removing thence to London.

Perhaps the most interesting of Barclay's compositions, however, is the much earlier 'To William Lessius', composed shortly after 1606. Dedicated to a young Scottish student, it allows the poet – in a manner obviously

[26]   Lord Hailes, *Sketch of the Life of Mark Alexander Boyd* (Edinburgh, 1787); R. Donaldson, '"M. Alex: Boyde": the Authorship of "Fra Banc to Banc"', in A.A. MacDonald, M. Lynch and I.B. Cowan (eds), *The Renaissance in Scotland: Studies in Literature, Religion, History and Culture* (Leiden, 1994), pp. 344–66; and I.C. Cunningham, 'Marcus Alexander Bodius, Scotus', in L.A.J.R. Houwen, A.A. MacDonald and S.L. Mapstone (eds), *The Palace in the Wild: Essays on Vernacular Culture and Humanism in Late-Medieval and Renaissance Scotland* (Leuven, 2000), pp. 161–74.

[27]   Allan, *Philosophy and Politics*, pp. 69–72; *Musa Latina Aberdonensis*, eds and trans. Sir William Duguid Geddes and William Keith Leask, 3 vols (Aberdeen, 1892–1910), vol. 3, pp. 3–20 [hereafter *MLA*].

redolent of Buchanan's fond address to Francois Olivier – to reflect upon a close friend's absence as he pursues his studies through the great intellectual centres of the Continent:

> Lessius, chief crony mine, you were born in a region where poets might place their Tempe, where the climate is ever mild and the Lossie threatens the ruined cathedral of Elgin. Moray will not hold you, nor Mar. Go to the now long famous Dutch, give Meursius and Heinsius a hearing; if their marshes breed a loathing, go to Louvain with its memories of Lipsius; if to France, most pleasant land of France, prithee turn aside to Douay. Then betake yourself to Paris; how could I sing its praises! You may care to see Italy, but Paris holds me and my friends.[28]

The effortless classicization of the landscape of northern Scotland is, of course, a striking reflection of the personal perspectives of a neo-Latin poet from Banffshire. But more intriguing is Barclay's conclusion. A Catholic in Continental exile, as is hinted at by the reference to Paris, he encourages his subject to prefer Counter-Reformation Europe to the no doubt alluring scenes of north-east Scotland. In other words, the conventional philosophical antithesis, turning on the moral superiority of the countryside and the provinces, has actually been reversed by Barclay. Now it is the cities and their seats of learning that are truly to be admired: Lessius, as a result, can safely choose a foreign university over his native Moray.

Thomas Dempster was another Aberdeenshire neo-Latinist for whom an unyielding attachment to Catholicism and thus, because of the Reformation, the life-transforming experience of long-term exile, were critical factors informing his art. Once again, the biographical details are sketchy, an indistinctness exacerbated by Dempster's unrivalled gift for re-inventing his own past – for example, to have been the twenty-fourth of 29 children, to have learned the alphabet in one hour at the age of three, and to have personally published fifty separate works (for fewer than two-thirds of which there is any credible independent evidence).[29] What is certain is that his career was marked by serial peregrination, often propelled by self-induced misfortunes: as a consequence, and although he was still to die relatively young, he managed either to study or to teach, sometimes for more than one period, at Cambridge, Paris, Louvain, Rome, Douai, Toulouse, Nîmes, Pisa, and Bologna. Among Dempster's most interesting poetic compositions were two that were directed to the difficult task of winning the favour of his own monarch in London. The 'Panegyric to the Most August and Mighty Prince, James I, King of Great Britain, France

---

[28] Ibid., vol. 3, pp. 10–14.
[29] *ODNB*.

and Ireland', which adopted another conventional mode for neo-Latin poetry – the poem in praise of a bountiful patron – can be attributed to the period around 1615 when he was briefly resident in England and was awarded a financial consideration by James. On this occasion Dempster's verse insists that the king's interest specifically in classical scholarship and literature is directly connected with his apparent success as a monarch:

> Under your rule Scotland enjoyed peace. You banish sloth, mould your early life on virtue, seeking in the chase the school of future war, or quitting the grove you woo the Muses. The work of Greece, the fall of Rome, the triumph of Rome from east to west, from north to south – all was child's play to you. You drank deep of Greek and Roman poetry. Such your early training, but now by your writings you shew yourself a noble example to kings.[30]

A second piece addressed to the same subject, the 'Appeal to the Most August and Mighty King James V', is, however, rather more cutting. Indeed, it develops as a passionate rhetorical assault by Dempster upon the dangers that can arise when a badly-advised royal ear allows itself to become deaf to the worthy pleas of poets and scholars:

> is the Prince's mind turned from the Muses, and is that band of no account which shines by honoring Apollo? Has virtue no reward, and are arts despised, which before were wont to raise their head under your protection?[31]

In other words, Dempster, who suggests that he already enjoys the applause of the rest of Europe ('Paris counts me among men of distinction, to academic Toulouse my name is known, and Nismes with its crystal fount shews me respect'), has now unaccountably been abandoned by his own king – as indeed had happened, the incurably-fractious poet's precarious position at court having been successfully undercut through the machinations of his numerous Protestant enemies.[32]

If Dempster was in many respects the prince of Scotland's exiled Catholic scholars, then the neo-Latin tradition also provided several other Scots poets who were not adherents of the old religion with the means to demonstrate their literary virtuosity as well as to consider their own circumstances in full view of the wider world. John Leech, who was responsible for, among other things, an epigram 'To Thomas Dempster, Professor of Jurisprudence at Bologna', was another notable

---

[30] *MLA*, vol. 3, pp. 44–50.
[31] Ibid., vol. 3, p. 51.
[32] Ibid., vol. 3, p. 52.

exponent of the art.[33] In this case an education in Aberdeen and at Paris and Poitiers, and much time subsequently spent in London, whence he was one of many to follow James VI's lead, were the background to numerous verse compositions in Latin that appeared in successive publications – *Lachrymae* (1617) (a copy of which he presented to the king), *Nemesis poetica* (1617) and *Musae priores* (1620).[34] Thomas Reid, an ancestor of the Enlightenment philosopher of the same name, and who studied in Rostock and Leipzig before settling in London as James's Latin secretary, was likewise the author of a paraphrase of Psalm 104 (printed by Barclay in the *Judicium de certamine* (1620)) and of a number of his own compositions that appeared posthumously in the *Delitiae*.[35]

Arthur Johnston himself, who had studied at Heidelberg and taught for many years at Sedan before returning to Scotland, eventually finished his own complete translation of the Psalms (1637) – inevitably the main basis for the subsequent comparisons between himself and Buchanan – and oversaw the final appearance of the *Delitiae* in the same year. And among the latest and most prolific of the major Scottish Latin poets was Johnston's schoolfriend David Wedderburn, who taught humanity at Marischal College and then at Aberdeen Grammar School. A noted educationist and grammarian, over a lengthy career which continued into the 1640s, Wedderburn produced several hundred verses, the best-known of which remain, appropriately for a man appointed poet laureate of Aberdeen, a series of occasional pieces – another particularly common form in the neo-Latin tradition – including ones on the death of Prince Henry in 1612 (*In obitum summae spei principis Henrici, Jacobi VI*), on James's return to Scotland in 1617 (*Invictissimo et potentissimo monarchae Jacobi VI, Britanniae magnae* and *Propempticon charitum Abredonionsium*), and on Charles's ill-starred visit in 1633 (*Vivat rex*), as well as no fewer than six elegies lamenting the death of Arthur Johnston (1641).[36]

IV

The epigram 'On the Bees Making Honey in the Temple of the Muses of Sir John Scot of Scotstarvet', composed by John Leech in or shortly after 1637, was an occasional piece of a slightly different kind. For it marked the publication of the *Delitiae poetarum Scotorum*, in which were gathered

[33] Ibid., vol. 3, pp. 289–90.

[34] T.A. Birrell, 'Some Rare Scottish Books in the Old Royal Library', in MacDonald, Lynch and Cowan (eds), *Renaissance*, p. 405; *ODNB*.

[35] *ODNB*.

[36] *ODNB*.

together, among the efforts of no fewer than 37 of the nation's diverse
Latin poets, exquisite examples of the skills of Leech, Barclay, Dempster,
Reid, Wedderburn, and, of course, Johnston too – who, with Scotstarvet,
lay behind this far-sighted enterprise. As Leech figuratively described the
editing process:

> While Scot prepares the publication of the Scottish Sons of Song, collecting
> their scattered remains from various quarters, the bees, quitting their hive in
> wonted style, settled together where a scented laurel discloses its green foliage.
> Then in a body again, it is a portent that I tell, the mass following their leader
> selected a definite spot at the top of Scot's house, where his library preserves
> the sacred singers.[37]

Leech's celebratory offering – with its ingenious and elaborate central
metaphor recalling the discussion of bee-keeping in the fourth book of the
Georgics as well as Seneca's image of the acquisitive reader in the *Epistolae
morales*; with its playful allusions to the Muses' location in rural Fife and
to Scotstarvet's willing accommodation of them; with its well-crafted
structure and its complete command of the Latin tongue – encapsulated
in a few lines the tradition he was describing at its most mature and most
impressive. It may now be hard to engage with such unfamiliar modes of
expression, much less to sympathize with such extravagant leaps of the
imagination; but this was exactly what so many contemporaries, and later
admirers, so esteemed in the Latin verse compositions of the sixteenth and
early-seventeenth centuries. It was clearly the case, as Boswell reported
that Samuel Johnson had insisted at St Andrews in 1773, that 'Buchanan
had spread the spirit of learning amongst us', and that the resulting verse
'shewed that there was then an abundance of learning in Scotland'.[38] It
follows, by the greatest of ironies, that a properly nuanced understanding
of the country's early-modern culture is impossible without at least in part
finding oneself sharing Johnson's judgements about the history of Scottish
literature.

---

[37] *MLA*, vol. 3, pp. 283–4.
[38] Johnson and Boswell, *Journey and Journal*, p. 187.

PART II
Texts

Allegory and Reformation poetics in David Lindsay's *Ane Satire of the Thrie Estaitis* (1552–54)

Amanda J. Piesse

David Lindsay's *Ane Satire of the Thrie Estaitis* (1552–54) is a morality play.[1] It describes how its protagonist, Rex Humanitas, sets out to be a good king; how he is tempted, through falsehood, deceit and flattery, to fall into the embrace of sensuality, and how he is redeemed from his fall by correction, by diligence, by good counsel and by taking heed of the common good. The play has English and Anglo-Irish generic counterparts: John Bale's *King Johan* (1538) shows its twelfth-century king in desperate need of advice from his country and the commonality in order to withstand papal sedition; the remaining fragment of the earlier Anglo-Irish *Pride of Life* (1400, lost in the Dublin Four Courts explosion of 1922 and only surviving in a photographed fragment made in 1891) shows its king relying on his stalwarts, strength and health, with an occasional dose of mirth, to fortify him as death approaches. Another anonymous and justly famous play of 1470 shows mankind being led so far astray by the devil's mischief that he forgets the promise of redemption and only just extricates himself from certain suicide by throwing himself back upon God's mercy, the promise of which he has wholeheartedly embraced at the beginning of the play.

Each one of these plays is to a greater or lesser degree concerned with reformation, both of its protagonist and of the church. One of them, *King Johan*, refers to a real historical character and reasonably accurately describes a set of historical events (even if, uniquely for this particular monarch, Bale's King John of England is a good king); one of them, *Ane Satire of the Thrie Estaitis* is deliberately ambivalent about its historical

---

[1] For an introduction to the genre, see Robert Potter, *The English Morality Play: origins, history and influence of a dramatic tradition* (London, 1975). For an accessible collection of the four major late medieval morality plays from Britain, see Peter Happé, *Four Morality Plays* (1979; reprinted, Harmondsworth, 1987). For the location of Lindsay's play within the genre, see Greg Walker, *Plays of persuasion: drama and politics at the court of Henry VIII* (Cambridge, 1991).

verisimilitude, with identifiable historical references that have been variously interpreted both to prove and disprove that Rex Humanitas is loosely based on the early life of James V of Scotland.[2] Each of them is written in the allegorical mode.[3] The virtues or vices that inhabit each play are all fully realized as characters on stage, and I present the accounts of them in the manner that I do above partly to draw attention to the subtlety of the allegorical mode. It is relatively easy to accept that flattery, an abstract term, can bring about the fall of a king, or that a similarly intangible notion, mischief, when set in train by the devil, might lead to the abandonment of any idea of mercy. In allegorical representation, with the personification of these qualities, the alignment of universalities and individual experience is ably demonstrated by the duality of word as character and character as word. The audience senses, and easily accepts, the double valency of the terms.

Not all reformation writing in the allegorical mode is this unproblematic, though. William Tyndale, in the closing stages of his extensive essay on the tensions between temporal and spiritual obedience, *The Obedience of A Christian Man*,[4] tackles the issue head on and casts considerable light on the intellectual difficulties a reformer might have with the notion of allegory. Complaining (understandably, I think) that the practice of fourfold exegesis ultimately obscures scripture rather than illuminating it, that once the expositor has run through the senses literal, tropological, allegorical and anagogical,[5] 'the literal sense is become nothing at all' (56), he goes on to single out allegorical interpretation as the most inimical of the four:

> Beyond all this / when we have found out the litterall sence of the scripture by the processe of the texte or by a lyke texte of another place. Then go wee & as the scripture boroweth similitudes of worldly things even so we agayne borrow similitudes or allegories of the scriptures and apply them to oure purposes?*

---

² For an overview of the running discussion between 1806 and 1973, see Joanne Spencer Kantrowicz, 'Encore: Lindsay's *Thrie Estaitis*, Date and New Evidence', *SSL*, 10 (1972–73), pp. 18–32. Kantrowicz's article provides the references for the main contributions to the debate, which centres around the dating of the play but uses the relationship between the historical King James V and the figure Rex Humanitas as a focus for the dating debate.

³ For an overview of the shifting definitions and applications of allegory at this time, see Jon Whitman, *Allegory: The dynamics of an ancient and medieval technique* (Oxford, 1987).

⁴ See William Tyndale, *The Obedience of a Christian Man* (1528; reprinted Menston, 1970). This is a facsimile edition in black letter type. For a more readily accessible edition which does not however preserve the original spelling or layout, see William Tyndale, *The Obedience of a Christian Man*, ed. David Daniell (Harmondsworth, 2000).

⁵ This is the system developed from Origen: see Whitman, *Allegory*, pp. 62–3.

which allegories are no sence of the scripture: but fre thinges besydes the scripture and al to gether in the liberte of the spirite. Which allegories I maye not make at all the wilde adventures: but must kepe me with in the compasse of the fayth and ever apply myne allegory to Christ and to the fayth. (fo. cxxi Riii)

Tyndale's difficulty here is that anything beyond the literal sense of scripture is fallen language, which makes exposition difficult.[6] Any elaboration, gloss, explanation is a movement away from the essential revealed word, because it superimposes humankind's interpretation on God's word. Once the signifier begins to meander between the sign and the signified, the signifier becomes deceptive: at worst, the signifier draws all the attention to itself so that both the point of departure and the intended goal are obscured by the process of the journey itself. This, obviously, is not a problem peculiar to Tyndale.[7] The issue of fallen language, of the insufficiency of any post-Edenic naming to come close to expressing what is intrinsically ineffable, is one that preoccupies a variety of Renaissance and reformation writers, usually on either the subject of religious writing or when justifying the privileging of the vernacular.

Lindsay, it seems to me, recognizes Tyndale's problem for what it is and comes pretty close to achieving a solution, and the purpose of this chapter is to try to demonstrate how he goes about it, to show the degree to which he writes reform not only in the content of his exposition but also in a wider sense, in terms of how we come to know what we know. If vernacular scripture allows non-clerical interrogation, allows the layperson direct access to the word, Lindsay's *mise-en-scène* encourages the layperson to acknowledge and accept knowingly the rhetorical effect of his writing. In order to reveal a moral and a social set of truths about the nature of humankind, some kind of process of signification is necessary. By embracing the morality tradition, Lindsay is setting himself up to be knocked down; the use of the universal to speak to the specific, of the outward and visible sign to articulate the inward invisible presentiment,

---

[6] For a discussion of the theory of the 'fallen vernacular' see Ruth Evans *et al.*, 'The Notion of Vernacular Theory', in Jocelyn Wogan-Browne *et al.* (eds), *The Idea of the Vernacular: An anthology of Middle English literary theory 1280–1520* (Exeter, 1999), pp. 314–30.

[7] The anonymous writer of the *Cloud of Unknowing*, for example, in extolling the virtues of the *via negativa*, expresses a desire for 'bot a litil worde of o silable; for so it is betir [th]en of two, for euer [th]e schorter it is, [th]e betir it acorde[th] wi[th] [th]e werk of [th]e spirite'; George Herbert observes in his poem 'The Flower' that '[God's] word is all, if we could spell' ; John Donne, in his 'Sermon of Valediction at My Going Into Germany at Lincolns-Inne, 18 April 1619' warns 'therefore thy memory looks not far enough back, if it stick only upon the Creature, and reach not to the Creator'.

is surely to run the risk of the sign becoming the focus of attention, rather than the conduit to meaning. What Lindsay does is to draw attention to his own deception as playwright, by encouraging the audience, at the end of the play, to acknowledge that it has been manipulated by both the form and the content of the play. By drawing attention to the seductiveness of both language and form, Lindsay educates the audience in how to avoid this kind of seduction.

Manipulation of this kind is nothing new: in *Mankind* (1470), the audience is seduced, in the early stages of the play, into preferring the active tomfoolery and vivid vocabulary of the vices to the static and frankly rather boring preaching of Mercy. Further, the audience is inveigled into singing a smutty song along with the vices by virtue of repeating the lines after them. The song begins innocently enough, but the willingness on the audience's part to sing each line without considering what it is singing soon leads it into uncleanness.[8] It is not difficult to see how this might be a reference to unthinking repetition led from the altar; how the aping of a mostly unintelligible Latin mass might lead the participants into error. Only towards the end does the playwright begin to overwrite the vices so that Mercy's elevated language and explicit emotive connection to Mankind becomes by contrast more attractive.

The point I'm trying to make here is that in *Mankind*, the playwright persuades the audience to empathize with his protagonist, to experience the same kind of seduction, to realize how easy it is to be seduced into this kind of behaviour, making the audience's experience of the play mimic Mankind's own experience. And after all, the allegorical leap of imagination here is that the audience *is* Mankind – the audience is representative of humankind just as the figure of Mankind is a synecdoche, so, if the playwright has done his job effectively, of course the audience experiences what Mankind experiences. The *Mankind* playwright achieves a wonderful mimesis.

Where Lindsay supersedes this predecessor intellectually is in his ability to manipulate the rhetoric – the intrinsic persuasiveness – of form and structure as well as content. It is after all not just that which is said that persuades, seduces, but the framework and context in which it is said, who says it and how they say it, and the order and process of revelation. One way to draw attention to this is to place certain scenes, situations and ideas in a deliberately incongruous context, thereby making habitually accepted practices strange.

I want to bring four different areas of Lindsay's playwrighting in *Ane Satire of the Thrie Estaitis* to bear on this idea. They are the structure of

---

[8]   *Mankind*, ll. 335 ff., in Mark Eccles (ed.), *The Macro Plays*, EETS 262 (London, 1969).

the four parts of the play; repeated motifs; the interplay between word and character; and the stage directions.

There are four parts to the play: the Banns, the First Part, the Interlude, and the Second Part. It has a huge cast of 44 characters, necessitating at least 22 players. The Banns, advertising what is believed to have been the first performance of the play in 1552 at Cupar in Fife,[9] name the date, time and place of the play. The banns also include a kind of 'trailer', a mini play, which is not an excerpt from the play proper, but which deals with a theme from it, marital unchastity, in a realistic (as opposed to allegorical) way. The themes of faithfulness and chastity are picked up in the First Part, which is highly allegorical, and deals with the protagonist, Rex Humanitas, being seduced by Sensualitie, Flatterie, Falset and Dissait, with the representative characters of Sowtar and Tailor struggling with the idea of chastity, and, towards the end, the appearance of Correction. An Interlude is then performed to keep the lower classes happy while the more elevated members of the audience take a comfort break.[10] The interlude is a brief, politicized attack on the Church's practice regarding death duties, and is self-consciously realistic.[11] The Second Part shows Rex Humanitas's actions to reform the 'thrie estaitis' (Spiritualitie, Temporalitie, and Merchand, in this account) ending with the hangings of three deceivers and a sermon from Folly, who appears to be flown in simply to deliver this speech.

Structurally, there is a deliberate movement from the representative into the allegorical mode, a disruption of the allegorical mode that draws attention to the fact that the play has been operating in it, and then a modified, more restrained allegorical performance. Diligence, at the beginning of the first part, performs a commonplace apologia:

---

[9] Some commentators believe that an account of a 1540 play refers to something substantially similar to extant versions of Lindsay's *Ane Satire*. The debate takes place in the articles cited above regarding dating and identity; for an account, see Kantrowicz, 'Encore: Lindsay's *Thrie Estaitis*'. While the debate about this report continues, it is certain that Lindsay's play was performed in 1552, which is the date I give here.

[10] 'Sen ye haif heard the first pairt of our play, Go tak ane drink and mak collatioun .../And ye ladies that list to pisch, / Lift up your taill, plat in ane dish' (ll. 1919–20, 1926–27). All quotations from *Ane Satire* are taken from Sir David Lindsay, *Ane Satire of the Thrie Estaitis*, ed. Roderick Lyall (Edinburgh, 1989).

[11] Both Carol Edington and Joanne Kantrowicz draw attention to specific historical analogues for this particular issue. See Carol Edington, *Court and Culture in Renaissance Scotland* (Amherst, MA, 1994), pp. 181–2, and Joanne Spencer Kantrowicz, *Dramatic Allegory: Lindsay's Ane Satyre of the Thrie Estaitis* (Lincoln, NE, 1975), p. 43. The specific historical references are discussed below.

Tak na man greif in speciall,
For wee sall speik in generall,
For pastyme and for play.
Thairfoir, till all our rymis be rung
And our mistoinit sangis be sung,
Let eveie man keip weill ane toung,
And everie woman tway! (i.71–7)

This announces the move to universality. The audience is required to think about the tension between fleshly reality and abstraction in the figure of Sensualitie, who comes to seduce the king away from his good intentions. She is vividly physical and draws attention to her own physicality: she shimmies into the playing area with 'Luifers awalk! behald the fyrie spheir, / Behauld the naturall dochter of Venus; / Behauld, luifers, this lustie ladie cleir' [i.271–3]. The audience is required to think further about the deception inherent in allegory as it watches the vices disguise themselves not just by a process of dressing up but with all the business of a parodic baptism. The play is dealing with deception by formula, not just the petty deception of enactment.

FALSET
Wee man do mair yit, be Sanct James,
For wee mon all thrie change our names.
Hayif me, and I sall baptize thee.
DISSAIT
Be God and thair-about may it be!
How will thou call me, I pray the tell?
FALSET
I wait not how to call my-sell!
DISSAIT
Bot yit anis name the bairn[i]s name.
FALSET
Discretioun, Discretioun, in Gods name!
DISSAIT
I neid nocht now to cair for thrift;
Bot quhat salbe my Godbairne gift?
FALSET
I gif yow all the devilis of hell!
DISSAIT
Na, brother, hauld that to thy sell!
Now sit doun, let me baptize the-
I wait not quhat thy name sould be.
FALSET

Bot yit anis name the bairn[i]s name.
DISSAIT
Sapience, in ane warld[i]s schame!
FLATTERIE
Brother Dissait, cum, baptize me.
DISSAIT
Then sit doun lawlie on thy kne.
FLATTERIE
Now brother name the bairn[I]s name.
DISSAIT
Devotioun, [in] the Devillis name!
FLATTERIE
The Devil resave the, lurdoun loun!
Thou hes wet all my new-shawin croun.
DISSAIT
Devotioun, Sapience, and Discretioun:
We thre may rewll this regioun.
We sall find monie craftie thingis
For to begyll ane hundreth kings;
For thow can richt weil crak and clatter
And I sall feinye, and thow sall flatter. (i. 778–805)

The audience is invited to stay outside of the action and to acknowledge its suspension of disbelief. The baptism scene, with its solemn, proper wording in direct tension with the mad horseplay that is evidently going on, is important: a process need not be coherent with its intention just because due process, and even due wording, is observed. Having offered his audience this lesson (and having allowed them to be amused by it) Lindsay proceeds to Advanced Allegory for Beginners. First we see the newly-named Sapience forget his name: he calls himself Thin Drink, because Sapience sounds like *sapeins*, which means dregs, or lees. The word can be mistaken if you pay attention only to its sound, and not to its meaning. On we go to the next lesson: representative townsfolk figures are aligned with the allegorical figures, and the dislocation between sign and misinterpreted figure is made plain again. Tailor and Sowtar converse with Chastity, who has come to see if she can find lodging with the prioress for just one night (she can't); Tailor's Wife and Sowtar's Wife hear that their husbands are conversing with a bonny woman, and that they seem very taken with her. They are suspicious, but only become enraged when they find out that their husbands are intending entertaining Chastity in their homes. This is the bouleversement in action; surely the women should be dreading infidelity? At a basic level, this is a demonstration of artisan-class minds working only on a literal level. The women in the play react first to the idea of their menfolk chatting to a bonny strange woman; that is realistic. But what enrages them is simultaneously physical and allegorical: if their husbands embrace Chastity/chastity, there will be, they complain no more *chalmer-glew* for them, the wives. Lindsay has the women move from performing as mimetic characters to a direct interaction with the allegorical process.

For the audience, the conundrum is this: what is of primary significance? The appearance of an attractive strange woman, at the mimetic level, the assumption of what she stands for (at a mimetic imagined level), or what she really stands for in terms of the allegorical paradigm of the play? What really interests me about this moment is that it is very easy to grasp, but almost impossible to explain. The allegorical mode can work a charm that literal language struggles to articulate. We are dealing here with 'a language that calls attention to its own hesitancy',[12] which relies on a particular mode of understanding to demonstrate what it means. As the First Part draws to a close, a messenger appears. He says that Correction is about to make his presence felt, and his language is close to being a replication of Diligence's introduction to the suspension of disbelief at the beginning of Part One. With this stylistic shift back towards the realistic mode in which the play started, it is signalled that the audience is assumed to have been through a process of conscious shifts in paradigm. It is assumed to have been seduced, to have aligned itself with the characters within the text, to have need of being addressed in the same register as the characters. At this point the vices run away, Dissait steals a money box and Rex Humanitas is woken from his postcoital doze in the arms of Sensualitie.

This moment is important too. Rex Humanitas has said at the beginning of Part One, as he stands waiting to enter the play, 'I knaw my days indure bot as an dreme', again hinting that what we are about to see is only one version of reality. Sensuality has, as we have seen, exhorted the audience to wake up to her attractions (signalling a sensual awakening, and indeed the King becomes sexually aware at this moment); moments later, the King himself wakes up Wantonness; Veritie, arriving with Chastitie and clutching to her bosom a vernacular gospel, has implored God to awake and aid them; and now Rex Humanitas is called upon to reawaken from the slumber into which Sensualitie has lulled him.

There is a clear invocation of the neoPlatonic notion of the waking dream here. This whole episode in Rex Humanitas's life has been a shadow (in every sense) of his ideal form. The series of awakenings maps out a path of decline, realignment and restoration, signifying the shift in

---

[12] Laurie Finke, 'Truth's treasure: Allegory and meaning in *Piers Plowman*', in Stephanie Trigg (ed.), *Medieval English Poetry* (London, 1993), pp. 84–9. Finke is commenting on Augustine's discussion of ineffability in *On Christian Doctrine*.

and out of allegorical lapse and realistic recognition. This is one of the repeated tropes that inhabit the play, and it is significant, not least because of its clear connections with the English morality tradition. In *Mankind*, Titivillus only finally secures Mankind's fall by putting him to sleep and whispering a dream vision of Mercy's death into his ear. In *Mankind* there is one dream vision – not a *Piers Plowman*-revelation of goodness on a higher plane, as all good dream visions should be, or an Anglo-Saxon *swēme*, a trance that reveals a spiritual truth like the *Dream of the Rood*, but a perverted version of that, a reversal of the expected trope.[13] In *Thrie Estaitis*, the different possibilities of kind are laid out in turn: the audience is invited to differentiate, to see how the motif functions as well as observe its effect.

The First Part draws to a close with Rex Humanitas calling for Wisdom and Discretion to help him confront Correction. The audience sees him learn that he has been deceived by these false figures. Having had on his side only false Wisdom and Discretion, both qualities have been in reality lacking, and he therefore could not see that what was before him was neither wisdom nor discretion, but in fact falsehood and deceit. He is told that Good Counsel, Diligence and Correction are far more important to the task that lies ahead of him. Then comes a vital stage direction: 'The King embraces Correction with an humbill countenance.' What the audience *sees* on stage is a simple embrace; what it *understands* is the assimilation of a quality. The very end of Part One shows an almost satirical return to reality, as the audience is invited to be aware of its physical existence in the most basic terms – the invitation to eat, to drink, and to relieve full bladders that is quoted above.

There are two more observations to make about the allegorical working of Part One. One is that the unholy Trinity of Flattery, Falset and Dissait continually refer to themselves as 'we three'. When they are replaced in Part Two by a trio of virtues, that trio refers to itself, without exception, as 'us three'. I think that there is a possibility, given the absolute consistency of the pronouns, that this is an early direct reference to the group of fools.[14]

---

[13] For a detailed account of kinds of dreaming see Steven F. Kruger, *Dreaming in the Middle Ages* (Cambridge, 1992); for a brief account of the kinds into which Macrobius sorts dreams, see *Chaucer: Sources and backgrounds*, ed. Robert P. Miller (New York, 1977), pp. 49–52. I am grateful to Professor V.J. Scattergood for providing me with these references.

[14] It is Malone who first comments on 'we three at loggerheads' in a note to II.iii.17, *Twelfth Night* in his 1790 edition of Shakespeare's works: 'I believe Shakspeare (sic) had in his thoughts a common sign, in which two wooden heads are exhibited, with this inscription under it: "We three loggerheads be." The spectator or reader is supposed to make the third.' Of a painting bearing the title 'Wee three Logerh[ea]ds', which shows two grinning fools in caps and bells, one

If that is the case, it would suggest a precise proposition on Lindsay's part; even the choice of a pronoun can make all the difference in signification, because of assumptions made through custom and resonance.

The second point is with the pattern regarding sleeping, or dreaming. The vice figures continually suggest that a character tempted to virtue is either dreaming (the significance of which we know) or with the Queen of Faery – that is to say, totally outside of the realms of reason. Lindsay tempts us to disregard the figure of the dream by trivializing it. Sleeping – not recognizing the possibility of operating in a different paradigm – is not the same as being away with the fairies, but if the two are juxtaposed often enough, they will come to seem contiguous, and a rhetorical trick of proximity will enable an intellectual deception. The vice figures then act in opposition to the playwright's project, continually inviting the audience to reject the possibility of alternative paradigms of experience as irrational.

The First Part of the play, then, works hard to establish a number of paradigms of representation, and to draw attention to the paradigms it is manipulating. The Interlude continues this project. Although it is scripted, and, like the rest of the play, in verse, it is supposed to seem spontaneous and realistic.[15] The idea is that while everyone is taking their break, a ('real') pauper who has been a spectator until now breaks through the crowd in protest onto the playing field and climbs up onto Rex Humanitas's throne, hurling abuse at the actor playing Diligence. What matters here is that momentarily the audience believes the hurlyburly to be true; it is a formal indication of the kind of debate that will take place in the interlude, the space between the two parts of the play, a serious, current argument about death duties. It is also partly a warm-up for Part Two, when Johne the Common-weill – Lindsay's Joe Public – will outline the real problems for which the newly and properly awakened Rex Humanitas will provide real solutions. But the reality trope attaching to this section is undermined by a guest appearance by the Sowtar and his wife, who wander in to the argument looking for a divorce from the Pardoner who is one of the

---

of them holding a mirror, Michael Hattaway explains 'Wee three Logerh[ea]ds [is] a visual joke at the viewer's expense ... The third loggerhead is the viewer who is tricked into asking where the third fool is. Continental prints of this trick survive from Shakespeare's time.' See Michael Hattaway (ed.), *A Companion to English Renaissance Literature and Culture* (Oxford, 2000), plate 12.

[15]   There are cases of this elsewhere. Servants, apparently waiting at table before the interlude to *Fulgens and Lucres* (1497) begins, step up to introduce the play and take roles in it. Roper's *Life of More* (?mid 1550s) tells how the young Thomas More would extemporize among the players at Cardinal Morton's household (for which, incidentally, *Fulgens and Lucres* is thought to have been written). In 1998 I was in an audience that was utterly convinced we were being interrupted by rowdy teenagers demanding to be allowed to participate in a jousting tournament at the Puy du Fou in the Vendée.

objects of Pauper's abuse. The divorce is granted, but only after Sowtar and his wife have gravely kissed one another's backsides, the outward and visible sign required by the Pardoner to seal the divorce. Their appearance, and the nonsense that surrounds them, throws the status of Pauper into disarray. How can we believe that he is not an actor if he interacts with characters from the play as characters, rather than as actors? Or does it work the other way around; does the alignment of the two sets of characters confer an *a posteriori* realism on Part One? The confusion itself raises the important questions: the audience must question process as well as product.

Part Two begins with the Thrie Estaitis answering Rex Humanitas's summons. They enter, famously, 'gangand backwart', elaborately demonstrating that a reversal is needed if proper order is to be maintained. Also invited to the realignment of the state is Johne the Common-weill. He arrives from among the audience, leaping over the ditch that separates them from the players – quite literally crossing notional boundaries. The voice of reality, of the real people, the audience, is being translated into the play. There follows a stichomythic exchange – the only one in the play.

REX
Schaw me thy name, gude man, I the command.
JOHN
Mary, Johne the Common-weil of fair Scotland.
REX
The Common-weil hes ben amang his fais!
JOHN
Ye, Sir, that gars the Common-weil want clais.
REX
Quhat is the caus the Common-weil is crukit?
JOHN
Becaus the Common-weill hes bene over-luikit.
REX
Quhat gars the luke sa with ane drerie hart?
JOHN
Because the Thrie Estaits gangs all backwart. (ii. 2442–9)

It's like a catechism, and Johne knows all the answers, and what's more he can rhyme – be exactly consonant – with Rex Humanitas. The outward and audible form mimics the accord of their inward sentiment. As the debate continues, Johne supports his side of the argument with appropriate scriptural quotation, always translating what he has said in Latin into the Scots vernacular in the next line – a direct reversal from Act One, where the vices quote to suit their purposes and don't translate. On the

basis of Johne's evidence, Correction declares, 'Or I pairt aff this nation/
I sall mak reformatioun' (ii. 2676–7): the lords and merchants 'embreasse
John the Common weill' (SD at ii. 2722) but the spirituality declines, and
the real ecclesiastical debate begins. The spirituality admit they can't back
up their argument with scripture, since they've never read the Bible, but
counterattack by accusing John of being deficient in his faith and insisting
he recite his creed. He won't do it for them ('ye are not my ordinair' he
hisses [ii. 3010]) but when Correction plainly commands 'Schaw furth your
faith, and feinye nat' (ii. 3021) he recites his creed perfectly in rhyming
couplets in the Scots vernacular, grinding to a halt in a vital place:

> I beliefe in God, that all hes wrocht
> And creat everie thing of nocht,
> And in his Son, our Lord Jesu,
> Incarnat of the Virgin trew;
> Quha under Pilat tholit passioun,
> And deit for our salvatioun,
> And on the third day rais againe,
> As Halie Scriptour schawis plane;
> And als, my Lord, it is weill kend,
> How he did to the Heavin ascend,
> And set Him doun at the richt hand
> Of God the Father, I understand,
> And sall cum judge on Dumisday.
> Quhat will ye mair, Sir, that I say?
> CORRECTIOUN
> Schaw furth the rest: this is na game.
> JOHNE
> I trow *Sancte Ecclesiam*–
> Bot nocht in thir bischops nor thir freirs,
> Quhilk wil for purging of thir nears
> Sard up the ta raw and doun the uther.

This moment is interesting in terms of historical allusion. One of the
elements in the dating of this play (1540, 1552, 1554) is the reference
to the Paternoster controversy that arose and rumbled in the Fife area
between 1549–52, to do with the addressing of the Paternoster to the
saints as well as to God. When the controversy was resolved with the
publication of Hamilton's catechism in 1552, it was by avoidance; the
recommendation from the Provincial Council of the Scottish Catholic
Church, which authorized the catechism, was that the prayer be taught
and recited in the vernacular as a basic requirement. Its direction was left
silent. This episode and the shenanigans surrounding it, which involved

an exposé of a particular priest's inability to expound scripture properly, is recorded in the 1570 version of Foxe's *Acts and Monuments*.[16] Here, I think, Lindsay alludes, but does not replicate. That John knows his creed, in the vernacular, speaks for itself here.

As the play draws to a close, Diligence proclaims 14 numbered acts, one after the other, beginning with the nation's duty to 'manfully defend and fortify / The kirk of Christ and his religion'. Having refused to embrace Johne, the spirituality has left, and taken Sensualitie with them – which goes quite a long way to aligning them with the vices at the end of Part One. The acts go on to decree that bishops will be appointed on grounds of their learning, that there will be no death duties, that the bishop will live in his diocese and the priest in his parish, that priests might marry, but that there is to be no intermarriage between the spiritual and the temporal states (this is the last of the acts). The enumeration is unusual in a play; there is a real drive to plain speaking here and the notion of the spiritual and the temporal being kept apart is not just literal in its meaning.

Finally, the hanging scene. Order having been established, it is decided that some vices must be destroyed permanently. Flatterie does a deal, sells his friends, and walks free. More of that in a moment. When Thift, Falset and Dissait are hanged, there is a stage direction for each, and the detail is fascinating. The stage directions in each case are different: *Heir sal Thift be drawin up or his figour: Heir sal Dissait be drawin up or ellis his figure: Heir sal [Falset] be heiset up, and not his figure; and an Craw or an Ke salbe castin up, as it war his saull.* Here Lindsay draws specific attention to the material workings of the play. Twice the reader (or director – but not the audience) is offered the opportunity to differentiate between the allegorical mode and the physical mode by drawing attention to the fact that the figure might be hoisted in either physical or symbolic mode. But then the real body of Falset must be hoisted up. Why? And why the sign of the departing black soul? By showing death by figure and then by actor and then configuring a departing soul by a symbol, Lindsay is reiterating the possibilities available to the morality playwright. An honest account of representation must admit that between the idea and the reality falls the shadow. It is impossible to write in a way that is completely free of rhetoric; all representation is fallen, will work to its own agenda. Flattery, the figure who represents abuse of language most explicitly, therefore must be allowed to do a deal, to give up his companions to judgements, and to

---

[16] See Kantrowitz, 'Encore: Lindsay's *Thrie Estaitis*', pp. 26–7. On the matter of dating, Kantrowicz concludes, 'If we accept Foxe's dates, Lindsay must have been working on the play and have finished it sometime between November 1, 1551, when the controversy erupted publicly, and early June, 1552, when the play had its first performance'.

walk free. The question is perhaps further answered by the appearance of Folly at the end of the play. 'Allegory demonstrates language's inability to guarantee the signified, to wed once and for all the word and the thing', and the best we can do is to be aware that it is folly to try. Reformation drama in the hands of David Lindsay is the most honest form there is. The revelation of an inward, invisible presentiment has to rely on some kind of outward and visible sign. All we can do is to acknowledge that, accept the slippage between the sign and the signified, and be always ready to embrace correction.

CHAPTER 5

John Knox and *A Godly Letter:* Fashioning and refashioning the exilic 'I'

Rudolph P. Almasy

One of the more recent attempts to reevaluate John Knox's contribution to Reformation history was the 1998 book of 13 essays edited by Roger Mason, entitled *John Knox and the British Reformations.*[1] In James Kirk's essay in that volume, 'John Knox and the Historians',[2] there is a sense that Knox continues in the scholarly imagination as either a theorist for political resistance or as an abstract, cold and exacting reformer or as a 'grim ayatollah-like figure',[3] this last label the result of feminist reactions to *First Blast of the Trumpet Against the monstrous Regiment of women.* The goal of Mason's collection is to help scholars see John Knox as an individual with a diversity of attitudes and beliefs yet an integral player in the Protestant international of the sixteenth century.

Unfortunately, within the 13 essays there is hardly any talk of John Knox as a writer, except to repeat commonplaces: that there seem to be two sides to Knox, a public persona and a private persona; that he plays the role of an Old Testament prophet; and that it is best to see him as he labelled himself – God's trumpeter.[4] As for blowing God's trumpet, no one ever looks closely enough to notice that in the Old Testament there are four different ways trumpets appear: as accompanying exhortations to repentance, as signals of impending divine activity, as instruments of praise, and as instruments of destruction. This oversight should alert Knox scholars of the need to examine the ramifications of the scriptural intertexts and their contexts that are found throughout Knox's prose, as

---

[1]   Roger Mason (ed.), *John Knox and the British Reformations* (Aldershot and Burlington, 1998). All passages from Knox are taken from *The Works of John Knox*, 6 vols, ed. David Laing (Edinburgh: Bannatyne Club, 1846–64).

[2]   James Kirk, 'John Knox and the Historians', in Mason, pp. 7–21.

[3]   Ibid., p. 11.

[4]   W. Stanford Reid's well-known biography of John Knox is titled *Trumpeter of God* (1974), and the essays by Richard Kyle often begin with the notion that Knox consistently played the role of prophet. See Kyle's 'The Thundering Scot: John Knox the preacher', *The Westminster Theological Journal*, 64 (2002), pp. 135–49; and his 'Prophet of God: John Knox's Self Awareness', *The Reformed Theological Review*, 61 (2002), pp. 85–101.

well as the ramifications of the labels brought to bear on Knox's complex arena of discourse, an arena shared by other Scottish religious writers of the sixteenth century. As for scriptural intertexts, Knox used them artfully. He knew which trumpet he was blowing and the hoped for result.

One scholar recently has pursued a close reading of some of Knox's texts, namely Kenneth D. Farrow in his study *John Knox: Reformation Rhetoric and the Traditions of Scots Prose 1490–1570*.[5] Farrow argues that Knox is a good prose writer in need of a good public relations officer, and Farrow's task is to be that officer through an examination of the stylistic sophistication which Knox demonstrated. Farrow's study, therefore, focuses on words, sentences, and brief passages that identify and discuss Knox's deliberate images, metaphors, and rhetorical figures and devices. Farrow's goal is 'to establish something of the flavour of the prose'.[6]

I want to pursue a different kind of close reading while serving as yet another public relations officer arguing for the richness and complexity of the Knoxian text. I want to step back from sentences and paragraphs to describe the *dispositio* or arrangement of material within the text to see how, in constructing an artful text, Knox negotiated the new reformist literary terrain that problematized the authorial self. To suggest how Knox, as author, puts together a text is to describe the politics of that text. That is, texts perform relationships, often of power and purpose, in ways discernible by paying attention to the languages and constructions of power and positionality, authority and intention. Through the politics of discourse, we can see this particular writer constructing a text that demonstrates a characteristic of early reformist writing, for reformation writing was often shaped by the social and political moments – critical and extraordinary circumstances – reformers like Knox encountered as they longed to speak or were compelled to speak in crisis to fellow believers. Examining Knox in this light should also alert us to the artfulness of other Scottish Reformation writings, polemic and pastoral and otherwise, as those writings explore such rhetorical concerns as genre, voice, audience, and strategy.

The critical moments I am exploring are the years of Knox's exile from the island of Britain after Mary Tudor became queen in 1553. And there were a variety of critical moments and movements. Knox left in 1554, eventually for Frankfurt which he abandoned because he could not accept all of the Edwardian Prayer Book as the liturgy for the English

---

[5] Kenneth D. Farrow, *John Knox: Reformation Rhetoric and the Traditions of Scots Prose 1490–1570* (Oxford: Peter Lang, 2004).

[6] Ibid., p. 70. Another useful essay on the flavour of Knox's prose is R.D.S. Jack, 'The Prose of John Knox: A Re-assessment', *Prose Study*, 4 (1981), pp. 239–51. Jack also stresses Knox's use of imagery and figures while discussing Knox's bilingual inheritance and the range and power of his rhetorical techniques.

congregation he was helping to pastor in Frankfurt. What followed was a brief stay in Geneva and then a call back to Scotland, but only for a matter of months, until he was forced out by the Roman Catholic establishment. He then accepted the call to pastor the English congregation in Geneva for several years, finally returning to Scotland in 1559. And all this time he was writing what appear to be occasional pieces (Farrow calls them 'admonitory public epistles'), sometimes to the English congregations he had left behind, sometimes to Scottish Protestants, sometimes to his family, sometimes to rulers. There were at least nine tracts between 1553 and late 1558 when the *First Blast* appeared. To understand Knox as a writer (and to sense his gift to create texts), one has to examine each of these tracts to see how well notions of prophet and trumpeter hold up and to watch how it is that Knox negotiates the discursive arena he appropriates (perhaps discovers) for the various purposes he announces.

Observing the discursive arena, which almost always has a polemical edge to it (and thus an elevation of a rhetorical 'I'), is critical in understanding what a reformist writer like John Knox was trying to do – and why – because for a reformed Christian of the sixteenth century there may have been a problem in being a writer, especially a Calvinist self who turned too much attention to that self. After all, God was the sole author of anything worthwhile for the heart of the believer. A writer, or a preacher, was merely (but importantly) the instrument of the Holy Spirit. Knox admits, for example, at the end of *A Godly Letter of Warning or Admonition to the Faithful in London, Newcastle, and Berwick* which we are going to review in this essay that his admonition is actually a warning from the Holy Spirit, not from him. Knox writes: 'The God of all comfort and consolatioun, for Chryst Jesus his Sonnies sake, grant that this my simple and plaine Admonitioun (yea, rather the warning of the Holie Ghost) may be resaved and accepted of yow, with no less feare and obedience than I haif writtin it unto yow with unfained lufe and sorowful heart' (3.215). There was a danger in the rhetorical 'I' of an author as too humanist and therefore sinful. Whenever one wrote, one stood in need of authorization, as Kevin Dunn has argued in *Pretext of Authority: The Rhetoric of Authorship in the Renaissance Preface*.[7] And that authorization could not be a self-authorization. Catharine Randall Coats also deals with the problematics of the 'I' in Reformation writing, an 'I', as Calvin would say, which is part of a fallen world.[8] The dilemma of authorship for the

---

[7] Kevin Dunn, *Pretext of Authority: The Rhetoric of Authorship in the Renaissance Preface* (Stanford: Stanford University Press, 1994).

[8] Catharine Randall Coats, *Subverting the System: D'Aubigné and Calvinism* (Kirksville, MO, 1990), especially Chapter One, 'Literary Constructs for Theological Conventions: Authorizing the Word of the Self', pp. 1–24.

Reformation often revealed the problem of authorial self-image and was frequently solved by appropriating scriptural models and by manipulating the discursive arena in order to be absorbed into the text one is producing. Knox certainly secured his authorization to speak from scripture, but to appreciate Knox's textual landscape we need to go beyond generalizations to see what he actually does in his texts.

In this essay, I am interested in the first piece of writing Knox produced for English readers as an exile, interested especially in how the 'I' is displayed. And I use that word 'displayed' deliberately, for we are beginning to see that by mid-century Tudor writers were experimenting with being an 'I' – not necessarily an autobiographical 'I' as we would understand it today, but an 'I' attempting to find a self-promotional discursive space in order to speak from both the mind and the heart. Such speaking seems to be characterized by display. My hope is that as we follow through the politics of the 'I' on display in this letter we will find a productive entry into all the exilic writings – and perhaps into the writings of other Scottish reformers.

Certainly Knox does display himself in *A Godly Letter of Warning, or Admonition to the Faithful in London, Newcastle, and Berwick*, a letter Knox may have started as he was preparing to leave England in the Fall of 1553 and which was published May of 1554 at Wittenberg. R.D.S. Jack believes that this letter 'could fairly lay claim to be the finest short literary piece' that Knox composed.[9] The very first words we see in the letter name the author himself: 'John Knox, to the faithfull in Londoun, Newcastell, and Barwick' (3.165), Knox choosing to direct this his first admonition to members of three reformed congregations he had recently ministered to in England. In the face of an unprecedented reversal of fortune, Knox explores what needed to be said, how it should be said, and by what kind of writerly self or authorized 'I'. And what needed to be said is found in a pastoral letter which provides a site for public debate early in Mary's reign. In this pastoral letter, Knox mixes simultaneously the pastoral or intimate with the public, something he does repeatedly in his exilic writings. It is also not unusual for Knox to name himself, to draw attention to himself and to his writing. It may be the case that what gave him permission to name himself immediately was the voice of the prophet Jeremiah. The importance of Jeremiah to Knox is acknowledged by almost everyone who has examined Knox's writings.[10] But we should look closely at the extent

---

[9]   Jack, p. 247.

[10]   See especially Kyle, 'Prophet of God: John Knox's self awareness'. Kyle writes, for example, that 'the reformer saw himself as a preacher – a watchman – cast in the mold of the Hebrew prophets. More than any of the major reformers,

of the Jeremian voice in an admonition like *A Godly Letter*, as well as other exilic pieces.

It is fitting to begin with Jeremiah, especially since in the first half of *A Godly Letter* Knox relentlessly uses the Book of Jeremiah to draw the attention of his reader. He may have done this to teach his readers what this Old Testament book actually contained. Knox's initial task, typically reformist, is to compare Israel and England, two covenanted nations, by duplicating long passages from Jeremiah. But these passages are not necessarily for the wicked as we find in the Book of Jeremiah but for the faithful to whom Knox hopes to speak. It is important to note the difference here and in other exilic writings: Jeremiah (actually it is often the voice of God) thunders at the wicked of Israel, while Knox speaks to the faithful he left behind. The comparison between Israel and England demonstrates how England has become unapologetically wicked since Mary's ascension and how God will punish the idolatry of the mass eventually. Knox does play – or display himself as – Jeremiah, as a mouthpiece of God, condemning the 'stif-nekit and stuburne pepell' (3.165) and persuading the faithful – who may have their doubts – that the stiff-necked will be punished. Knox plays Jeremiah before the wicked but appropriates another voice, as we shall see, for the faithful he is, perhaps, most interested in.

There are some problems, however, in naming Knox as a Jeremiah or in general as a contemporary Old Testament prophet as so many do without seeing what Knox actually does in the text. First, as I have already suggested, we need to consider audience. Note that Jeremiah writes globally – O Jerusalem, O Israel, O Judah – writes to the 'kingdom', to the 'nation', the prophetic always directed to the public and the global. That is, Jeremiah's view encompasses a wide landscape of multiple abominations, of unrelenting wickedness over decades of turmoil and disappointment. He emphasizes almost exclusively God's vengeance and Israel's inevitable destruction, for Jeremiah concludes that no faithful can be found in Israel. Knox quotes from Ezekiel: 'from the preist to the propheit, everie man dealleth disceitfullie. Behold, thair earis ar uncircumcisit thay can not advert ... Thay haif committit abominabill mischief; they can not repent' (3.173). If there is to be repentance – something highly unlikely – it must be national. As for the notion of the remnant which Jeremiah mentions infrequently, there are two groups for whom the remnant label is used, and for both Jeremiah counsels passivity: there are those exiled to Babylon and those left behind as too useless for exile.

Despite Knox's lengthy comparison in the first part of the letter between England and Israel, Knox does not write to a nation or a kingdom. Not

---

Knox most strongly identified himself with the prophetic tradition' of admonition and prediction (p. 85).

unlike other English reformers such as Tyndale and Askew and Bale, he writes, as the first sentence of the letter indicates, to a small group: the faithful in 'London, Newcastell, and Barwyck'. But then Knox adds that he is also writing to 'utheris within the realme of England, that luffeth the cumming of oure Lorde Jesus'. This is not, however, the whole nation, only some, certainly a minority, within the realm but beyond the specific congregations who love the Lord with an intensity Knox would approve. While Jeremiah's voice is expansive, Knox prefers the local or the confined in these exilic writings, even in the somewhat anomalous *First Blast of the Trumpet*. We might think for a moment that the faithful of England is the remnant mentioned in Old Testament prophecy. But this comparison also does not quite work. The faithful in England are not counselled to remain passive in the face of divine activity, nor are they exiled, nor do they flee to the greener pastures of some contemporary Egypt. Knox's faithful are in specific locales, specific congregations – or churches (perhaps we ought to be thinking of Paul rather than Jeremiah) – and, as we shall see, Knox wants them to do something specific in upholding the covenant, but not something extravagant as we find among the prophets.

The message exposing abomination and promising desolation is not really about the faithful nor entirely appropriate for what Knox will ask of the faithful. So why does he begin with such intense prophetic exhortation? And it is good to remind ourselves that, despite shifting within multiple audiences, Knox's writings are always well-organized to suggest that he knew exactly what he was doing. He might have begun this way to warn the vulnerable faithful not to backslide, or perhaps to remind them, once again, that God will eventually punish the papists, or perhaps to assure them that their wicked neighbours would not triumph over them for long. But there might be something else going on through the text.

In this his first piece of exilic writing (*A Godly Letter* appears to be only his second effort at preparing something for publication), Knox needed to be taken seriously as a writer. As a good reformist, he needed a scriptural voice. He needed to be welcomed as the self-proclaimed messenger of God, especially since he had fled to the relative safety of Protestant Europe where he was planning other essays. In exile, without benefit of the intimacy of the pulpit, Knox writes initially not as himself but as Jeremiah; he can disappear within the text and texture of prophecy; he can stand separated from the wicked nation – and be noticed. Here is a self displayed yet grounded in scripture. Jeremiah and his language enable Knox to be an 'I' on display when a reformist writer had to be careful about that 'I' and about self-promotion.

In this way, too, the self-exiled Knox can argue for the importance of the particular historical – and divine – moment, and this is an argument that only the faithful (who could also be called the elect) can hear and truly understand. As Jeremiah found himself at a moment when the prophetic needed to be heard, so too does Knox find himself in an analogous situation when a prophetic-like voice could convey the biblical message: 'For the Lord hes appoyntit the day of his vengeance, befoir the whilk he sendis his trompettis and messingeris, that his elect, watcheing, and praying, with all sobrietie, may, be his mercie, eschaipe the vengeance that sall cum' (3.168). Knox must speak of God's promised vengeance on England precisely because he has assumed the prophetic pose and is confident of what that pose enables him to do as he addresses a nation which has broken its holy covenant. Yet, simultaneously Knox seems to invite the faithful to assume, like him, the prophetic role as messengers of Jeremiah's warning that God punishes when his grace has been offered but refused, as with present day England. After all, Knox does asks: 'What man then can ceis to prophesie? The Word of God planelie speikis' that the wrath of God 'salbe kendillit aganis' the wicked (3.169). Not only does the word of God plainly speak, but Knox makes sure how plain it is through the relentless quoting from Jeremiah and Ezekiel and the inescapable comparison of England and Israel. The faithful as priests in their own right are invited into the enterprise of survival and can assume the voice of the prophet to warn and condemn those in their community who will listen. All the faithful can blow trumpets. If we want to think of Knox (and others) as a thundering trumpet, this particular trumpet at this particular moment in the text signals impending (and perhaps destructive) divine activity. But one question prompted by this Jeremian message is whether, by the end of Knox's text, the elect are perceived or constructed as merely watching for the coming divine vengeance about which Knox was educating them. Such a cosmic moment feels different from the historic/historical moment of Knox's letter in which the brethren struggle to survive.

Knox does stress the singularity of the moment and his intimate relationship to that moment by revealing biographical details that draw the congregation into the personal: how he was one of Edward's preachers, how he knew Northumberland, how he could spot the true preachers at court, how he warned what Mary Tudor might bring, how he knows those faithful ministers now being tortured in the Tower of London. To display himself as a Jeremiah gives Knox permission boldly to put himself right in the middle of what is happening back in London. As he writes, 'I may be admittit for a sufficient witness; for I heard and saw, I understude and knew ... the manifest contempt and craftie devyces of the Devill agains those most godlie and learnit Preacheris that this last Lent, Anno M.D. LIII., wer appoyntit to preache befoir the Kingis Majestie' (3.175). And he stills knows it all, even though he is absent from England. His display as Jeremiah invites the dearly beloved to think about him – about Knox – while they read or heard the letter: 'Consider now, Deir Brethren, the estait of Godis trew Prophet; what anguische wes this in his hart, whan not onlie wer his admonitionis contempnit, but almost everie creature was conjurit aganis him ... In the middis of these stormie trubillis, no uither comfort had the Prophet than to complane to his God' (3.186). And he indicates there will be more writing to come about those wicked Edwardian politicians: 'But now will I not speik all that I knaw; for yf God continew my lyfe in this trubill, I intend to prepair ane dische for suich as than led the ring in the Gospell' (3.177). Continuing to draw attention to himself, Knox can proclaim as Jeremiah did that 'no man will wey, ponder, and consider the cause. This people will not heare my worde. Thay walk in the wicked invention of thair awn hartes'. The language is prophetically extravagant: 'But in England, I heir of none ... that dar put thair hands betuix the blude-thristie lyonis and thair pray: that is, betuix those cruell tirantis that now ar lowsit from thair dennis, and the pure sanctis of God' (3.189). Displaying himself as a Jeremiah further authorizes him to ask for action from various groups, but perhaps more importantly it enables him to suggest that his 'trubil' (as he is self-exiled in Protestant Europe) is somehow similar to the troubles of 'the pure sanctis of God' and, thus, they can and should still listen to him as they listened to him from the pulpit. Here we can see that Knox's text begins to reflect multiple possibilities and multiple audiences. There is throughout a call for repentance, a call to forsake idolatry, but this call is not relevant for 'the pure sanctis of God', understood above as 'pray'. There is also the hope that God will 'bring upon [the wicked] the plagues that he had threatnit' (3.187). Finally, there is the hope that Knox can inspire some to dare to put their hands between 'the blude-thrislie lyonis and thair pray', a hope that informs the *First Blast*.[11]

But this hope of rescuing the 'pray' is articulated less in *A Godly Letter* than it would be later in something like the *First Blast*. As the people revolted back to idolatry after Jeremiah's death, so it would not surprise Knox in *A Godly Letter* that the same would happen in England without him, even to that 'small and soir trubillit flock' he is most interested in.[12] As Jeremiah was not allowed to enter the Temple, so is the self-exiled

---

[11]   It is also possible to identify yet another group Knox hoped to speak to in his Jeremian voice. Knox cites Romans 1 where Paul condemns not only those who commit iniquity 'but also suche as consentis to the same'. Knox asks rhetorically: 'Who can deny but suche men as daylie dois accompany wickit men, and yit never declairis thame selves offendit nor displeasit with thair wickitnes, does consent to thair iniquitie' (3.190). Perhaps it is for this group that the prophetic voice of the letter has spoken warning and vengeance. That is, the only way to challenge this group of fence sitters or 'double dissemblers' is to speak as a Jeremiah about the dangers of dancing with the devil.

[12]   Indeed, this is what happened if we are to believe Knox's 1558 *Epistle to the Inhabitants of Newcastle and Berwick*, who allowed themselves to be seduced

Knox absent from the English temple. As Jeremiah's sermons were read out loud in the Temple by Baruch, so too will Knox's 'letter' be read aloud (quite literally) if a Baruch can be found, he says. As Jeremiah was commanded to write, so too is Knox commanded. The use of Jeremiah is more than merely sounding like a Jeremiah. It is a rehearsal of a call by God to minister, Knox finding a scriptural model which reflects his life as well as one of his voices, a scriptural model he can be absorbed into, Jeremiah as the prophetic text into which he disappears and into which his readers are also invited to be absorbed. As Knox appropriates the Jeremian voice, his exile becomes irrelevant, for the voice enables him to stand apart, separated as Jeremiah was from the wicked nation, an absent presence so to speak.

But Knox, although absent, must not appear to be really separated ('imprisoned' like Jeremiah) from the 'small and soir trubillit flock' who are, I believe, his principal audience. Thus, something other than the expansive, prophetic voice of a Jeremiah needs to speak to the faithful, and speak intimately. We begin to hear this voice as Knox constructs the second part of the letter, which I would argue deliberately leaves behind the Old Testament prophetic display for something more subdued. Knox must have known that the prophetic Jeremian voice that speaks globally would not do in saying to the faithful what needed to be said at this critical moment after it was clear that Mary was intent on returning England to papal obedience but before, as we now know, the burnings at Smithfield. In the second half of the text the reader finds Knox more deliberately addressing 'Belovit Brethrene' or 'Deir Brethrene' or 'Deirly Belovit'.[13] With such language Knox is not separated from the 'Brethrene'; instead, he begins to play another role, the role of the pastor, urging the brethren to avoid idolatry and to consider alternatives for their difficult situation. We may sense here, therefore, a shift from the Jeremian to the Pauline, Knox deliberate and artful with voice or persona for the needs of the critical moment and relying on the personal and intimate which Jack observes.[14]

One alternative – and it can be found in various Pauline letters – is to 'avoyd all fellowship with idolatry, and with the maintainers of the same' (3.192). In other words, Knox has moved from condemning a nation of stiff-necked and stubborn to counselling a small group to be careful in their relationships with others. In the surrounding passages which emphasize

---

by Satan and returned to the bondage of idolatry. Knox's solution in this *Epistle* is to threaten plagues and urge repentance.

[13]   Each of these phrases appears at 3.189 which serves rhetorically as a transitional section to the letter's second part.

[14]   As Jack remarks, Knox can be 'the most personal of writers, revealing himself and his religious beliefs simultaneously' (p. 250).

God's grace, the believer's salvation, the work of the Holy Spirit, and the assurance of divine mercy for the children of faith, Knox does not appear as an 'I' on display as he was in the first part of *A Godly Letter*. The extravagance of prophetic condemnation has given way to quieter teaching about faith and idolatry. Having established himself earlier as a voice and hoping that he was now being heard from a distance, Knox as teacher does not need to draw any further attention to himself. There is clearly a shift from the unavoidable 'I' of the prophetic to the pastoral that speaks to a defined community of laity. That is, the global voice which proclaims the need to slay idolaters is reduced to a quiet, domestic voice urging the faithful to avoid the company of the wicked.[15] As his proof-text, Knox cites Paul's first letter to the Corinthians, chapter 10, which not only warns of temptations but also asks for readers to examine their relationships with others, and to be careful, as Paul writes in verse 31, to 'do all to the glorie of God. Give none offense'.[16]

The call finally is not from a prophet condemning a broken covenant and urging national repentance but from a pastor asking the faithful to join him as one of the saints of God, to act the role of the elect. The saints are cautioned to avoid idolatry, but finally they hear something far more Pauline – an emphasis on inward faith.[17] And here, then, at what could be considered the heart of the tract, Knox asks plainly for the first time in *A Godly Letter* 'What sall we do now, in this the battel for our Soverane Lord?' The saints are to give confession, but only 'when time and necessitie requyreth', and that apparently is not now on every street corner in London or Newcastle or Berwick. A living faith can be declared 'in tyme convenient' (3.198). 'In tyme convenient' – to me this utterance reduces or circumscribes the confessional landscape. The 'deir brethrene' do not declare daily for twenty or thirty years as Jeremiah did, but perhaps only once, quietly, if they must before stiff-necked officials. And in that

---

[15] Surely, here is one of those 'quieter moments' admired by Kenneth Farrow who believes the true literary value of so much of Knox's writings is found in such places rather than in the bombast of the prophetic. See his 'Humor, logic, imagery and sources in the prose writings of John Knox', *SSL*, 25 (1990), pp. 154–75.

[16] 3.194. Knox writes: 'But of yow is requyreit onlie to avoyd participatioun and company of thair abominationis, as well in bodie as in saule; as David and Paule planelie teachis unto yow.'

[17] For example, Knox writes: 'The voice of the Holie Spirit joyneth togidder faith, as thinges that be inseperable the one from the other; and thairfoir dare I not tak upon me to dissever thame; But must say, that whair trew faith is, that thair is also confessioun of the samyn when time and necessitie requyreth; and that whair confessioun is absent, that thair faith is asleip, or ellis … far frome home. For lyke as eiting, drinking, speiking, moving, and utheris operationis of ane lyveing bodie, declairis the bodie to be alyve, and not to be deid; so dois confessioun, in tyme convenient, declair the faith to be lyveing' (3.198).

witness the faithful might speak the pastoral, for in the reformist sense they are all potential priests. Clearly, in this second part of the letter as Knox draws upon various scriptural passages to demonstrate the importance of testifying and bearing witness, his goal – more Pauline and less prophetic – is to inspire from a distance the faithful Baruchs and enable them to remain together as a reformed community, at the centre of which must be an informed and indispensable laity.

But I think we need to ask what action it is that Knox wants to inspire, and in answering we need to read the text closely. It may be that from time to time Knox's extravagant language and his prophetic enthusiasm get the best of him. One could point to passages that invite the faithful to be modern-day Jeremiahs like Knox, declaring 'hatred and alienatoiun … aganis all ydollis and wirschipping of false goodis'. As Knox writes: 'Considder, deare Brethren, what God requyris by his Prophet of his pepill whan thai wer in the middis of thair enemyis wha wer ydolateris. Will He not requyre the same of us, being in oure awn countrie, and amangis suche as suld be Christianis?' (3.201). Knox's prophetic display can get out of hand. For example, in his enthusiasm to condemn the mass – a single idolatry substituting for the multiple abominations in the Book of Jeremiah – and to have the faithful join him in this condemnation, he urges them with these words: 'Ye sall say it, and that sall ye do, not privilie, but opinlie to thame that put their trust in such vanitie'(3.202).

But then he pulls back from his 'passionate exhortation', as Jane Dawson calls it[18] – pulling back which is what the rhetoric of the second half of the letter seems always to be doing. Knox catches himself here. After pointing to how Daniel and his three friends boldly condemned King Nebuchadnezzar's idol (and landed in the hot furnace) Knox says: 'I requyre not so mekill, foir I constrane no man to go to ydolateris in the tyme of thair ydolatrie, and to say, Your Godis maid neither Heavin nor Earth, and thairfoir sall thai perische, and ye with them, for all your wirschipping is abominabill ydolatrie. But I requyre onlie that we absent oure bodies … frome all suche diabolicall conventionis', that is the mass.[19] And where should they be? In their homes, in territory more confined and specific and local than Jeremiah's territory which is all of Israel and Judah. The faithful are not to preach publicly about their faith, are not to condemn the mass on the street corners of London, Newcastle, and Berwick, are not to shout for the death of Mary Tudor. They are urged here by Knox to get off the streets – that's Jeremiah's place – and into their houses. Their chief and

---

[18]   Jane E.A. Dawson, 'The Two John Knoxes: England, Scotland and the 1558 Tracts', *Journal of Ecclesiastical History*, 42 (1991), pp. 555–76.

[19]   3.202. Since it is so early in Mary's reign and before the Smithfield burnings, such a call for patience and passivity is understandable.

perhaps sole responsibility, so it would appear, is to embrace the domestic and educate their children in the truth of reformist doctrine. As Jeremiah saw the future in terms of destruction and return, Knox hopes merely for the survival of the next generation, and in this hope displayed in *A Godly Letter* he is far less radical than he would show himself to be in *First Blast of the Trumpet* four years later.

How are blessedness and happiness for the next generation achieved? Through divine vengeance? Apocalyptic action? National repentance? Political action? The particular moment of crisis in early 1554 requires the following, to use Knox's words: 'The onlie way to leive our children blissit and happie, is to leif thame rychtlie instructit in Godis trew religioun' (3.203). Although Knox has permission through the figure of Jeremiah to view a broad national canvas and to think of himself as a prophet, the faithful, according to Knox, can best be called 'scolemasteris' (3.204), a title suitable also to Knox himself whether he is teaching what the Book of Jeremiah was all about or instructing fathers on what to do to guarantee the future. Indeed, Christian behaviour is finally at moments of crisis more important than the thunderings of prophets: 'Patience and constancie sal be a louder trumpet to your posteritie, than wer all the voyces of the prophetis that instructit yow: and so is not the trompet ceissit sa long as any baldlie resisteth ydolatrie' (3.208).

But we need to ask – as is seldom done in Knox studies – what does this particular trumpet signify? 'So is not the trompet ceissit.' It is no call to repentance, no instrument of destruction, no medium of praise. That leaves only the trumpet as sign that divine activity is to begin. And in this insight arises that tension which appears in so much reformist writing. If divine activity is about to happen or is happening, what role human effort? If God is in control, the faithful, apparently, need do little else than be faithful in their small community, the true church as persecuted minority, to be content and faithful in the home where children learn about the battle which their God is waging outside. God will take care of that battle, for it is his power which will be seen by both the righteous and the unrighteous. 'I am commandit to stand content, for it is God himself that performis the word of his awn trew messengeris' (3.206).

Knox's goal here – and in other pieces of exilic writing – is to create an intimate community, not to condemn a nation. Furthermore, he becomes an intimate part of that community, that 'privy kirk', not as prophet Jeremiah but as pastor, Knox as writer not burdened in the discursive arena by a single (autobiographical) identity.[20] Initially he seizes an authorial (and

20   The always perceptive Patrick Collinson writes that 'while Knox, with Old Testament in hand, presumed to correct and direct nations and national Churches, his natural and circumstantial environment belonged to the imaginary world of

authoritative) voice to speak as a contemporary Jeremiah; he could get lost in that voice and in the Jeremian text which is so faithfully duplicates. But then in determining what really had to be said at a particular moment to the people who mattered, he appropriates another scriptural model. That model is Paul as pastor writing to isolated, small congregations, urging them with the 'I' of a pastor – an 'I' far less on display than the 'I' of an imposing prophet – urging them to embrace the local, the congregational,[21] and like Paul urging believers to go about the business communally of living the faith and waiting patiently as God acted.

As he ends his letter, Knox does return to a prophetic stance with a call for repentance, a warning of backsliding, and the promise that the wicked shall be destroyed. But these standard prophetic themes are not conveyed with the bombast of the Old Testament but with reference to the New Testament and the words of Jesus: 'He that denyis me befoir men, I will deny him befoir my Father. He that refuseth not himself, and takis not up his croce and followis me, is not worthie of me. No man putting his hand to the pleweh, and luiking bakward, is worthie of the kingdome of God' (3.210). As Knox exhorts to 'remember the dignitie of oure vocatioun', his tone has become personal; as he invokes 'the Lordis tabill', the scene is communal and intimate. And in that worshiping community – so different from the prophetic landscape of vengeance and destruction – all are disciples who 'incalleth the name of the Lord' to be saved. Lay disciples do not extravagantly call for national repentance on the street corners but 'baldlie confess Chryst befoir men' (3.213) only when necessary. The few left to rightly worship and witness in London, Newcastle, and Berwick follow in the footsteps of those catalogued in Hebrews 11 (which Knox cites in the margin) who lived by faith and whom Knox finally elevates as models for righteousness.[22] The text has led Knox to speak less as an 'I' and more as an 'us'. In drawing attention in the closing paragraph to his 'sore trubillit heart, upon [his] departure from Deipe', he admits in not knowing of his future – 'whither God knaweth' – and so is like his English

---

the New Testament, finding its home in the "Privy Kirks" and still more in the inchoate and unstructured house groups and conventicles which preceded the Privy Kirks'. 'John Knox, the Church of England and the Women of England', in Mason, pp. 74–96; quotation from p. 76.

[21] Michael F. Graham identifies this as 'committed urban cells'. See his 'Knox on Discipline: Conversionary Zeal or Rose-tinted Nostalgia', in Mason, pp. 268–85.

[22] 'Did God comfort thame, and sall his Majestie dispyse us, gif in fichting aganis iniquitie we will follow thair futstepis? He will not, for he hes promissit the contrarie, and thairfore be of gud corage, the way is not so dangerous as it appeareth; prepair in tyme, and determyne with your selves to abyde in Chryst Jesus, and his croce sall never oppress you as presentlie ye feir.' 3.214.

disciples. Whatever his personal future is, he seeks to join together with other saints, for 'baith you and I sall be comforted, when all suche as now molestis us sall trembill and schaik'.[23] The letter is signed 'Your Brother in the Lord.'

Knox does authorize himself as he moves through the text from prophet to brother, fashioning and refashioning his 'I'. He appropriates scriptural models, especially the prophetic, but the prophetic may not be the most important of his voices, certainly not the only one. It is true that prophetic language and the task of self-promotion may often be in control of the discourse, but that language is not the only language heard. Knox does use the trumpet imagery, but it is important to determine why the trumpet is blown. Readers need to watch the geography of the Knoxian 'I': sometimes the 'I' is centre stage, on display, sometimes it is absorbed in the textual material, other times it is there but hardly noticed, at times moving from 'I' to 'us'. Knox's texts do indeed have a politics to them which the critic needs to observe. It is more than what he says. What may be most interesting and artful is what he does in the discourse and with the languages he uses, whether scriptural or religious, polemical or political. As in William Tyndale and other early English reformers, there are multiple purposes, multiple audiences, multiple identities (rather than one complex character), multiple displays depending on audience, but the landscape is often narrowed finally to the intimate and the few faithful elect, as in the writing of John Bale. Knox's ultimate goal – and it is not all that extreme – may be to create a community that will survive as the faithful are asked to avoid idolatry and to educate their children. Above all, survival was his ardent hope during the five years of his exilic writings.

Knox's literature of exhortation emerges from specific historical moments when that urgent moment and the need to speak to the beloved determine discursive strategy. As we review other reformist writings, Scottish and English, we should identify the controlling historical moment and understand its textual influence. As I hope my brief comments on this one Knoxian piece demonstrates, these moments also created rich and exciting texts worthy of review by literary scholars as well as historians. Observing Knox's various discursive strategies and scriptural voices alerts us to be skeptical of easy generalizations about this writer and to place Knox within his context, historical and rhetorical, in order to understand

---

[23] 3.215. Emphasis mine. In these last sections, Knox easily moves from speaking to his congregations – 'The battail shall appeare strang, which ye are to suffer, but the Lord hym selfe shall be our comfort' – to joining with them in hope and confidence: 'For the Lord himself sall cum in our defence with his michtie power; He sall gif us the victorie when the battell is maist strang; and He sall turn our teares into everlasting joy.'

Knox's contribution to creating reformist texts for a lively textual culture. Knox does, in a sense, celebrate the specific historical moment but the specific moment as always a part of the divine moment. To respond to those moments, Knox both invites the faithful to participate alongside him in God's work and, depending on the scriptural pattern he appropriates, separates himself from the faithful as a lone crier in the wilderness. But all scriptural models he appropriates validate him, as he turns the scriptural into the personal to reflect the reformist experience.

CHAPTER 6

Theological controversy in the wake of John Knox's *The First Blast of the Trumpet*

Kenneth D. Farrow

Knox's *The First Blast of the Trumpet Against the Monstrous Regiment of Women*[1] was published in Geneva in 1558, probably by Jacques Poullain and Antoine Rebul,[2] and remains, to this day, one of the Reformer's most controversial productions. Even those who shared Knox's religious orientation were uneasy in their response. For instance, John Foxe entered into correspondence with Knox over it (4.352) and the English Reformer, John Aylmer, saw fit to write an entire tract controverting it (which we shall be looking at in due course). Calvin, too, had cause to regret its publication, and to rebuke Knox for setting it forth, for, in 1559, when his *Commentaries on Isaiah*, which had originally been dedicated to Edward VI, was sent instead to Queen Elizabeth I, she received it icily, largely because she had been deeply offended by certain Genevan publications such as Christopher Goodman's *How Superior Powers Ought to be Obeyd*, and, of course, Knox's resounding *The First Blast*.[3] Elizabeth, it should be added, took offence *personally* to such publications; she was far from seeking to turn the world of the sixteenth century upside down, and her animus should not be regarded as evidence of proto-feminism!

---

[1] All passages from Knox are taken from *The Works of John Knox*, 6 vols, ed. David Laing (Edinburgh: Bannatyne Club, 1846–64); selections from Quintin Kennedy's *Ane Oratioune* are also to be found in Laing's edition of Knox, vol. 6. N.B.: such quotations, from the Reformer, and the other writers discussed in this paper, are derived from original sixteenth-century printed sources. At no point have spellings been modernized. Rhetorical terms and their definitions can be found in L.A. Sonnino (ed.), *A Handbook to Sixteenth Century Rhetoric* (Oxford, 1968).

[2] The text displays no publisher's name, however, and Laing implies that it was Jean Crespin; see Laing vol. 4, p. 352. Pierre Janton concurs; see *John Knox (ca. 1513–72): L'homme et l'oeuvre* (Paris, 1967), p. 517.

[3] For a full study of the two texts, see Jane E.A. Dawson, 'Trumpeting Resistance: Christopher Goodman and John Knox', in Roger A. Mason (ed.), *John Knox and the British Reformations* (Aldershot and Burlington, 1998), pp. 130–53.

Perhaps at this point, it might be appropriate to look at *The First Blast* itself, to establish what kind of text it is, and why it caused such offence. Certainly, it is not a highly structured work, but it can be internally divided into sections. There is a preface to the main body of argument, and the latter part makes its purpose clear through its heading. The pamphlet, Knox says, was written 'to awake women degenerate' (Laing IV: 373), although, properly speaking, the 'target' is not so much women themselves, as those who would advocate their cause as rulers and monarchs. (An important point about *The First Blast*, often overlooked in these days of feminist resurgence, is that it is *men* who are its primary addressees, although, of course, women do not altogether escape the fury of Knox's tongue). In the preface, Knox shows that he knows full well how controversial his undertaking is (4.370), but for all this, he will persevere in his task, primarily out of a sense of duty:

> Wonder it is, that amongst so many pregnant wittes as the Ile of Grete Britany hath produced, so many godlie and zealous preachers as England did sometime norishe, and amongst so many learned, and men of grave judgement, as this day by Jesabel are exiled, none is found so stowte of courage, so faithfull to God, nor loving to their native countrie, that they dare admonishe the inhabitantes of that Ile, how abominable before God is the Empire or rule of a wicked woman, yea, of a traiteresse and bastard; and what may a people or nation, left destitute of a lawfull head, do by the authoritie of Goddes Worde in electing and appoynting common rulers and magistrats (4.365).

This is *inopinatum*: Knox is, at some length, expressing his amazement at a certain situation which is full of seeming contradictions, and his ubiquitous and well-attested sarcasm is not far from the surface. He 'sets up' his sarcasm by opening with the word 'wonder', which will immediately attract readers who want to know more; indeed, who does *not* want to know more about that which is 'wonderful', even if the word is used in a negative sense? (Compare, for instance, Edmund's comment in *King Lear*: 'an *admirable* evasion of whoremaster man'; Act 1, Sc. 2.) He reinforces his opening by using the phrase 'so many', which suggests an unspecified but extreme degree, and repeating it twice thereafter. With each repetition comes an intensification of the wonder he is discussing. Then comes the crux of the paradox; out of 'so many', there are '*none*' who will act with courage (italics added).

The language is obviously from the very harshest extreme of the preacher's register, both highly pejorative and inflammatory ('Jesabel', 'abominable', 'wicked woman', 'traiteresse' and 'bastard'). All of these items refer very specifically to Mary Tudor, and it is clear that Knox is using *congeries* to lead up to the last term, which attacks not only Mary's legitimacy, but also, by implication, the nature of her behaviour. Bastards act basely. (Indeed, the implication is more sustainable than the direct meaning when we are talking about the daughter of Catherine of Aragon, unless one would follow Henry VIII's reasoning!)

A deeper artifice, however, becomes apparent when we realize that Knox is in fact using two distinct 'lines' of *congeries*: a negative one (the above) and a positive one, evident in the strand of adjectives which precede: 'godlie', 'zealous', 'stowte', 'faithfull', 'loving'. Both lines are in a sense 'rising' ones (if we allow that their overall effect on the reader is cumulative), but they balance each other to such an extent that the reader is spared uninterrupted exposure to denunciation. Reading the whole passage, and what follows, leads us to the conclusion that, even after the semicolon, which marks a natural pause, Knox continues to be amazed, now at what people may do (as opposed to what they *haven't* done) in the name of God: that which in fact is in direct contradiction of His word. Here, sarcasm still prevails. So even Knox's introductory comments give us a comprehensive insight into the scope and nature of his forthcoming undertaking.

The remainder of *The First Blast* reveals it to be a sombre, highly scholarly undertaking which relies heavily on the citation of scripture, and more especially, the Church Fathers, such as Augustine, Chrysostom, Origen and Tertullian, as well as Aristotle and Basilius Magnus. But it is not merely an example of rigorously sustained arguments backed up by antiquity. As a text, it is noticeably not without its own dramatic gestures, most evident in the artifice with which Knox maintains his anonymity. Of this tactic, he says:

> Yf any wonder why I do concele my name, let him be assured, that the feare of corporall punishment, is nether the onlie, nether the chief cause. My purpose is thrise to Blow the Trumpet in the same mater, if God so permitte: twise I intend to do it without name; but at the Last Blast to take the blame upon myselfe, that all others may be purged (4.371).

This is as much as to say that avoiding 'corporall' or bodily punishment *is* a factor (only a fool would not fear it), but it is not the primary concern. Knox assures the reader of his prudence; he is not about to invite arrest for treason, but he retains the high ground of a determined advocate who none the less 'dares damnation', as it were. He is also, it seems, aware of the symbolic and functional significance of his (proposed) threefold action. We have a beginning (this text), a middle stage, and an ending. Knox will not reveal his identity until the end stage, thus making his ultimate revelation all the more sweeping and powerful. And, in a sense, he can also speak with a hint of morality, for he is neither so corrupt nor cowardly that he will allow another to take the blame for his actions. However, we also notice how Knox makes sure the reader *knows* this!

The drama of this elaborate device is caught up again with the final line of the pamphlet, which is almost an open challenge to all-comers: 'And therefore let all man be advertised, for THE TRUMPET HATH ONES BLOWEN' (4.420). (*The First Blast*, indeed, should be regarded as a European phenomenon, the influence of which was not limited to Britain. After all, in addition to issuing from Geneva, it was composed in Dieppe, and its impact was felt in places such as Basel and Antwerp, as well as Edinburgh and London!)[4] Even the typographical presentation augments the universal challenge and thereby allows Knox to reveal the deafening loudness of his tone in a graphic or visual way. In a sense, Knox has no choice but to make his readers 'see' a sound, and thus he comes close to a *synaesthesia* of sorts. Of course, as things turned out, Knox never wrote the second and third blasts, which is undoubtedly just as well. One was damaging enough to his reputation, and it is difficult to see what he could have added to a theme which he had already explored so thoroughly.

One author who did take up the challenge of *The First Blast* was John Aylmer (1521–94), who had been tutor to Lady Jane Grey, and who, like Knox, was a Protestant exile from Mary's England. He returned to his native country on Elizabeth's accession and pursued a fairly distinguished career that culminated in his becoming Bishop of London.[5] He assisted John Foxe in translating his *Book of Martyrs* into Latin, but his reputed harshness led to him being adversely portrayed in literary works such as Spenser's *Shepherd's Calendar*.[6] His response to *The First Blast* was

---

[4] Some of the issues raised by Knox in *The First Blast* were alluded to by Peter Frarin in his *Oratio Petri Frarini male reformandae religionis nomine arma non sumpserunt sectarii nostris temporis habita*. It was translated into English by the publisher, John Fouler, as *An Oration against the Vnlawfull Insurrection of the Protestantes of our time, vnder pretence to Refourme Religion* (Antwerp, 1566) (see *STC I*, 11333); see also 4.360. Foxe was in Northern Switzerland when he received a copy of Knox's *Blast*; 4.352.

[5] For Aylmer's biography, see John Strype, *The Life and Acts of the Right Reverend Father in God, John Aylmer* (Oxford, 1821). Given Aylmer's expressed views on women in general, there is some irony in the fact that he rose to prominence under Elizabeth. As Roderick Graham observes: 'his diplomacy … in this case having done his chances of elevation no harm'; see Roderiock Graham, *John Knox: Democrat* (London, 2001), p. 113.

[6] See Edmund Spenser, *The Shepheardes Calendar* (Menston, 1968), a facsimile of the original edition printed by Hugh Singleton, London, 1579, ff. 26v–31v, under 'Iulye'. For the association of Bishop Aylmer with 'Morrell', see Paul E. McLane, *Spenser's Shepheardes Calendar: A Study in Elizabethan Allegory* (Notre Dame, 1961), pp. 188–202. McLane argues that Spenser's estimation of Aylmer is much less negative than is commonly supposed.

written during his exile, however, in Switzerland. His tract against Knox was entitled *An Harborovve for Faithfull Subjects agaynste the late blowne Blaste, concerninge the Gouernment of Wemen* (1559).[7] Like Knox's work, it was published anonymously.

Right from the start, Aylmer speaks mildly of Knox. This mildness surfaces in numerous places: 'I mynd to use such modestie that I seke to defend the cause, and not deface the man', whose 'error rose not out of malice but of zele' (sig. B2v) (to modern readers, of course, zeal is hardly more defensible than ill-will, but evidently not so for Aylmer!). Furthermore, he acknowledges Knox's appeal to the intellect and the openness of his challenge, which he combines with faint praise: 'For I haue that opinion of the mans honestie and Godlyness: that he will not disdayne to heare better reasons' (sig. B2v). Aylmer shows that he is familiar with the technique of how to contrive a text from an apparently casual comment: '*Happening* therefore not longe agone to rede a lytle booke, strangly written by a Straunger ... ' (sig. B2v) (italics added).

He certainly knows of Knox's Scottishness, and, it seems, he was no lover of his island cousins, calling them 'the pydling Scottes, which are alwayes Frenche for their lyues' (sig. Q3v), 'the scoruy Scot' (sig. P2r) and 'Scottishe skyttes' (sig. N2v). Indeed, the fact that Knox had been, in some senses, an alien in England, gives Aylmer a reason for ruling his arguments out of court without even engaging with them:

> The voyce of a straunger, is to be hard in the pulpit so long as he speaketh Gods worde: but a straungers voyce is not allowed ... in the parliament about pollicie, by cause he is not a citezen. This I saye not to philip you, as though you meant euill to vs ... but I meane to monish you, that being a straunger you disturbe not our state: lest you giue occasion to them that know you not, of suspicion. It is a great enterprise (and as they say no balle playe) to pulle a quenes crowne of hir head: and specially such a ones [Elizabeth's], as many ages haue not sene ... (sig. F2r; square parentheses added).

Aylmer, then, is willing to allow Knox's preaching, but not insofar as it contains any overtly political statement. He begins by speaking generally, but with the second sentence, it is obvious that he is addressing Knox directly and personally. He wants to make it clear that his concerns are not trivial ones; he rejects all implication of petty mischief on his own part by using the verb 'philip', defined in *O.E.D.* as 'a flick, a movement made by bending the joint of a finger against the thumb', as in Hooker's comment 'There is not a meane subject that dare extend his hand to fillip a peere of

---

7   For Aylmer's text, see *STC I*, no. 1005.

the realme' (1586),[8] but Aylmer's tone is overwhelmingly schoolmasterish. In short, he is patronizing. He means to 'monish'. This is mitigated or off-set a little by his attempt at understatement in the latter part of the extract ('no balle playe'), but a reader can judge for himself if he is successful in refuting Knox by such methods. How effective is an argument that says one is not bound to answer the adversary at all?

I suggested earlier that Knox's addressees were men. He says very little directly about women in a way that separates them from his thesis. Pejorative comments *can* be found: some women have 'died for sodein joy', 'some for unpacience ... have murdered themselves', 'some have ... burned with inordinate lust' (4.376). But they are not frequent, and as we shall see in a moment, they are not even *that* severe. For Aylmer writes, admittedly of women 'of the wurst sort', that they are:

> ... fond, folish, wanton, flibbergibbes, tatlers, triflers, wauering, witless, without counsell, feable, careles, rashe, proude, deintie, nice, tale bearers, euesdroppers, rumor raisers, euell tonged, worse minded, and in euery wise, doltified dregges of the Deuills dounge hill ... (sig. G4v).

This is surely far in excess of anything Knox ever said about women. And does it refute Knox's arguments? Certainly not. It is perhaps one of the most amusing ironies of literary history, that Knox should be (mistakenly) labelled a misogynist because of *The First Blast*, when the man who took up the cudgels against him in his own day, is apparently more of an egregious misogynist even than any of today's chauvinists (as Diarmid MacCulloch reminds us, Knox's life-situation marked him out as 'very much 'effeminate' by the standards of the sixteenth century').[9]

But in its context in the treatise, the above does have an argumentative function, which may not be immediately apparent to modern readers. In essence, this is *intended* to be a *concessio*; a concession to the adversary, and can only perform its function on Aylmer's side insofar as it shows the reader that he is open-minded (!) and willing to defer a little to the opponent. Its ultimate effectiveness comes when its force 'swings back' into the counter-argument, which is being launched by a man whom the audience now knows to be 'reasonable'. But Aylmer's misjudgements are even greater than Knox's. He has gone too far, conceding much, *much* more than Knox would ever expect, or perhaps even want, to be said.

---

[8]   *New English Dictionary on Historical Principles (O.E.D.)*, ed. J.A.H. Murray (London, 1888–1933), vol. 4, p. 217.

[9]   See Diarmid MacCulloch, *Reformation: Europe's House Divided, 1490–1700* (London, 2003), p. 656; and for a fuller study, P. Collinson's 'John Knox, the Church of England and the Women of England', in Mason, pp. 74–96.

Aylmer's passage, to be sure, *is* a 'blast', but it's from a shotgun, and entirely off-target.

Nevertheless, if we were to stop here, we would do Aylmer something of an injustice. For all the lack of judgement and restraint behind it, the above passage (if one has the stomach for it), represents wonderful invective, in the genre *vituperatio*. Aylmer is brilliant at alliteration; indeed, no worse than the best I have seen).[10] Aylmer builds up patiently to his final scatological denunciation, which invokes Satan as well as disgusting human or beastly elements. Rhetorically, we first detect the device *articulus*, a use of single words punctuated only by commas, and, on a larger scale, we have *conglobatio*, or many definitions of one thing, which maintain their force not by 'likes' and 'unlikes', but by consistently direct statements. Aylmer is most effective against Knox, however, when he fights logic with logic.

> ... whatsoever is natural, the same is universal. But that woman shuld not rule is not universall, Ergo, it is not naturall. If to rule in woman be unnaturall: then not to rule is naturall. But not to rule is not universal. Ergo it is not natural. That it is not universal we haue proved by a great number of histories ... (sig. G1v).

Obviously, Aylmer is heavily dependant on the formalized language of syllogism. Here we have a three-step categorical, followed by a four-step hypothetical (steps, as opposed to premises), but Aylmer gets himself into trouble with his reader by relying too heavily on negation and his vocabulary is highly repetitive (four 'naturall's, one 'un-natural' and four 'universall's). More than this, he has to justify the penultimate step of his second syllogism by referring to external authorities. He may be just as competent a logician as Knox,[11] but his foundations are not so sure. (Here, I hasten to add, being 'logical' is not synonymous with being 'right'!)

The real truth behind Aylmer's controversy with Knox is that Aylmer simply could not defeat Knox's argument (and to say so, is of course, to endorse critically *neither* of the positions adopted by the writers!).

---

[10] Some other examples: 'rotten bones of Romysche Martirs' (sig. C1v), 'contrafaited Confessores' (sig. C1v), 'braynsick beast' (sig. E5v), 'clatteringe Clargie' (sig. F1r), 'spirituall spiders' (sig. F1r), 'swarmes of Sathanistes' (sig. H2v), 'venymous vipers' (sig. N4v).

[11] For Knox's use of logic, see P. Janton, 'L'art et la technique du syllogisme chez John Knox', in *Théologie pratique et Société. Mélanges à la mémoire de Michel Péronnet* (Montpellier, 2003), t. II, pp. 69–80; and K.D. Farrow, *John Knox: Reformation Rhetoric and the Traditions of Scots Prose 1490–1570* (Oxford, 2004), pp. 104–6, 242–3.

The closest he comes is to achieve a kind of stalemate (which, I suppose, is a draw). This is it:

> ... the male is moore mete to rule then the female, well, what infer you? ergo, the woman vnmete. I denie that argument[;] you should saye the woman is not so mete, that we could graunt you, and not a whyt hurt our cause: for otherwyse no man will reason, as to say this man is better learned than the other: ergo thother is unlearned. Chalke is whyter than cheese: ergo cheese is black. No man that knoweth what comparison is, will bryng two contraries in one comparison, as to saye pitche is blacker than snowe or fyre is whotter than watter ... (sig. I3v)(square parenthesis added).

What we have here is primarily *reductio ad absurdum* (in fact, there are six individual examples of it) with a limited *concessio* at the centre of the argument. Aylmer's illustratrions are all reasonably humorous; in fact, they are not far from *good* humour. His figurative language is colourful without being savage or denigratory, and it is drawn from a context which is immediately recognizable to all. Here, Aylmer scores his greatest success over Knox, but it is far from dialectical victory.

But it is almost as if he senses his arguments have been, at best, inconclusive. Although C.S. Lewis does not seem to be aware of Aylmer, he says rightly of *The First Blast*: 'No one wanted the thing to be said, yet no conscientious doctor could answer it in the resounding style which alone would satisfy Queen Elizabeth.'[12] In a final push, Aylmer, it seems, attempts to sweep Knox out of the way on a tide of English patriotism. At one point, fittingly, towards the conclusion, he achieves a resounding *coup* by alluding not only to his opponent's nationality, but uniting the allusion to one of Knox's own central metaphors, thus turning it back on its author, all under the auspices of loyalty to his own country: '... though it be the propertie of *Northern blastes* to coole and freese: yet in the hartes of ... *true Englishmen* ... it can do nothing' (sig. M1r; italics added).[13]

A more effective antagonist of Knox was Ninian Winzet (1518–92), who certainly did not share his general religious orientation, and it is to the work of this Catholic controversialist that we now turn. He was from Renfrew and probably attended Glasgow University for a time, but left without a degree. He later became schoolmaster of Linlithgow, but his

---

[12] See C.S. Lewis, *English Literature in the Sixteenth Century (Excluding Drama)* (Oxford, 1954), p. 200.

[13] Ninian Winzet also used patriotism as a weapon against Knox; see J.K. Hewison (ed.), *Winzet's Works*, 2 vols (Edinburgh and London, 1888–90), vol. 1, p. 138. All subsequent references to Winzet are taken from this two-volume edition.

opposition to the Reformation led to his removal from office in 1561. His composition of theological tracts and provocative letters led ultimately to his being exiled from Scotland, but he too pursued a distinguished career (albeit abroad), teaching at the University of Paris and conducting further study at Douai. He was finally appointed to the abbotship of the Benedictine monastery of St James at Ratisbon, where he stayed until his death in 1592.

It is another amusing irony of literary history that the final blast which Knox envisaged was actually written by his most famous adversary in the vernacular, for a text by Winzet entitled *The Last Blast of the Trompet of Goddis Worde aganis the usurpit auctoritie of Iohne Knox and his Caluiniane brether intrudit Precheouris* ...[14] was delivered to an Edinburgh printer in 1562. Aylmer was evidently not the only controversialist to pick up on Knox's titles and metaphors! Sadly, however, the whole of this document never saw the light of day, as the printer was arrested, and the author himself had a narrow escape from the authorities.[15] Only a few sheets now survive. Also, their contents are disappointing, because, despite the title, the regiment of women is not even one of Winzet's topics, although he does deal with this subject elsewhere.[16]

But it is still an interesting 'book', and can be used as a general introduction to Winzet's more substantial writings. Winzet tells us specifically why he chose the title: to propose three questions, and one of them concerns the lawfulness of Knox's vocation to preach (1.39). Winzet, indeed, raises this issue repeatedly, because he never received a satisfactory answer to his assertion that Knox had no right to take the office upon himself. We shall have to leave such challenges aside, but for now, we can use *The Last Blast* to establish some preliminary points about Winzet's style.

Two things emerge immediately: he has a master's control of metaphor and alliteration (like Aylmer). Some examples: 'sweit *venum* of deuyillish eloquence' (1.40), '*drest* and *deckit*' (1.45), '*fra fals fenzeit* hypocrisie' (1.44), '*sueinging* in thair *stinkande styis infectis* the tender *burgeonis* of the zong *wynis*' (1.45). And in the following, alliteration combines with metaphor, personification and *anapodoton*: 'Bot of the twa *proude princes, Dame Heresie* and hir *sister, we wyll not talk*' (1.44) (italics added). We shall now see how Winzet uses such skills in a major work, entitled

---

[14]   See *Works*, vol. 1, pp. 35–45; there is a facsimile of the printer's title page on p. 35.

[15]   John Leslie has written of this in his *De Origine, Moribus et Rebus Scotorum*, and the narrative is well-known in the vernacular translation of Father James Dalrymple; see *Works* 3: xli.

[16]   See, for example, 1.121–2; Question no. 73.

Certane Tractatis for Reformatioun of Doctryne and maneris, set furth at the desyre, and in ye name of ye afflictit Catholikis, of inferiour ordour of Clergie, and layit men in Scotland (1562).

The opening to *Certane Tractatis* is one of the most eloquent passages of prose one can find in the whole field of sixteenth-century controversy (at least in English or Scots). The state of religion in Mary Stewart's kingdom, is, Winzet says:

> ... na thing mair lyke than to ane schip in ane dedely storme enforsed be contrarius wyndis betuix maist daingerus sandy beddis on the rycht hand and terrible rolkis presenting deth alrady on the left; quhilk, gydit thir mony zeris be sleuthfull marinaris and sleipand sterismen (we mean of the pastores of the Kirk, and, in that part, of their promoueris) is euyl crasit on the schaldis. Quhairat sum effrayit, and almaist desperat of thair awin and vtheris lyues in the samyn schip, hes pullit the rudder and gouernment fra the formare rewlaris, maist vnworthy thir mony zeris of that name; and be our jugement fleing fra the sandy beddis, speidis baith with airis and erect salis, to brek in splendaris the schip on the feirful rolkis. For the quhilk perrel we now mair effrayit than we and they wes for the vther, may not contene vs for na feir of man, sen the mater standis in dangeir of our bodies and saulis, bot exhort the latter marinaris, albeit impatient other of repreif or aduertisement, to lat down ane grete dele thair hie sailis, and hald to wyndwart, returning thair course fet by the first set compasse, and direct it to sum mair sure harbery place then thay first intendit (1.3–4).

This too contains a concession, to Knox's and Willock's Reformation, in that it freely acknowledges the corruption of pre-reformation churchmen. As J.H. Burns says of Winzet, he: 'never doubted that properly conceived reform was essential to the life of the Church'.[17] But, as is clear from the above, the reform that finally came, in the form of Protestantism, was, for Winzet, quite misguided, and would lead to disaster; indeed, to adopt his own figure, to complete shipwreck. Noticeably, he uses the same imagery ('harbery') as his predecessor, Aylmer.

But we introduced the above by commenting on the style. It is surely very impressive. This is written in the grand style: *supra* or *magniloquens*. The genre is *narratio rhetorica* and the specific form of the above, *similitudo*. We have here three sentences (not all of the opening sentence is quoted), of 107, 60 and 83 words respectively. So evidently, Winzet uses his most pregnant sentence first, as is fitting. By comparison, Knox opens the preface to *The First Blast* with a longer individual specimen (118 words), but both have a firm control of the 'long' sentence. Winzet aims for a shorter 'middle' sentence, which consolidates or reinforces the content of the first,

---

[17] See J.H. Burns, *Ninian Winzet* (Glasgow, 1959), p. 23.

and the third deals with the consequences of the situation outlined in its two antecedents. So the inner progression is slow, smooth, evenly paced and naturally consequential.

Like the best similitudes, it is exceptionally vivid (about a quarter of its vocabulary refers specifically to the illustration). It is highly developed, and so inevitably shades into *allegoria*: priests equal bad sailors, ship equals Church, or religion in general, Reformers equal mutineers, Protestantism equals rocks, and ruin for the ship. Indeed, one could go on until we had an interpretation worthy of St Augustine, but there is no need to do so. Winzet's quality and skill are self-evident. This granted, we shall leave his more direct dealings with Knox for another occasion, and concentrate now on the work of another Catholic scholar and polemicist who has unfortunately received less attention than Winzet: Quintin Kennedy.

Kennedy (*c.*1520–64) is generally regarded as a non-existent figure in the history of Scottish literature. Of course, he is known to historians and lexicographers, but literary textbooks almost never mention him at all. After all, he didn't write any memorable literary 'sound bites', such as Winzet is famous for,[18] but he was every bit as keen an adversary of Knox. It is the contention of the present writer that, although a very minor figure in the literary scheme of things, Kennedy is well-worthy of attention.

He was the son of Gilbert Kennedy of Dunure, second Earl of Cassillis, and he studied at St Andrews and Paris. He became the abbot of Crossraguell, in Ayrshire, in 1549, and he took part in a memorable debate with John Knox, in Maybole, in 1562. The proceedings were published by Knox. A handful of other, less well-known, texts in the vernacular can be attributed to him. We shall begin by looking at *Ane Oratioune in favouris of all thais of the Congregatioune, exhortand thaim to aspy how wonderfullie thai ar abusit be thair dissaitfull prechouris* which was addressed to the nobility in Scotland in the immediate post-Reformation period (1561).

This is an exceptionally accomplished work, and even a cursory reading reveals high artifice. We meet a very large range of rhetorical devices (many more than we find in Winzet). For example, a favourite technique of Kennedy is obviously *geminatio*: '*Haif pietie, haif pietie* for Christ's sake ...' (6.160), '*Failyeande tharof, recant*, for schame, *recant* (ye famouse Precheouris) ... ' or '*recant*, in tyme *recant*, as ye lufe your salvatioun ... '. He is especially effective when he uses imagery (which he often combines with alliteration: 'breid in ane *baxtaris buyth* wyndo ... ', 'to be a *schielde* and *buklar* to thair lustis and heresies ... ' (6.164), 'the rest, plays the *jugleour* ... ' (italics added). But one passage rises above others: 'Alace! alace! with sorofull hart, weping, and teris, I am

---

[18] Winzet's famous address to John Knox, (1.138) (see also fn. 14), has often been violently wrenched out of context because of its memorability.

constranit to desist fra further aggravatioune of this miserable purposs; for gif I had all the eloquence that ever had Cicero or Demostenes, I amme nocht hable to discrive the hundreth part of the samin' (4.162). We have *exclamatio*, *lamentatio* and *adynaton*, all rolled into one. There is also a use of *judicatio*, coming in behind them all (for there is an implicit tribute to the great orators of the past, and a total condemnation of the seditious Reformers).

Kennedy's *Ane Compendius Tractiue conforme to Scripturis of almychtie God, ressoun, and authoritie, declaring the nerrest, and onlie way to establische the conscience of ane christiane man* ... (1558)[19] is a much more substantial work than *Ane Oratioune* but that is not necessarily to say that it is better as literature. Right from the start, the abbot seems to raise fundamental questions in a manner which must be characteristic of him. For example: '*Mark, gude Redare*, that our Salveour spekis heir to the Apostolis in the personage and place of all utheris cheif ministeris and rewlaris, quhilkis wer to succeid in thair place be authoritie and office, to the ende of the world. *For quhy*' (116) (italics added). As C.H. Kuipers observes, such passages are 'suggestive of the habitual speaker'.[20] The italicized phrases have the effect of focusing the mind by invoking one's own presence. Once this is done, Kennedy presents us with important information and challenges us (and himself) on its veracity. He is using *rogatio*: he asks a question but immediately answers it himself in what follows.

But in other works, such as *Ane Compendious Ressonyng, be the quhilk is maid manifest, truelie and propirlie, conforme to the scripturis of almychtie God ... the mess to be Institute be Iesu Christ our salueour in the latter supper* ... (1561),[21] Kennedy shows an even higher degree of artifice. This is because it is a literary dialogue (not a *viva voce* debate such as that which actually took place between Knox and Kennedy). It is ostensibly between two brothers, Quintin (Q) and James (I) Kennedy. Quintin naturally represents the author, who speaks for traditional Catholic beliefs, but James is given the role of spokesman for the 'new' Protestant faith. Kennedy's purposes, however, are not heuristic in the Platonic sense, but overtly didactic, more in the Aristotelian mode. One might expect such a debate to be rather wooden, and to be sure, Kennedy cannot wholly

---

[19] *Ane Compendius Tractiue* was published in *The Miscellany of the Wodrow Society*, ed. David Laing (Edinburgh, 1842), and all references concerning it are to this text.

[20] See C.H. Kuipers (ed.), *Quintin Kennedy (1520–1564): Two Eucharistic Tracts* (Nijmegen, 1964), p. 100. All further references to Kennedy are from this text.

[21] See *Two Eucharistic Tracts*, pp. 149–83.

escape the charge, but there are spontaneous moments which lift the text out of such danger.[22] On occasion, Kennedy writes very 'literary' prose, like this, which is in answer to James's query as to why the Reformation conflict arose at all:

> Q: Ye sall wit that thare Is kirkmen evin as Iudas was ane apostle, sua that the speciall caus, efter my Iugement, of all kynd of variance in religioun and mischeif amangis christiane men for the fayth, Is that princis has vendicat dispositioun of benefices, disponand thame to vnqualifeit men as temporale revarde. Haif we nocht seyn in our dayes Ane bletour stert vp to be ane bischop, Ane awn to be ane abbote, Ane pultroun to be ane priour, ane pelour to be ane persone, Ane veill to be ane vicar, Ane kow to be ane curate? Quhen sic monstruous ministeries, blindit in Ignorance, drownit in lustis, ar appoinctit to haif authoritie in the kirk of God, quhat wonder is it that the world be confundit with hereseis, factioun, and opinioun as it is? (171)

Kennedy's editor rightly identifies this as standing in the tradition of 'flyting', and observes: 'if more of its vividness had entered his tracts, they would have been considerably more attractive from a literary point of view'.[23] But there is more at work here than 'flyting' techniques. There seem to be four parts to the passage. The first contains the fairly standard allusion to Judas as the corrupt religious (in the classical tradition, Sinon performs the role of archetypal traitor). The second part entails an outspoken denunciation of the system of bestowing benefices unworthily. Kennedy had done this elsewhere, and even as an orthodox churchman, he is not alone in his criticisms.[24] The system, he says, is open to extreme corruption and the perpetration of injustice (like Winzet, he's not above honest social commentary). The third part involves the central question and the 'flyting' section. The fourth employs a subsidiary question and widens the sphere of reference while retaining vestiges of the derogatory language ('monstruous ministereis'). Both questions are *interrogatio*; they require no answer, merely acquiescence.

In the opening sections, Kennedy is sensibly selective of his material. We notice how he identifies 'the speciall caus' (James's is a huge question!). He balances this by emphasizing that his is a personal assessment ('efter my Iugement'). Thus, he can both defend it, if necessary, as merely subjective, and use it to assume full responsibility for what he has said. And it is the vocabulary and the alliterative correspondences that make what follows

---

[22] See, for example, pp. 154, 157, 171.

[23] See p. 100.

[24] See *Ane Compendius Tractiue*, ch. 14, pp. 150–51, and also John Major's *History of Greater Britain*, ed. A. Constable (Edinburgh: SHS, 1882), p. 136.

so powerful. Kennedy, for the most part, chooses an animal image to correspond to a Church office (in two cases, with 'pultroun' and 'pelour', or coward and thief, he does not, but the words are every bit as pejorative as the other images). So the 'bletour', sheep, is a bishop; the 'awn', ass, is an abbot (and Kennedy need not wince at his own satire here!), a 'veill', calf, is a vicar, and lastly, a 'kow' is a curate. (With the last, Kennedy, strictly speaking, does not alliterate, but the sounds correspond.) The pace of the denunciation augments the comedy and the satire to such an extent that the final question is superfluous. If the passage is reminiscent of anything, indeed, it may not be of another Kennedy's 'flyting' with William Dunbar,[25] but Sir David Lindsay's *The Testament and Complaynt of the Papyngo* (1538), in which churchmen, in the guise of ravenous birds of prey, devour the still-warm corpse of a parrot.[26]

This brings us to the end of our analysis of Kennedy's work, but we are not quite ready to take leave of our learned Scots abbot himself. As we have heard, Knox published *The Copie of the Reasonyng which was betwix the Abbot of Crossraguel and Johne Knox, in Maybole, concerning the Masse* (1563). Here is a sample of how Knox dealt with Kennedy's arguments when he actually encountered them head on. The abbot has been using a technique called *necessaria concludentia*, a favourite form of his,[27] in an attempt to show that the wine brought forth to Abraham by Melchizedek, after his expedition against Chedorlaomer (*Genesis* 14: 18–20), prefigures the Mass. Knox responds:

> What I have answered, the benevolent reader shall after judge; to the present conjecture of my Lorde, I answer, That if Melchisedec allone without al company had broght onely furth so much bread and wine as he was able goodly to carie, yet sal it not be necessarilie concluded, that therefore he brought it not furth to gratifie Abraham; for an smal portion may oftentymes be thankfull to many, but my Lorde appeareth to shoote at that ground, which I have not laid for my principal. And, therefore, albeit his Lordship shuld win it, yet my formare strength were litle deminished (in my judgement) for onles his Lordship be able to prove by the plaine wordes of the text, that the bread and wine wer broght furth to be offered unto God, my principall ground does alwayes abyde (4.207).[28]

---

[25] See William Dunbar, *Selected Poems*, ed. P. Bawcutt (London and New York, 1996), pp. 262–76.

[26] See *The Works of Sir David Lindsay*, 4 vols, ed. Douglas Hamer (Edinburgh and London: STS, 1931), vol. 1, pp. 56–90; in particular vol. 2, pp. 1144–85.

[27] See, for example, the argument concerning Kennedy's interpretation of Malachi, pp. 156–7.

[28] Calvin responds to this issue in an *academic* context; see *Institutes of the Christian Religion*, 2 vols, trans. Henry Beveridge (Grand Rapids, 1989), vol. 2,

Although he was (obviously) perfectly well aware of debating techniques, it is clear that Knox does not need any intellectual gymnastics to substantiate his argument. And in any case, he has placed the burden of proof firmly on his adversary. He opens with *permissio*, and Knox is envisaging a tangible future text, a 'hardcopy' of the controversy, if you will. Moreover, his lucidity is admirable; there are no long, contorted, over-prolix sentences which the reader finds hard to follow. Only on one occasion does he tend towards a slightly complex 'strand' of thought, with a double negative. But, if we simply remember that one negative cancels out another, we can proceed. Knox invokes two concepts; the first is beloved of the English masters, *relevance*, and the second, *eternity*, of theologians. And this brings us to the end of our textual analysis.

We have seen John Aylmer attempting to refute Knox, despite the fact that, by and large, he *agreed* with him, and only wanted to make an exception for Elizabeth,[29] or to apply Knox's comments about female rulers in general to Mary Tudor in particular.[30] A situation in which two writers who have, superficially at least,[31] so much in common with each other, square-off, leads to what is, in the end, one of the best examples of the futility of controversy to be found anywhere. Ninian Winzet, on the other hand, had a real quarrel with Knox, and the skill to make it a keen one. Sadly, however, he did not produce such a large and doctrinally concentrated body of work as the Reformer. But, in any case, he was obviously prepared to leave his great rival aside on many occasions, and tackle the Protestant 'heresy' in general.

Quintin Kennedy's works belong to an earlier phase of the Reformation conflict than Winzet's, but he was obviously a man of considerable ability. Had there been more works such as *Ane Oratioune ...*, *Ane Compendius Tractiue* and *Ane Compendious Ressonyng*, by numerous Catholic authors, then they might indeed have turned the tide, at least slowing down the process of Reform, if not halting it altogether. When we return to Knox, and to his living encounter with Kennedy, we witness the clash of two champions. The power of Knox's own rhetoric is well-established, and we

---

p. 608 (Book 4.18.2).

[29]   Knox was more than willing to concede this point; see Letter XV, 'Knox to Queen Elizabeth', (20/07/1559), in vol. 6, pp. 47–52.

[30]   Again, Knox is not far from making a similar statement concerning *The First Blast* in his comment to Mary, Queen of Scots: ' ... that Book was written *most especialie* against that wicked Jesabell of England'; vol. 2, p. 279 (italics added).

[31]   Although a Protestant, who was early influenced by Reformation doctrine, Aylmer was, none-the-less, often opposed to both Puritan and Catholic factions. 'Thomalin', Morell's (Aylmer's) adversary in *The Shepheard's Calendar*, is generally taken to be a Puritan; see McLane, p. 189.

now know what Kennedy was capable of. He turned all his skill on Knox, and met a brick wall.

In the course of this essay, then, we have seen some striking examples of the multiple 'reformations' in Scotland and beyond. All of the writers considered are among the least irenical and most satirical of controversialists, but obviously none is devoid of imagination or a sense of the dramatic. In the end, though, one truth emerges. *After* beliefs have been well-formed, most men will believe what they *want* to believe, no matter what arguments they encounter, and some forms of argument, no matter how intrinsically meritorious in their own right, can never prevail over other forms, if there is no real point of contact between them. Herein lies the Reformation tragedy.

CHAPTER 7

King James VI and I as a religious writer

Astrid Stilma

King James VI of Scotland liked to consider himself a deeply religious monarch with a more than common understanding of theology and harboured, in the words of his biographer D.H. Willson, 'a pardonable ambition to make these qualities more generally known'.[1] However, for a sixteenth-century ruler religion was inevitably not only a matter of theology or even of personal faith, but also one of politics. For James, religion and politics were inextricably linked both in terms of internal Scottish affairs and foreign policy. His tense relationship with certain ministers of the Presbyterian Kirk – who never entirely trusted this son of the Catholic Mary, Queen of Scots – was made even more problematic by James's ideas about the relationship between church and state; as he advised his son in his kingship manual *Basilikon Doron* (1599), it was a monarch's task to control the church and never allow it 'to meddle … with the estate or pollicie'.[2] The Kirk, on the other hand, considered it a duty to 'meddle', and its ministers were openly critical of James whenever they disagreed with his policies or the company he kept. They tended to be especially ready to denounce any 'Catholic sympathies' they detected in their king; a tendency which irritated James, not in the last place because such rumours might damage the impeccably Protestant reputation he was in the process of building. This essay will focus primarily on two texts written by James to help strengthen his image as a Protestant monarch: *Ane Frvitfvll Meditatioun contening ane Plane and Facill Expositioun of ye 7.8.9 and 10 versis of the 20 Chap. of the Reuelatioun in forme of ane sermone* (1588) and *Ane Meditatioun vpon the xxv, xxvi, xxvii, xxviii, and xxix verses of the xv Chapt. of the first buke of the Chronicles of the Kingis* (1589).[3] Like James's later writings on kingship, these early theological works were

---

[1]   D. Harris Willson, *King James VI and I* (London: Jonathan Cape, 1956), p. 63.

[2]   *Basilikon Doron*, in Johann P. Sommerville (ed.), *King James VI and I: Political Writings* (Cambridge: Cambridge University Press, 1994), p. 45. All references to *Basilikon Doron* will be to this edition.

[3]   The two meditations were reprinted in a rather sloppily anglicized version in London in 1603, and again in the folio edition of the King's collected *Workes* (1616). All references will be to the original Edinburgh editions in their Scottish spelling.

steeped in the practical political concerns of late sixteenth-century Scotland as well as being linked to international diplomatic relations. Although until recently they have generally been neglected by modern scholarship, James's religious writings offer valuable insights into a Renaissance monarch's perspective on the interplay between religion and politics.[4] A discussion of these texts and the process that led to their publication – including the relationship between James and the Presbyterians at this time – will show how King James used religious treatises both as an opportunity to display his theological learning and as a political tool in his attempt to manage his reputation through the medium of print.

James had been brought up to be an ideal Protestant monarch. Placed on the throne at the age of thirteen months after his mother's forced abdication, he was moulded into the kind of king his Protestant guardians wished to see. His education became the responsibility of the celebrated humanist scholar, poet and political thinker George Buchanan and the Geneva scholar Peter Young, whose combined efforts were meant to instil in the young King of Scotland both the Reformed doctrine and an awareness of his duties rather than his rights as a monarch. However, although the effects of his education would stay with James throughout his life, as an adult he came to insist on his dignity and autonomy as a king. James's advocacy of Divine Right – the idea that kings are appointed by God and are answerable only to Him – is well documented, and it is hardly a surprising standpoint for someone whose mother had been deposed and who had himself had to deal with being lectured, berated and indeed on occasion kidnapped by his subjects. Much to James's annoyance, however, the Kirk refused to submit quietly to his authority and insisted on calling him to account, not only on matters of policy that directly involved religion, but also regarding his personal life. Although he was willing to concede the ministers' point that divine authority outweighs that of secular monarchs, James challenged their sole right to represent that authority. Ministers had the important task, as God's 'heraulds', to spread the word of the Lord, but the divinely appointed monarch was no

---

[4]   Recently the importance of James's theological writings has increasingly tended to be acknowledged, for instance in Malcolm Smuts, 'The Making of *Rex Pacificus*: James VI and I and the Problem of Peace in an Age of Religious War'; Daniel Fischlin, '"To Eat the Flesh of Kings": James VI and I, Apocalypse, Nation, and Sovereignty', both included in Daniel Fischlin and Mark Fortier (eds), *Royal Subjects: Essays on the Writings of James VI and I* (Detroit: Wayne State University Press, 2002); and Jane Rickard, 'The Word of God and the Word of the King: the Scriptural Exegeses of James VI and I and the King James Bible', in Ralph Houlbrooke (ed.), *James VI and I: Ideas, Authority and Government* (Aldershot and Burlington: Ashgate, 2006). Surprisingly, the early meditations have not been included in any of the recent scholarly editions of James's works.

mere layman: his special position as 'God's lieutenant' left him subject to none, not even to the Kirk.[5]

The first major crisis of confidence between king and Kirk was connected to James's distant cousin, the French nobleman Esmé Stuart, Sieur d'Aubigny, who arrived in Scotland in 1579 and soon became the king's closest companion; he was created Earl and later Duke of Lennox and was given what looked to the outside world like virtually unlimited power. James's enthusiasm soon gave rise to concerns about the extent of Lennox's influence over him. As George Buchanan put it, even a king as promising as James might yet be corrupted by 'evil company, the fawning foster-mother of the vices'.[6] Despite Lennox's conversion to Protestantism, he was widely considered to be an agent of James's maternal relations, the French Catholic Guise family. In the words of the church historian David Calderwood, Lennox was obviously being paid by 'the Pope, the King of France, and the Guisians' to dissolve Scotland's 'amitie with England', 'to procure an associatioun betuixt the young king and his mother in the government', and 'to alter the state of religioun'.[7] Whether or not such fears were grounded in reality, Lennox's rise led to persistent rumours that James had Catholic sympathies and might even be persuaded to convert, and the influence of the favourite certainly contributed to the deterioration of the king's relationship with the Presbyterian ministry. Even James's public affirmation of his Protestantism in the form of the Negative Confession, a fiercely anti-Catholic confession of the faith signed by the King and the court in January 1581, proved not to have a lasting effect.[8] Lennox's influence finally came to an end when James was kidnapped in the so-called Ruthven Raid of August 1582 and effectively held prisoner

---

[5]   James refers to ministers as 'heraulds' in *Basilikon Doron* (p. 19), and to kings as 'God's lieutenants' or even 'little Gods' on several occasions throughout his published works.

[6]   Roger A. Mason and Martin S. Smith (eds), *A Dialogue on the Law of Kingship among the Scots: A Critical Edition and Translation of George Buchanan's De Iure Regni apud Scotos Dialogus* (Aldershot and Burlington: Ashgate, 2004), p. 3.

[7]   David Calderwood, *The History of the Kirk of Scotland*, 8 vols, ed. Thomas Thomson (Edinburgh: Wodrow Society, 1842–49), vol. 3, pp. 460–61.

[8]   The *Negative Confession* did have an afterlife, however. It was reprinted and signed again on several occasions when James wished to emphasize his Protestantism; it circulated widely in the form of broadsheets, a quarto booklet and an appendix to John Craig's popular *Short Summe of the whole Catechisme*, and was translated into Dutch (1581 and 1603), French (1603), and German (1604) as evidence of James's wished-for commitment to the European Protestant cause. The confession would later come back to haunt James's son, Charles I, when it was used as the basis of the National Covenant in 1639.

for nearly a year while Lennox was forced to return to France.[9] When the king finally managed to escape and proceeded to deal with his former captors and their allies, among other things by introducing the 'Black Acts' that established royal control over the church, several ministers of the Kirk found the atmosphere so hostile they decided to flee the country.

In the late 1580s, however, the climate at the Scottish court had changed considerably. The regime of the powerful Earl of Arran, who had organized the backlash against the Ruthven Raiders and who was widely believed to be dealing with Catholic France and the exiled Queen Mary, had fallen in 1585 and James, now advised by his new Secretary Sir John Maitland of Thirlestane, was beginning to pursue a policy of reconciliation with the Kirk and closer relations with Protestant England. The execution of Mary in 1587 not only put a final stop to rumours that James might consider sharing the government of Scotland with his mother, but it also left him one step closer to the English throne. Historians have disagreed about the extent to which James's prospects in England influenced his policies at this early stage.[10] However, whether he was motivated by domestic issues or by his hopes regarding the English succession (or both), it is clear that in the late 1580s a solidly Protestant reputation became increasingly important to James. This change of gear is also reflected in the king's writings. Before this time, James had mainly written poetry, gathering around him a coterie of court poets usually referred to as the 'Castalian Band'[11] and publishing his early efforts – including a treatise on Scots poetics – in the collection *The Essayes of a Prentise in the Divine Art of Poesie* (1584). In the latter half of the 1580s, however, he turned his attention to more weighty forms of writing and composed three theological prose works: *A Paraphrase vpon the Revelation* (written at some point in the 1580s but left unprinted until the folio edition of James's collected *Workes* of 1616), and the meditations on Revelation (1588) and the Chronicles (1589).

A Paraphrase vpon the Revelation is probably the most 'technical' of James's theological writings. Written in the persona of the apostle St

---

[9]   Although the Ruthven Lords are often described as ultra-Protestant, their main link with the Kirk appears to have been a shared loathing of Lennox. See Alan R. MacDonald, *The Jacobean Kirk, 1567–1625: Sovereignty, Polity and Liturgy* (Aldershot and Burlington: Ashgate, 1998), pp. 23–4.

[10]   For an overview of the debate, see Susan Doran, 'James VI and the English Succession', in Houlbrooke (ed.), *James VI and I*, esp. pp. 25–8.

[11]   The phrase 'Castalian Band' is still a convenient shorthand but, as Priscilla Bawcutt has pointed out, it is a later construction and was not used by the poets themselves in this context ('James VI's Castalian Band: A Modern Myth', *SHR*, 80 (2001), pp. 251–9.

John, it consists of a rewording of the entire final Bible book.[12] Although James hastens to explain that in contrast to certain commentators who 'wrest and conforme the meaning thereof to their particular and priuate passions', he has interpreted the Revelation using only Scripture and 'nothing of my own coniecture', the reading offered in the *Paraphrase* is by no means a neutral one.[13] James proceeds to do exactly what he denies to have done – using Scripture for his own ends – by providing a strongly anti-Catholic reading of the text, based on what was by this stage an established Protestant exegetical tradition.[14] Initially, Protestant discussions of the Book of Revelation had concentrated on the identity of its author and hence its canonicity, but commentators in England and on the Continent soon began to focus on the possible religio-political applications of the prophecies.[15] However complex and well researched their actual theological contents might be, the main selling point of such commentaries was their identification of the Church of Rome with the Whore of Babylon. The Zürich reformer Heinrich Bullinger's influential treatise *A Hvndred Sermons vpon the Apocalipse of Iesu Christ*, for instance, is popularly summarized in the prefatory verses to its English edition as showing:

That Rome is Babylon,
the beastes with her heades all:
The whore sitting theron,
is Pope that downe shall fall.[16]

---

[12]   For a more detailed discussion of the contents of this text, see Daniel Fischlin, 'To Eat the Flesh of Kings'.

[13]   *A Paraphrase vpon the Revelation*, in *The Workes of the Most High and Mightie Prince, Iames* (London, 1616), pp. 1–2.

[14]   For a more detailed discussion of James blurring the distinction between his own authority and that of the Scriptures, see Rickard, 'The Word of God and the Word of the King'.

[15]   On the tradition of Revelation commentary, see, among many others, Irena Backus, *Reformation Readings of the Apocalypse: Geneva, Zurich, and Wittenberg* (Oxford: Oxford University Press, 2000); Crawford Gribben, *The Puritan Millennium: Literature & Theology, 1550–1682* (Dublin: Four Courts Press, 2000); and Richard Bauckham, *Tudor Apocalypse: Sixteenth-Century Apocalypticism, Millennarianism* [sic] *and the English Reformation: from John Bale to John Foxe and Thomas Brightman* (Abingdon: Sutton Courtenay Press, [*c*.1978]). On apocalyptic prophecy in Scotland, see Arthur H. Williamson, *Scottish National Consciousness in the Age of James VI: The Apocalypse, the Union and the Shaping of Scotland's Public Culture* (Edinburgh: John Donald, 1979).

[16]   Heinrich Bullinger, *A Hvndred Sermons vpon the Apocalipse of Iesu Christ* (1561) (London: John Day, 1573), sig. A4r. James owned a copy but does not

King James, too, explains in his introductory 'Epistle to the Whole Church Militant' that he considers the Book of Revelation 'a speciall cannon against the Hereticall wall of our common aduersaries the Papists'. By commenting on this particular Bible book, James had chosen a religious topic that almost inevitably carried political overtones.

The *Paraphrase* itself, as we have seen, did not appear in print until 1616, but the two meditations that James did publish immediately after they were composed are at least as strongly anti-Catholic and even more overtly political. Written as a reaction to the Armada crisis, they were about more than theology. Their publication was a political act, in keeping with James's policy of seeking the approbation of the Kirk, and it served to put him on the map as a prominent member – and potentially a leader – of the European Protestant community.

As the subject of his first published theological text, *Ane Frvitfvll Meditatioun* (1588), James chose one of the most popular passages of the Revelation: Chapter 20:7–10. The passage in question deals with Satan being released from his prison after a thousand years, to join with Antichrist and the figures of Gog and Magog (often linked to the Ottoman Turks) to plague the saints and the beloved city before finally being cast into a lake of fire and brimstone. Protestant commentators were drawn to this passage because it naturally invited comparisons between the persecution of the 'saints' in the text and the persecution of Protestants, as well as speculation about the identity of Antichrist and the chronology of the Latter Days. This latter aspect of Revelation commentary was of minor importance to James; having no wish to encourage millenarianism, which he saw as the province of radical movements that might destabilize the established order of the commonwealth, James took care not to mention specific dates or dwell on the chronologies that so fascinated his contemporaries.[17] In all other respects, *Ane Frvitfvll Meditatioun* offers a fairly traditional exegesis that combines elements of popular and scholarly interpretation and draws on various biblical texts to explain the passage in question to a non-specialist audience as a continuation of Old Testament prophecies.

The main tenor of the meditation, however, is firmly political: it is set up to lead the reader to the inevitable conclusion that the Pope is Antichrist and that the tyranny of the Church of Rome is soon to disappear into the

---

appear to have followed this or any other source in terms of content, although his meditation does cover exactly the same passage as Bullinger's eighty-ninth sermon.

[17] For a more detailed discussion of this issue, see e.g. Luc Borot, 'James VI & I and Revelation: How to Discourage Millenarian Aspirations', *Anglophonia* 3 (1998), pp. 23–36.

lake of fire and brimstone mentioned in verse 10. The list of symptoms James provides as evidence that the Latter Days are imminent includes the rise of Antichrist and his claim to supreme power, the persecution of the faithful, and the final attack involving what James calls 'ane new sort of vermine' to plague the world; a reference to the Jesuits, whose portrayal as agents of evil was rapidly becoming a tradition. On the basis of these symptoms, James presents his own conclusion – with the same self-assurance he displayed in his *Paraphrase* – as the inevitable outcome of a careful reading of the biblical text: 'Now quhither the Pape beiris thir markis or not, let ony indifferent man iudge: I think surelie it exponis the self' (sig. B2r). More concrete evidence of the identity of Antichrist, according to James, can be found in a series of events in contemporary Europe, culminating in the sailing of the Spanish Armada:

And ar nocht presentlie ye armies amassit, zea vpon ye verie point of thair executioun: In France against the saintis thair: In Flanders for the lyke: and in Germanie, be quhom alreddie ye Bischop of Colleyne[18] is displacit: And quhat is preparit and cum fordwart against this Ile: Do we not daylie heir: and be all appearance shortlie sall see: Now may ze iudge gif this be not ye tyme quhairof this place that I have maid chois of doeth meane. (sig. B2v)

The meditation concludes with a rallying cry to European Protestantism in general and Scotland in particular:

with guide conscience we may, being in ye tentis of ye saintis & belouit citie, stand in our defence: Incourage ane another to vse lawfull resistance, and concur in ane with another as warriouris in ane camp and citizenis of ane belouit citie, for mantenance of ye guid caus God hes cled vs with, and defence of our liberties, natiue countrie, and lyfes. (sig. B4r)

The militant tone of this meditation was understandably appreciated by various groups of Protestants on the Continent, who took it as a hopeful sign of James's much-needed support for their cause. The text was translated into French (1589), Latin (1596; reprinted twice in 1603) and Dutch (1603), and provided with introductions and liminary verses

---

[18]   Gebhard Truchsess, Bishop of Cologne, had decided to marry a Protestant woman in 1582 and was forced to flee to the Netherlands in 1583. The Latin edition of *Ane Frvitfvll Meditatioun* is dedicated to Truchsess, and its prefatory epistle explicitly agrees with James's reference to the bishop's misfortunes as evidence that the Pope is Antichrist.

which encouraged James to put his excellent theories into practice.[19] *Ane Frvitfvll Meditatioun* thus became the most widely disseminated of James's texts before *Basilikon Doron*, and its importance in terms of his European reputation is not to be underestimated.

The image of Scotland as an exemplary Protestant nation, connected to a European community of the faithful 'as warriouris in ane camp', was driven home the following year in the *Meditatioun vpon the Chronicles*. This second meditation celebrates the defeat of the Armada, to which James refers as a 'blissit comedie' (sig. B3v), by depicting Scotland as an elect nation led by a godly king as Israel was led by King David. Whereas James's comments on Revelation had constituted a call to arms, his meditation on King David dancing before the Ark of the Covenant has an air of triumph (and, indeed, of self-congratulation) about it. It is also more inwardly focused on Scotland than the earlier text with its frequent references to the European Protestant cause. On one level, *Ane Meditatioun vpon the Chronicles* offers a theological exegesis of the passage in question, explaining, for instance, that the Ark of the Covenant should be seen as a figure of Christ, and that David's dancing signifies his 'feruent and zealous mynd ... fullie to promoue the glorie of God' (sig. A3v). However, James mainly concentrates once more on parallels between the biblical passage and recent events. The Catholic powers of Europe, for instance, can be identified with the Philistines, and Scotland with Israel:

> Ar they nocht as Philistinis adoreris of legionis of Goddis, and rewlit by ye foolish traditiounis of men? Haue they not as ye Philistinis bene continuallie ye perseweris, and we as Israell ye defenderis of our natiue soill and patrie? (sig. B3v)

This identification works even in the details, as both the Philistine army and the Armada were destroyed by a 'michtie wind' sent directly by God. Thus James deftly appropriates for Scotland a triumph in which it had not played that substantial a part, and in the process even argues – with more enthusiasm than modesty – that the recent victory over the Armada has 'bene far mair notabill then that of Israell' (sig. B3v).

In addition, the meditation sketches specific links between the structure of David's government and sixteenth-century Scotland. Three different groups of Israelites are mentioned in the biblical passage: the elders, the captains over thousands, and the priests and Levites. The former group, comprising mostly magistrates in walled towns and tribal chieftains, was

---

[19]   For a more detailed discussion, see my *A King Translated: James VI and I and the Dutch Interpretations of his Works, 1593–1603* (Aldershot: Ashgate, forthcoming).

charged with dispensing justice, 'not vnlyke to twa of the estaitis of our kingdome, the Barroun and the Burges'. The captains over thousands are comperable to the King of Scotland's military advisers: 'godlie and valiant men, quho vnder the King did rewle in tyme of weir: had the custodie of ye Kingis persone: and faucht his battailis' (sig. A4v). The priests, of course, correspond to the ministers of the Kirk. This section of the meditation begins to resemble James's later political writings in its preoccupation with good kingship. For example, the history of King David is said to show that 'ane godlie King of his godlie foirsicht in choosing guid vnderrewlaris reapis this profite & pleasure, that as he gois befoir, so his with zealous hartis do follow' (sig. B1r); issues of good counsel and the king's responsibility to be an example to his people are similarly emphasized in James's handbook on kingship, *Basilikon Doron* (1599). Although such remarks on kingcraft in the meditations are mostly commonplace and too general to be seen as a direct foreshadowing of the king's later writings, it is clear that James was already considering some of the issues of government that he would later discuss in more detail. His focus, however, is at this stage firmly on cooperation rather than the control issues that characterize *Basilikon Doron*. This is especially striking in his comments on the relationship between David and his priests. One of his conclusions is that

> This is to be markit weill of Princes, and all thois of ony hie calling or degrie that mellis to do in Goddis caus: Dauid dois nathing in matteris apperteining to God without ye presence and speciall concurrence of Goddis Ministeris appointit to be spirituall rewleris in his Kirk. (sig. B1r)

Such statements could hardly have failed to please – even though the phrase "appointit to be spirituall rewleris" would have done little to reassure radical Presbyterians of James's intentions for the Kirk, since it can easily be taken to refer to Episcopalian bishops. As James's dispute with the Kirk over church government became more heated in the course of the 1590s, the Scottish ministry could be forgiven for thinking that the king was not exactly following his own advice. In 1589, however, it was clearly still in his interest to seek their approval.

The importance James attached to the approval of the Kirk is witnessed by the fact that his meditations are introduced to the reader by two ministers: both texts are prefaced by Latin verses by John Malcolm, then regent of St Leonard's College, St Andrews, and introductory epistles by the Perth minister Patrick Galloway. One of the 'seditious preachers' with whom James had been in a state of continual conflict a few years earlier, Galloway had preached incessantly against the royal favourite, Lennox; one sermon in 1582 had even provoked the Duke so much that he had to be physically restrained from attacking Galloway in the pulpit.[20] Not surprisingly, the minister found it prudent to leave Scotland in the aftermath of James's escape from Ruthven Castle, when Lennox's former enemies became 'the men ... most hated by the court'.[21] After his return from his brief exile, however, Galloway's relationship with the court soon became considerably more amicable. In 1588 and 1589, he contributed introductions to James's meditations, endorsing the texts as 'ane witnes of [James's] vpricht meaning in the caus of Christ' and praising their royal author as both a true child and a 'nuresing father' to the Kirk, whose good example might 'prouoke vther kingis to yeild to the treuth'.[22] Galloway even hints that his involvement went beyond merely endorsing the king's efforts: he implies that the initiative to seek publication was his own and that he could only hope 'his Maiestie may weill allow of this my doing'.[23] Of course, a scenario in which Galloway obtained James's meditations and published them without authorization, hoping for the king's post-factum approval of this 'boldnes', is extremely unlikely, considering the importance James attached to controlling the circulation of his writings. In any event, the king was anything but offended by the minister's actions: Galloway was offered a position as court preacher in 1590 at James's personal request. It clearly served the royal interest to allow Galloway to 'discover' the meditations and to publish this evidence of the king's commitment to Protestantism with the Kirk's seal of approval.

In fact Galloway's influence may have extended even further than his introduction implies. Differences between the printed meditations and their manuscript versions suggest that before publication the texts were fine-tuned with the Kirk's sensibilities in mind.[24] Apart from considering shorter biblical passages and being less clearly structured, the manuscript versions of both meditations lack the numerous cross-references to other books of the Bible that characterize the printed texts, and they provide a far less detailed exegesis. The nature of the additional printed material suggests that James may have consulted a professional theologian – and a Calvinist one at that. The print of *Ane Frvitfvll Meditatioun*, for instance, includes a new section of nearly half a page in length on the elect, identifying them as the 'saintis' in the scriptural passage, since they 'ar in

---

[20]   The incident is described in Calderwood, *History of the Kirk*, vol. 4, p. 113.

[21]   Calderwood, *The History of the Kirk*, vol. 4, p. 38.

[22]   *Ane Meditatioun vpon the Chronicles*, sig. A2r.

[23]   *Ane Frvitfvll Meditatioun*, sig. A2r.

[24]   The manuscript versions of the meditations are in MS Bodley 165, preserved in the Bodleian Library, Oxford. They are the subject of a forthcoming article in which I will discuss the issue in more detail.

the lufe of God selectit, and be grace ingrauit in Christ, in quhome they ar comptit and fund iustifeit, worthie of loue and endles glorie' (sig. A4v). By contrast, the doctrine of election is not even mentioned in the manuscript. In the *Meditatioun vpon the Chronicles*, there are long additional passages on, for instance, David's exemplary zeal (sigs A3v–A4r) and the reasons why the Ark of the Covenant should be seen as a figure of Christ (sigs B1r–B2v). Furthermore, the link between Israel and Jacobean Scotland was made much more explicit in print. Nearly the whole of the second chapter of the meditation, describing the persons who accompanied David and likening them to Scotland's Three Estates (sigs A4v–B1r), is absent from the manuscript, as are certain phrases emphasizing that David acted 'with concurrence of his haill estaite' (sig. A3v). One of these additions is the passage quoted above about David doing nothing in matters spiritual 'without ye presence and speciall concurrence of Goddis Ministeris'. Between the initial conception of the meditations and the start of the printing process, then, James not only ensured his arguments were well presented and contained impressive amounts of exegetical detail and biblical cross-references, but he also emphasized the importance of cooperation between the secular and spiritual authorities.[25]

Despite James's best efforts, however, his attempt to present himself as a champion of Protestantism was only moderately successful within Scotland, as his unambiguous statements in print were not necessarily followed by similarly decisive policies. The General Assembly of 1590 may have broken out into fifteen minutes of spontaneous applause when the king asserted he would defend 'the sincerest kirk in the world … so long as I bruike my life and crowne', but James's credit with the Presbyterian ministry was far from unlimited.[26] In 1591, for instance, James apparently felt his Protestant reputation was still too fragile to survive the publication of his epic poem *The Battle of Lepanto*, which has the Spanish Catholic Don Juan of Austria as its hero, without the assurance in an explanatory introduction that it would be 'cleane contrarie' to the intentions of its royal author to read *Lepanto* as a poem 'in praise of a forraine Papist bastard'.[27] Clearly James could not rely on his readers to accept this as a

---

[25] I do not wish to suggest that the alterations to the meditations were made by anyone other than James, but we cannot be certain of who was or was not involved in the editing process, and a close cooperation between the king and a minister of the Kirk – perhaps Galloway – does present itself as a possibility.

[26] Calderwood, *Historie of the Kirk*, vol. 4, pp. 98, 106.

[27] James Craigie (ed.), *The Poems of James VI. of Scotland*, 2 vols (Edinburgh: STS, 1955–58), vol. 1, p. 198. There has been much speculation about James's intentions in writing the *Lepanto*. It has most often been seen as a sign of his wavering between personal Catholic sympathies and the exigencies of ruling a Protestant country, or as an early sign of his ecumenical desire to heal Christian

matter of course. When the next major Catholic scare after the Armada, the affair of the Spanish Blanks, came to light in 1593, many saw it as an inevitable result of James's laxness in taking real measures against Catholics. Some of the same ministers who had applauded James three years earlier now readily believed that this plot supporting a Spanish invasion of England via Scotland had James's 'expresse or tacite consent', or at least that the conspirators had, as Calderwood put it, 'perceaved him inclynned that way, wherupon they have presumed'.[28] Several of James's Calvinist subjects reproached him for not fulfilling the promises made in his meditations. John Napier of Merchiston, for instance, used the preface to his own commentary on the Revelation to lecture the king about his duty to reform his country by setting a good example:

> and first (taking example of the princely Prophet Dauid) to begin at your M. owne house, familie and court, and purge the same of all suspicion of Papists, and Atheists or Newtrals ... For shall any Prince be able to be one of the destroiers of that great seate [i.e., Rome], and a purger of the world from Antichristianism, who purgeth not his owne house?[29]

In one of the bitterest attacks on James's 'fayr promeissis and protestations', the minister John Ross called the king 'the maist fynest, and maist dissembling hypocreit' and even thundered in the royal presence that he 'wald crave of God that his words war fewar, and his deidis war in greater nomber'.[30] Sermons, as Peter McCullough has rightly pointed out, can after all be used 'both to trumpet and to shout down royal policy'.[31] Such admonitions failed to produce concrete results, however, and in the course of the 1590s the relationship between James and the Kirk deteriorated ever further as they clashed repeatedly over matters of church government.

---

differences, although in my opinion the poem is more unambiguously Protestant than is often realized. The most detailed recent discussion of the *Lepanto* can be found in Peter C. Herman, '"Best of Poets, Best of Kings": King James VI and I and the Scene of Monarchic Verse', in Fischlin and Fortier (eds), *Royal Subjects*; see also Astrid J. Stilma, '*The Battle of Lepanto*: the Introduction of James VI of Scotland to the Dutch', in Houlbrooke (ed.), *James VI and I*.

[28]   Calderwood, *History of the Kirk*, vol. 5, p. 231.

[29]   John Napier, *A Plaine Discovery of the Whole Revelation of St John* (Edinburgh, 1593), sigs A3v–A4r.

[30]   *The Historie and Life of King James the Sext: Being an Account of the Affairs of Scotland, from the Year 1566, to the Year 1596, with a Short Continuation to the Year 1617* (Edinburgh: Bannatyne Club, 1825), pp. 317–18, 322.

[31]   Peter E. McCullough, *Sermons at Court: Politics and Religion in Elizabethan and Jacobean Preaching* (Cambridge: Cambridge University Press, 1998), p. 2.

James's early meditations, in short, were the products of a particular moment in his career, when he made a concerted effort to re-invent himself as what Jenny Wormald has termed 'the most Protestant king in Europe'.[32] From the late 1590s onwards, he was to focus predominantly on issues of government, without much thought of pleasing the Kirk. These later texts always dealt extensively with religion as well, but their main focus in this respect tended to be the relationship between kingship and divine authority and the need to establish royal control over the church. The political tract *The True Law of Free Monarchies* (1598), James's earliest defence of Divine Right theory, is invariably discussed as a work of political theory, but like the earlier meditations it largely consists of a politically applied exegesis – in this case of a passage in the Book of Samuel dealing with the Israelites' demand that God appoint a king to rule them.[33] The substantial religious component of *Basilikon Doron* mainly emphasizes the importance of a monarch's personal piety and the political application of that piety in governing the church. Since a king's 'office is … mixed, betwixt the Ecclesiasticall and ciuill estate', he should use his thorough knowledge of the Bible to keep the church from exceeding its authority: if ministers should urge their flock 'to embrace any of their fantasies in the place of Gods word, or would colour their particulars with a pretended zeale', the king must 'grauely and with authoritie redact them in order againe'. James was thus using the Presbyterian insistence on scriptural authority against them by claiming for himself the same right to interpret the Bible, to the extent of attributing to kings the responsibility of ensuring that ministers 'vague not from their text in the Pulpit'. The prospect of being second-guessed by a royal critic in the congregation would have done little for James's popularity with the clergy; but then, the King complained, certain 'fierie spirited men in the ministerie' had always been publicly critical of him anyway, 'not for any euill or vice in me, but because I was a King, which they thought the highest euill'.[34] If ministers such as Ross, of whom James may well have been thinking here, felt that they had waited 'over lang' for their 'carnall Prence' to repair the 'disorderit'

---

[32]   Jenny Wormald, '"Tis True I am a Cradle King": the View from the Throne', in Julian Goodare and Michael Lynch (eds), *The Reign of James VI* (East Linton: Tuckwell Press, 2000), p. 249.

[33]   On *The True Law* as a response to George Buchanan, see e.g. Roger Mason, *Kingship and the Commonweal: Political Thought in Renaissance and Reformation Scotland* (East Linton: Tuckwell Press, 1998); on the tract as a response to Robert Parsons's tract *A Conference about the Next Succession*, see Peter Lake, 'The King (the Queen) and the Jesuit: James Stuart's *True Law of Free Monarchies* in Context/s', *Transactions of the Royal Historical Society*, 14 (2004), pp. 243–60.

[34]   *Basilikon Doron*, p. 52; p. 19; p. 45; p. 26.

commonwealth, James in turn had given up on them as well; one can easily imagine him heaving a long-suffering sigh as he advised his son not to waste time arguing with Presbyterians, 'for I haue ouer-much surfeited them with that, and it is not their fashion to yeeld'.[35]

Despite acknowledging the futility of 'surfeiting' the opposition with arguments, as King of England James did not lose his taste for theological discussion, especially when it touched on Divine Right and the limits of royal power. Such discussions took place on an increasingly international scale as James argued with the Pope and Cardinal Bellarmine in *An Apologie for the Oath of Allegiance* (1607), and attempted to stop the Dutch Arminian theologian Conrad Vorstius, whose works he considered 'monstrous blasphemie and horrible Atheisme', from becoming Professor of Divinity at Leiden in 1611.[36] James also published two further meditations (on the Lord's Prayer and on verses from St Matthew), which were added to his collected *Workes* in 1620. By his own admission, these late meditations are theologically less solid than the texts of the 1580s; they are concerned with general issues such as charity and forgiveness or the burdens of kingship rather than 'wading' as before in scriptural matters so deep 'an Elephant may swimme' in them.[37] James's reputation as a theologian-king, in short, remained important to him throughout his reign, but the focus and tone of his religious writings changed with his priorities, increasingly dwelling on issues of kingship and reflecting concerns that were now more pressing to James than pleasing the Scottish Kirk. While in Scotland the king had literally sat at the foot of the pulpit and his engagement with what he heard there had by necessity been a process of negotiation, later in his reign he was able to exert authority in more direct ways.[38] His early meditations, however, remained relevant not only to those who continued to refer to them through quotation or translation, but also to James himself – as witnessed by his decision to include them in the folio edition of his collected *Workes* in 1616. Recent scholarship has started to recognize the importance of sermons and exegesis as 'the most frequent and influential literary enterprise' at the Jacobean court, as well as their importance in creating and reinforcing James's public image.[39] There can be little doubt that James, who was said in 22 years on the English throne to have

---

[35] *Historie of King James the Sext*, p. 319; *Basilikon Doron*, p. 45.

[36] See *A Declaration Against Vorstius*, in *The Workes*, pp. 347–80.

[37] *A Meditation upon the Lords Prayer*, in *The Workes*, p. 571.

[38] On the significance of church architecture, see McCullough, *Sermons at Court*, pp. 28ff.

[39] McCullough, *Sermons at Court*, p. 2; Mary Morrissey, 'Presenting James VI and I to the Public: Preaching on Political Anniversaries at Paul's Cross', in Houlbrooke (ed.), *James VI and I*.

'heard more sermons, than all the Princes before him in two hundred',[40] had a discerning palate for matters theological. It is therefore all the more important to remember that he did not only consume exegeses but produced them as well, and that we should engage with these productions as seriously as his contemporaries evidently did.

---

[40] Phineas Hodson, *The Last Sermon* (1625), quoted in McCullough, *Sermons at Court*, p. 118.

CHAPTER 8

Calvinism, counter-Reformation and conversion: Alexander Montgomerie's religious poetry

Mark S. Sweetnam

The Scottish court of James VI is one of the most complex of the loci of Reformation. The King's family connections and the complexity of his diplomatic manoeuvrings – conducted with one eye on the English succession, and the delicate balance of power on the European continent – add a further layer of complication to the difficult and debated issues of survivalism and recusancy which existed even when a monarch pursued an unambiguous programme of Reformation.[1] In spite of this complexity, Alexander Montgomerie, soldier, poet, ambassador and outlaw, is an outstandingly problematic figure.[2] Both 'the Jacobean paragon and the Jacobean excommunicate', Montgomerie was an intimate of the King, his

---

[1]   The author wishes gratefully to acknowledge the generous support of the Irish Research Council for the Humanities and Social Studies. I would also like to thank Prof. Eiléan Ní Chuilleanáin for her insightful and helpful comments on an earlier draft of this work.

For the developing discussion of these issues see *inter alia* Eamonn Duffy, *The Stripping of the Altars* (New Haven and London: Yale U.P., 1992); John Bossy, 'The Character of Elizabethan Catholicism', in Trevor Aston (ed.), *Crisis in Europe 1560–1660* (London: Routledge and Kegan Paul, 1965); and Alexandra Walsham, *Church Papists: Catholicism, Conformity and Confessional Polemic in Early Modern England* (Woodbridge: The Boydell Press, for the Royal Historical Society, 1993).

[2]   For biographical information on Montgomerie see R.D.S. Jack, *Alexander Montgomerie* (Edinburgh: Scottish Academic, 1985); idem, 'Montgomerie, Alexander (early 1550s–1598)', *ODNB*, [http://www.oxforddnb.com/view/article/19052, accessed 4 Oct 2005]; David J. Parkinson (ed.), *Montgomerie's Poems*, 2 vols (Edinburgh: STS, 2000), vol. 2, pp. 11–15; H.M. Shire, *Song, Dance and Poetry of the Court of Scotland under King James VI* (Cambridge: Cambridge University Press, 1969); Roderick J. Lyall, 'Alexander Montgomerie and the Netherlands, 1586–89', *Glasgow Review*, 1 (1993), pp. 52–66; Mark Dilworth, 'New Light on Alexander Montgomerie', *The Bibliotheck*, 4 (1965), pp. 230–35, and John Durkan, 'The Date of Alexander Montgomerie's Death', *Innes Review*, 34 (1983), pp. 91–2.

poetic mentor, and the chief architect of James' new Scottish prosody.[3] He was a courtier, dependent on the goodwill of the King for his pension, drawn from the bishopric of Glasgow, and an emissary for the King to the Spanish court. However, he was also a convert to Catholicism, who became increasingly militant, until, at the end of his life, he was involved in armed rebellion against James, declared an outlaw, and denied 'Christian burial'. After his death, he again became the object of James's interested intervention, both in the regularization of his interment and the provision of an epitaph for this 'prince of poets'.[4] Montgomerie's verse proves as complex as his life, eliding the simplistic efforts of some critics to remake it in the form of Counter-Reformation propaganda. Rather, a careful consideration of Montgomerie's religious writing reveals a complex imbrication of the concerns of the Calvinism, in which he was raised, with the doctrinal stresses of his adopted Catholicism.

Montgomerie was born in the early 1550s. There is no record of his attending any Scottish college, and his subsequent styling as *eques montanus* and as captain suggests that, like the younger sons of many noble families, Montgomerie spent some time soldiering. If the 'MountGomerye' mentioned in a surviving letter by Sir Thomas Cecil, Governor of Brielle refers to Alexander, as both R.D.S. Jack and Roderick Lyall conclude, it seems that he fought on the side of the Protestant Low Countries in their war against Catholic Spain.[5] His upbringing was Calvinist, and it is unclear at what point in his life he converted to Catholicism. It is possible, however, that this event took place during a conjectured visit to Spain in the 1580s. Montgomerie became a servitor of Esmé Stuart, Sire d'Aubigny, later Earl of Lennox, and a courtier at the Scottish court. His 'literary production crosses political and cultural thresholds in spanning both the Marian and Jacobean decades. He contributed prominently to the cultural inauguration of James' reign through allegorical masque-like narrative which celebrates the iconicity of James' new kingship'.[6] Montgomerie subsequently became the King's mentor, and the central figure in James's project of creating a distinctively Scottish form of poetry. In the pursuit of this goal, James gathered around him a coterie of poets, the 'Castalian Band', with the King as their leader, but with Montgomerie as their

---

[3]   Sarah M. Dunnigan, *Eros and Poetry in the Courts of Mary Queen of Scots and James VI* (Basingstoke, Hampshire and New York: Palgrave Macmillan, 2002), p. 125.

[4]   Montgomerie, *Poems*, vol. 2, p. 11.

[5]   R.D.S. Jack, 'Montgomerie and the Pirates', *SSL*, 5 (1967–68), pp. 133–6; Lyall, 'Alexander Montgomerie and the Netherlands, 1586–89', *Glasgow Review*, 1 (1993), pp. 52–66.

[6]   Dunnigan, *Eros and Poetry*, p. 126.

acknowledged superior and poet laureate. His importance was attested to by the prominence given to his work as exemplars of the King's new programme in his *The Essayes of a Prentise in the Divine Arte of Poesie* (1585). A further evidence of James's esteem was seen in his sympathetic interpretation of the prevailing legal situation in granting Montgomerie a pension from the bishopric of Glasgow.

In 1586, Montgomerie was given permission to travel in Europe, and it seems likely that this permission was given in order to allow him to act as a secret ambassador to the Spanish court, on James's behalf. In June, Montgomerie was captured off the Brielle, on a ship loaded with contraband. The exact events that took place during his absence from Scotland are somewhat obscure, but it appears that he may have been imprisoned for a time. When Montgomerie returned to Scotland, circumstances had become unfavourable to him. Anti-Catholic feeling had increased, and the Protestant claimant to the see of Glasgow had claimed Montgomerie's pension, depriving the poet of his financial support. Montgomerie engaged in legal action to recover his stipend. This action dragged on until 1593, narrated by a series of increasingly polemical and bitter sonnets addressed to the legal representatives on both sides and to the king. In 1593 Montgomerie finally lost his case. Disappointed, he left Scotland, and took refuge amongst the Scottish Benedictines in Würzburg, where, for a time he contemplated taking religious orders. Subsequently, Montgomerie returned to Ayrshire, and became involved in a military action to secure the strategically important island of Ailsa Craig in the Firth of Clyde, in support of the rebellion of the Earl of Tyrone. This action was quelled by the forces of the king, and Montgomerie was outlawed. Shortly afterwards he died. His funeral arrangements became embroiled in controversy, and the king, whose perceived betrayal had been documented in Montgomerie's poetry, intervened to ensure that the poet received an orderly burial. James recorded his continuing esteem for his erstwhile laureate in a work calling on the Castalian Band to recognize the poetic genius of Montgomerie:

> Though to his buriall was refused the bell,
> The bell of fame shall aye his praises knell.[7]

Such, then, are the contours of Montgomerie's life. They provide a picture not lacking in elements of excitement and adventure, following, in Sarah Dunnigan's phrase, 'a dramatic and changeful trajectory'.[8] For the student

---

[7]   *The Poems of James VI of Scotland*, ed. J. Craigie, 2 vols (Edinburgh: STS, 1955–58), vol. 2, p. 108.

[8]   Dunnigan, *Eros and Poetry*, p. 126.

of literature, however, the question of interest is the extent to which this commitment to Catholicism and the Counter-Reformation found expression in his writing. It may be worth asking whether we should, in fact, expect such a congruence between a largely private belief and a very public poetry. We must remember that, even for prominent Protestants, the system of court patronage demanded a great deal of circumspection even in the expression of orthodox doctrine.[9] Montgomerie's early dependence on the pension granted by James, and his later hopes of regaining it, were also likely to moderate any very forthright expression of Catholic belief. Indeed, the experience of Montgomerie's friend and fellow-poet Henry Constable was a cautionary tale against too lightly making such an avowal.[10] In this regard, it is worth remembering that Montgomerie's one incontrovertible act of insurrection came close to the end of his life, and only at the point when his pension was clearly irretrievable. In this context, we might legitimately expect any discussion of Catholicism to be indirect at most.

There are, on the other hand, factors that would lead us to expect that such a discussion would take place at some level. If we apply, with due reservation, John Bossy's taxonomy of post-reformation English Catholicism to the Scottish context, Montgomerie falls into the second category, that of 'alarm spiritual'.[11] Bossy distinguishes this second wave from the survivalism of an insular Catholicism rooted in bastard-feudalism and the big house. The second generation, in Bossy's reading, tended to be converts, often to be clerks, and always heavily interlinked with European religion and politics. These missionaries saw themselves as the 'instrument of the enterprises of God'. Montgomerie fits well into this description. Though not in clerical orders, he was a convert to Catholicism, accustomed to military activity, and *persona grata* at the court of Phillip of Spain. For Bossy this 'muscular Christianity' had its intellectual counterpoint.

> This metamorphosis of the clerk into the man of action could not be allowed to suppress his character as a man of thought and scholarship. The mission itself demanded books: simple explanations of doctrine, books of spiritual

---

[9]   See Jonathon Goldberg, *James I and the Politics of Literature: Jonson, Shakespeare, Donne, and Their Contemporaries* (Baltimore: Johns Hopkins Univ. Press, 1983), pp. 132, 133; Guy Fitch Lytie and Stephen Orgel (eds), *Patronage in the Renaissance* (Princeton: Princeton Univ. Press, 1981); and Marla Hoffman Lunderberg, 'John Donne's strategies for discreet preaching', *Studies in English Literature 1500–1900*, 44 (2004), 97–119.

[10]   Ceri Sullivan, 'Constable, Henry (1562–1613)', *ODNB*. [http://www.oxforddnb.com/view/article/6103, accessed 4 Oct 2005].

[11]   Bossy, 'Elizabethan Catholicism', p. 231.

encouragement and direction, statements on doubtful points of practice, manifestoes, martyrologies.

Similarly, Caroline M. Hibbard suggests that 'the quantity and quality of Catholic literature ... reflect the vigor of Stuart Catholicism. The clandestine conditions in which this literature had to be produced and distributed did not prevent a lively trade in books printed secretly in England or smuggled in from the continent.'[12] This move for Counter-Reformation, then, both demanded and valued the contribution of literature. Thus, a poet of Montgomerie's skill and stature may well have been assumed to have made what contribution he could to this aspect of the struggle.

A more compelling, and yet more problematic reason for expecting Montgomerie's corpus to contain forthright and unapologetic defences of Catholicism is found in Latin verses discovered by Mark Dilworth.[13] These verses were written by Thomas Duff, a monk of the Scottish Benedictine monastery at Würzburg, Franconia. They have proved an invaluable resource, providing a great deal of fresh information on Montgomerie's life. It is to Duff that we owe the information that Montgomerie was a convert to the counter-reformation faith, that he had gained distinction in military service, and that he was contemplating taking orders before his untimely death. More problematically, they state:

> Hostis eram gravis haereseon semperque perodi
> Falsa, Picarditas carmine Marte premens.
> [I was a strong enemy of heretics and I always hated [their] falsehoods, attacking 'Picarditas' with sword and poetry.][14]

Most critics, with the notable exception of Dilworth, have noted that '"Picardi" seems to have been used in Catholic circles as a generic term for Protestants.'[15] Indeed, 'Duff does seem to equate the terms in another poem.' In spite of the fact that 'there was a rebellion in Picardy in which Montgomery could have been involved, so that the surface meaning also remains possible', most critics have thus interpreted this statement as meaning that Montgomerie was engaged in the literary defence of his faith.[16] On this basis, they seem to suggest a defence of Catholicism satisfactory to the most demanding of Catholics. The difficulty is that

[12]   Caroline M. Hibbard, 'Early Stuart Catholicism: Revisions and Re-Revisions', *The Journal of Modern History*, 52 (1980), p. 12.

[13]   Mark Dilworth, 'New Light on Alexander Montgomerie', pp. 230–35.

[14]   Thanks are due to Prof. Eiléan Ní Chuilleanáin for supplying this translation.

[15]   Lyall, 'Montgomerie and the Netherlands'.

[16]   Jack, *Montgomerie*, p. 127.

'such impassioned religious polemic cannot entirely be substantiated from Montgomerie's poetic relics'.[17]

This unfortunate fact has led some critics to exercise what might well be regarded as an unseemly amount of ingenuity in identifying such doughty defences in Montgomerie's work. The most ingenious and, at times, tendentious attempts have been made by Helena M. Shire in her *Song, Dance and Poetry of the Court of Scotland under King James VI* (1969). The tone for her interpretation is set by her glossing of the lines quoted above as 'He assailed Protestantism with sword and song', without drawing attention to the assumption that by 'Picardi' Duff did, in fact, intend Protestants. As Professor Jack is careful to stress, this hypothesis is 'quite likely', but a hypothesis nonetheless, and some indication that Shire's reading relies on such an assumption is sadly wanting.[18] Having established this premise for her approach to Montgomerie, Shire finds the polemic to support her reading in Montgomerie's most substantial work, the dream-romance, '*The Cherrie and the Slae*'. For Shire, this work is 'a poem of serious import, nearly concerned with "mighty matters", religious and hence politic, in Scotland in the age of Counter-reform'.[19] She supports this by an analysis of the allegorical imagery in the poem, especially of the 'cherrie' and of the 'slae', which she aligns respectively with Catholicism and the Reformed faith. '[T]he cherry was heavenly fruit', and 'the white and red of its flesh and juice ... could eloquently figure the body and blood of Christ, of the sacrament.' The 'bitter/black' Slae is obviously a far less attractive option, in spite – or perhaps because of – the fact that it was 'low and accessible on its Bush'. This bush, moreover clinches Shire's allegorical interpretation – 'the bush, the 'burning bush', was chosen as heraldic badge on the seal of the Reformed Church of France', although she fails to suggest what else the poet might have reasonably depicted a sloe growing on.[20]

Shire then uses a comparison of the two extant versions of the poem to suggest that it had, indeed, been read by its original audience as a forceful and dangerous commentary on the comparative attractiveness of Catholicism and the reformed faith. She argues that the composition of this 'early "unfinished" version ... would have been watched with keen interest in the newly assembled court of 1583 and 1584. With the turn affairs took in 1585 – towards Protestant dominance at court – it comes as no surprise that the poem was severed or silenced.'[21] Montgomerie,

17   Dunnigan, *Eros and Poetry*, p. 127.
18   Jack, *Montgomerie*, p. 127.
19   Shire, *Song, Dance and Poetry*, p. 118.
20   Ibid., p. 126.
21   Ibid., p. 130.

she suggests, later returned to the poem, and revised it in a spirit of despair, having appreciated that the conversion of James was no longer within the sphere of practical ambition. This, in her contention, positively identifies Montgomerie's polemical activities against the Reformation – an identification that ought to be obvious when due allowances are made for 'the old-style manner of his poetic expression'.[22]

Shire's reading is, as we have said, tendentious, and it is scarcely surprising that other scholars have demurred from it. Professor Jack, in his valuable book-length study of Montgomerie, moderately identifies some of the difficulties with Shire's reading, pointing out that 'neither the Cherrie nor the Slae is an obvious symbol for the monarchy, Catholicism or Protestantism. ... Indeed the Slae ... does [not] at any point provide the real opposition suggested by the dignity of the Scottish crown or the power of Protestantism.'[23] Charles B. Gullins, reviewing the volume for the *Renaissance Quarterly*, was less moderate, but scarcely less accurate:

> [Shire's] interpretation of Montgomerie's 'The Cherrie and the Slae' illustrates [an] aberration of scholarship, the wilful misinterpretation of text to fit a thesis. Mrs. Shire pretends to explain much of the allegory by pointing out that animals and plants which occur in the text have allegorical or iconographic significance in other poets or poems, yet gives so many diverse significations that it is impossible to ascertain what specific meaning applies to Montgomerie.[24]

It should be stressed that we are not denying the possibility of reading a religious significance to '*The Cherrie and the Slae*', nor indeed are we querying the validity of such a reading. Nonetheless, it seems clear that any reading of the poem on its own terms will fail to provide the forthright defence of Catholicism, or the attack on the Reformed faith that Duff's lines lead us to expect. It seems, therefore, that we must look elsewhere for Montgomerie's literary defences of his adopted faith.

Roderick Lyall posits another possibility, more convincing, yet still unsure, relying, as it does, on the attribution of two anonymous sonnets attacking the Protestants, which were thrown into the pulpit at St Giles Church and into the house of John Cairns, the incumbent.[25] Lyall's identification of Montgomerie as the writer is well-argued and convincing, and the sonnets are certainly couched in forceful language, attacking

---

[22]   Ibid., p. 137.

[23]   Ibid., pp. 126–7.

[24]   Charles B. Gullins, 'Review of *Dance and Poetry of the Court of Scotland under King James VI*', *Renaissance Quarterly*, 25 (1972), p. 98.

[25]   Roderick J. Lyall, 'Alexander Montgomerie, Anti-Calvinist Propagandist?', *Notes and Queries*, new series, 49:2 (2002), p. 210.

prominent Calvinist clergy by name, and concluding with a damning comparison between these prominent religious figures and those upbraided in the gospels:

> Ye scorne but Christ, your Counterye, kirk, and kinge,
> Prescryband points as Scribes in euerye thinge.[26]

These forthright denouncements are clearly congruous with Duff's description, and could we be certain of the validity of ascribing them to Montgomerie, we would, perhaps, be justified in feeling that a missing piece of the jigsaw had been supplied. As it is, however, it is difficult to rest here with any complacency.

It remains, therefore, a question whether we are in fact missing a piece from Montgomerie's *oeuvre*. True, Duff's words are uncompromising enough. However, critics in interacting with them have paid insufficient attention to Mark Dilworth's cautious comment on the stanzas: 'It will be evident that the artificial verse form draws, as it were, a fairly thick veil over the historical facts, while the robust sectarian spirit of the author does not lend itself to objectivity.'[27] Both form and content, then, should make us cautious regarding any assumptions about the nature of Montgomerie's religious poetry. Duff was writing as a eulogist, and his stanzas provide abundant evidence of the 'robust sectarian spirit' remarked by Dilworth. We would surely be better advised to pay prior attention to the content of Montgomerie's work, and draw our conclusions about the nature of his attack on Protestantism from what he wrote, rather than being seduced by one source, of dubious objectivity, to excesses of critical ingenuity. Such an examination leads us to the conclusion that

> Although the devotional poems are clearly the work of a devout Catholic, they do not breathe a combative, missionary spirit. Essentially personal, they consistently choose the Catholic means to salvation rather than the Protestant but they do not emphasise major doctrinal conflicts in a belligerent manner. Personal consolation founded on basic Catholic teaching rather than direct conflict with opposing creeds seems Montgomerie's aim.[28]

Indeed, we can go further than this, and observe that Montgomerie looks at his Catholic faith in a distinctively Calvinist way. Perhaps unsurprisingly, given the relatively mature age at which Montgomerie shifted his confessional allegiances, his new faith does not appear to have entirely

---

26   Lyall, 'Anti-Calvinist Propagandist', p. 210.
27   Dilworth, 'Fresh Light', p. 231.
28   Jack, *Alexander Montgomerie*, p. 71.

displaced the teaching of his youth. Inevitably, these stresses emerge most clearly in Montgomerie's religious verse, and within the confines of the present study, we will examine the 'doctrinal universe' of those explicitly religious lyrics that we can, with certainty, attribute to Montgomerie.

Prima facie, these lyrics are eloquent of Montgomerie's commitment to religious poetry. The origin of the arrangement of his poems in the Ker manuscript is a matter of some conjecture, but it is at least a possibility that they were ordered by Montgomerie himself. Certainly, Jack contends that the compiler 'knew the poet's work well and almost certainly had access to his papers'.[29] Similarly, while David Parkinson is somewhat more cautious about attributing the arrangement to Montgomerie, he stresses that the 'clarity and ease' of the way in which the scribe 'draws the reader's attention to innovations in versification' implies scribal familiarity with, and commitment to, the poet's practice. They suggest ... that [the Ker manuscript] is not far from Montgomerie's own copies.'[30] In the resulting arrangement, religious lyrics have 'been given a position of extreme importance'.[31] Six explicitly religious lyrics open the collection, and a further two (whose authorship has been called into question by Parkinson) close it, providing a frame for the secular works which make up the preponderance of the manuscript.[32] This framing is as much thematic as physical.

> [I]f the secular works concentrate on human misfortune, injustice and mutability, these six [opening] poems by way of contrast stress divine benevolence, mercy and eternal life. ... [T]he last two sound out a note of triumph in contemplating the divine love offered to those who reject the world and become brides of the Lamb.[33]

In addition, the lyrics themselves provide evidence of Montgomerie's estimation of the value of his religious lyrics. 'A godly prayer' articulates his understanding of his poetic ability as a talent given by God, and to be used for His glory:

> ... mak my Tongue the Trompet of thy truth
> And lend my verse sik wings as are divine.
> Sen thou hes grantit me so good Ingyn
> To Loif the, Lord, in gallant style and gay

---

29   Jack, *Alexander Montgomerie*, p. 37.
30   Montgomerie, *Poems*, vol. 2, p. 4.
31   Jack, *Alexander Montgomerie*, p. 68.
32   Montogomerie, *Poems*, vol. 2, pp. 5–6.
33   Jack, *Alexander Montgomerie*, pp. 68–9.

Let me no moir so trim a talent tyne.
Peccavi Pater, Miserere mei.

Thy Spirit my Spirit to speik with speed inspire.
Help holy Ghost, and be Montgomeries muse.
Flie doun on me in forked tongues of fyre
As thou did on thy oune Apostills vse
And with thy fyre me fervently infuse
To laud the, Lord, and longer not delay.
My former foolish fictiouns I refuse. (4, ll.43–55)[34]

These stanzas are noteworthy for a number of reasons. They are clearly retrospective, and are, to some extent, a retraction. In this context, it is interesting that the compiler has chosen to place this poem close to the start of his collection. It seems, therefore, to undermine the validity of the remaining works – Montgomerie's 'former foolish fictiouns'. This suggests a value system that sees religious poetry as hugely more valuable than any secular work. The difference in values comes as a concomitant of the different sources of inspiration. The significance of the line 'help Holy Ghost, and be Montgomeries muse' is especially marked when we recall the invocations of classical deity that saturate the work of the Castalian Band. Clearly, Montgomerie's religious poetry is no mere ancillary to his more voluminous secular works.

In the context of Duff's remarks on Montgomerie's religious poetry, the imagery of the poet's tongue as the 'Trompet of [God's] truth' is surely worthy of note. The trumpet has, of course, martial connotations, both chivalric and Biblical. This image appears to suggest a bold and warlike declaration of God's truth, as understood by the Catholic Church. In the wider context, however, we see once again the lack of 'combative, missionary spirit' remarked by Jack. Montgomerie is less interested in doctrinal warfare than in the glorification of God, whom he desires to 'Loif' and to 'laud'. It must be acknowledged that the public nature of Montgomerie's manifesto seems, to some extent, poorly to accord with the essentially private nature of his religious poetry. Nevertheless, we must measure this statement of intent against the actual achievement.

The two lyrics that open the Ker manuscript further complicate an attempt to press an identification of Montgomerie as a poet of the counter-reformation. The metrical versions of the first and second psalms seem to integrate Montgomerie with the quintessentially Protestant tradition of vernacular psalmody. It was not the case that Protestantism had any

---

[34]   The text and numbering of Montgomerie's works follows Parkinson's edition of *Poems*.

monopoly on the use of the Psalms. Rather, they were utilized by Catholics and by Protestants 'as a vehicle for basic moral and religious instruction' and as a part of 'a devotional tradition in which [they] provided a nucleus for the private prayers of the laity'.[35] Nonetheless, as early as 1549, Thomas Sternhold had identified the freedom for a layman to engage in vernacular translations of the psalms as one of the chief blessings of life in a Reformed kingdom: ' ... rendrynge thankes to almyghtye God, that hath appoynted us such a Kynge and gouernour, that forbyddeth not laye men to gather and leaze in the lordes harvest.'[36] More especially, however, it was the 'congregational singing of metrical psalms [that] encapsulated many of the guiding principles of the Reform movement', and which was so typical of the Reformation's stress on vernacular scripture.[37] Clearly, Montgomerie's very accomplished versifications occur rather as personal meditations. However, Professor Jack draws our attention to evidence which suggests that these lyrics are initial efforts in a far more ambitious programme projected by Montgomerie. The General Assembly of the Scottish church have left on record their appreciation of Montgomerie's poetic abilities, and of his becoming modesty in pursuing this project: 'Alexr Mongomerie had a singular vaine of posie, yet he tuik a more modest course, for he translated bot a few for a proofe, and offered his travels in that kynde to the kirk.'[38] So, then, we are not simply dealing with verse translations of the Psalms intended for the enjoyment of the poet, or of a limited coterie. Rather, we are presented with a poet who is offering his services to the Reformed kirk of Scotland, and, what is more, offering those services in the furtherance of the most Protestant of innovations. It would not, perhaps, avail much to engage in speculation as to why he should be moved to do this. Nonetheless, it is surely not excessively cynical to wonder whether the poet was actuated by considerations of the financial gain or of the increased fame that would inevitably result if he succeeded in obtaining Scotland's leading poetical franchise. The point of central importance, however, is that he did do so. This seems indicative of a degree of accommodation in his approach to matters of religion that is difficult to reconcile with the doctrinaire defender of the Catholic faith by sword and song.

---

[35] Rivkah Zim, *English Metrical Psalms: Poetry as Praise and Prayer* (Cambridge: Cambridge U.P., 1987), p. 3; and see, on the Psalms as a vehicle of religious instruction, pp. 30–34, and as private prayer, pp. 27–30.

[36] Quoted in David W. Music, *Hymnology: A Collection of Source Readings* (Lanham and London: Scarecrow Press, 1996), p. 72.

[37] David Greer, Review of Robin A. Leaver, '"*Goostly psalms and spirituall songes*": English and Dutch Metrical Psalms from Coverdale to Utenhove 1535–1566', in *Renaissance Quarterly*, 47 (1994), p. 713.

[38] Quoted Jack, *Montgomerie*, p. 68.

Amongst the themes which dominate Montgomerie's religious lyrics is the need for fruitful faith that is effectual in the production of good works. 'The Poets Dreme', the third lyric in the Ker collection, is a meditation on the necessity of meritorious action if the poet is to be amongst the limited company to find a place in Heaven. The first stanza calls for a commencement of such actions – the narrator resolves to

> ... sleep na mair in sleuth and sin
> Bot rather ryse and richtly rin
> That hevinly wedfie for to win
> Vhilk he prepairs for his. (3, 5–8)

Montgomerie draws on Revelation 19:8, where the Church is granted to wear 'fine linen, clear and white', glossed by John's angelic interlocutor as 'the righteousness of the saints', and aspires his 'spousing garment for to spin'. In the second stanza, Montgomery calls upon the Calvinist teaching of his youth. As he speaks of the limited number likely to find a place in Heaven, he echoes, whilst subverting, Calvinism's teachings on the elect:

> The way is strait, the number small,
> Therfor we may not entir all. (9–10)

Here, the soul's final arrival in Heaven, and place amongst this limited number is not dependent on an unchanging election, but rather on a 'faith [that] brings furth gude frute' (12). And the production of such fruit can only be guaranteed by constant and consistent exertion:

> Tak tym in tyme or tym be tint
> To stryve with sin and never stint...
> As raynie dropis do pierce the flint
> Throu falling oft and not throu dint,
> Of hope if thou hold fast the hint
> Thou sall prevail at last. (17–24)

This insistence on the importance of hope leads, in the following stanza, to the Augustinian exhortation 'presume not nor despair to speid' (25).[39]

---

[39]   '[L]et none despair, but let none presume in himself. Both the one and the other are sinful. Let thine unwillingness to despair take such a turn as to lead thee to make choice of Him in whom alone thou mayest well presume', Augustine, *Tractate 49* (John 11:1–54), *Nicene and Post-Nicene Fathers*, 14 vols, First Series, Volume 7, ed. Philip Schaff, (Peabody, MA: Hendrickson publishers Inc., 1995; repr. of 1888 edn), p. 271.

'A walking from sin' enunciates a very similar understanding of soteriology. Once again, Montgomerie touches on the idea of a select band who win salvation – 'The goatis ar many thought the Lambis be thin' (30). Similarly, he returns to the theme of repentance and reparation in time – 'turne in tym, and not so rekles run / Or thyself in Condemnation cast' (14–15). 'Death is debt', and that day of reckoning will involve being called to account by a Divine creditor (25). In spite, however, of this use of the trope of sin as a debt which must be paid, it is notable that Montgomerie seems not to envisage the possibility of a posthumous reparation. The judgements dispensed on the 'dreidfull day' are 'endles pain of endless joy' (27, 29). Intriguingly, there seems little thought of Purgatorial redress. So, while the Catholic emphasis of lines like 'obey his blessed bidding from above / So thou sall Purchess profit to betuene' is very evident, the doctrine of the poem cannot be said to be wholly, and certainly not stridently, Catholic (35–6).

Montgomerie clearly does see the way of salvation as being through good works, and thus he is more in accordance with Catholic teaching than with the Protestant insistence on *sole fide*. However, it could be argued that, even in relation to this issue, he stops short of a definitive declaration of Catholic teaching on the merit of good works, and while his point of view would have been repugnant to Luther and the more evangelically inclined reformers, it would have provoked little dismay in the *via media* Protestantism favoured by James. Indeed, John Donne, writing in 1610 against the Catholic views of merit, adumbrates a view of works very consonant with Montgomerie's, and similarly stressing the importance of fruitful faith:

> Yet there is more Devotion in our Doctrine of good works, then in that of the Romane Church ... we acknowledge that God doth not onely make our faith, to fructifie and produce good works as fruits thereof, but sometimes begins at our workes: and in a mans hart morally enclined to doe goode, dooth build up faith.[40]

Montgomerie's estimation of the value of Scripture is also worthy of consideration. We have already remarked on his interest in vernacular Psalms, and his other poems echo repeatedly with Scriptural allusion. So, for example, while the penultimate stanza of 'The Poets Dreme' claims historical validity for the 'godly fathers', by stressing their continuity as 'heires of Abraham' (3.34–5), his assurance to the fearful soul that 'Thy warand is the word' would scarcely disquiet the most Biblicist of

---

[40]   John Donne, *Pseudo-Martyr* (1610), ed. Anthony Raspa (Montreal and Kingston: McGill-Queen's University Press, 1993), 88.

reformers (40). Similarly, 'A godly prayer', which we have already noted as Montgomerie's poetic manifesto, comfortably combines very obvious echoes of Catholic liturgy – 'Peccavi Pater, Miserere mei', 'Sed salvum me fac dulcis fili Dei' and 'In me cor mundum crea' – with a sustained focus on Scripture (1, 14, 71). Thus, in the second and fifth stanzas, Montgomerie explicitly refers to 'Luk' and to the 'Psalmist' (15, 48). Similarly, the fourth stanza demonstrates Montgomerie's familiarity with scripture, and the accomplishment with which he uses it. Verses from Psalm 139 are conflated with the identification of the Earth as Christ's footstool from Isaiah 66 (25–32). Again, the sinner's assurance of the possibility of redemption and forgiveness is based squarely on Scripture – 'as witnessis thy sacred holy writ' (36).

Another issue that is very clearly foregrounded in these lyrics is the role of grace in the life of the believer. Both Montgomerie and the compiler of the Ker manuscript draw our attention to the importance of this subject. We have already remarked that the manuscript opens with Montgomerie's metrical translation of Psalm 1. In the contemporary Bishops' Bible, the opening verse of the Psalm reads thus:

> Blessed is the man that walketh not in the counsell of the vngodly: nor standeth in the way of sinners, nor sitteth in the seate of the scornefull.

Montgomerie's rendering expands a little on this:

> Weill is the man,
> Yea blessed than,
> Be grace that can
> Escheu ill Counsell and the godless gait,
> That stands not in
> The way of sin
> Nor does begin
> To sitt with mockers in the scornefull sait. (1.1–8)

The poet's introduction of grace is very striking, partly because of the prominence given to it at the start of the poem, but also because of its suggestion that grace is essential in the life of the blessed man, vital for the development of the characteristics lauded in the Psalm. And, our attention having been drawn to this concept, it emerges as a dominant theme throughout these lyrics. It is given an equally prominent place in the third poem 'The Poets Dreme' – 'God grant me grace for to begin / My spousing garment for to spin', where Montgomerie significantly goes beyond the lines quoted above by making it explicit that a God-pleasing life cannot begin without grace – a concept whose importance we will shortly remark (3.1–2). Again, in 'A godly prayer' the poet prays that God will grant him grace to the end that Satan might be 'begyld' of his prey (4.7). In the third stanza of this poem, the poet gains assurance from the historical grace of God, who, 'of [His] grace ... sent [His] Sone our penalty to pay' (21–2). In the immediately following lyric, 'A walkning from sin', the primacy of grace is stressed again – 'To call for grace betyms at god begin / Befor thou folou on the flesh too far' (5.3–4). Tellingly, in the last of these opening religious lyrics 'A lesone hou to lierne to die', there is no mention of grace, and God is an unyielding judge, requiring the poet's 'Checker compt', while 'Justice halds the Balance evin' (6.52, 67).

Clearly, then, grace has a vital role in Montgomerie's soteriological understanding. Given the centrality of grace in the Reformation debate, it is interesting to investigate whether this understanding is allied more closely with Catholic or with Protestant thought. There can be little doubt that Protestant thought gives a greater prominence to grace – *sole gratia* was, after all, one of the five *solae* of the Reformation. In the Reformed understanding, humanity was, in Calvin's phrase, totally depraved, utterly incapable of bringing pleasure to God unless suffused with Divine prevenient grace. This is very clear in Calvin's own account of the value of human merit:

> There is no doubt that whatever is praiseworthy in works is God's grace; there is not a drop that we ought by rights to ascribe to ourselves. If we truly and earnestly recognize this, not only will all confidence in merit vanish, but the very notion. We are not dividing the credit for good works between God and man, as the sophists do, but we are preserving it whole, complete, and unimpaired for the Lord. To man we assign only this: that he pollutes and contaminates by his impurity those very things which were good. For nothing proceeds from a man, however perfect he be, that is not defiled by some spot.[41]

It is considerably more problematic to summarize the Catholic understanding of grace. This understanding was far from static, and any attempt at a monolithic definition would be foolhardy.[42] However, it can be contended that, historically, the Church 'adhered in her teaching to the conviction ... that natural man is capable of performing some naturally good works

---

[41]   John Calvin, *Institutes of the Christian Religion*, 2 vols, ed. John T. McNeill, trans. Ford Lewis Battles (Philadelphia: Westminster, 1960), vol. 1, pp. 790–91.

[42]   Roger Haight, *The Experience and Language of Grace* (Dublin: Gill and Macmillan, 1979), provides, in its earlier chapters, a helpful overview of the role of grace in Catholic theology.

without actual grace, and particularly without the grace of faith'.[43] More specifically, in the context of Montgomerie's milieu, we are able to attach a good deal of weight to the redefinition of grace that had been undertaken by the Council of Trent in 1546. While the *Decree on Justification* insisted on the importance of grace in a way that was not entirely dissimilar from the teaching of the Reformers, there was a crucial difference in statement of the primacy of grace. The decree endorsed the view that 'human beings are active and cooperate with grace through stages of preparation for justification'.[44] So, John Donne, preaching in 1624, complained that 'they proceed in the Romane Church ... to tye the grace of God, to the action of the man'.[45] Thus, while both traditions stressed the importance of grace in rendering human effort acceptable to God, only Protestantism insisted that grace was necessarily prior to meritorious accomplishment. Hence, Montgomerie's emphasis on a grace that allows him to begin a life that would please God seems more at home with a Calvinist understanding of the human standing than it does with a Catholic viewpoint.

The complexities of Montgomerie's work are neatly summed up in 'A leson hou to lierne to die'. This poem adds generic ambiguity to the doctrinal palimpsest of the other works. The '*ars moriendi*' tradition, of which this poem is an inflection, had an important significance for Catholics and Protestants alike.[46] From its medieval origins, the genre was to prove influential and popular with both Calvinists and Catholics. Indeed, Thomas Becon's *The Sicke Mannes Salve*, a Calvinist take on the form, 'was one of the top best sellers among Elizabethan devotional books in general'.[47] Subsequently, the genre returned to its Catholic roots, as during the Counter-Reformation 'the practice of methodical religious meditation had become an important spiritual discipline for Roman Catholics'.[48] These works received a 'cordial reception' in Protestant Britain, and were widely influential in editions purged of specifically Catholic doctrine. However, Beaty identifies some very radical differences between the Calvinist and Counter-Reformation versions of these works.

[43]   'Actual Grace', in *Catholic Encyclopedia* (New York: Robert Appleton, 1907–1912), *s.v.*

[44]   Haight, *Experience and Language of Grace*, pp. 110–11.

[45]   John Donne, *The Sermons of John Donne*, 10 vols, eds Evelyn M. Simpson and George R. Potter (Berkeley and Los Angeles: University of California Press, 1953), vol. 6, p. 92.

[46]   For the definitive survey of this influential genre see Sr Mary Catherine O'Connor, *The Art of Dying Well: The Development of the* Ars Moriendi (New York: Columbia U.P., 1942).

[47]   Nancy Lee Beaty, *The Craft of Dying: A Study in the Literary Tradition of the* Ars Moriendi *in England* (New Haven and London: Yale U.P., 1970), p. 110.

[48]   Ibid., p. 157.

She identifies in the Calvinist versions of this literature a 'zealous, even aggressive didacticism', and 'a rigid focus of soteriology, at the expense of warm devotion to either the human Jesus or the living Christ'.[49] By contrast to this, she accounts for the popularity of Counter-Reformation works by suggesting that they provided 'just those affective elements most conspicuously lacking in comparable Protestant works'.[50]

In the light of this, and given Montgomerie's Counter-Reformation loyalties, we might expect the affective element to predominate in this poem. In view, however, of those elements of his work that we have already considered, it is not entirely surprising that Montgomerie's vision of the *ars moriendi* corresponds far more closely with Calvinist rigour than with Catholic affective piety, a stress clearly revealed in the repetition at the close of each stanza of the phrase, 'Without contineuing of Dayis'. Montgomerie's focus on last things concentrates almost entirely on the confrontation between the sinner and an affronted God; only in the final stanza is Christ mentioned, and then without any reference to either His sufferings or His love. Instead, Montgomerie peoples his vision with a series of threatening personifications – Death, Conscience and Justice, and with an accusing Devil. On this day, 'Conscience brings furth his Books … reveiling both thy good and evil' (6.19, 26). Misused gifts of 'Beutie, Riches, Wit and Strenth … sall caus the cry alace at lenth', damning the soul because not used in the glory of God (49, 51). In this evaluation, 'Thoght, word and Deid sall be weyde' (43), and this weighing determines the soul's final destination:

> Quhen Justice halds the Balance evin
> Sho mettis no inshis with the ell.
> The hevy saulis ar had to hevin
> The light alace ar hoyde to hell
> Quhair Belzebub in burning brayis
> In wter darknes vhair no day is. (67–72)

The lesson at the heart of Montgomerie's didacticism echoes a strand that runs through all his religious lyrics – that preparation for death and for the 'Euermair' must begin in time, and requires thoughtful diligence. In this context, 'Prayers, almesdeids and tearis' must, of necessity, occupy the individual. The closing stanza, however, deals less with works of merit than with the acceptance of Christ, in a way as amenable to Protestant preaching as to Catholic dogma:

---

49   Ibid., p. 112.
50   Ibid., pp. 157–8.

... hear vhill Chryst knokis at thy hairt
And open it to let him in
Or thou sall abill efteruard
Crave entrie vhair thou sall not win. (85–9)

Very clearly, there is little of the affective about this work, and it is both as didactic and as resolutely soteriological as any Calvinist engagement with the genre.

At this point, then, it is difficult to concur with Duff's very considerable claims about the nature of Montgomerie's art. Rather than the doctrinaire defender of the Counter-Reformation faith, we are left with a poet whose work indicates a fascinating imbrication of influence; a poet who is quite clearly a Catholic, but who, equally clearly, is a Catholic who still thinks like a Calvinist, who has never quite broken the mould in which his upbringing made him. Nor is it at all clear that this should surprise us. In the first place, we must remember that the evidence suggests that Montgomerie's conversion took place when he had attained to mature adulthood. In addition, we must recall that much of his time had been spent in a milieu where Catholicism was repressed, and where opportunities to meet with other Catholics and, more especially, to enjoy the ministry of an ordained priesthood can only have been occasional. In this context, it is hard to see why Montgomerie's modes of thought would have changed very radically from those inculcated in his youth. Nor can his situation have been a particularly unusual one. It is, perhaps, a reminder that understanding the experience of conversion during the Reformation raises difficulties that critics are only imperfectly equipped to deal with.

Critics should, however, have been better equipped to deal with Duff's verses. By assuming that these verses expressed the impartial and objective truth about Montgomerie's work, they have condemned themselves to the attempt to force his poems into a straitjacket that, quite evidently, will not fit. Duff was simply doing what eulogists invariably do: engaging in *ad hominem* praise of his subject. How familiar he was with Montgomerie's work, we cannot say. Doubtless, he was able to enjoy Montgomerie's articulation of Catholic values and beliefs, muted though it was. However, had he possessed, or been anxious to express the disinterested objectivity that critics have imputed to him, it scarcely seems likely that he would have extolled his friend as the warrior-poet, who fought the Protestants 'with sword and poetry'.

CHAPTER 9

English bards and Scotch poetics: Scotland's literary influence and sixteenth-century English religious verse

Deirdre Serjeantson

His Maiesties poeticall exercises at vacant houres, the second collection of poetry by James VI of Scotland, appeared in 1591 to the polite acclaim of laudatory verse.[1] The volume opens with the King's letter to the reader, which is succeeded by a series of commendatory poems from four authors. By comparison with the more substantial pageant of praise which preceded the poetry in James' earlier work, the 1584 *Essayes of a prentise*, it is a modest list – but it is also an intriguing one, and one which, I suggest, has consequences for our understanding of the development of religious poetry in England in the succeeding decades.[2]

Of the poets featured, William Fowler's name is perhaps the most obvious inclusion. He had already contributed a sonnet to the *Essayes*; and, an Edinburgh man, a courtier, and a member of James' 'Castalian Band' of poets, he was close, in literary and political terms, to the King. Hadrianus Damman, who contributed a Greek and two Latin epigrams to the volume, was also living in Edinburgh, where he was Professor of Law at the University.[3] He was a native of Bistervelt in Flanders, and had taught at the young university of Leiden in the late 1580s;[4] however, he was known to the King from his appointment to the entourage of Anne of Denmark: his role had been to entertain James with his Latin conversation. Damman

---

[1]   James VI of Scotland, *His Maiesties Poeticall Exercises at Vacant Houres* (Edinburgh: Robert Waldegrave, 1591).

[2]   James VI of Scotland, *Essayes of a Prentise, in the Divine Art of Poesie* (Edinburgh: Thomas Vautrollier, 1584).

[3]   James K. Cameron, 'Some Continental Visitors to Scotland' in *Scotland and Europe 1200–1850*, ed. T.C. Smout (Edinburgh, John Donald, 1986), pp. 45–61 (p. 49).

[4]   Willem Otterspeer, *Groepsportret Met Dame I: Het Bolwerk Van De Vrijheid De Leidse Universiteit 1575–1672* (Amsterdam: Uitgeverij Bert Bakker, 2000), pp. 144, 150; J.A. Van Dorsten, *Poets, Patrons and Professors: Sir Philip Sidney, Daniel Rogers and the Leiden Humanists* (Leiden: Publications of the Sir Thomas Browne Institute/Leiden University Press, 1962), pp. 79–80, n.3.

had cultivated a literary relationship with the King, and the previous year, he had produced a book of verse commemorating the royal wedding, published – like the present volume – by Richard Waldegrave.[5] As with Fowler, his appearance in the *Poeticall Exercises* occasions no surprise.

The two remaining poems are by Englishmen. Henry Constable's sonnet is printed at the head of the dedications, possibly in deference to his reputation as a poet (his sonnet sequence, *Diana*, was ranked by his contemporaries next to Sidney's *Astrophel and Stella*), but more likely because of his superior social rank. Constable was a member of a prominent Nottinghamshire family; his father, Sir Robert Constable, a one-time Marshal of Berwick, was Master of the Queen's Ordnance; he himself was a favourite of Elizabeth, an intimate of Arabella Stuart and a member of the Sidney circle. His association with the Scottish court was of long standing. He had visited on diplomatic missions in 1583 and 1589, and on these visits had written four sonnets addressed to the King, later printed in *Diana*.[6] The sonnet which appears in the *Poeticall Exercises* is one of these poems, and must have been taken from a manuscript copy: the first (unauthorized) printed edition of *Diana* was not to appear until the following year.[7] If Constable's appearance among the prefatory materials of the volume seems incongruous, this is only in retrospect. The printers in Edinburgh could not know that he was in the process of becoming an embarrassment to the book, but even as it was published in 1591, Constable had converted to Catholicism and gone into exile on the continent. His praise, to judge by his initial reception from James when he next visited Scotland in 1599, subsequently lost something of its lustre, but as the *Exercises* went to press, he was still entirely respectable, both as poet and courtier.[8]

The final sonnet of this commendatory group is squeezed by the printer into half the space allowed to the other poems; but although the name subscribed, one 'Henrie Lock', is not accorded the same status as his fellow contributors, the bare fact of his inclusion begs a question. Why Henry Lok? In his later years, and into the seventeenth century, Lok (*c*.1560–*c*.1608) achieved a measure of fame as the author of a prodigious body of religious verse. More recently, his work has attracted critical attention as a precursor

---

[5]   Hadrianus Damman, *Schiediasmata Hadr. Dammanis ... De Nuptiis Scot. Regis Jacobi VI. et Annae. II. De Tempestate ... VI. De Introitu* (Edinburgh: R. Waldegrave, 1590).

[6]   Henry Constable, *Poems*, ed. Joan Grundy (Liverpool: Liverpool University Press, 1960). For an account of his status among his contemporaries, see pp. 61–2; for his family history, pp. 16–20; for his early career, pp. 21–34. The 1589 sonnets addressed to James are on pp. 140–43.

[7]   *Diana. The Praises of His Mistres, in Certaine Sweete Sonnets. By H.C.* (London: J. C[harlewood] for R. Smith, 1592).

[8]   Constable, *Poems*, p. 40.

of Donne's *Holy Sonnets* and the devotional poetry of George Herbert. And yet, in 1591, this was all in the future: Lok's two published works, the *Sundry Christian Passions Contained in Two Hundred Sonnets*, and the *Ecclesiastes*, which included a further hundred sonnets, did not appear until 1593 and 1597 respectively;[9] and although these were to form the most substantial body of religious sonnets in English, they cannot account two years earlier for Lok's presence among the tributes to James. The only other work ascribed to Lok is a sonnet of commendation in a manuscript collection of psalm translations by his cousin, Michael Cosworth, which is again likely to be later than the 1591 sonnet, and which, in any case, seems too slight a work upon which to build a literary reputation sufficient to attract attention in Edinburgh.[10]

Nor does Lok, by contrast with his fellows in the collection, initially appear to have more than the slightest connection with Scotland. He may have had continental links: he was descended on both sides from prominent London merchant families with dealings in the Low Countries, and both his mother and paternal aunt were Marian exiles who had lived in Antwerp and Geneva.[11] There is a Scottish dimension through the friendship of his

---

[9]   Henry Lok, *Sundry Christian Passions Contained in Two Hundred Sonnets. Divided into Two Equall Parts: The First Consisting Chiefly of Meditations, Humiliations, and Praiers. The Second of Comfort, Joy, and Thanksgiving* (London: Richard Field, 1593), and *Ecclesiastes, Whereunto Are Annexed Sundrie Sonets of Christian Passions Heretofore Printed, and Now Corrected and Augmented, with Other Affectionate Sonets of a Feeling Conscience of the Same Authors* (London: Richard Field, 1597). All quotations from Lok are taken from these editions. For the sake of brevity, when citing in the text I indicate the three separate centuries of sonnets in Arabic, and the place of the sonnet within the sequence, in Roman, numerals. Sonnet 1.i is therefore the first sonnet in the *Meditations, Humiliations, and Praiers*.

[10]   British Library, Harleian MS 6906. This is undated, but is likely to be earlier than 1601, when Cosworth is called a psalmist in Richard Carew, *Survey of Cornwall* (London: Printed by S. S[tafford] for Iohn Iaggard, 1602), fol. 145^r. It is worth mentioning that Sidney Lee, in the 1893 edition of the *Dictionary of National Biography*, vol. XXXIV (London) notes that Lok has occasionally been identified with the H.L. whose initials appear in a volume of poetry called *Of Love's Complaints with the Legend of Orpheus and Eurydice* (London, 1597). Lee concludes, however, that the reference is to the printer, Humfrey Lownes. In any case, 1597 is too late to have a bearing on the *Poeticall Exercises*.

[11]   For an account of the life of Lok's grandfather, Stephen Vaughan, see David Daniell, *William Tyndale: A Biography* (New Haven and London: Yale University Press, 1994), pp. 209–17. His paternal grandfather, William Lok, and his uncle Michael Lok, both have entries in the *ODNB*. Anne Lock's time in Geneva is well-documented: see the biographical introduction in Susan Felch (ed.), *The Collected Works of Anne Vaughan Lock* (Tempe, Arizona: Arizona Center for Medieval and Renaissance Studies, 1999). For his aunt Rose Lock, see J. Shakespeare and M. Dowling, 'Religion and politics in mid-Tudor England through the eyes of an

mother, the poet Anne Lock, and John Knox;[12] but Knox was long dead by the 1590s, and although it is speculated that she retained contact with his circle, the extreme religious and political views of men like Christopher Goodman meant that they could hardly provide Lok with an *entrée* to the Scottish court.[13]

In the event, the answer to the mystery comes via Lord Burghley and his intelligence network. Biographical information on Lok is scanty – there is a nineteenth-century account of his life in Grosart, and notices in successive editions of the *Dictionary of National Biography* which have changed relatively little over the years.[14] However, it has long been known that Lok was employed by Burghley, and later by his son, Robert Cecil: he appears in the Calendar of State Papers for the late 1590s and early 1600s as their agent in Bayonne and their somewhat disgruntled petitioner.[15] The early 1590s were a blank – until James Doelman unearthed Lok's name in the British Library MS *Transactions between England and Scotland in the years 1590, 1591, etc, to the year 1[6]03*, and found him already working for the Cecils, serving as messenger between the English Government and the Earl of Bothwell: in other words, Lok was in Scotland, and at court.[16]

Doelman's discovery goes some way towards solving the puzzle of the *Poeticall Exercises*, as it provides a geographical basis for Lok's presence in the volume. It also allows for a potential network of literary connections in Scotland: Lok's association with Bothwell suggests that he may have known Fowler, also one of the Earl's clients, and one of the poets included with him in the collection. It might even be inferred that Lok had a reputation as a poet before the publication of the works now extant. His reference, in 1597, to the 'vainer theames' of his youthful poetry, rejected there in favour

---

English protestant woman: the recollections of Rose Hickman', *Bulletin of the Institute of Historical Research*, 55 (1982), pp. 94–102.

[12] See, for instance, Patrick Collinson, 'The Role of Women in the English Reformation Illustrated by the Life and Friendships of Anne Locke', in idem, *Godly People: Essays on English Protestantism and Puritanism* (London: The Hambledon Press, 1983), pp. 273–87, and Susan Felch, '"Deir Sister": The Letters of John Knox to Anne Vaughan Lok', *Renaissance and Reformation*, 19 (1995), pp. 47–68.

[13] Collinson, 'The Role of Women', p. 285.

[14] 'Poems by Henry Lok, gentleman', *Miscellanies of the Fuller Worthies' Library*, ed. A.B. Grosart, 4 vols (1870–76), vol. 2, pp. 1–389.

[15] For Lok's correspondence with Cecil from *c*.1596, see *Calendar of State Papers, Domestic Series, Elizabeth 1595–97* (London: Longman, Green, Reader and Dyer, 1869), p. 348; *1598–1601*, pp. 25, 60, 72, 74, 172, 201, 246, 262, 332, 361, 426, 495, 509; *James I 1608–10*, pp. 244, 307, 431, 463.

[16] James Doelman, 'Seeking "the Fruit of Favour": The Dedicatory Sonnets of Henry Lok's *Ecclesiastes*', *ELH* 60 (1993), 1–15. This information has not yet made its way into the *ODNB*.

of sacred subjects, has (in the absence of any surviving secular works) been seen as merely conventional;[17] however, such was James's interest in poetry that writers were often chosen to be part of embassies to his court. Salluste du Bartas, for example, was a tactical inclusion when Henry of Navarre sent envoys in 1587 to negotiate the marriage of his sister and the Scottish King. Cecil's choice of Lok as his agent could be taken to indicate that these early works in fact existed, but are lost. However, whether or not Lok had been known for his writing before he came to Edinburgh, it is clear from his appearance in the *Exercises* that he attempted to become involved in the literary milieu of the court on his arrival. His political mission was a failure: by 1593, James had detected his involvement with 'Bothwell and others of his Rebells' and had informed the English ambassador 'in some warm colour' that 'he esteemed Mr Lock his great enemy'.[18] Lok's usefulness as an agent in Scotland may have come to an end – but his publishing career in England was just beginning. It is to this new body of work that I now turn.

My contention is that these four names among the prefatory material of the King's poems are not themselves the mystery, but rather, that they – and especially Lok – are the clue. The relationship between English and Scottish writing in the years before James' accession to the English throne, particularly from the perspective of purely literary influence, has been overlooked while scholars have measured their texts against continental models. The presence of two Englishmen in this Scottish collection adds to the evidence, already amassing, for traffic of texts across the border. The particular significance of Lok's name in this context is that he returned to England to engage in a literary field about to refashion itself completely. Religious poetry underwent a major transformation in the 1590s, and, as will transpire below, certain critics have suggested that Lok played a small part in this process. I am about to argue that, in fact, he played a highly important part; that the religious poetics he had encountered in Scotland were a major factor in his writing; and that, through him, they were to become an element in the emerging aesthetic of English devotional writing.

---

[17] See the sonnet to the Marquess of Northampton, *Ecclesiastes*, sig. Xviii[v].

[18] *Transcripts of Papers Relating to Scotland from the Cottonian MS, c. 1590–1603*, British Library MS Harley 4648. See the entry marked 'Conference between the K of S and the L. Zouch. 1593. fol 169', pp. 166–79 (p. 173).

Religious writing in England

It has been a convenient critical maxim that Protestant writing is concerned with simplicity. Certainly, the imperative driving the translation of the Bible into vernacular languages was that it should be comprehensible to all, and this urge towards clarity extended to liturgical texts too: Elizabeth I ordered that revisions be made to the *Book of Homilies* 'for the better understandyng of the simple people',[19] and Thomas Cranmer insisted that the new rite in the *Book of Common Prayer* be written 'in suche a language and ordre, as is most easy and plain for the understandyng, bothe of the readers and hearers'.[20] At the same time, however, a Latin version of the *B.C.P.* was licensed for use in university chapels, for a readership to whom (at least in theory) Latin was as simple and transparent as the vernacular. In other words, the much-vaunted 'plain speech' of Protestant writing was highly dependent upon its audience and its function. Thus, the elaborate psalm translations of a Wyatt or a Surrey, intended for private consumption among an educated readership, could coexist with the simple diction of the Sternhold and Hopkins psalter, which was designed for common use within religious services.

Nonetheless, it is the case that even court literature in England from the mid-century onwards can be heard to profess an allegiance to simplicity in regard to religious writing. The issue was rendered more complex by other associations surrounding the concept of plain speech. So, for instance, Tyndale's plea for clarity in the translation of scripture for the sake of 'unlearned laypeople' also suggests that ornate diction is a ploy by Catholics to obscure the word of God: they 'darken the right way with the mist of their sophistry', he says, thereby turning unadorned language into the shibboleth that would distinguish Catholic and Protestant.[21] Sophistry also concerned Calvin: his inference from the Bible, that simplicity was the index of truth, had implications for literary language,

> For this also was not done without the singular providince of God, that the hye misteries of the heavenly kingdom should for the moste part be uttered under a contemptible basenesse of word, least if it hadde ben beautified with more glorious speache the wicked shoulde cavill that the onely force of eloquence doeth reigne therein. But when that roughe and in a maner rude simplicitie

---

[19]   Ronald B. Bond (ed.), *Certain Sermons or Homilies (1547) and a Homily against Disobedience and Wilful Rebellion (1570)* (Toronto: University of Toronto Press, 1987), p. 9.

[20]   *The boke of the common praier* (Worcester: John Owen, 1549), sig. Aiii^r.

[21]   William Tyndale, 'Preface to the Pentateuch, 1530', in *Documents of the English Reformation*, ed. Gerald Bray (Cambridge: James Clarke & Co. Ltd, 1994), pp. 32–40 (p. 33).

dooeth rayse up a greater reverence of it selfe than any rhetoricians eloquence, what may we judge, but that there is a more myghty strength of truthe in the holye Scripture, then that it nedeth any art of wordes.[22]

'Eloquence' and 'skilful words', the fabric of literary writing, do not come well out of this encounter with biblical *simplicitas* and truth, to the extent that they are nudged into opposition with the religious register. Within the field of religious poetics, there were a number of rhetorical stances available to the sixteenth-century writer. One, which pursues the implications of Calvin's system, was to insist on the incompatibility of literary language and sacred subjects. Within this system, the sacred and the simple are not only opposed to the Catholic, but also to the ornate and the fictional, which encompasses all of secular literature. Ideas of an opposition between sacred and secular writing were not unique to Protestant thought: they are also apparent in the literary manifestos of some Catholic writers of the period, and they are pervasive in early Christian tradition.[23] Conversely, nor were they universal within Protestant culture. However, a very vocal advocacy of the Christian plain style was widespread in England, and it was an important influence on religious poetry of the mid-to-late century.

In respect of English Protestant Tudor writing, plain style is most readily defined through negatives. The refusal of elaborate diction manifested itself in the choice of plain words and simple rhythms: ornaments, neologisms and complex rhyme schemes were all avoided. Allusions to secular literature were also eschewed, and in many cases there was careful avoidance of any matter or devices which had no precedent within the sanctified language of the Bible. This latter cannot entirely be attributed to a desire for simplicity, however: the cento prayers and gospelling plays which are built out of biblical quotations point to another element in reformation poetics – that is, to the question of *inventio*.[24] Questions about the nature of literary

---

[22] Jean Calvin, *The Institution of Christian Religion, Wrytten in Latine by Maister Ihon Caluin, and Translated into Englysh According to the Authors Last Edition*, trans. Thomas Norton (London: Reinolde Wolfe and Richarde Harison, 1561), fol. 16ʳ.

[23] See Alison Shell, *Catholicism, Controversy and the English Literary Imagination, 1558–1660* (Cambridge: Cambridge University Press, 1999), pp. 59 ff. for a discussion of this opposition in the works of Robert Southwell, S.J. Lily Bess Campbell provides a comprehensive survey of the same dichotomy in Protestant thought in *Divine Poetry and Drama in Sixteenth Century England* (Cambridge, Berkeley and Los Angeles: Cambridge University Press, University of California Press, 1959), although her very literal-minded approach fails to accommodate the practice of the age as well as the theory, and ignores the secular poetry which coexisted with the religious in the works of many of the poets she examines.

[24] Examples of texts written entirely in cento include Thomas Becon's *A Newe Dialog Betwene Thangell of God, and the Shepherdes in the Felde* (London: John Daye, 1547). Edmund Bunny, *The Coronation of David* (London: Thomas Orwin

inspiration are not connected to plain diction, but they are nonetheless an issue of the plain style. A classical poet, or his legion of renaissance imitators, could invoke the inspiration of his muse; for a religious poet to do likewise risked venturing on to secular terrain. More pressingly, it violated the tenet so rigorously worked out in Protestant doctrine, that man was incapable of creation, literary or otherwise.[25] Scriptural paraphrase neatly avoided the problem of claiming independent creative agency by celebrating instead that which was already created. Writers in this tradition were reluctant to describe themselves as poets, preferring to emphasize the purely didactic value of works they claimed to have put into metre rather for ease of memory, than for any more aesthetically-motivated reason.[26]

Invocations of a specifically Christian muse, such as Du Bartas's *Urania*, were not current in English Protestant writing up to the 1590s, and nor was there a Protestant literature of devotional poetry which was imaginative rather than scriptural; however, by the seventeenth century, this had changed. Milton invoked a Heavenly Muse in *Paradise Lost*. Herbert's *The Temple* was published in a format designed to echo the *Book of Common Prayer*, although its contents were not strictly liturgical or biblical. The border between the sacred and the secular had been breached. While there were still writers espousing the plain style, an alternative was available within the mainstream of Protestant writing. It is clear that a critical change occurred towards the end of the sixteenth century, and critics have attempted to account for the factors behind the transformation. Jesuit poetics have been looked to for one possible solution. Louis Martz suggested in his *Poetry of Meditation* (1954) that Robert Southwell's writing introduced a new religious aesthetic to England, and more recently, Alison Shell noted that his work 'helped to create a climate in which non-biblical religious verse became increasingly acceptable'.[27]

Domestic factors, as well as the influence of the Counter-Reformation style imported from the continent, contributed to this change. Rivkah Zim and Ramie Targoff both point to the importance of Philip Sidney in the

---

for Thomas Gubbin and John Perin, 1588) is more typical (if less spectacular), featuring cento psalms.

[25] See A.D. Nuttall, *Overheard by God: Fiction and Prayer in Herbert, Milton, Dante and St. John* (London and New York: Methuen, 1980), for a probing investigation of the problem.

[26] For instance, William Baldwin, *The Canticles or Balades of Salomon, Phraselyke, Declared in Englysh Meters* (London: Edward Whitchurch, 1549); Francis Seagar, *Certayne Psalmes Selected out of the Psalter of David, and Drawen into Englyshe Metre* (London: Wyllyam Seres, 1553).

[27] Louis L. Martz, *The Poetry of Meditation*, 2nd edn (New Haven and London: Yale University Press, 1974), p. 185; Alison Shell, *Catholicism, Controversy and the English Literary Imagination*, p. 57.

transformation of English religious poetics. Targoff's *Common Prayer* (2001), a study of the language of English worship and writing from the Reformation to the mid-seventeenth century, examines the emergence of a self-consciously literary form of prayer in the 1590s. She attributes this to Sidney's *Apology for Poetry*, suggesting that 'what marks the Apology as a significant intervention in England's reception of the Psalms, is its extended and polemically charged insistence on the Psalms' poeticality independent of their devotional content'.[28] Sidney's defence of the literary qualities of the Psalms made it possible to apply secular poetic standards to the writing of religious verse, she argues. Targoff perhaps does not give due weight to the authority of writers earlier than Sidney who also championed the poetic value of the psalms;[29] however, her sense of the transformative effect of Sidney's work is not uncommon among critics of the religious verse of the period. Zim also credited Sidney's influence with effecting a literary revolution, suggesting that he, and to a lesser extent, his sister, Mary Herbert, 'regenerate[d] their contemporaries' expectations of psalms as poetry'.[30]

It is in this context that Henry Lok's name makes another of its brief appearances. Targoff is interested in the emergence of the English religious sonnet sequence, and cites examples by Lok and by Barnabe Barnes, author of *A Divine Centurie of Spiritual Sonnets* (1595), which she sees as illustrative of a new literary self-awareness in sacred poetry. She comments on the incongruity of sonnets on spiritual subjects, within the context of the 1590s, when – in the wake of the publication of *Astrophel and Stella* (1591) – the vogue for petrachan sequences was at its height, and the sonnet was identified with romantic love. Lok's eagerness to justify his use of the sonnet as a vehicle for devotional expression indicates that he was fully cognizant of its significance.

> As for the apt nature of Poetry, to delight, to contrive significatively in few words much matter, to pierce and penetrate affections of men, with the aptness thereof, for help of memory, I will not say much; but for my deducing these passions and affections in Sonnets, it answereth best for the shortness, to the nature, and common humor of men.[31]

---

[28] Ramie Targoff, *Common Prayer: The Language of Public Devotion in Early Modern England* (Chicago: University of Chicago Press, 2001), pp. 73–74.

[29] For instance, Origen, Augustine, Jerome and Petrarch. For a full discussion, see James Kugel, *The Idea of Biblical Poetry: Parallelism and Its History* (Baltimore and London: Johns Hopkins University Press, 1998), particularly Chapter 6.

[30] Rivkah Zim, *English Metrical Psalms: Poetry as Praise and Prayer, 1535–1601* (Cambridge: Cambridge University Press, 1987), p. 152.

[31] Henry Lok, 'Letter to the Christian Reader' in the 1597 printing of his sonnets, as cited in Targoff, *Common Worship*, p. 75.

The emphasis Lok placed on the utility of his work allies it with the functional nature of writing in the metrical psalm tradition; nonetheless, he also conceived of his text in specifically literary terms, referring to 'Poetry' and 'Sonnets'. Targoff moves on at this point to explore works by Michael Drayton; however, there is more to be said about Lok, firstly, in respect of the literary qualities of his sequence, which represents a more dramatic innovation in religious poetry than could be accommodated within Targoff's short account, and secondly, in relation to the timeline of influence as she and Zim propose it, a chronology which Lok significantly disturbs.

To begin with the literary nature of Lok's poetry, his preface, the 'Letter to the Christian Reader' quoted above, sets the tone for the volume. His protestations of the spiritual utility of his work, however sincere, are countered by his obvious pleasure in the ornate and the witty. Lok's Christian Reader has already encountered the dedicatory verses, addressed to the Queen: both are pattern poems, the first, with the words arranged in two columns which can be read horizontally or vertically, the second, in a grid, which can be read in a variety of patterns (including a St. Andrew's cross) and yet still makes sense, and still (albeit a little less than fluently) approximates a poem in praise of his dedicatee. Pattern poems have courtly connotations. Puttenham discusses them at some length in his *Arte of English Poesie* (1589) and considers them as 'fittest for the pretie amourets in Court' and useful to keep 'delicate wits' from the evils of 'idlenesse'.[32] Puttenham's account of the genre associates it with love poetry, and with human art and inventiveness, neither of which accords readily with the ideals of Lok's predecessors in reformed versification.

The body of the text presents a similar mixture of established practice and literary departure. Many of the poems are based on the Bible. Some are spoken in the personae of characters from Scripture, like Samson or the Prodigal Son; more are sown with quotation and paraphrase; others turn on scriptural allusion. These poems are interesting in themselves, perhaps particularly in Lok's frequent adoption of the female voice: he writes from the perspective of the Samarian woman at the well and Mary Magdalen, amongst others. In the context of English reformation poetics, however, it is the poems which range outside the boundaries of the Bible that command more attention. Lok was far from avoiding reference to secular literature or learning. In his choice of the sonnet, he had aligned himself with one of the most worldly forms of his day. There is much critical discussion of the usurpation of petrarchan motifs by religious

---

[32] [George] Puttenham, *The Arte of English Poesie (1589)* in *Elizabethan Critical Essays*, ed. G. Gregory Smith, 2 vols (Oxford: Clarendon Press: 1904), vol. 2, p. 95.

poets in the seventeenth century, with the intention of undermining them through the technique of sacred parody;[33] however, Lok does not discredit petrarchism. He makes some use of petrarchan devices, such as a rejection of the white and red of roses as a suitable comparison for the beauty of Christ, but such examples are rare.[34] More prominent is his use of classical allusion, which is an equally dramatic departure, requiring some degree of classical learning in the reader, and violating the principle of separating the Christian and the pagan. Christ is addressed as 'Phoebus' and 'Apollo'; the state of human sinfulness is compared to the dangerous 'laberinth' of Daedelus; the token of the sibyl, guiding Aeneas through the underworld, is likened to the Bible: '… thy word was Sibyls braunch to mee, / Through hell and death away to let me see, / To Elizian fields'.[35] Typically, Lok uses the figures of classical literature as allegory for the Christian world, but he is also capable of folding the two worlds into one, as here, where Old Testament and Greek literature merge:

> As sauage beasts by Orpheus harpe were tamde;
> Yong Dauids harpe, Sauls furious spirit shamde,
> And Dolfins did Aryons musicke heare.
> Such sympathie in all things doth appeare … (2. lxiv)

Most of these references appear in the second part of the series. The first century, 'Consisting Chiefly of Meditations, Humiliations, and Praiers', consists largely of explorations of Lok's own, or mankind's, sinfulness, and remains relatively close to the biblical text. The second hundred, 'Of Comfort, Joy, and Thanksgiving', consists of hymns of praise, as does the further hundred which he appends to the second edition of the sonnets in Ecclesiastes. These sonnets grapple with the problem of praise in the face of the inadequacy of language, an issue explored at length in the secular sonnet sequences of the period, but not readily associated with Protestant religious verse. Lok has been counted among those writers for whom simplicity, not adequacy, of language was the major concern, perhaps because in his first sonnet he rejects poetry as a means of salvation.[36] However, he also rejects prayer:

---

[33] See Rosemund Tuve, 'Sacred "Parody" of Love Poetry, and Herbert', *Studies in the Renaissance*, 8 (1961), pp. 249–90, for what is still the most subtle treatment of the subject.

[34] Lok, *Sundry Christian Passions* (1593), Part 2, Sonnet xxxv.

[35] Lok, *Sundry Christian Passions* (1593), Part 2, Sonnets xxxvi, xii.

[36] See Anne Ferry, *The 'Inward' Language: Sonnets of Wyatt, Sidney, Shakespeare, Donne* (Chicago and London: University of Chicago Press, 1983), p. 225.

> It is not Lord the sound of many words,
> The bowed knee or abstinence of man,
> The filed phrase that eloquence affords,
> Or Poets pen that heauens do pearce, or can ... (1.i)

This is orthodox Protestant doctrine. Nothing can effect salvation, except for grace. A rejection of poetry's potency in this respect is not the same thing as a rejection of poetry, and Lok's work shows a pronounced literary consciousness. Like a secular poet, he refers to his muse, and he acknowledges the poetic nature by referring to his writing in the technical terms of literary criticism.[37] His defence of his work at 2.lxxvii turns on his knowledge of classical rhetoric. The division of speech into three styles, the simple or plain, the middle and the grand, demanded a corresponding level of diction.[38] The colloquial language of the reformed texts was identified, as we have seen, with the plain style; however, Lok rejects 'common speech', and thus, the English Protestant poetics of his day, for something more ornate:

> For common matter common speech may serue,
> But for this theame both wit and words do want,
> But thou O Lord who cloven tonges did send..
> Shall guide my stile, as fits thy glory best. (2.lxxvii)

Lok's rhetorical treatment of his theme is proof of his intent to write in a literary manner; his pre-emptive defence of his approach in his preface ('only I would satisfie them first in the cause of my writing them in verse') demonstrates that he was aware that this represented a departure from the established mode. Among comparable endeavours by Barnabe Barnes, by Robert Southwell and by Philip Sidney, Lok's work is perhaps most notable because it is so early. Southwell's highly-influential lyrics did not appear in print until after his death in 1595, and although some writings circulated in manuscript beforehand, these were dangerous texts in their unedited form, and appear to have been confined to a circle of Catholic readers.[39] Barnes's sequence was also published in 1595. The Sidney *Psalms* were in private circulation: we know that John Harington, for instance, saw

---

[37] Lok, *Sundry Christian Passions* (1593), Part 2, Sonnet viii.

[38] For a detailed discussion of the distinctions in rhetorical style, see Brian Vickers, *In Defence of Rhetoric* (Oxford: Oxford University Press, 1988), pp. 80 ff.

[39] There is a discussion of the scribal publication of Southwell's writings in Nancy Pollard Brown, 'Paperchase: The Dissemination of Catholic Texts in Elizabethan England', *English Manuscript Studies 1100–1700*, 1 (1989), pp. 120–43.

one in 1600, and that the same year, a presentation copy in manuscript was prepared for the Queen.[40] Harington was part of a close-knit literary circle surrounding the Sidneys, however. There is nothing to suggest that Lok could have had comparable access to these particular translations. Similarly, the *Apology for Poetry*, with its important claims for the poetical nature of the Book of Psalms, was also not printed until 1595, and it had particularly limited circulation in manuscript before that date.[41] Several of these texts could have had a bearing on Lok's 1597 sonnets, which is the edition most commonly cited by scholars; however, the first edition of his sequence (which includes the poems quoted above) originally appeared in 1593, so that they represent a disruption to these hypothesized literary genealogies.

The transformation of religious poetry did not come about through a single influence which passed in order along a chain from a Sidney or a Southwell; nor is it likely to have originated with any one writer or work. Sidney and Southwell both represent factors in the change, but Lok, working independently of them, suggests the presence of another set of influences, hitherto neglected. His circle included various writers, the most important of whom was his mother, Anne Lock, herself the author of a sequence which merged the sonnet form with the Book of Psalms. Her *Meditation of a Pentitent Sinner* (1560), which appeared in a volume of her translations of Calvin's sermons, is a rendering of Psalm 51 in the form of a 21-sonnet sequence, with an original preface also framed in sonnet form.[42] However, there is nothing about Anne Lock's approach which suggests any blurring of the boundaries between human invention and the plain style of scriptural exposition. She makes no claims for inspiration or for the literary status of her work. Her allusions are biblical, rather than classical, and she does not comment on the formal qualities of her verse, only their content. Indeed, it has been speculated that she was unaware of

---

[40]   Gavin Alexander, '*The Triumph of Death*. A Critical Edition in Modern Spelling of the Countess of Pembroke's Translation of Petrarch's *Trionfo Della Morte*', *Sidney Journal*, 17 (1999), pp. 2–18 (p. 2). An account of this presentation copy is given in Margaret Patterson Hannay, '"Princes You as Men Must Dy": Genevan Advice to Monarchs in the Psalmes of Mary Sidney', *English Literary Renaissance*, 19 (1989), pp. 22–41.

[41]   H.R. Woudhuysen, *Sir Philip Sidney and the Circulation of Manuscripts, 1558–1640* (Oxford: Clarendon Press, 1996), pp. 234–35.

[42]   The poems appear in Anne Lock, *Sermons of John Calvin* (London: John Day, 1560), starting at sig. Aa1ʳ. There is a discussion of the circle of women writers around Anne Lock, which includes members of her (and hence Lok's) immediate family, in Micheline White, 'Women Writers and Literary-Religious Circles in the Elizabethan West Country: Anne Dowriche, Anne Lock Prowse, Anne Lock Moyle, Ursula Fulford, and Elizabeth Rous', *Modern Philology*, 103 (2005), pp. 187–214.

the sonnet as a genre.[43] Whether or not this was the case, it was certainly true that the English sonnet of the mid-century did not have the strong associations with love poetry which it had acquired by the time her son was forced to defend his use of the form in his sequence. Lok quotes his mother's work in his own sequence; it seems likely that he also responded to the rhetorical force and conviction of her work, and that she was the earliest model he would have known for religious poetry. And yet, in respect of poetics, she represented an approach entirely distinct from that which he would take.

Spenser's *Faerie Queene* mingles the epic style with religious matter, particularly in Book I, which was published in 1590. It was an immediately popular text, and it is likely that Lok encountered it; however, whether the allegorical style in which Spenser represented the drama of salvation would have appeared analogous to Lok's direct and personal devotions is debatable. A more likely model is the Huguenot poet, Salluste du Bartas. Although his highly diffuse account of creation, *La Sepmaine* (1578), and its sequel, the unfinished *Seconde Semaine* (1584), were designed as Christian epics and are more immediately comparable with the broader scope of the *Faerie Queene*, Du Bartas's version of Protestant poetics bears a close resemblance to Lok's. His first volume, *La Muse chrétienne* (1574), was named for one of the poems it contains, which describes the poet's meeting with Urania, the Christian Muse (a position to which he co-opted the classical muse of astronomy and astrology). The text functions as a poetic manifesto, in which Du Bartas announces his intention to write sacred verse; the fusion of pagan and Christian culture in the title indicates his commitment to using all of the resources of human language and learning in this endeavour.

Despite the widespread popularity and influence of Du Bartas's work across Protestant Europe, his works were relatively slow to appear in England. The earliest edition produced by an English printer was a small pamphlet containing *Urania* in parallel French and Latin texts, published in 1589, fifteen years after the poem was first printed.[44] In 1591, a Latin translation of the *Sepmaine* appeared, a reprint of the 1583 French translation by Gabriel de Lerm.[45] The first English translation, Josuah

---

[43] See Michael Spiller, 'A Literary "First": The Sonnet Sequence of Anne Locke (1560)', *Renaissance Studies*, 11 (1997), pp. 41–55.

[44] Guillaume de Salluste Du Bartas, *L'Uranie ou Muse Celeste de G. de Saluste Seigneur du Bartas / Urania Sive Musa Coelestis Roberti Ashelei de Gallica G. Salustij Bartasij Delibata* (London: Iohannes Wolfius, 1589).

[45] Du Bartas, *Guilielmi Salustii Bartassii Hebdomas a Gabriele Lermaeo Latinitate Donata. ... Opus Argumentum Sacrum, Stylo Perelegans, Doctis Gratum, Studiosae Iuuentuti Perutile* (London: [Printed by John Windet?] apud Robertum Dexter, 1591).

Sylvester's *Canticle of the Victorie … at Yvry*, was not a religious poem, so it was not until Sylvester's next essay into Du Bartas' work, the *Triumphe of Faith* (1592) that Du Bartas's syncretic approach to religious verse appeared in English, in printed form.[46]

It may be that Lok encountered Du Bartas through one of these texts, or through their French originals; however, despite his manifest sympathy with Du Bartas's religious poetics, it is perhaps telling that he does not mention him in his writing. Protestant poets in England were beginning to use Du Bartas's name to flag their aesthetic allegiances. Barnabe Barnes, for instance, that other Protestant sonneteer, prefaced his *Divine Centurie* with very favourable notice of 'divine Salust the true learned frenche Poet'.[47] It is interesting that, although he couches this introductory letter in syncretic terms, alluding for instance to the 'spirituall Pegasus of celestiall poesie', he is careful to confine his sonnets strictly to biblical, rather than classical, allusion. Lok's approach is altogether more assured, and he pays tribute to no specific model. It seems more likely that he was affected by familiarity with a poetic milieu in which Du Bartas's syncretism was general; and the Scottish court, where he was writing his laudatory sonnet to James even as the Latin Sepmaine was published in London, was just such a place.

Reformation poetics in Scotland: 'A gallant Style and Gay'

The literary relationship between England and Scotland in the early modern period has been largely overlooked. There has been some interest in the political uses of the poetry which travelled across the border: James's cousinly sonnet to Elizabeth (*c*.1586), and the contributions of the Scottish court to the Cambridge volume of tributes to Philip Sidney (1587) have

---

46   Du Bartas, *A Canticle of the Victorie Obteined by the French King, Henrie the Fourth. At Yvry. Written in French by the Noble, Learned, and Deuine Poet, William Salustius; Lord of Bartas, and Counsailor of Estate Vnto His Maiestie,* trans. Josuah Sylvester (London: Printed by Richard Yardley, 1590). This was followed by *The Triumph of Faith the Sacrifice of Isaac. The Ship-Wracke of Ionas. With a Song of the Victorie Obtained by the French King, at Yvry* ([London]: Printed by Richard Yardley, and Peter Short, 1592). It was said after his death that Philip Sidney had begun a translation of the *Sepmaine*, which would have been the earliest English translation, although unlikely to have been printed before his death; however, the manuscript, if it ever existed, was lost by the 1580s: for an account, see the excellent edition of Josuah Sylvester's *The Divine Weeks and Works of Guillaume De Saluste Sieur Du Bartas*, ed. Susan Snyder, 2 vols (Oxford: Oxford University Press, 1979), vol. 1, p. 70.

47   Barnabe Barnes, *A Divine Centurie of Spirituall Sonnets* (London: John Windet, 1595), sig. A3[r].

been carefully sifted for the diplomatic manoeuvring they may conceal.[48] English texts addressed to James in the years surrounding his accession to the English throne have – with some reason – been read as bids for patronage.[49] The subtexts have been examined; it is the texts themselves which continue to require attention.

Scottish writing has often been excluded from accounts of sixteenth-century literature in English, or else it has been treated alongside English poetry, as though the two were part of a single, common endeavour, rather than the distinct and only occasionally overlapping literatures they in fact embodied. The case of Du Bartas is a relevant one in this connection. Various important studies of Du Bartas's influence on English poetry have offered bibliographies of translations of his work into English, beginning with Thomas Hudson's translation of *Judith* (1584) and the version of *Urania* in James VI's *Essayes of a Prentise* in the same year. These Scottish publications are not differentiated from the English editions noted above;[50] however, they not only predate these texts, but they were received into a literary circle operating within different parameters, with different assumptions and a religious aesthetic that, as shall be shown below, did not rely solely on Du Bartas's model for its sympathy to syncretism. Scotland's close association with France affected its literary climate. Whereas the influence of the Italian vernacular tradition was dominant at the English court, the primary influences behind Stewart court poetry were French.[51] This led to an important divergence with regard to religious verse. Counter-Reformation, Catholic, Italian aesthetics were an ineligible model for Protestant writing in England, until they were naturalized in a heavily-edited form via Robert Southwell in 1595; the alternative model,

---

[48] The Cambridge collection is *Academiae Cantabrigensis Lachrymae Tumolo Nobilissimi Equitis, D. Philippi Sidneii Sacratae*, ed. Alexander Neville. This is discussed, and the text of the 1586 sonnet is given, in Peter C. Herman, 'Authorship and the Royal "I": King James VI/I and the Politics of Monarchic Verse', *Renaissance Quarterly*, 54 (2001), pp. 1495–1530.

[49] James Doelman, 'The Accession of King James I and English Religious Poetry', *Studies in English Literature, 1500–1900*, 34 (1994), p. 19.

[50] Anne Lake Prescott, 'The Reception of Du Bartas in England', *Studies in the Renaissance*, 15 (1968), 144–73. Despite her title, Prescott includes the Scottish poems in her study. See also the bibliography for the *Sepmaine* in *The Divine Weeks and Works*, ed. Susan Snyder (Oxford: Oxford University Press, 1979), vol. 1, pp. 70ff.

[51] Morna R. Fleming, '"And So Her Voice and Shape Alike Were New": Montgomerie, Stewart of Baldynneis and James VI and Their Translations of French Lyric Poetry', *SLJ* 26 (1999), pp. 77–95; Jonquil Bevan, 'Scotland', in *The Cambridge History of the Book, 1557–1695*, eds John Barnard, D.F. McKenzie and Maureen Bell (Cambridge: Cambridge University Press, 2002), pp. 687–700 (p. 688).

that of the French Protestants like Du Bartas, was established in Scotland before it became popular in England, and the sophistication of Scottish reformation poetics reflects this early adoption.

Other elements affected the reception and writing of Scottish religious poetry. The King's literary tastes tended towards sacred verse; moreover, in the Castalian Band, he gathered a group of poets to produce a new Scottish literature to his prescription. R.D.S. Jack has commented that the publication of James's *Reulis and Cautelis to Be Observit and Eschewit in Scottis Poesie* (1584) established a professional coterie of writers focused on the King, and that this professionalism, as much as James's personal taste, 'produced a more analytic and self-consciously erudite kind of art than that practised in England'.[52] The emergent literary self-awareness which Targoff and Zim trace in English religious poetry in the mid-1590s was already well developed in Scotland.

It would be strange if English writers had not felt the difference between the devotional poetry of the Scottish court and the plain style prevalent in England; and Lok and Constable were not the only ones to be involved in Scottish affairs in the 1580s and 90s, or to experience Castalian poetry at first hand. Sidney was active in Scottish diplomacy (although his gift to the King was not a laudatory poem, but a pair of bloodhounds).[53] He could have encountered Scottish poetics through George Buchanan, the King's former tutor, who, through James as well as through his own work, had a formative influence on Scottish writing. Buchanan's reputation in continental Europe is recognized; he also had connections in England. His writing circulated among Sidney, Spenser, Dyer and Daniel Rogers, with positive effect, and Sidney praised him in the *Apologie for Poetry*.[54] Constable's connections with Scottish writing encompassed more than the poetry of praise exemplified in his various sonnets to James: Alexander Montgomerie, in effect the Scottish poet laureate, counted him as his closest friend.[55] One of Constable's sonnets appears in the Ker manuscript, our chief witness to Montgomerie's poetry, so we can assume that the

---

[52] R.D.S. Jack, 'Critical Introduction: Where Stands Scottish Literature Now?' in *Mercat Anthology of Early Scottish Literature, 1375–1707*, ed. by R.D.S. Jack and P.A.T. Rozendaal (Edinburgh: Mercat Press, 1997), pp. xvi–xvii.

[53] He was involved in Walsingham's negotiations over Elizabeth's pension to James in 1585. Herman, 'Authorship and the Royal "I"', p. 1508.

[54] James E. Phillips, 'George Buchanan and the Sidney Circle', *The Huntington Library Quarterly*, 12 (1948–9), 23–55; Philip Sidney, 'The Defence of Poesy', in Sir Philip Sidney, *The Oxford Authors*, ed. Katherine Duncan-Jones (Oxford: Oxford University Press, 1989), pp. 212–50 (p. 241).

[55] Roderick J. Lyall, *Alexander Montgomerie: Poetry, Politics and Cultural Exchange in Jacobean Scotland* (Tempe, Arizona: Arizona Center for Medieval and Renaissance Studies, 2005), pp. 177–9.

exchange of verse was an element in their friendship.[56] And it was not only the diplomats and courtiers who had access to Scottish works. Scottish poetical treatises were being read and considered by English poets – Gabriel Harvey's copy of the *Reulis and Cautelis*, heavily marked with his approving comments, survives in the library of Magdalene College, Cambridge.[57]

England's literary debts to Italy, to France, to Spain and the Low Countries, have all been painstakingly sourced and acknowledged. There may be many reasons why we lack a similar evaluation of what is owing to Scotland. One is certainly the tendency to fold early-modern Scottish writing, other than that in Gaelic, into the canon of 'English' literature. However, at least to some degree, the omission must be due to the complex politics of Scottish literary criticism.[58] Recent years have seen scholars attempt to tease out the conflicting definitions of 'Scottishness' which have shaped competing accounts of the Scottish Renaissance. The Presbyterian, Knoxian version which dominated historiography throughout the nineteenth century was challenged in the twentieth by critics like Hugh MacDiarmid and Edwin Muir, who rewrote the religious convictions of Scottish literature, defining it as that which was produced by 'the opponents of Calvinism or men out of sympathy with it'.[59] Nationalist concerns with the autheticity of the language of literary texts eliminated 'anglicized' writers, such as Knox himself, or James VI, just as efforts to prioritize 'popular' literature over court writing conversely pitched Knox and James against each other. Recent readings have attempted to reinstate Calvinism, and theological writing more generally, at the centre of a canon which encompasses both court and common reader. This, pace Muir and MacDiarmid, represents an approach more faithful to the character of early modern Scottish writing; nonetheless, it will hardly prove useful unless taken in conjunction with a broad view of Protestant poetics in the period.

Knox's supremacy in Scottish writing has been challenged. However, the assumptions which appear to underlie scholarly readings of Scottish poetry suggest that the association of Protestantism and the plain style

---

[56]   *Alexander Montgomerie: Poems*, ed. David J. Parkinson, 2 vols (Edinburgh: STS, 2000), vol. 1, p. 4.

[57]   Library of Magdalene College, Cambridge, Shelfmark Lect. 26. The *Reulis* are contained in the 1584 *Essayes*. For a detailed discussion of the marginalia, see Eleanor Relle, 'Some New Marginalia and Poems of Gabriel Harvey', *RES* 23 (1972), pp. 401–16.

[58]   See Crawford Gribben, 'The Literary Cultures of the Scottish Reformation', *RES* 57 (2006), pp. 64–82.

[59]   Edwin Muir, *John Knox* (London, 1929), p. 71.

continues to be accepted uncritically. It can only be from this perspective that Alexander Hume's 'Of the Day Estivall' (1599) is seen as 'highlight[ing] the shift from high Renaissance classicism ... toward a poetics compatible with his Calvinist distrust of secularized and idolatrized aesthetic practice'.[60] There is some evidence for such a claim, hinging on lines 108–12 of the poem, as follows:

> Nocht guided be na Phaeton
> Nor trained in a chyre
> Bot by the high and holy On,
> Quhilk dois all where impire.[61]

Hume's rejection here of pagan Phaeton for Christian God might be seen to invite a symbolic reading, in which the secular world is rejected for the sacred; however, such a reading cannot withstand Hume's own statement on literary practice in the introduction to the volume in which this poem appears, where he comments, 'I contemne not the moderate and trew commendation of the vertuous, and noble actes of good men: nor yet the extolling of liberall sciences.'[62] By any definition, the liberal sciences include the traditional trivium subjects of grammar and rhetoric; that is, the study of those verbal arts associated with 'high Renaissance classicism' and 'secularized ... aesthetic practice'. This inclusive approach is borne out in the poetry, where Hume was free with his use of classical imagery; and if, in his religious verse, he was careful to indicate that Mercury, Neptune and Aeolus are all inferior to the Christian God, he still resorted to the classics to characterize him: 'Their is na Iupiter but he.'[63]

Knox's public writings and private correspondence, and the highly popular hymns of the *Gude and Godlie Balletis*, demonstrate the existence of Scottish religious literature in the plain style. And yet, Hume did not occupy an isolated position either. His work built on that of a generation of writers, including the King, who largely identified their work as Protestant, but who perceived no incompatibility between sacred subjects and secular style. This was partly due to the ideas discussed above, the intellectual nature of Castalian poetry, the French influence at the court,

---

[60] Gerard Carruthers, 'Form and Substance in the Poetry of the Castalian "Band"', *SLJ* 26 (1999), pp. 7–17 (pp. 10, 14).

[61] Alexander Hume, *Hymnes, or Sacred Songs Wherein the Right Vse of Poësie May Be Espied. ... Whereunto Are Added, the Experience of the Authors Youth, and Certaine Precepts Seruing to the Practise of Sanctification* (Edinburgh, 1599), sig. C4ᵛ, ll. 108–12.

[62] Hume, *Hymnes*, sig. A4ᵛ.

[63] Hume, *Hymnes*, sig. Fᵛ.

James's admiration for Du Bartas. There was a further model of reformed poetics readily available in the works of another court writer, the King's tutor George Buchanan.

Buchanan's religious writing was engaged with classical literature from the first. In the 1540s, while teaching at the Collège de Guyenne in Bordeaux, he wrote his *Jephthes sive votum tragoedia*. This was a biblical play based on Judges 11.30–40 but recast in terms of classical tragedy: his model was Euripides' *Iphigenia in Aulis*.[64] The Greek ancestry of the work was intended to be obvious to the audience: Buchanan altered the biblical story to conform with *Iphigenia*, changing the order in which events unfold, and adding characters to mirror the personae of the original play. His debt to secular literature was not just structural: he availed himself of all of the rhetorical techniques, of all the colourful language of the original to ornament his work. This syncretic approach was not confined to his plays – Buchanan's psalm paraphrases demonstrate the same willingness to incorporate classical references into religious material. His precedent was much imitated. There were multiple translations of the play into the vernacular languages of Europe.[65] Jean de la Taille was one of Buchanan's students when he taught at Boncourt, and his work clearly owes a debt to his master in its blend of biblical and classical: *Saul le furieux: tragedie prise de la Bible* (*c*.1563) is based upon Seneca's *Hercules Furens* – a relationship alluded to on the title page, which describes the play as 'faicte selon l'art & a la mode des vieux autheurs tragiques'.[66] Theodore Beza also produced a play in the same mould. He knew Buchanan's play in manuscript, and his *Abraham Sacrifiant* (1550) shows its descent from both *Iphigenia* and *Jephthes*. It is a mark of the doctrinally-controversial nature of Buchanan's poetics that Beza's work displays a conspicuous unease with the fusion of worldly and religious language. His preface is full of the oppositions familiar from Calvinist theory, marshalling the petrarchan and profane together on one side, and the godly and biblical

---

[64]   For a full discussion of the play and its Greek elements, see Debora Kuller Shuger, *The Renaissance Bible: Scholarship, Sacrifice, and Subjectivity* (Berkeley and Los Angeles: University of California Press, 1994), pp. 134–66. It should be noted that the college was not a Protestant institution; however, Buchanan's Protestant leanings were already clearly in evidence from his *Franciscanus* (1536).

[65]   There is an account of the translations in I.D. McFarlane, 'George Buchanan and European Humanism', *The Yearbook of English Studies: Anglo-French Literary Relations Special Number,* 15 (1985), 33–47 (p. 44).

[66]   'Created according to the art and manner of the ancient tragic authors.' The play is reproduced in Donald Stone (ed.), *Four Renaissance Tragedies* (Cambridge, Mass.: Harvard University Press, 1966).

on the other;[67] and he is eager to disavow any association with classical writing, denying the presence of the accoutrements of Greek tragedy: 'I haue made a songe without a chorus, nother haue I vsed the termes of Strophies, Antistrophies, Epirrhemes, Parecbases, and other such wordes ...'[68] Beza's protestations are a useful reminder that the Protestant aesthetics associated with plain style are not exaggerated or isolated, but fall well within a valid range of stances available throughout the period. Given Beza's importance as a Protestant authority, it is unsurprising that syncretism was not immediately and universally adopted, in Scotland or elsewhere. However, at the Scottish court, under the influence of Buchanan himself, fostered by the importation of French humanist writing and later by the poetry of Du Bartas, syncretism was well-established by the time Henry Lok was sent north by the Cecils.

It would be misleading to suggest that the religious poetry produced by the Castalian Band was homogenous in its variety, just as it is inaccurate to read Scottish reformation writing as uniformly plain. There are elements of a Calvinist aesthetic in the moral poetry of Stewart of Baldynneis, and the King himself clearly kept the Geneva Psalter (1558) – that standard-bearer of the plain style – at his side when engaged in his own psalm translations: there are verbal echoes of that edition in his texts which could not come from any other version of the psalms.[69] However, he also makes the psalms into a vehicle for poetic ingenuity: James avoids the common metre associated with the psalter – for the thirty psalms he translated throughout his life, he employed 28 stanza different forms, a richness of variety more often associated with the Sidney Psalms, in which there are only four examples of metrical repetition.[70] James Craigie notes of the King's psalm metres that 'most of them [are] his own invention and some of them [are] of considerable complexity of structure'.[71] Alexander Montgomerie imitated this metrical complexity in his own psalm versions,

---

[67] 'It would become them better to sing a song of God, then to counterfet a ballet of Petrarks': Théodore de Bèze, *A Tragedie of Abrahams Sacrifice, Written in French by Theodore Beza, and Translated into Inglish, by A*[rthur] *G*[olding] (London: Thomas Vautroullier, 1577), sig. A3ᵛ.

[68] De Bèze, *A Tragedie of Abrahams Sacrifice* (London, 1577), sig. A4ᵛ.

[69] See for instance James's interpolation of the phrase 'fade nor fall' in his translation of Psalm I, which is only precedented in the Geneva version of Sternhold's rendering of the text.

[70] James VI of Scotland, *The Poems of James VI of Scotland*, ed. by James Craigie, 2 vols (Edinburgh: STS, 1955), vol. 1, p. xx; *The Collected Works of Mary Sidney Herbert, Countess of Pembroke*, ed. by Margaret P. Hannay, Noel J. Kinnamon and Michael G. Brennan, 2 vols (Oxford: Oxford University Press, 1998), vol. 1, p. 57.

[71] *The Poems of James VI of Scotland*, ed. Craigie, vol. 1, p. xx.

which were offered to (and refused by) the Kirk: he took the tune, the Solsequium, as the basis of his stanza form, accommodating his verse to the irregular line-length of the popular melody.[72]

This metrical virtuosity might have been related to a religious source, the *Gude and Godlie Balletis*, which similarly does not employ common metre for its psalms; however, the emphasis on learning and poetic skill among the court poets suggests a more literary model. James's translation of Psalm 104, which appears in the *Essayes*, is a text of unimpeachable reformed credentials. He asserted his orthodoxy by signalling his use of Immanuel Tremellius' Latin translation of the Hebrew psalms as his source text. (Because of his knowledge of Hebrew, Tremellius' version was felt to represent the most 'authentic' scriptural language: Beza, for instance, used it as the basis for his psalm paraphrases.) The King's psalm is arranged in 12 stanzas of eight decasyllabic lines rhyming *ababbcbc*. This same rhyme scheme is discussed a few pages earlier in the *Reulis and Cautelis*: 'For an heich & grave subiectis, specially drawin out of learnit authoris, use this kynde of verse following, callit *Ballat Royal*.'[73] In such a deliberate and literal-minded text, it cannot be accidental that ballat royal appears a second time in the volume, in the translation from Book V of Lucan's *Pharsalia*. The shared metre unites the two poems, sacred and secular, on account of their 'heich & grave' matter, and it implicitly compares their literary value; but it also serves to break down any barrier between the classical and the scriptural work.

This lack of distinction between sacred and secular writing meant that the two were discussed in the same literary terms, even with regard to the matter of poetic inspiration, so problematic in English writing. Alexander Montgomerie's 'A godly prayer' is a telling example, as he invokes divine aid

> ... mak my Tongue the Trompet of thy treuth
> And lend my Verse sik wings as ar divyne.
> Sen thou hes grantit me so good Ingyn
> To Loif the, Lord, in gallant style and gay
> Let me no moir so trim a talent tyne.[74]

---

[72] Alexander Montgomerie, *The Mindes Melodie Contayning Certayne Psalmes of the Kinglie Prophete David, Applyed to a New Pleasant Tune* (Edinburgh: Robert Charteris, 1605).

[73] 'Ane Schort Treatise, conteining some reulis and cautelis to be obseruit and eschewit in Scottis Poesie' in *The Poems of James VI of Scotland*, ed. Craigie, vol. 1, pp. 65–83 (p. 80).

[74] Montgomerie quotations are taken *Poems*, ed. Parkinson, vol. 1. See no. 4, ll. 43–7.

The galanterie of courtly verse has not been readily associated with the Scottish court, and those readers conditioned to expect a plainer manner have attempted to assign Montgomerie's desire for 'a gallant style and gay' to the Counter-Reformation poetics of his Catholic co-religionists. In fact, although the court was broadly tolerant of Catholicism, Montgomerie was anxious throughout his career not to risk too sectarian an expression.[75] His religious poetry focused instead on the common language of Christian prayer, and this poem, evoking the penitential psalms, was acceptable to his Protestant readership in both matter and style. The alternative Protestant poetics of the Castalian circle was not unamenable to a brave or gallant hymn.

Perhaps the most interesting allusion in the poem is to an assumption underlying issues of style. The 'ingyn' to which Montgomerie refers is glossed as 'intellect' in Parkinson's edition of the poems, and the *O.E.D.* gives 'native wit' as its primary sense, but its use at the Scottish court suggests a more technical application, associated with ideas of poetic ability and invention. We see it in the Reulis, where 'Ane rype ingyne' is the first quality named in the 'Sonnet Decifring the Perfyte Poete';[76] and in the preface to his translation of the *Uranie*, James explains that because God had refused him the 'lofty and quick ingyne' needed to emulate Du Bartas, he intended to make his poems known 'to this yle of Brittain (swarming full of quick ingynes)', so one more able could take up the task instead.[77] Montgomerie similarly employs the term in reference to his own poetic gifts. In one of his (not infrequent) complaints, he expresses his frustration that he has been given 'a goldin grave Ingyne / Both for Invention and for utterance apt', which he is unable to use to its full potential.[78] The talent reference, similarly, can be taken to allude to the parable in Matthew 25, in which the talents apply metaphorically to the whole range of human potential. In respect of the poet, however, the most obvious application is to his writing. Montgomerie's allusions to his 'good Ingyn' and 'trim' talent explicitly demonstrate a concern with the aesthetics as well as the subject of his religious writing: otherwise, his own abilities would be irrelevant. Furthermore, they assume that man's creative powers should be involved in sacred verse: it is not, as Herbert would later suggest, waiting 'ready

---

[75] R.J. Lyall provides a theological analysis of Montgomerie's poetry in *Alexander Montgomerie* (2005), chapter 8. See further Mark Sweetnam's essay in this volume for a study of the Calvinist palimpsest underlying Montgomerie's work.

[76] 'Reulis and Cautelis', in *The Poems of James VI of Scotland*, ed. Craigie, vol. 1, pp 65–83 (p. 69).

[77] *The Poems of James VI of Scotland*, ed. Craigie, vol. 1, p. 16.

[78] Alexander Montgomerie, *Poems*, ed. Parkinson, vol. 1, 10 ll. 26–7.

penned' in the Scriptures. This contravenes the orthodox poetics of the English reformation, but also provides a model for Henry Lok's evident interest in his own poetic ability. The inspirational power of the muse, the ornaments of rhyme and the authority lent by allusion to classical texts would be unnecessary for the poet who believed the job was already done.

Conclusions

Could Lok have found his models elsewhere than Scotland? The similarity of Montgomerie's conception of religious poetry to ideas expressed (if less explicitly) in Sidney's *Apology* demonstrates that he could have imbibed his poetics outside the Scottish court, whether from a hypothesized Sidney manuscript, or from one of the continental or classical sources in the hinterland of both 'Godly Prayer' and the Sidney *Psalms*. Lok's achievement, however, was not confined to recognizing a new development in religious writing. His use of the sonnet form is revolutionary in English poetry; and through his choice of the sonnet, he identifies his work more closely with the Castalian Band.

The distinction between the English and the Scottish sonnet has tended to be occluded in the rare modern editions of lesser-known sequences. Holger Klein's edition of *English and Scottish Sonnet Sequences of the Renaissance* (1984), for instance, does not attempt to differentiate between the two; and although his selection of italianate love sonnets is an accurate reflection of the typical English sequence of the 1590s, the Scottish examples, William Alexander's *Aurora* (1604) and David Murray's *Caelia* (1611), are far from representative.[79] The *Reulis* envisaged quite another use for the sonnet than these late and petrarchan sequences with their anglicized orthography can embody. Rather than associating it with love, which he suggested be treated in 'Commoun verse', James chose to recommend the sonnet for 'the compendious praysing of any bukes, or the authouris thairof, or ony argumentis of uther historeis, quhair sindrie sentences, and change of purposis are requyrit'.[80] There were Scottish love sonnets, just as there were English sonnets of dedication; however, the Scottish sonnet had a wider range of employment than was typical in England. It was used in flytings and satire as well as dedications. A sonnet by William Stewart introduces the psalms in the Scottish prayer book, and

---

[79] Holger M. Klein (ed.), *English and Scottish Sonnet Sequences of the Renaissance*, 2 vols (New York: Hildesheim, 1984).

[80] 'Reulis and Cautelis', in *The Poems of James VI of Scotland*, ed. Craigie, vol. 1, pp. 65–83 (p. 81).

this relationship of sonnet and religious theme was borne out in a series of religious sonnets by the King, Montgomerie and James Melville, among others.[81] The Scottish poets appear unapologetic about their use of the sonnet form. They had, it is true, a precedent in various French sonnet sequences on religious themes. Lyall traces likenesses between poems by James and Montgomerie, and Huguenot Marin Le Saulx, but there were other examples available to them in the works of Marot and Beza, for instance.[82] These poems were equally available to English readers, who were, however, less ready to emulate them: it seems likely that the broader associations of the sonnet in Scotland made the religious sonnet a less problematic model for the Castalian poets – and hence, for Henry Lok.

The particular form of Lok's sonnets is also suggestive. While the rhyme scheme of the sonnet allowed for some variation, English and Scottish sonnets tended to finish on the distinctive couplet. The arrangement of rhymes within the body of the poem is less constant, although it is notable that the interlocked 'Spenserian' pattern (ababbcbccdcdee) appeared both north and south of the border.[83] This is the scheme most often adopted by Lok; however, he seems more likely to have learnt it from Scottish models. Spenser's sonnets (or, at least, those in Spenserian form) did not appear in print until 1595, and furthermore, Lok could not have acquired from them one of the more unusual characteristics of his verse, his taste for internal rhyme. About half of his sonnets conform to the pattern illustrated below, in lines 12–14 of sonnet 2.xxxiv.

> And thy regard my wandring will shall *tame*,
> Yea I will *blame*, And scorne each other thing,
> Saue what shall me vnto thy fauour bring.[84] (my italics)

The concluding couplet rhymes, but there is also a rhyme between 'tame' at the end of line 12, and 'blame', in the middle of the next line. In every case, Lok stresses this echo with a caesura, forcing the reader to pause and note the patterning. Internal rhyme is used in French sonnets, but the French scheme diverges dramatically from the Scottish model in its placing

---

[81]   Church of Scotland, *The forme of prayers … used in the English Church at Geneva, approued & receiued by the churche of Scotland* (Edinburgh: Robert Lekprevk, 1565), unpaginated.

[82]   Lyall, *Alexander Montgomerie*, pp. 307 ff.

[83]   Maria Philmus has concluded that the Scottish form predated the English, but that they both developed independently. Maria R. Rohr Philmus, 'The Case of the Spenserian Sonnet: A Curious Re-Creation', in *Spenser Studies: A Renaissance Poetry Annual XIII*, ed. Anne Lake Prescott and Thomas P. Roche (New York: AMS Press, 1999), pp. 125–37.

[84]   Lok, *Sundry Christian Passions* (1593), Part 2, Sonnet 2.xxxiv.

of the couplet in the middle, rather than at the end, of the poem. There is a Scottish precedent for internal rhyme in their native medieval verse; and whether the Castalians were looking to this example, or to the French, in their poetry, the result is much closer to Lok's work than the unmediated French poem could be. The Flyting between Montgomerie and Polwarth is rich in examples:

> Thy scrowis obscuir ar borrowit fra sum buik.
> Fra Lyndsay thow tuik, thow art Chawceris cuik.[85]

Here, the internal rhyme is part of a competitive display of poetic skill. Lok's adoption of the device is a further indication of his interest in using his sacred sonnets to demonstrate his own poetic skill, and also, of his commitment to marrying religious themes with human effort. However, it also serves to point to the influences he imbibed during his time as Burghley's agent at the Scottish court.

Lok's first sonnet sequence appeared in print in 1593, and did not remain unique for long. Barnabe Barnes followed it with a sequence of holy sonnets two years later, and, also 1595, Robert Southwell's devotional poems were published, with, as discussed above, important effects for sacred verse in England. The wider circulation of Sidney's texts in the late 1590s also made way for a more literary approach to religious writing. In 1603, James assumed the English throne and set about the unification of the two nations, and his presence in England changed English writing, as poets vied to please his tastes. The space in which Lok, with his Scottish poetics, might effect some transformation is narrow, or so it seems. Nonetheless, he was well-known in his day. The popular anthology, the *Belvedere or the Garden of the Muses* (1600), as we shall see, is only one of the texts to include him in the company of Spenser and Sidney.[86] He was influential in Barnes's *Divine Centurie*, and his sonnet on the parable of the talents might be considered as the model for Milton's 'Talent' sonnet, previously traced to Barnes's later version.[87] Thomas P. Roche has suggested that Herbert based one of the poems in the *Temple* on a sonnet from Lok's sequence.[88] This continuing influence is only part of the story, however.

---

[85] Alexander Montgomerie, *Poems*, ed. Parkinson, vol. 1, 99:I: 44–5.

[86] John Bodenham, *Bodenham's Belvedere or the Garden of the Mvses, Publications of the Spenser Society* (Manchester: Charles Simms and Co., 1875).

[87] James L. Potter, 'Milton's "Talent" Sonnet and Barnabe Barnes', *Notes and Queries*, 202 (1957), p. 447.

[88] Thomas Roche, *Petrarch and the English Sonnet Sequences* (New York: AMS Press, 1989), pp. 160–62.

Perhaps as important as Lok's sonnets, as I suggest at the opening of this essay, is that his circumstances are a clue to a wider phenomenon.

Henry Lok was not the only English poet to encounter Scottish writing. We have seen that Sidney, Constable and Harvey knew some Scottish texts, and it is likely that others in their circles knew of their reading. It is also clear that Scottish poetics were distinct from English literary theory, even before James so explicitly stated in the *Reulis* that he wished to create a literature distinct from England's.[89] The close relationship between Scottish and French writing has made it more difficult to tease out instances where English writers were learning from their Scottish neighbours; however, the likelihood is that their debt has been underestimated. There was regular traffic among all three countries, and although France had a greater geographical proximity to London, not all of English literary production took place in the south-east corner, and nor did her poets confine themselves to home. Certain communities of English writers living abroad have been recognized, in post-colonial studies of Spenser and Ralegh in Ireland, in accounts of Marian and Catholic exiles, and in Van Dorsten's work on the extraordinary convergence of literary figures in Leiden in the 1580s. The traffic between England and Scotland has yet to be systematically examined, but promises to yield fruitful results.

The border-town of Berwick-upon-Tweed, for instance, was the scene of a most remarkable confluence of literary figures of both nations from the mid-sixteenth century. John Knox was there, preaching and courting, in the 1550s. Constable's father, as we have seen, was Marshal of Berwick from 1576–78. The diplomat Thomas Randolph spent the year 1576 travelling back and forth between Edinburgh and Berwick, and sent home to Sidney works by his friend Buchanan; it is not implausible that he also communicated something of the poetry of James Melville, whom he had known in Paris in the 1550s. Melville himself fled religious persecution in Scotland in 1584, and took shelter in Berwick. The poet Thomas Churchyard was writing to Christopher Hatton from the town in June 1581: it is tempting to think that the translation of Du Bartas's *Premier Jour* to which he alludes in *Churchyards Challenge* (1593), but which is now lost, was prompted by contact with some of his Scottish admirers there. Barnabe Barnes, with his customary perversity, was in hiding in 1596 following an attempt to murder the Recorder of Berwick.[90] And

---

[89] 'For albeit sindrie hes written of it [Poesie] in English, quhilk is lykest to our language, zit we differ from thame in sindrie reulis of Poesie', 'Reulis and Cautelis', in *The Poems of James VI of Scotland*, ed. Craigie, vol. 1, pp. 65–83 (p. 67).

[90] Having initially attempted (without success) to poison him with a glass of sack, Barnes, undaunted, offered him a poisoned lemon, thereby raising the suspicions of his intended victim. More of Barnes's exploits are available to the

Henry Lok lived in Berwick as secretary to Henry Carey, Lord Hunsdon, Marshal of Berwick after leaving Scotland in about 1591. He appears to have stayed there until 1597, and there is evidence of his literary life there: Elizabeth Carey, Henry Carey's wife is the Lady Hunsdon to whom Lok addresses a dedicatory sonnet in the *Ecclesiastes*, the terms which strongly suggest she knew his other writings.[91]

There is perhaps little to be gleaned about Lok's innovative 1593 sequence from this tangle of interconnections at Berwick, since his stay there postdates the writing of that work. Rather, Berwick gestures towards the broader issue of literary exchange between the two countries – an issue which is certain to be explored and clarified over the coming years, as scholarly interest in the intertwined histories of the three kingdoms of Ireland, Scotland and England continues to grow.[92] To date, much investigation in this field has related to the political relationship between the countries as expressed in their literatures: religious poetics, which partake of both political and literary discourses, are highly relevant in this context, and Lok's example remains significant. Aesthetics, especially when involved in religious doctrine, must tend to require more than one impetus towards change. The transformation of English devotional verse at the end of the sixteenth century still owes debts to forces exemplified in the Sidneys and in Southwell; but Scotland must be taken into account, for the reason that contemporary writers evidently perceived Scottish poetics as something distinct from English writing.

Lok, as we have seen, was sufficiently well-known to be included in Bodenham's *Belevdere* (1600), in illustrious company: the names which appear alongside him all continue to be generally recognizable today. Lok was also sufficiently well-known to be satirized on stage. At Christmas 1601, the scholars of St John's College, Cambridge played the *Return from Pernassus*, in which Lok's literary attainments are evaluated:

> Locke and Hudson, sleepe you quiet shavers, among the shavings of the presse, and let your bookes lie in some old nookes amongst old bootes and shooes, so you may avoyde my censure.[93]

---

reader of Mark Eccles's wry account of his life in *Thomas Lodge and Other Elizabethans*, ed. Charles J. Sissons (Cambridge, Mass.: Harvard University Press, 1933), pp. 165–242.

[91] Lok, 'To the Right Honourable, the Ladie of Hunsdon', *Ecclesiastes*, sig. Yii[v].

[92] See particularly John Kerrigan's pioneering work in this field, *Archipelagic English: Literature, History, and Politics 1603–1707* (Oxford: Oxford University Press, 2007).

[93] Anon., *The Returne from Pernassus, or, the Scourge of Simony. Publiquely Acted by the Students in Saint Iohns Colledge in Cambridge* (London: G. Eld, for

The comment comes in the midst of an evaluation of the poets of the moment. Again, the names are familiar, and relatively few of them come in for censure.[94] John Marston is treated most harshly, probably in recompense for his recent and scurrilous collection of satires, the *Scourge of Villanie* (1598). Marlowe's skill is commended, but his 'vices sent from hell' are noted.[95] Lok and his companion in ignominy, by contrast, seem merely to be the victims of the anonymous playwright's taste. He appears to have preferred love lyrics: he admires 'sweet hony dropping Daniell', 'Draytons sweete muse' and remarks of Spenser that he was 'a sweeter swan than ever song in Poe'.[96] Lok and Hudson are the only poets treated in tandem, presumably because they were perceived as sharing traits of style or theme – and it was not the 'sweet' or 'sugred' love sonnets of English tradition. Hudson is Thomas Hudson, an English musician who was employed at the Scottish court, and whose translation of Du Bartas's *Judith* was commissioned by James VI in 1584.[97] He contributed a laudatory sonnet to the King's *Essayes of a Prentise* that same year. It may be that the *Pernassus* playwright was aware of this common background in Scottish court poetry; it seems much more likely that he perceived in the two poets a similar style and a comparable approach to their religious subjects. Whether or not he identified their poetics as Scottish, he seems certainly to have understood them to be distinct from the other works of which he treated. Sixteenth-century readers disagreed with his evaluation of their worth: Lok's sonnets went into a second edition, and Hudson's *Judith* was printed eight times by 1641. The devotional poetry of the next decades suggests that their gallant and gay poetics had its influence; and once more, the curious company kept by Henry Lok's name hints that some part of that influence derives from the royal court of Scotland.[98]

Iohn Wright, 1606), sig. B2ʳ.

[94] The writers evaluated are Spenser, Constable, Thomas Lodge, Samuel Daniel, Michael Drayton, Thomas Watson, John Marston, Christopher Marlowe, John Davies, Ben Jonson, Shakespeare, Thomas Churchyard and Thomas Nashe.

[95] *Return from Pernassus* (1606), sig. B2ᵛ.

[96] *Return from Pernassus* (1606), sig. B2ʳ.

[97] Guillaume de Salluste Du Bartas, *The Historie of Iudith in Forme of a Poeme*, trans. Thomas Hudson (Edinburgh: Thomas Vautroullier, 1584).

[98] My thanks are due to Eiléan Ní Chuilleanáin, Mordechai Feingold, Richard Serjeantson and Mark Sweetnam, and to the Irish Research Council for the Humanities and Social Sciences, whose generous support facilitated the writing of this article.

CHAPTER 10

Hume of Godscroft on parity

David Reid

David Hume of Godscroft (1568–1629/31?) was the most impressive thinker of the second wave of Genevan Reform in Scotland in the late sixteenth and early seventeenth centuries. He is an exceptionally formidable arguer, but a witty and engaging one. Like George Buchanan, he was a distinguished Latin poet, and like him also a distinguished historian and political theorist. But he has never had his due. Nowadays among literary people he is better known as the father of Anna Hume, the translator of Petrarch's *Trionfi*, than for his own writing. In his own day, he could not get his major works published or did not wish to. The Marquis of Douglas, for whom Godscroft had written *The History of the Houses of Douglas and Angus*, his most sustained piece of writing, held back publication because of its Presbyterian views on kings and subjects. In 1644, the year of the Solemn League and Covenant, when its political views might have chimed with the mood of the moment, Anna Hume tried to bring it out, but the Marquis managed to stay publication for two years and the moment passed. Anna Hume edited away much of her father's expressive style and its Scots forms. A great deal of its material, abridged and revised, found its way into David Calderwood's *History of the Kirk of Scotland*, and it is naturally to this factually more reliable source that professional modern historians turn, Godscroft's contribution lying unnoticed.

Obviously I cannot repair this crumbling away of Godscroft's work in a short paper. Nevertheless, I hope by recommending as an essay in political theory his letters to James Law, Bishop of Orkney, to do something for the recovery of his intellectual achievement.[1] Above all, the letter of 10 April, 1610, is a remarkable piece of writing, not just for its ideas about democracy, but also for the manner in which it argues. The six letters are not hard to come by. David Calderwood collected them in his *History of the Kirk of Scotland*, six out of the 12 he says Godscroft wrote to Law on

---

[1] In its original form this paper was delivered in July 2005 to the 11th International Conference on Scottish Language and Literature (Medieval and Renaissance) at Brock University, St Catharines, Ontario. It has benefited from the comments of Professor Roger Mason of the University of St Andrews and Professor Arthur Williamson of California State University, Sacramento.

episcopal innovation between 1608 and 1610 (Calderwood, 7:145).[2] But except for Arthur Williamson's remarks on Godscroft in *Scottish National Consciousness in the Age of James VI*, they seem to have escaped notice.[3] Of course that is a large 'except'; anyone who knows Williamson's book will not think it odd of me to say that his few pages on Godscroft have enough penetration and weight to supply starting points for many articles and books. But articles on Godscroft's correspondence with Law do not seem to have followed, and that being so, I am not ashamed to go over some of the ground he has covered and develop some of the things he has touched on.[4]

James wrote in his *Basilicon Doron* of 1598 that the Reformation in Scotland,

> not proceeding from the Princes ordour, as it did in our neighbour country of England... ; some fierce spirited men in the ministerie, gote such a guyding of the people at that time of confusion, as finding the guste of gouernment sweete, they begouth to fantasie to themselues, a Democratick forme of gouernment, and hauing... bene ouer-well baited vpon the wracke, first of my Grandmother, and next of my mother, and after vsurping the liberty of the time in my long minority, settled themselues so faste vpon that imagined Democracie, as they fed themselues with the hope to become *Tribunis plebis*: and so in a populare gouernment by leading people by the nose, to beare the sway of all the rule. (1:75)[5]

The 'imagined Democracie' James speaks of is the idea of church government sketched in Andrew Melville's *Second Book of Discipline* (1578), which replaced an episcopal hierarchy with a hierarchy of church courts. Ministers would not be subject to regulation by fellow ministers promoted to episcopal rank but to courts in which all ministers had an equal voice and decisions were made by majority vote. Such is the principle

---

[2] David Calderwood, *The History of the Kirk of Scotland*, 8 vols. (Edinburgh: Wodrow Society, 1842–49), 6:727–31, 746–51; 7:64–9, 69–90, 139–45, and 145–9.

[3] *Scottish National Consciousness in the Age of James VI* (Edinburgh: John Donald, 1979), pp. 132–4.

[4] But see Williamson's essay 'Education, Culture and the Scottish Civic Tradition', forthcoming in Arthur Williamson and Allan Macinnes (eds), *The Stuart World, 1603–1714: The Atlantic Connection* (Leiden: Brill, 2005), pp. 33–54, which he kindly let me read in advance. Though the focus is not on the correspondence with Law, it develops Williamson's discussion of Godscroft's civic humanism, an important context for the ideas I shall be looking at.

[5] *The Basilicon Doron of King James VI*, ed. W.A. Craigie, 2 vols. (Edinburgh: STS, 1944–50).

of parity that Hume and the Melvillian Presbyterians contended for and that James saw as the 'the mother of confusion, and enemy to Vnitie which is the mother of ordour' (1:77). There had been a short period in the late 1580s and early 1590s when, uneasily, it is true, James got on fairly well with the Presbyterians among the Kirk leaders; the so-called Golden Act of 1592 effectively replaced bishops with presbyteries. But the protests of these leaders against James's conciliatory treatment of the Catholic earls and the popular riot in Edinburgh in 1596 convinced James, if he needed convincing, that he must govern the Kirk through bishops and silence criticism of his policies in its assemblies. From 1597 James took a hand in regulating General Assemblies and excluding the intransigent Presbyterians. At first his policy was to combine bishops and presbyteries, a policy which seems to have been widely accepted. But from 1602 his policy took a more determinedly episcopal direction and he moved to get rid of church government through deliberative assemblies and replace it by rule through bishops. This actively Erastian subordination of the Kirk to monarchical rule seems to have been less acceptable and had to be implemented by manipulation, threats and bribes as well as banishment of unruly ministers; certainly it was unacceptable to committed Presbyterians like Andrew Melville and his nephew James and Hume of Godscroft, who thought the Kirk was being overturned.[6] One of the trusted agents of James's campaign was James Law, promoted to Bishop of Orkney in 1605. To him, Godscroft wrote to discover, he says, what the principles behind the new measures were (6:728). We do not have Law's replies, but from Godscroft's letters it is clear that he follows the line on parity and order set out by James. Deliberately or not, in arguing with Law, Godscroft is arguing with his King. In doing, so he argues on political and constitutional grounds. No doubt he felt that the Presbyterian position was surely grounded in scripture and the history of the primitive church. In passing, he seems to accept Theodore Beza's theological arguments for parity in church government and dismisses Hadrian Saravia's attempt to refute them as dishonest.[7] But his controversy with episcopacy deals with

---

[6] For the historical background, see Alan R. MacDonald, 'James VI and the General Assembly, 1586–1618' in *The Reign of James VI*, eds. Julian Goodare and Michael Lynch (East Linton: Tuckwell Press, 2000), pp. 170–85.

[7] The controversy between Saravia and Beza goes back to the controversy stirred up by Beza's answer, *c.*1580, to Lord Chancellor Glamis's query concerning church government, *De Triplici Episcopatu* (see Gordon Donaldson, 'Lord Chancellor Glamis and Theodore Beza', *Miscellany of the Scottish History Society*, 3rd series, 8 (1951), pp. 87–113). Glamis had written while the Regent Morton's management of the church was being criticized by Andrew Melville. Beza's reply was taken up by English as well as Scottish Presbyterians. Saravia weighed in for episcopal government with *Examen tractatus de episcopatuum triplici genere* (1587) and,

acts of Parliament and General Assembly and with political principles. Although the distinction cannot be a categorical one, his thought is political rather than theological.

Godscroft engages to keep Law's correspondence to himself: 'I sall not communicat your letters with anie; I sall not carie them abroad with me; and at home, they sall ly in a lockfast kist; and if there be anie thing needfull for secrecie, that yee may be in suretie to write freelie whatever your minde diteth' (6:747). One wonders how Godscroft's letters came into Calderwood's hands and how he could place them in his history as if they were public statements. Still, as we do not have Law's replies, Godscroft must have been as good as his word and kept them private, while probably allowing his own letters to circulate in what must have come close to one-sided manuscript pamphleteering.[8] Yet however public on his side the exchange, the private letter form gives rules of openness which, I shall argue, help to give shape to the conversation he wishes to engage Law in. Besides, his not venturing into print meant that he had not exactly engaged in political agitation; no doubt he still risked punishment for the opinions he expressed but in fact he suffered nothing worse than having his last letters lie unanswered.

I shall begin my commentary by talking about Godscroft's manner, which is remarkable for the character he bears as a controversialist.

At the end of the seventeenth century, after about eighty years of controversy over episcopacy and presbytery, the extruded episcopal party sometimes turned to publishing their case in the form of letters from one gentleman to another.[9] By doing so, writers escaped the forms of academic disputation and wrangling over terms that ecclesiastical controversy had fallen into. In writing a letter to a friend, the writer might be presumed to say what he really thought without the point-scoring and hair-splitting of standard polemic and without the consequent loss of significance in a bitter war of words. That at least was the presumption. At the beginning of the century, Godscroft, in writing to Law as to a friend, has already arrived at an understanding about the spirit in which an argument has to be conducted if reasonable conclusions are to be reached.

---

in reply to Beza's reply, with *De diversis ministrorum evangelii gradibus* (1590), works found a useful prop by the Scottish as well as the English bishops.

[8]   Godscroft attempted a similar correspondence with William Cowper, Bishop of Galloway, who felt compelled to make a public answer in his *The Bishop of Galloway, his Dikaiologie* (London, 1614).

[9]   See, for example, *An Account of the Present Persecution of the Church in Scotland* (London, 1690).

In addition, he is binding himself to rules of civility and plain-dealing such as might inform a civic ideal of human association.[10] By contrast, Jacobite and Episcopalian public letter writing at the time of the Whig Revolution (1688–91) was a polemical device, a device of civil war in words if not in arms, rather than a means of carrying on a civic-humanist political debate: the form of letters between friends managed to imply that the opposition was excluded from the conversation or writing of gentlemen and at the same time allowed the writer to carry off every expression of contempt for the other side as what was called for by the indignation honest and candid friends should share. Godscroft's use of the letter form is free at least of that rhetorical guile. Although he addresses Law as a friend, Law is a friend who has chosen the other side. Godscroft is writing, not to share publicly a party understanding of a quarrel but, he insists, to arrive at an understanding of the principles that actuate the other party, to find out what they think they are doing and what they mean by what they say. There is a good deal of remonstration with Law's proceedings as a bishop and leader of the Episcopalian party going on behind Godscroft's inquiry into the truth, and he does not think it part of writing in a spirit of friendship and plainness to spare Law a formidable analysis of what he has written or done. Still, whereas most controversialists of the Seventeenth Century, Presbyterian or Episcopalian, are disfigured by their animus, Godscroft treats his opponent in a respectful manner that wins himself and his arguments respect.[11] And though his protestations of Christian and brotherly love may sound unctuous or false to our ears, he did make a pretty stout effort to keep straight-forward rational human conversation going at a time when compulsion, secrecy and fear were the order of the day and when argument tended to lose itself in pedantry and acrimony.

Godscroft's use of Scots plays a part in establishing his plain-dealing character. 'I love to use the Scottish language', he says, 'als good as English, if my countreis love blinds me not' (7:87). His Scots is anglicized to a considerable extent and specifically Scots spellings and words are in fact quite thin sown, at least as Calderwood preserves them. But preserve them he did to some extent (unlike the editors of Godscroft's *History of the Houses of Douglas and Angus*), perhaps because Godscroft's use of Scots was recognized as a sterling mark of his being a spokesman for the

---

[10] On this subject particularly, see Williamson's article specified in note 4, above.

[11] One might add that William Cowper's *The Bishop of Galloway, his Dikaiologie*, a reply to a similar attempt of Godscroft's to examine the principles behind the episcopal innovations, shows most of the faults of tone and temper of the later controversialists.

anti-court party, much as half a century earlier, Winzet had made play of his honest Scots tongue in controversy with the anglicizing innovator, Knox.[12] At any rate, the scattering of Scots in Godscroft's letters is enough to give them the flavour of someone who writes without affectation, in touch with the way he and his reader naturally turn their thoughts, even at quite a high level of abstraction: parity in church government lets 'men see their mutuall mister' [need for each other] (7:77); Godscroft wonders how people are 'ather so untentie [careless] not to advert, or so wilfull not to acknowledge' that one man, one vote, is the universal rule in deliberative assemblies (7:74); definitions are 'verrie kittle in their strict lawes, and nothing worth without them' (7:80); 'And not to fyle my feet with farre gates ... [does Law's argument mean] our [Court of] sessioun ... [has] no order in the world in it [?]'. The mixture of quite a formal English register and a colloquial, easy Scots one, is attractive. Again there is an analogy with a later seventeenth-century development, when English writers like Dryden learnt to modulate between an elegant and formal register and syntax and colloquial turns of upper-class speech. But Godscroft's modulation between formal and colloquial is without class swagger. Its ease is the ease of someone whose intellectual confidence is based on having thought things through for himself and who feels he has a good enough case to address others without disguise or mannerism. The contrast with Hawthornden's manner in *Irene* (see the passage quoted below, p. 204) is perhaps too broad to be sharp but useful enough to illustrate my point.

---

[12]   Even in the MS of his *History of the House of Douglas, in David Hume of Godscroft, The History of the House of Douglas*, 2 vols., ed. David Reid (Edinburgh: STS, 1996), which may be taken as close to what he wrote, Godscroft's Scots is anglicized if measured against, for instance Bellenden's translation of Boece (pp. xlvii–lvi), but it keeps a good deal more in the way of Scots spelling and word forms than the pieces Calderwood has collected. Calderwood's policy is generally to reduce the material he edits to fairly standard Southern English; that he has left so much Scots in the case, not only of Godscroft's letters to Law, but also in the case of his colloquy with the Eighth Earl of Angus over the subject's right of insurrection against a tyrant (Calderwood, 4:466–83) is a good reason for thinking that Godscroft's use of Scots in writing was recognized as distinctive and worth preserving. It is unfortunate that the 'Larger MS' (BL Additional MSS, 4734–6), the compilation from which Calderwood condensed the MS in the British Library that was edited by Thomas Thomson for the Wodrow Society edition, stops at 1586 and so does not contain the letters in a form that might have preserved more of Godscroft's Scots. I should add that Godscroft's use of Scots is also a patriotic gesture of a rather complex sort. He had belonged to the anglophile party of the exiled Lords while he was attached to the Eighth Earl of Angus and wrote in favour of the union of Scotland and England, but a union in which Scots forms of government, above all church government, were jealously guarded. His use of written Scots seems to be partly a deliberate resistance to union as assimilation to England.

Hawthornden's highly artificial literary manner and distance from the way he or his countrymen talked is the voice of one chanting in the wilderness, more concerned with the cultivation of his chant and its plangencies than with conversing with other minds. Godscroft's plain style, by contrast, with its traces of Scots, is the style of someone who has found a way to be himself among other men in writing and who writes to carry on a reasonable conversation with them.

As important as style and language for carrying on reasonable conversation is Godscroft's understanding of those vices of discourse that get in the way of a genuine exchange of views. He insists that he and Law should deal sincerely with each other. He appeals to 'our old familiaritie' as an excuse for addressing Law 'freelie and friendlie' (6:728). He asks Law to consider what he says 'in good sadnesse' (7:84), that is 'seriously'. He says that he calls Law 'right beloved brother' 'unfainedlie'. This is of course the language of Christian fellowship but it goes with a care for good talk in general, that it should be without those disguises and pretences by which conversation is used to jockey for advantage or undermine. Godscroft is eager that he should really meet with Law in the matter of Church government and not have 'strive[d]' or 'staved with a shadow' (6:750; 7:65). He knows how the spirit of genuine discussion is easily lost in disputation: 'contention ... never wanteth words' (7:64).

Godscroft's unusually developed concern with the way discussion may be vitiated probably owes something to the Humanists' critique of the scholastic philosophers' pursuit of dialectic as a means of arriving at truth. The remark about definitions being 'verrie kittle', which I have already quoted, is the sort of thing Valla or Erasmus might have said to express their disdain for the uses of language cultivated in the schools.[13] In their spirit too is his refusal to define the word 'order' and his turning to the ordinary use of words: 'who would weill defyne order I darre not presume, and thinke it the worke of a refynned ingyne. It is eneugh how we know how the word is used' (7:80–81). Godscroft's use of 'refynned' has an almost eighteenth-century ring to it, deprecating artifice and metaphysical subtlety. Or again, '[I] use names as I may, nather ever have will to stand on words ... suche exact pressing of definitiouns, and use of words according

---

[13]   See Petrarch, 'A Disapproval of an Unreasonable Use of the Discipline of Dialectic', trans. Hans Nachod, *Renaissance Philosophy of Man*, ed. Ernst Cassirer *et al.* (Chicago: University of Chicago Press, 1948), pp. 134–9; Lorenzo Valla, *Dialectical Disputations*, for which, see Jerold E. Seigel, *Rhetoric and Philosophy in Renaissance Humanism* (Princeton: Princeton University Press, 1968), p. 164; and Erasmus, *Antibarbarorum Liber* in Albert Hyma, *The Youth of Erasmus* (Ann Arbor: University of Michigan Press, 1930), pp. 239–41. See also Hanna-Barbara Gerl, *Rhetorik als Philosophie: Lorenzo Valla* (Munich: Fink Verlag, 1974).

to the pressed definitiouns, gives als muche caus and mater of contentioun as light in things' (7:84).[14]

Though Godscroft, the disciple of Buchanan, is certainly a fine product of Scottish Humanism, his concern for the 'right use of words' (6:727, 749) is by no means limited to the thought that scholastic logic is a science of logomachy, of contention about words, as for example in the wake of Locke, Scottish eighteenth-century teachers of rhetoric came to say.[15] For one thing, Godscroft knows that rhetoric, the Humanists' preferred art of discourse, is capable of representing opposites in equally splendid colours, and instead of glorying in this power, he brings it up both to deflate the conventional praise of hierarchy and to suggest the unaptness of that sort of commendation since equality might similarly be praised. He wants a plain discourse that avoids the vices both of dialectical logic-chopping and of rhetorical manipulation of appearances:

> Our speech I allow be simple, and without flowres of rhetorick, (except such as serve for cleerenesse, not for ornament,) without fard or bastard logick, direct, without diverting by digressiouns or by-wayes; loving without hatred, at least of persounes of men, calme without storminesse; of affectiouns, sweete without bitternesse, or taxing even of taxing; popular without curiositie, or so scholastick subtiltie of words; as farre as may be plaine, without ambiguitie of words or phrases. So shall it be shortest, soundest, and soonest brought to the point, which otherwise men can never come to, thought they spend whole volumes. (6:748)

---

[14] Ramus took over much of the Humanists' critique of Scholasticism, above all their disparagement of the medieval use of Aristotle and their complaints about the divorce of philosophy from rhetoric; among other things, Ramus remarked of the schoolmen that 'ordinary people do not talk like that' (*Aristotelicae animadversiones* (1543), ff. 4, 79, cited in Walter J. Ong, S.J., *Ramus, Method, and the Decay of Dialogue: From the Art of Discourse to the Art of Reason* (Cambridge, Mass.: Harvard University Press, 1958), p. 54. Godscroft graduated from St Andrews in 1573, the year before Roland MacIlmaine, another graduate of St Andrews, published the first English edition of Ramus's *Dialecticae libri duo* and a translation, *The Logike of the moste Excellent Philosopher P. Ramus*. Whether that means Godscroft had been already introduced to 'Ramism' as an undergraduate or not, it is unlikely that his awareness of the precariousness of rational discourse did not owe something to the stir that Ramus made. Though Ramism was popular among Calvinist intellectuals, George Buchanan did not include Ramist reforms in his plan for St Andrews; on the other hand, Andrew Melville introduced Ramist reforms at the University of Glasgow in the 1570s (see Wilbur Samuel Howell, *Logic and Rhetoric in England, 1550–1700* (Princeton: Princeton University Press, 1956), pp. 179–89, and Ong, pp. 46, 48–9).

[15] See, for example, George Campbell, *The Philosophy of Rhetoric* (London, 1850), pp. 69–70. See also Wilbur Samuel Howell, *Eighteenth Century British Logic and Rhetoric* (Princeton: Princeton University Press, 1971).

Williamson remarks that the East Lothian schools, where Mair had been taught retained a tradition of dialectic that trained Godscroft's formidable powers of argument.[16] The plain manner that Godscroft calls for is not only an absence of logical pedantry but also a manner that respects the spirit, if not the method, of dialectic. When Law apologizes for arguing for hierarchy on 'logicall grounds' rather than from scriptural authority, Godscroft is quick to reply that 'I compt a logicall argument a good argument, and logick it self a good handmaid or servant to authoritie' (7:84). Further, Godscroft, unlike the controversialists of his day and of the next generations, who felt that 'a horse-load of citations' added weight to their cause, protests that he acknowledges 'reasoun onlie for the tuiche of truthe, not the persouns of men' (7:80), and adds refreshingly that too much citation 'imports prejudice', that is, interferes with judgement of the matter under discussion.

For all his disclaiming of subtlety in matters of definition, Godscroft shows himself to be a very competent dialectician, as far as I can judge, able to deal with questions about the essence of parity and its supposed logical absurdities with briskness and acumen (7:65). Moreover, his appeal to the common sense of words does not keep him from speculative boldness. When Law, following James, charges parity of rank and function among pastors with going against order, Godscroft grants that this is 'a verie odious thing appearandlie, as though it were therefore unorderlie and confused' (7:79). 'But what', he asks, 'if they [disorder and confusion] be not ill ay? What is the mater then? Why sould we contend for words?' God is infinite and all infinity is against order and confused. At first, this sounds idle point-scoring, as if one were to reply to an accusation of self-contradiction that opposites coincide in God and so what appeared to human sense absurd must be divinely cogent. But Calvinists dwelt on the unaccountable and indeterminable nature of God's power and Godscroft may quite seriously have seen in God's infinity, rather than in the conventional notion of God's

---

[16] Note 14, p. 175; Mair's school was Haddington, Godscroft's Dunbar. 'Ramism', of course, combined a great deal of what had been taught as rhetoric with dialectic and in doing so, according to Ong, hopelessly muddled and diluted the old scholastic discipline of dialectic. I cannot find any trace in the letters to Law of Godscroft's following specifically Ramist directions (his way of reducing documents to heads in *The History of the Houses of Douglas and Angus* might, however, be one such). In any event, my argument is not that Godscroft is a product of Humanism or of 'Ramism' or of residual scholastic dialectic, or for that matter of resurgent neoscholastic dialectic (see Quentin Skinner. *The Foundations of Modern Political Thought, Volume II, The Age of Reformation* (Cambridge: Cambridge University Press, 1978), p. 321, on the revival of scholastic method in the 1570s among Huguenot defenders of the right of resistance such as Beza and Mornay), but that he arrived at a fine critical intelligence about rational discussion through using the disciplines of his time with discrimination.

creating the world through a hierarchical procession, a pattern for the Church.[17] At any rate he saw something rationally defensible in the decision-making of assemblies of equal members and may have felt that in the deliberation of a whole membership, rather than in the decisions of single men set in authority, there was an analogy with divine infinity and potentiality: the voice of the whole is the voice of God.

I am arguing that Godscroft, not only shared with the Humanists an idea of how human reasoning must run according to the rules of good conversation and the ordinary sense of words, but that he might also draw on a scholastic dialectical tradition of searching analysis of terms and even turn to metaphysical theology. The metaphysical bent comes out also in Godscroft's play with mathematical ideas, in his analogy for instance between arithmetical proportion and parity of voting and geometrical progression and weighting of votes by hierarchical rank, or in his argument by analogy with circles and spheres that perfect order need not have a first and last.[18]

The sort of mind that we have to deal with in Godscroft cannot be pressed into limited categories and then fitted into a standard intellectual history. He can be aligned with the Humanists and with a critical line of thinking about human discourse and talk about talk running from them through Godscroft's contemporary, Bacon, to the Enlightenment and beyond. But Godscroft has a range of intellectual competence that allows him to use, rather than be used by, the scholastic discipline of logic attacked by Humanists, and even to bring in ideas from speculative theology and mathematics. We have to do with someone admirably cultivated in the intellectual disciplines of his time and able to use them to think intelligently about matters he held to be of first importance to Scottish citizens. All this comes out from looking at the sort of arguments he engages in and his ways of talking about them. It is now time to turn to the arguments themselves. What he had to say about parity in Church government is as interesting as his way of talking about it. If the most impressive thing about his way of arguing is his critical concern with rational discussion, the most impressive thing about what he argues for, parity, is that it is a condition of rational discussion.

---

[17] Like Luther, Calvin took a severely scriptural line with theological argument and was hostile to human philosophical speculative traditions. Godscroft's recourse to God's infinity is then by no means a conventional Calvinist tack. But though infinity is not a keyword in Calvin's *Institutes*, nevertheless Fulke Greville, Godscroft's English Calvinist contemporary, makes frequent use of it to speak of God's unbounded power; see *Caelica*, LXXXVIII, XCVII, XCIX, and CI.

[18] For arithmetical and geometrical proportion, see Calderwood, 7:70, for interminable circles and spheres, Calderwood, 7:81.

The seventeenth-century Scottish controversy between bishop and presbytery, between hierarchy and parity, is not one that any longer enlists many people's intelligence or passions. Moreover, where constitutional history is concerned, Godscroft is more categorical than he ought to be: Knox, as Bishop Cowper, and later Bishops Spottiswoode and Sage maintained, was more Episcopalian than Presbyterian.[19] Until 1592, the government of the reformed Church of Scotland involved bishops, even if they were called 'superintendents'. And consequently Godscroft's contention that James's imposing of bishops was a turning upside down of the constitution of the Kirk is in need of qualification, if not wrong. It would be easy, then, to write off Godscroft as a man of party who argued only to confirm himself in narrow and ill-founded views. But Godscroft's ideas about Church government are important and new ideas about government in general and they take a striking new direction in his political thought. It is as if in the framework of ecclesiastical government, Godscroft was free to think freshly in ways that attachment to 'kindly' Scottish feudal traditions ruled out when he thought about secular politics.[20]

As a political theorist of secular government, Godscroft was the heir of Buchanan. In his *History of the Houses of Douglas and Angus*, he records, or works up, a conversation he had with the eighth Earl of Angus on the right of subjects to rebel against tyrants.[21] This is a wonderfully lively defence of the most notorious of Buchanan's ideas about the Scottish constitution. But Godscroft's theory of the constitution, like Buchanan's, is

---

[19]   The superintendents had originally been appointed by the Kirk and to a Melvillian, who held that the two kingdoms of Church and State were separate, would be an entirely different thing from bishops appointed by the King; nevertheless what is at issue in Godscroft's letters is parity and clearly a superintendent is not quite on the same footing as the pastors or synod he superintends. See 'Of Superintendents' in the Book of Discipline presented to the Convention of January 1561, in John Knox, *The History of the Reformation in Scotland*, ed. William Croft Dickinson, 2 vols. (Edinburgh: Nelson, 1949), 2:291–5, and John Spottiswoode, *The History of the Church of Scotland* (Edinburgh: Spottiswoode Society, 1851), 1:342–45); Calderwood in his copy of the Book of Discipline cannot bring himself to put down this section but records instead the election of John Spottiswoode as Superintendent of Lothian (2:291–295); Gordon Donaldson, *The Scottish Reformation* (Cambridge: Cambridge University Press, 1960), pp. 102–29, 183–225; William Cowper, *The Bishop of Galloway, his Dikaiologie* (London, 1614); Spottiswoode, 2:44–6, 184; John Sage, *The Fundamental Charter of Presbytery, as it hath been Lately Established in the Kingdom of Scotland, Examin'd and Disprov'd* (London: Brome, 1695), pp. 23–38.

[20]   On the importance of 'kindly', see Williamson, *Scottish National Consciousness*, p. 133.

[21]   David Hume of Godscroft, *The History of the Houses of Douglas and Angus* (Edinburgh: Tyler, 1644), pp. 414–29.

limited, first of all because it is a theory only of emergencies.[22] Power may corrupt and kings may always be in danger of becoming tyrants, but actual occasions for rebellion such as, for Godscroft, the misrule of Mary or the Earl of Arran, are after all exceptional. Godscroft, like Buchanan, makes no provision for the ordinary course of government. On the evidence of his *History*, he simply wants strong, competent monarchical rule, but gives no thought to its forms beyond the notion that the Earls of Douglas or of Angus are the King's natural servants and that to deprive them of office is to go against justice and so justify aristocratic rebellion. And that brings up the second limitation. Even more than Buchanan, Godscroft assumes that those who have the right of rebellion are the magnates of the realm. He has no democratic feeling. The people are the rude multitude, which the aristocracy may gratify with shows of brutal retributive justice.[23] As for new men, which include gentry such as the Maitlands, raised to office in recognition of their ability, Godscroft regards them as creatures of misused power, either dependent on and therefore servile to their creator, or unprincipled manipulators.

When it comes to the constitution of the church, though, Godscroft does bend his mind to ordinary government. His defence of parity among ministers is a defence of democratic decision-making in regularly convened assemblies of divines as against hierarchical administration by bishops. It is true that Godscroft argues for parity in church assemblies by saying that they blend aristocratic and democratic principles, aristocratic in that pastors are to their flocks as lords are to their followers and dependents, and democratic in that among themselves they are equals. But Godscroft is not just making ecclesiastical parity palatable by saying it has an

---

[22] My account of Buchanan's views is heavily indebted to Roger A. Mason, '*Rex Stoicus*: George Buchanan, James VI and the Scottish Polity', *New Perspectives on the Politics and Culture of Early Modern Scotland*, ed. John Dwyer, Roger A. Mason and Alexander Murdoch (Edinburgh, [1982]), pp. 19–20. In his Introduction to *A Dialogue on the Law of kingship among the Scots: A Critical Edition and Translation of George Buchanan's* De Iure Regni apud Scotos Dialogus, ed. and trans. Roger A. Mason and Martin S. Smith, Mason draws an important distinction between 'the feudal-baronial conciliarism' of Buchanan's political views in *Rerum Scoticarum Historia* and the much more radical ones in *De Iure*; something like this distinction, holds between the political views to be found in Godscroft's *History of the Houses of Douglas and Angus* and those in the letters to Law, though one could not describe him, even at at his most democratic, as 'radically populist' (p. lxix). See also my article 'Hume of Godscroft on Kings and Subjects' in *Older Scots Literature*, vol. III, ed. Sally Mapstone (East Linton: Tuckwell Press, 2005), pp. 601–3.

[23] See for example the plan for the execution of Riccio and the hanging of Kirkcaldy of Grange, *The History of the Houses of Douglas and Angus*, pp. 289, 329.

admixture of aristocracy. He is thinking boldly and corrosively about forms of government and about terms used to describe them. Aristocracy itself has a democratic side, since nobles are peers in the King's council with equal votes and voices. Words for types of government, Godscroft says, are like words for physiological complexions: no actual case of a melancholy temperament is constituted purely by black bile (Calderwood, 7: 85). This scepticism about names for types of government undermines Law's attempt to characterize episcopal and Presbyterian rule by their essences, to classify them as types of order and disorder and to argue, by analogy with an order of nature for the rule of bishops. It is not that Godscroft disdains arguments from nature: 'Nature and reason so sib as they are, and agreing so weill in one voice' (6:72), furnish arguments for parity. It is just that the clear-cut categories that Law looks for in nature are not to be found there. Nature, in fact, is order in flux and assemblies with temporary moderators elected for the occasion accord with its working as much or more than fixed hierarchy (Calderwood, 7:81).

Godscroft, then, has a philosophy of nature to ground his ideas and his practical intelligence about how words make sense only in context and according to current occasion. It allows him to make what, for the early seventeenth century, is an unusual defence of the word, 'democracy', to distinguish it from ochlocracy or mob rule and to face down the scorn attached conventionally to words like 'confusion' and 'disorder' (Calderwood, 7:86–7).[24]

---

[24]   Godscroft is, however, perhaps expanding on a passage on civil government in John Calvin, *The Institutes of the Christian Religion*, trans. Ford Lewis Battles, ed. John T. McNeill, 2 vols. (Philadelphia: Westminster Press, 1960), Bk. 4, ch. 20, 2:1493–4: 'I will not deny that aristocracy, or a system of aristocracy and democracy, far excels all others: not indeed of itself, but because it is very rare for kings so to control themselves that their will never disagrees with what is just and right; or for them to have been endowed with such great keenness and prudence, that each knows how much is enough. Therefore, men's fault or failing causes it to be safe and more bearable for a number to exercise government, so that they may help one another, teach and admonish one another; and if one asserts himself unfairly, there may be a number of censors and masters to restrain his wilfulness.' Calvin himself is probably adopting Aristotle's remarks on mixed constitutions in *The Politics*, trans. T.A. Sinclair, rev. Trevor J. Saunders, rev. ed. (Harmondsworth: Penguin, 1992), III, xv:1286a36; IV, ix:1294b14; xi:1295a34–b13; xii:1297a6. It is tempting to think that Godscroft's boldness may have owed something to reading Machiavelli. He certainly read Machiavelli's *Prince*, but only to reject him in a fairly conventional point by point rebuttal in *Apologia basilica* (1626); there is no proof that he read *The Discourses*. His theoretical idea that confusion might not be evil in government need not derive from Machiavelli's historical observation (*The Discourses*, ed. Bernard Crick, trans. Leslie J. Walker, S.J., rev. Brian Richardson (Harmondsworth: Penguin, 1974), Bk. 1, ch. 6, p. 124) that the discord between the plebs and the patricians made Rome more powerful any more

But even more remarkable than his acuity about how words must be used in debate is his practical understanding of how democratic assemblies work. He rejects the easy scorn of able and ambitious men for less able, or at least less ambitious, ones and argues that solid decisions are reached through the interaction and exchange in conversation of diversity of ability. To bring out how exceptional what Godscroft is doing here, I have collected a number of passages treating political order arising out of diversity. All make an analogy with diverse parts that go to make a building. Godscroft's is much the earliest one and the one with the most solid political insight. The others, in comparison, seem more concerned to put a rhetorical spin on a generality they approve of than to argue closely for a practical form of politics.

The first of these passages is from Hawthornden's *Irene*, written in 1638 in response to the national Covenant and the seizure of power by the magnates leading a Presbyterian resurgence against the government of Charles I and its Laudian church policies. More than a quarter of a century after Godscroft's letters on parity and more than forty years after his colloquy with the Earl of Angus on the right of resistance to tyranny, his political ideas became operative. Hawthornden uses some of the ideas of that appear in Godscroft's letter of 10 April, 1610 but to opposite ends:

> The Soueraigne creator of this All making no thing but in order, and order not being but where there is difference and diversitie; yea, not onlie this Universe in generall, but there is no creature in it, not a bodye, not a simple that is not composed and existing with some diversitye. Gemmes, gold, the mineralles, the elementes existe not pure: the planetes have a motion contrarye to the first moveable: yet is there a perfect harmonie in all this great frame and a discording Concord maketh all the parcelles of it delightfull. Of the diversitie and varietie which is in this World ariseth that beautie so wonderfull and amazing to our eyes. In architecture diversitie doth not destroy Uniformitie: the limmes of a noble fabricke may be correspondent enough, though they be various. Wee find not two persones of one and the same shape, figure and lineamentes of the Face, lesse of the same conditiones, qualityes, humoures, though they be of the selfe same parentes, and why do we seeke to find men all of one thought and one opinion in formalityes and matteres disputable? or if they shall be found dissonant and disagreeing from the vulgarlie receaved opiniones, or errores, why should wee by our fancye and lawe of Power banish, proscribe, designe or expose them to slaughter?[25]

---

than his readiness to defend 'democracy' need derive from Machiavelli's judgement that the masses are more knowing and more constant than is their Prince (Bk. 1, ch. 58, p. 252).

[25]   William Drummond of Hawthornden, *Poems and Prose*, ed. Robert H. MacDonald (Edinburgh: Scottish Academic Press, 1976), p. 186.

Ideas of nature and human temperaments as mixtures of elements and of good order arising from the play of variety are at work, but at work to reproach the new order, which based itself on Godscroft's principles, if not his actual writings. Godscroft wrote as a politically engaged defender of Presbyterian church government and of aristocratic curbing of royal power. Drummond uses similar turns of thought to deprecate the intolerance of the politically engaged and to recommend an acceptance of compromise attractive to his cultivated withdrawal from the political life of his country, attractive also perhaps to the Royalist party in retreat, but only as an agreeably disengaged fiction of moderation about the world they had lost or the order they would bring back. It is a wistful rhetorical remonstration rather than an argument closely engaging with the political situation or putting forward a theory of monarchical government as moderating extremes.

Milton wrote his *Areopagitica* in 1644 to defend the press in Parliamentarian London against censorship. Seeing in the intellectual ferment of the city and the spate of controversial tracts a general and brotherly search after truth, he launches into a magnificent praise of the attempt to build a new political order out of disorder:

> Yet these are the men cry'd out against for schismaticks and sectaries; as if, while the Temple of the Lord was building, some cutting, some squaring the marble, others hewing the cedars, there should be a sort of irrationall men who could not consider there must be many schisms and many dissections made in the quarry and in the timber, ere the house of God can be built. And when every stone is laid artfully together, it cannot be united into a continuity, it can be but contiguous in this world; neither can every peece of the building be of one form; nay rather the perfection consists in this, that out of many moderat varieties and brotherly dissimilitudes that are not vastly disproportionall arises the goodly and the gracefull symmetry that commends the whole pile and structure. Let us therefore be more considerat builders, more wise in spirituall architecture, when great reformation is expected.[26]

Milton is usually more abrasive than Godscroft about the multitude. But here his characteristic feeling for the freeing of impulse and liberation of individual energy as expressions of a divine unboundedness takes a more generous direction towards shared activity and joint effort than is usual with him.[27] That makes the passage so noble and attractive that one does

---

[26] John Milton, *Areopagitica*, ed. Ernest Sirluck in *Complete Prose Works of John Milton*, Vol. 2, 1643–8 (New Haven: Yale University Press, 1959), p. 555.

[27] Like Godscroft, Milton has a religious or metaphysical notion of divine infinity that may take in confusion and uses it to justify radical political ideas; see for instance his dismissal of episcopacy in the light of the unconstraint in heaven,

not wish to inquire too closely how the rhetoric tallies with the political reality. One takes it as a lofty expression of political idealism more than as a political insight or a practical theory of government.

The passage from Marvell's 'The First Anniversary of the Government under H.H. the Lord Protector' of 1655 perhaps takes a hint from Milton and is even more magnificent.[28] It celebrates Cromwell's Instrument of Government of 1653 as like Amphion's bringing together the stones of Thebes by the strong music of his lyre; so Cromwell was able by his political magic to bring together the disparate and discordant elements of the country into a working constitution.

> The commonwealth then first together came,
> And each one entered in the willing frame;
> All other matter yields, and may be ruled;
> But who the minds of stubborn men can build?
> No quarry bears a stone so hardly wrought,
> Nor with such labour from its centre brought;
> None to be sunk in the foundation bends,
> Each in the house the highest place contends,
> And each the hand that lays him will direct,
> And some fall back upon the architect;
> Yet all composed by his attractive song,
> Into the animated city throng.
>
> The commonwealth does through their centres all
> Draw the circumf'rence of the public wall;
> The crossest spirits here do take their part,
> Fast'ning the contignation which they thwart;
> And they, whose nature leads them to divide,
> Uphold this one, and that the other side;
> But the most equal still sustain the height,
> And they as pillars keep the work upright;
> While the resistance of opposèd minds,
> The fabrick (as with arches) stronger binds,

conveyed in oxymorons such as 'eccentricall equation' and 'invariable Planet' in *The Reason of Church Government*, ed. Ralph Haug, *The Prose Works of John Milton*, 8 vols. (New Haven: Yale Univ. Press, 1953–82), 1:74–81, 752. As with Godscroft, there is no evidence that this way of exalting political confusion owes anything to Machiavelli's *Discourses*.

[28]   That Marvell took a hint from Milton is the contention of the note to ll. 89–96 in *The Poems and Letters of Andrew Marvell*, 3rd edition, ed. H.M. Margouliouth, rev. Pierre Legouis and E.E. Duncan Jones (Oxford: Clarendon Press, 1971), p. 322, followed by Nigel Smith in *The Poems of Andrew Marvell* (London: Pearson, Longman, 2003), p. 290.

Which on the basis of a senate free,
Knit by the roof's protecting weight agree. (ll. 75–98)[29]

It is possible that Marvell's praise of Cromwell's Instrument of Government owed something to ideas of a balanced constitution circulating and published in 1656, the year after Marvell's poem, in Harrington's *Oceana*.[30] But Marvell's flight soars beyond political reality. In the first place, the image of a semi-divine constitutional architect eclipses any libertarian constitutional ideas. Vaulting ambition is a normally masked or ironized side of Marvell's personality; here it escapes forthrightly in his admiration of Cromwell. In the second place, the Instrument of Government was a failure and it should already have been apparent that Cromwell was as little able to manage deliberative assemblies as Charles I. If there is serious constitutional thinking behind the passage, encomiastic hyperbole takes over from it. Of course, this can hardly be blamed in a celebratory poem.

Godscroft's defence of heterogeneity in politics is not without eloquence.

And therefore, perhaps, has wisdom himself made choice of this sort of governement ratherest, in that diversitie yee write of graces which he has givin, and thus diversified, not to distinguishe degrees so muche, as to mixe gifts in the governement of his kirk by manie, according, as by harmonie, one with another: other where they are good, suppleing where defects are, ballancing and counterposing where imperfectiouns and infirmiteis are, rather than to concredit the government therof ather to one or to a few.

We can give a reasoun, ay, and it is eneugh that he thus of that way ordeanned things [i.e. in scripture]. Yitt may it be seene to the sight of the eye [i.e. to natural reason], this equall power of governement in unequall things not to be so farre out of purpose as we will declame, but of a wisdome rather to be admired, letting men see their mutuall mister, and making them furnishe mutuall helpe. Subtilitie and quicknesse in one (least it may vanish) fixed with the soliditie of another soliditie, and grosser humour of this stirred up with the spiritinesse of that other ambitioun; heere soaring up to the cloudes, drawin doun therre by a counterweight wisdom and learning, least they might debord; in some, holdin with more exquisite bonds of sinceritie, in another sinceritie again, least it might become simplicitie, sharpened by the whetstone of the wiser and more learned. Loe nature, loe the voice of reasoun. (7:76–7)

Godscroft is not, however, writing celebratory poetry, like Marvell, or, like Hawthornden or Milton, deliberately attempting rhetorical elevation. The analogy, if indeed it is present, of the building made with different stones

---

[29]   The text follows Smith, pp. 289–90.

[30]   See Jonathan Scott, *Commonwealth Principles: Republican Writing of the English Revolution* (Cambridge: Cambridge University Press, 2004), pp. 142–3.

is present only glancingly in a pun on 'edify', from the Latin *aedificare*, 'to build'. When he uses analogies it is for witty clinching of a point ('no flowres of rhetorick, (except such as serve for cleerenesse, not ornament')) (6:748). His is a plain, closely argued style. The series of antitheses showing how different sorts of minds balance and correct each other is an unusually expanded amplification for Godscroft, but little more than is required for his rapid and sinewy exposition of his idea[31] and in any event strikingly spare in comparison with Drummond's leisurely and copious series of balances expatiating on his idea of comprehension of diversity; strikingly spare too in comparison with Milton's violent and sublime forcing of a scriptural parallel through puns on 'schisms' and 'dissections', where the much railed-upon divisions of the schismatics and sectaries are compared to the masons' hewing of the stones of Solomon's temple.[32]

Moreover, the idea Godscroft is putting forward also seems to be more in touch with political experience than Hawthornden's or Milton's or Marvell's and more solid. He is justifying parity in deliberative assemblies against Law's idea that it is fitter that the ablest should rule. Having questioned the grounds on which ability might be assessed – age eloquence, experience, learning – and suggested that rank might induce people to discern outstanding gifts rather than outstanding gifts be the cause of elevation to rank, he comes up with an idea of communicative reason, to borrow Habermas's term.[33] The rationality and good judgement of deliberative assemblies does not lie in the pre-eminent ability of an individual but in the interaction of the whole body of various individuals. In the same spirit, elsewhere, he argues that it is only in such a free market

---

[31]   Professor Mason has pointed out to me that Godscroft may be working with Aristotle's idea of the mean (*Nicomachaean Ethics*, II, vi–ix); Godscroft's application of Aristotle's idea of individual virtue to virtuous government would, however, be his own development; it is not the application Aristotle himself makes of the idea of the mean in *Politics*, IV, ii:1295a34. See also Godscroft's debt to Calvin, indicated above, note 24; Calvin is perhaps glossing Aristotle's remarks (*Politics*, III, xi:1281a39–b32; xv:1286a21) on the wisdom of collective judgements, but Calvin's hint, splendidly developed by Godscroft. is vastly more interesting than Aristotle's platitude.

[32]   Sirluck, *Areopagitica*, p. 555, notes another typically Miltonic violence. Milton appropriates a scriptural place usually employed to enjoin conformity and to forbid controversy; all hewing of wood and stone was banished from the building site to the quarries and groves so that holy silence might be kept as the Temple rose.

[33]   See Jürgen Habermas, *The Philosophical Discourse of Modernity*, trans. Frederick Lawrence (Cambridge: Polity, 1987), pp. 294–326.

of ability and opinion that the best judgements can prevail; hierarchy tends to distort or suppress the weight of what is being said.[34]

Obviously Godscroft is talking in ideal terms in appealing to nature and reason. His following appeal to use and experience, that the Kirk was better governed by parity than by hierarchy would be bitterly contested by James and his bishops (Calderwood, 7:77; cf. 89–90). Besides, without entering into that controversy, it seems obvious that if the Kirk did work democratically, it must, like other democracies, have done so partly through caballing, intrigue and backstairs politicking. Yet if they are to work, deliberative assemblies also need an ideal of communicative rationality. It is the unusual merit of Godscroft's letter of 10 April 1610, that it raises the contemporary issues that prompted him to write to what seems a still cogent defence of some aspects of such an ideal.

---

[34] Calderwood, 7:77–8; on p. 78 Godscroft has an interesting argument for thinking the assent of an assembly where parity is the rule answers to Aristotle's idea of distributive justice (probably *Politics*, III, ix:1280a21; xii:1282b23–b34): 'it most rightlie gives and distributes to everie man, according to the said proportioun, their own due regard and reverent respect; in greatest measure to the greatest gifts, power and government in equall measure to the greatest gifts, power and government to the whole, because whole are equal in it'. To clinch his argument that to give power of decision to bishops goes against distributive justice, he cites the tale in Xenophon's *Cyropaedia*, I, 3, 16–17, of the boy Cyrus, who was whipped by his tutor for taking a big coat that belonged to a little boy to give it to a big one; the tale is also cited in *Basilicon Doron*, 1:149, but in a different context.

PART III
Reception

CHAPTER 11

Political theatre or heritage culture? *Ane Satyre of the Thrie Estaitis* in production

Adrienne Scullion

Sir David Lindsay's *Ane Satyre of the Thrie Estaitis* is the most dramaturgically innovative and historically celebrated theatrical text of the Scottish Reformation. Formally highly stylized, thematically daring and politically sophisticated, the play is the masterpiece of Scotland's Reformation culture. With its heady combination of complex secular commentary, profound sacred drama, poetical sophistry and with the addition of knockabout farce it transcends modern genres and defies categorisation. However, despite the fact that literary scholars can readily claim it as an unrivalled high point of the nation's drama, the play has only a precarious foothold in the producing repertoire of theatre in Scotland – and, beyond the academy, is ignored elsewhere.[1] Radically satirical in its day, the play's very contemporaneity – along with its late-medieval dramaturgical form – meant that it fell quickly out of ideological and theatrical fashion and, when the play was finally revived, the values it sought to represent and promote were very different from the play's particular and political purpose at the sixteenth-century Scottish court. Instead of a play seeking to influence contemporary policy-making and policy-makers, its twentieth-century impact has been very different. Reviewing the play's modern stage history, one encounters a series of productions readier to draw on the values of heritage culture than of political theatre with this potential conservatism marked in staging, costuming and casting choices,

---

[1]   This essay draws on materials held in the Scottish Theatre Archive (STA), part of the Department of Special Collections of the library of the University of Glasgow. This collection holds a significant collection of primary material relating to the several twentieth-century productions of *Ane Satyre* ... including programmes, miscellaneous press cuttings, photographs and related correspondence, as well as some of the other publications and materials referred to in this essay.

While Joanne Spencer Kantrowitz is surely correct to attest 'a drama that scarcely exists outwith the groves of Academe', this essay will demonstrate that she overstates the play's production history when she argues that, from the mid twentieth century, it 'has enjoyed a vigorous stage life in Britain'. Joanne Spencer Kantrowitz, *Dramatic Allegory: Lindsay's Ane Satyre of the Thrie Estaitis* (Lincoln: University of Nebraska Press, 1975), p. 1.

as well as in production, editorial and directorial choices as regards the
text and language, staging and performance.

Early productions

The play is known to have been performed three times in the sixteenth
century: as an indoor interlude performance to the court at the palace of
Linlithgow in 1540, of which the text is lost and little detail known; and
then outdoors on Castle Hill in Cupar, Fife, in 1552 and on the Greenside
Playfield on Calton Hill, Edinburgh, in 1554.

Many scholars – including Anna Jean Mill, Roderick Lyall and Walker
himself – have explored and interpreted the text and contemporary stagings
of *Ane Satyre* in relation to Lindsay's close association with James V and
his various courtly roles, including that of Lyon King of Arms, as well
as the wider debate about religion, politics and society within sixteenth-
century Scotland.[2] This contextualizing scholarship underlines Lindsay's
status as a political playwright, not in a twentieth-century materialist
sense but instead as writing, reflecting on, testing and influencing policy-
making at the highest levels of his contemporary society and doing so with
a sustained critique of political will and process.

The mid sixteenth century was a period of religious and political debate
and upheaval in Scotland and *Ane Satyre* has been shown as operating at the
centre of this ferment. Lindsay's high-profile role at the heart of Scotland's
contemporary elite and his reformist religious politics are key points of
entry in understanding *Ane Satyre*: indeed, these two elements combine in
Greg Walker's argument that Lindsay's 'demands for reform were always
framed within the parameters of practical politics'.[3] It is, in Walker's view,
such a *real politick* that underpins Lindsay's complex play, delineating a
playwright who was both pragmatic about and aspirational in his politics.
It is this immediate and particular political imperative – with its complex
nexus of textual allusions and metaphors, as well as what might very
well be seen as archaic language and antiquated form – that presents the
modern production with clear challenges if it is to achieve something other
than an archaeologizing re-staging. Can this play's politics – critiquing

---

[2] For example, and in addition to the previous citation: Anna Jean Mill,
'Representations of Lindsay's *Satyre of the Thrie Estaitis*', *PMLA* 47 (1932),
pp. 636–51, and 'The original version of Lindsay's *Satyre of the Thrie Estaitis*',
SSL, 6 (1968/1969), pp. 67–75; John MacQueen, '*Ane Satyre of the Thrie Estaitis*',
SSL, 3 (1965/1966), pp. 129–43; and, Roderick Lyall (ed.), *The Thrie Estaitis*
(Edinburgh: Canongate, 1989), pp. ix–xiv.

[3] Greg Walker, *The Politics of Performance in Early Renaissance Drama*
(Cambridge: Cambridge University Press, 1998), p. 123.

power and challenging the responsibility of elites – be recovered in modern productions that are so removed from its original production contexts?

First revivals

It was only after four centuries of neglect and with the explicit aim of representing Scotland – and, by implication representing Scotland's cultural credentials and values – to a national (Scottish and UK) and to an international audience that *Ane Satyre* was brought back to the producing stage.

The Edinburgh International Festival (EIF) had been launched in 1947 – in the immediate aftermath of World War II – with the explicit aim of contributing towards post-War European reconciliation and reconstruction. The organizers sought to bring together the best of international music, dance and theatre for an arts event in one of the few great European cities left undamaged by the War. However, the first festival was criticized for its lack of Scottish representation. The organizers – who included the playwright James Bridie, founder and director the Glasgow Citizens' Theatre – moved to fill this perceived gap. For the second festival, in August 1948, the Festival's organizing committee invited the director Tyrone Guthrie 'to direct a company of Scottish actors in a Scots play; if possible, a classic'.[4] The repertoire of Scottish plays being notoriously limited Guthrie's reading list was, predictably, short: it consisted of Allan Ramsay's *The Gentle Shepherd* (1725) and John Home's *Douglas* (1756), and Lindsay's *Ane Satyre*. Determined 'to make a bold gesture in favour of Scottish Drama', Guthrie dismissed the first as having 'immense charm' but more 'Poetry Recital rather than a play' and the second as merely 'a dramatic curiosity'. Still searching for 'something larger and louder', Guthrie records that he 'sat down with a rather sinking heart to the two thick, squat, drab of volumes of *The Three Estates*, with their teasing, difficult spelling, their columns of "Notes", their much needed Glossary'.[5]

In his search for something 'large and loud' *Ane Satyre* certainly fits the bill – it is a huge text, full of great poetry, wicked humour and an eclectic cast of characters extending to some 44 speaking parts.[6] Perhaps unexpectedly, however, Guthrie also chose Lindsay's play for its performative potential: 'For all its difficulties,' he wrote, 'it was soon apparent that Lindsay knew

---

[4] David Lindsay, *The Satire of the Three Estates*, with an Introduction by Tyrone Guthrie (London: Heinemann, 1951), pp. vii–xi, p. vii.

[5] Lindsay, *The Satire of the Three Estates* (1951), pp. vii–viii.

[6] The most useful modern edition – Roderick Lyall (ed.), *The Thrie Estaitis* (Edinburgh: Canongate, 1989) – runs close to 5000 lines.

how to write for actors; and I thought that we had actors in Scotland who could do him justice.'[7]

Arguably, Guthrie is alluding to not only a quantity of actors active within the burgeoning Scottish theatre industry of the post-war period but also a quality, or style, in their stage presence and technique. In the introduction to the production he wrote for the festival's Souvenir Programme, Guthrie underscored his

> confident belief that good Scottish acting has a distinctive quality and can make a valuable contribution, not only as an amenity of Scottish life, but by interpreting Scotland abroad. But this can never occur so long as Scotland's professional actors have either to acquire an English metropolitan style or else be confined to 'dialect' character-parts and exhibitions of pawkiness labelled 'For Export Only'.[8]

Certainly the generation of actors that included Stanley Baxter (Correction's varlet in the 1948 production), Duncan Macrae (Flatterie, Pardoner), Lennox Milne (Veritie), Jean Taylor Smith (Chastitie) and Molly Urquhart (Dame Sensualitie) was a uniquely versatile one, emerging from a richly diverse amateur theatre sector, that drew on a similarly wide range of theatre traditions, and with proven ability to work across media and genres from mainstream film and public-service radio to agit-prop, pantomime and other popular forms that demanded rather different skills to communicate with an audience that those of the dominant British ('English') 'rep' style. As Guthrie's programme note makes explicit, it was this new generation, and just as importantly its emergent industry, that this production deliberately and explicitly presented to the world, albeit showcased in a four hundred year-old play.

Having made the decision in favour of *Ane Satyre* – and having expressed his confidence in the immediate acting community – Guthrie commissioned a new version of the text from Robert Kemp, an Edinburgh-based playwright with a strong reputation in respect of adaptation for both the stage and radio. Reflecting on his approach to the adaptation process Kemp argued that his 'guiding principle was to prune down to [the] action so that there should always be something happening on the stage'.[9] With this aim in mind he produced a new text redesigned to be 'actable by modern

------

[7]   Lindsay, *The Satire of the Three Estates* (1951), pp. vii–viii.

[8]   Tyrone Guthrie, 'The Satire of the Three Estates: the setting and presentation', *The International Festival of Music and Drama, Edinburgh 1948, Souvenir Programme* (Edinburgh: EIF, 1948), p. 21.

[9]   David Lindsay, *The Satire of the Three Estates*, the acting text prepared by Robert Kemp for Tyrone Guthrie's production at the Edinburgh Festival 1949,

actors and comprehensible to a modern audience': Lindsay's verse was substantially cut back and restructured and some of the extremes of tone were levelled out. This was achieved by cutting some of the knockabout elements of the play as well as its more lewd exchanges – although the Scots of the original was for the most part retained.[10] Of the adaptation process Guthrie recognized that 'cuts have had to be so drastic that there has often been need of some sewing up of gaping wounds, and some smoothing of raw edges'.[11] This was achieved by judicious interventions and rewrites. Kemp, for example, excised much of the theological debate and rhetoric – both formally alien to modern theatre audiences and rather overly specific to the immediate debates in and concerns of Lindsay's own society for ready understanding. He also recast the play into a two-part structure: 'the first dealing with moral and personal problems of conduct and conscience of the Individual, represented by King Humanity; the second [which incorporated the previously separate Interlude], with the political and social problems of The Group'. Two less obvious cuts were the removal of Folly, a late entry in Lindsay's original to begin with, while the violent hanging of the Vices is significantly compressed with their speeches and addresses cut. With an eye to the sensibilities of their modern audience – and, of course, to the requirements of the Lord Chamberlain – Kemp and Guthrie also cut Lindsay's 'coarse and rough' *entr'acte* sketches that included some of the play's more bawdy comedy.[12]

Even before rehearsals had begun Guthrie had galvanized some of the leading forces of cultural Scotland into contributing to and supporting his EIF production: Kemp was, of course, adapting the text; Bridie was championing the production on the Festival committee and, in some measure, acting as producer too; and, Cedric Thorpe Davie had been commissioned to write a new score. The cast consisted of just about every one of Scotland's nascent professional acting community – including Stanley Baxter, Archie Duncan, Moultrie Kelsall, Duncan Macrae, Lennox Milne, Bryden Murdoch, Jean Taylor Smith and Molly Urquhart who were already well-known figures on Scottish stages from the days of the Scottish National Players and, more recently, at the Citizens' Theatre, in commercial touring productions and in radio broadcasts. Official support

---

with an Introduction by Robert Kemp (Edinburgh: *The Scots Review*, [1949]), pp. i–vii, p. vi.

[10]   Lindsay, *The Satire of the Three Estates*, the acting text ([1949]), p. i.

[11]   Ibid., p. ix.

[12]   Lindsay, *The Satire of the Three Estates* (1951), p. viii. In passing, and while some of these cuts did edge back into the performed text over the years, it remains the case that Lindsay's play has not been performed in its entirety in modern times.

also came in the form of the Lord Provost of Edinburgh who addressed an early rehearsal telling 'the assembled actors of his confidence that theirs would prove to be an outstanding contribution to the Festival'.[13] Guthrie's call on establishment Scotland was further reinforced with his choice of playing space: the Assembly Hall of the Church of Scotland on The Mound in Edinburgh was a venue distinctively representative of Presbyterian Scotland, a room uniquely imbued with the values and meanings of the Reformation. However, and perhaps a little unconvincingly, Guthrie claims some counter-cultural potential in his chosen site:

> The entrance, grim, black, forbidding but impressive, with its endless stone stairs, was just the right prelude to the play. [...] The general air of solid, smug, well-fed respectability, the sage-green upholstery, the stained glass [...] the strong odour of sanctity [...]; were all so sharply opposed to the whole spirit and feeling of the play, so gloriously wrong, that, perversely, I was convinced of their rightness.[14]

Certainly, in 1948 British theatre, such a non-traditional choice of playing space – and the staging choices subsequently made within the space – was bold and added an extra element of interest for local and visiting audiences. Intriguingly most subsequent productions of the play have used this same venue. Arguably, though, with each revival, the play's associations have become less political, less satirical, and more conservative and containable. Further, it is revealing to note that not only have subsequent productions generally used the same performance site – and Kemp's adaptation and Davie's music – additionally most have also used – or at least borrowed heavily from – Guthrie's staging, including his innovative thrust stage, processions, connotations of the tradition of medieval mansions and entrances through the auditorium. As described by Guthrie:

> The play was given in the centre of the auditorium on a stage about twenty-five feet by fifteen feet, accessible from three of its four sides by shallow steps. The audience sat around threes sides of the stage: behind the fourth side there was a gallery approached by stairs from the main stage. On this gallery sat the Spiritual Estate. Beneath it was a curtained recess, into which the King and Courtiers retired with Sensuality and her train. Nobles and Merchants sat in a sort of jury boxes flanking this gallery. Entrances were made through the

---

[13]   Lindsay, *The Satire of the Three Estates*, the acting text ([1949]), p. i.

[14]   Lindsay, *The Satire of the Three Estates* (1951), p. x.

audience, down the aisles.[15] The Three Estates were three groups of singers. In addition to these Three Estates we showed a Fourth – the disfranchised Poor, who took place at the end of the stage furthest from their noble and wealthy kinsmen. They lay in squalid rags on the steps and, as the mob always will, noisily supported whichever party seemed temporarily in the ascendant. At this end of the stage were the stocks; and later the gallows.[16]

For Cordelia Oliver this staging signalled a daring and unconventional scenography and proxemics:

> Scenic realism was thrown out of the window; here, after all, is no demand for illusion, immediate contact with the audience being the very essence of the play in which the actors, as often as not, are addressing their audience directly.[17]

This actor-audience relationship – direct, reflexive and interrogative – was enabled through this 'immediate contact with the audience' and it is especially this aspect of the production that might be identified as particularly suiting Scottish acting talent, performance styles and traditions. It is not that there is an argument for some direct line of performance practice from the medieval to the modern but that, in the recovered indigenous and professional theatre industry of the twentieth century, performers very often came from or drew directly on the tropes, styles and conventions of the local popular traditions of pantomime, geggy and variety. For example, in recording the play's modern history 'of providing good Scottish players with opportunities for memorable performances', Oliver argues that Duncan Macrae's performances as Flatterie 'revealed to the full his brilliant clown's gift for the kind of comedy that can be engaging and disquieting at one and the same time'.[18] The roots of the popular in modern Scottish theatre go well beyond a dramaturgical propensity towards the local, the immediate, nostalgia, humour and use of dialect and, as Oliver intimates, also influences performance modes and styles.[19]

---

[15]   In one account 'the players came and went freely […] up and down the aisles' and did so 'often rumbustiously enough to send shocks through an audience unused to such intimacy'. See Cordelia Oliver, '*Ane Satyre of The Thrie Estaitis*', typescript of unidentified article (STA Cm Box 11/11).

[16]   Lindsay, *The Satire of the Three Estates* (1951), p. x.

[17]   Oliver, *Ane Satyre of The Thrie Estaitis*.

[18]   Oliver, *Ane Satyre of The Thrie Estaitis*.

[19]   For a variety of approaches to the place of the popular in Scottish drama see, for example: John McGrath, *A Good Night Out: Popular Theatre, Audience, Class and Form* (London: Eyre Methuen, 1981); Alasdair Cameron, *Study Guide to Scottish Theatre* (Glasgow: Department of Scottish Literature, University of Glasgow, 1988); Femi Folorunso, 'Scottish drama and the popular tradition', in

The 1948 production was revived – with most of the same actors in most of the same roles – at the 1949 and 1951 EIF and, with some new cast members, in 1959, being increasingly framed as 'a vital part of the Festival's history'.[20] At each production the same text, score, location and staging applied with actors either retaining a much-loved role or maturing into new ones: for example, Macrae played both Flatterie and the Pardoner in 1948, 1949, 1951 and 1959; and, Bryden Murdoch was the King in 1948 and 1949 but Gude-Counsall in 1959.[21]

Linking back to Guthrie's initial reaction to the play, it is clear that, however removed the words and their meanings might seem, with actors ambitious for their craft and industry, Lindsay's play was capable of communicating some strong messages about the capacity of post-war Scottish culture to people a local and an international cultural agenda.

The role of the EIF in presenting this new theatre culture to a wider and international audience should not be underestimated – actors tested their craft in a demanding text in an unconventional staging and in front of an informed and discriminating audience and they achieved huge success.

In 1950 the EIF commissioned a different production for the same slot and with essentially the same purpose of presenting the achievements of Scottish theatre to an international audience: the Citizens' Theatre presented a similarly celebratory production of Home's *Douglas* (1950) – one of the plays rejected by Guthrie for 1948 – in a production directed by John Casson and starring Sybil Thorndike and Lewis Casson with new music again composed by Cedric Thorpe Davie and other former *Ane Satyre* performers, including Stanley Baxter, James Gibson and Lennox Milne, in the cast. *Douglas* was played in rep with the premiere of Bridie's *The Queen's Comedy* – the first new Scottish play to appear at the EIF but one that was just as allegorical as Lindsay's in its exploration of war in both classical and modern times. While supervising the 1951 revival of *Ane Satyre* Guthrie even gave his second runner-up play, *The Gentle Shepherd*, an outing when it was given as a rehearsed reading, directed by Guthrie and with members of his *Ane Satyre* company.

By 1951, the year of Bridie's death, it would be fair to say that modern Scottish theatre had arrived. In the previous decade at least five theatres and one major theatre company had been started in Scotland; the government

---

Randall Stevenson and Gavin Wallace (eds), *Scottish Theatre since the Seventies* (Edinburgh: Edinburgh University Press, 1996), pp. 176–85.

[20]   Michael Billington, 'The Thrie Estaitis', *The Guardian* 14 August 1984, unpaginated press cutting (STA Cm Box 11/11).

[21]   This pattern continued in subsequent professional productions: for example, Walter Carr was Deceit in 1959 but assumed the roles of Flattery/Pardoner in 1983, 1985 and 1986; Lennox Milne was Veritie in 1948, 1949, 1951 and 1973; while Bryden Murdoch returned to the role of Gude-Counsall in 1973.

had begun to fund the arts through a system of direct state subsidy; the combination of this with the growth of regional broadcasting meant that the possibility of a Scottish acting profession had been opened up; as outlined, the EIF had begun, and Scotland's dramatic heritage had been displayed there without shame; there had also been a deluge of new plays on Scottish themes by Scottish writers – and these had begun to break through in the context of EIF and its 'fringe'. The retrospective of the classical repertory of Scottish theatre – this review of the dramatic heritage of the nation – came at the very time the theatre industry entered a new age of professional practice and mature, integrated infrastructure. The goal of the 1948 festival committee to programme something demonstrably 'Scottish' – in Guthrie's rather problematic terms something 'typically and authentically Scottish' – was certainly achieved with this production as was a recognition that Scottish professional theatre making had 'arrived': 'Reflecting on the occasion, Jack House wrote in the *Scottish Drama Year Book*: "It is difficult to say who were the more astonished – the Scots who thought that nothing good could be done by people they knew personally, or the London critics who thought nothing good could be done by people they didn't know personally."'[22] This achievement – in terms of a theatre culture – was immense, underlining a unique coming of age. But despite the production of Bridie's new play about war, still a raw issue for Europe in 1950, the success of *Ane Satyre* and its revivals, and the variations on its revivals, presented the Scottish theatre to the UK and international cultural community as a backward-looking culture. Here was an industry full of skilled workers and not wanting ambition but also one wherein history was denuded of politics and mined little in respect of exploring or critiquing contemporary society.

Guthrie's productions of *Ane Satyre* certainly raised the profile of Scottish actors, but his scenographic choices were significant too, with his open, apron-style staging proving particularly influential in subsequent theatre architecture, above all that architecture associated with Guthrie himself as he developed the idea further in the new builds of Stratford, Ontario and Minneapolis, which subsequently influenced the Sheffield Crucible and Leeds Playhouse. Meanwhile, the production itself coalesced in the wider culture as 'a symbol of regeneration in Scottish theatre'.[23]

In contrast, however, what reviewers, critics and recollections of the various revivals of Guthrie's production do not highlight is a social politics drawn out from the play text itself that might have messages for this

---

[22]   Allen Wright, 'Revival of *The Thrie Estaitis*' *The Scotsman* 13 August 1984, unpaginated press cutting (STA Cm Box 11/11).

[23]   Peter Easton, 'The Thrie Estaitis', *Scottish Theatre News*, 41 (1984), pp. 5–7, p. 5.

post-War society renegotiating social and class hierarchies and rebuilding structures of power and democracy. Indeed, and astonishingly quickly, a sense of *Ane Satyre* as an off-the-shelf flagship production coalesced and it was this theatrical rather than political legacy that was at least part of the motivation behind revivals of the play in the 1980s – when Scottish political culture was under pressure due to Thatcherism but the play instead connoted values of continuity – for example, casting through lines may be drawn clearly – and past glory. Before that, though, came two slightly different productions that merit some comment.

Other agendas

Between the pageant of Tyrone Guthrie/Tom Fleming productions in the 1940s and 1980s come two others: a 1969 production directed by academic James Arnott for the Glasgow-based semi-professional Arts Theatre Group and the Departments of Drama, Scottish History and Literature at the University of Glasgow; and, a production for the 1973 EIF, in a new version by Tom Wright, directed by Bill Bryden, but again played in the Assembly Hall with a familiar cross-section of Scotland's best-known performers.

1969

To stage *Ane Satyre* is a huge undertaking for any group of theatre makers. It has a large cast of characters and types, it is dramaturgically and theatrically ambitious, and for performers and audiences alike it is linguistically challenging and complex in meaning. Yet, by all accounts, the production led by Arnott, with his mixed cast of semi-professional performers, recent graduates and undergraduate students, fully realized its ambition.

The text was minimally adapted by Arnott from the first printed edition of Lindsay's play from 1602 relating to the 1554 production: again a key objective in the edit was to limit the size of the text with stanzas being edited out of long speeches and complete exchanges – for example, much of the scene between the Soutar and his Wife towards the end of act I and the Folly-Diligence exchange in act II – being cut wholly.[24] Nevertheless, a key element of Arnott's text that was inclusion of Lindsay's powerful sermon

---

[24] See annotated version of the script (STA Bk 8/1) and marked up copy of Sir David Lindsay, *A Satire of the Three States*. A play adapted by Matthew McDiarmid from the acting text made by Robert Kemp for Tyrone Guthrie's production at the Edinburgh Festival 1948 with music by Cedric Thorpe-Davie.

that, transcending the political allusions to sixteenth-century Scotland, fully distils the play's moral purpose into one powerful and compelling speech presented directly to the audience. The impact of the sequence remains strong in memories of the 1969 participants and audiences alike. Like Guthrie's production, the playing space was a found, non-theatre one: the Gilbert Scott-designed Victorian-Gothic Bute Hall at the University of Glasgow offered a large open playing space but with difficult sightlines and acoustic dead spots principally the consequence of a deep balcony running around three sides of the elegant, high-ceilinged hall. Arnott's staging solution was something of a variation on the traverse – with two proscenia at each end of the hall and a central raised dais. Whilst retaining something of the pageantry and the processions associated with the play this production did not use the mansion motif and static choruses of Guthrie's work, and reviewers and performers commented on the use of movement and, increasingly, gesture as bringing subtlety and human drama to the morality play.

> The first act was smooth, turbulent, syrupy and fiery in turns. In contrast, the second act with its attack on the Church's corruption was more static, producing the necessary contrast to the first which was sensuous – dependent on continuous flow [of performers and action through the playing space] for impact. In act two [...] the eye did not have to follow the movement but had to focus on one spot, with the audience concentration also fixed.[25]

Set and costume design were realized by a large team of volunteers and the high production values achieved were commented on by contemporary reviewers and are evidenced by photographs of the production and confirmed by those involved. An orchestra of some 16 supported the production with musical tones shifting from sixteenth-century recorder music to dramatic interventions by the hall's great organ.

The University's Department of Drama had been established only in 1966 and this production forged deliberate links between it and other parts of the University – the academic departments of Scottish History and Literature, Music, and English as well as University management, estates and service units.

Ane Satyre presented Arnott and his team with robust dramaturgical choices and staging demands that needed thoughtful solutions and lent themselves to a production of scale and, appropriately to mark the new

---

Introduction and notes by Matthew McDiarmid (London: Heinemann Education, 1967). (STA Hj 21)

[25]   Sheena MacKay, 'Estates – a triumphant pageant', *Scottish Theatre* (May 1969), p. 22 (STA Hm 10/3).

department, celebration. The challenge of the production was to declare theatre and drama – and, indeed, Scottish theatre and Scottish drama – as a legitimate locus for the academic exploration of place, image, representation and identity. It should not, therefore, belittle this production to identify it as an academic one – a practical exploration of text and staging making significant demands on participants and audiences and fully focused on exploring, interpreting and understanding Lindsay's play and his characters and their theatrical world.

1973

In 1973 Edinburgh's Royal Lyceum Theatre Company – at the time something of a powerhouse of Scottish theatre making and writing under the leadership of Clive Perry and his lieutenants, Richard Eyre and Bill Bryden – commissioned a new and arguably rather edgier adaptation of Lindsay's play from Tom Wright to be directed at the EIF by Bryden.[26] Key structural and tonal differences from Kemp's adaptation were the retention of at least part of Lindsay's long sermon in the middle, the inclusion on Folly towards the end and the recovery of some of the bawdiest of humour. Key similarities with Guthrie's' production included the EIF production context, its location in the Assembly Hall, and much of the cast. These similarities – and, in particular, continuity of casting – were an aspect of the production particularly significant in marketing terms as it signalled the production's heritage within the Scottish theatre industry and EIF, assured familiarity and promised 'quality' for audiences. Nevertheless, Bryden was keen to mark significant shifts in the industry and, at least implicitly, place the Lyceum's recent success story at the heart of the revival:

> One of the great things about his company [...] is that they know each other so well, and act together naturally. [...] Guthrie lives on in their memories. [...] They obviously loved him. He was older that most of them, and helped them recognise and develop their talents. [...] Guthrie gave them success and pride but there was not much future for them and they waited until the next production of 'The Three Estates' to make them famous again. Now there is a continuing vitality in the theatre in Scotland and we are doing 'The Three Estates' as part of it, instead of in isolation.[27]

---

[26] Numerous copies of the script – some annotated by members of the production team – are held in the STA – for example STA Gj29.

[27] Bill Bryden quoted by Allen Wright, 'Genesis with a cast of 100', *Scotsman* 20 August 1973, 'Edinburgh Festival Guide' p. ii.

Wright's text was cut even more than Kemp's and was generally interpreted as being closer in tone and sense to Lindsay's. Underlining the production's intention of focusing on the plight of the country and its people, one interesting addition to the second act drama was the recovery of a scene in the second act. Bryden and Wright 'reintroduced an episode deleted in the Guthrie version, in which the pardoner effects a divorce with obscene ritual, and this, together with the cheating of an honest poor man, shows the Church operating in risible fashion'.[28] This choice to focus on a drama of people – and, in particular, ordinary people – did not wholly convince although it was certainly Fulton MacKay's John the Commonweal that found the clearest political voice of the production with his 'splendidly vehement [...] denunciation of pride and oppression' that was 'almost alone [...] in giving Lindsay's superb polemic something of its fullness and force'.[29]

While Michael Coveney found the production 'a superbly integrated performance', Christopher Small saw 'a static costume display, with as much real feeling for times past as for the drama that brings them into the present as we would expect in a Hollywood pageant'.[30] Critics were divided as to the impact of the pomp and circumstance of the production with its processions, banners and trumpet fanfares. However, as had become familiar, most saw rich talent in the comedy – in particular, in this production, Rikki Fulton's turn as Flatterie – although challengingly Small hinted that 'the domesticated satire of pantomime' was undercutting the potential politics of the piece. Opinion, too, was divided on the central dramas of the piece: Coveney was amongst the few who saw 'a real dramatic force' in the human dramas of the narrative.[31]

Only one critic draws parallels between these two alternative productions and, predictably, Christopher Small finds little to redeem Bryden's choices:

> Comparisons are hardest to avoid, not this time with Guthrie's work, but with the magnificent university production of four years ago, which, more faithful, like the present effort to the original text [than Guthrie's], also brought back

---

[28] Michael Coveney, 'The Thrie Estaites', *The Financial Times*, 21 August 1973, p. 3.

[29] Christopher Small, 'Two Cheers for The Thrie Estaites', *Glasgow Herald*, 22 August 1073, p. 11.

[30] Coveney, 'The Thrie Estaites'; and, Small, 'Two Cheers for The Thrie Estaites'.

[31] Coveney, 'The Thrie Estaites'.

and even [...] multiplied the fiery demands sounding through the fun and bawdry, 'Mak reformatioun!'[32]

National heritage

A decade after Bryden's mixed success, the 1984 revival of *Ane Satyre* was commissioned by the incoming EIF director, Frank Dunlop. The production was conceived as a major pillar of his first festival in charge. For one critic it was a (financially) risky choice: 'it takes some nerve to install an often impenetrably Scottish production on the summit of The Mound for the full duration of the festival' observed Irving Wardle in *The Times*.[33] Everything else, however, seemed safe, conservative and risk free. Certainly there was nothing counter-cultural or provocative in Dunlop's choice of text or production team: indeed the production was to a significant degree the very same as Guthrie's – Kemp's script, Davie's music, and major elements of Guthrie's staging in the same distinctive venue were deployed by director Tom Fleming who had even acted in previous productions (as Divine Correction in 1959 and 1973). All this represented an explicit reference to the festival's history and, specifically, an appeal to previous festival successes. However, while connoting past glories and appealing to the festival's heritage, Dunlop also achieved another rather more pragmatic target: staging *Ane Satyre* employed a very large number of Scottish actors and musicians in a festival that was still regularly accused of ignoring indigenous talent, of investing in foreign culture makers not local ones. As in 1948, in 1984 *Ane Satyre* was mobilized to represent Scotland and the EIF to different audiences: not least among them the Scottish cultural community itself.

The revivals of *Ane Satyre* made during the 1980s – in 1984, 1985 and 1986 – were done so under the auspices of the Scottish Theatre Company (STC), a touring organization founded in January 1980 with clear ambitions as to cultural role, national status, and degree of anticipated subsidy. By 1984, and having just about survived some rocky times financially and, to some degree, critically too, the company was, at the very least, 'anxious to come of age'.[34] Presenting this flagship production – closely associated with Guthrie and impossible to dissociate from some of Scotland's best-known actors – at the world's leading arts festival could achieve this. More particularly, however, Fleming wanted the company he was directing to be a 'national' one – such flagship status would certainly have afforded

---

[32] Small, 'Two Cheers for The Thrie Estaites'.

[33] Irving Wardle, 'The Thrie Estaites, Assembly Hall', *The Times*, 14 August 1984, unpaginated press cutting (STA Cm Box 11/11).

[34] Easton, 'The Thrie Estaitis', p. 5.

the company authority, prestige, and funding of a wholly different order. Presenting what was seen as a uniquely Scottish text – in some sense *the* uniquely Scottish text given its pre-Union origins – in a thoroughly tried-and-tested production that involved a cast of Scotland's leading performers in the General Assembly Hall during the Edinburgh Festival very deliberately and very visibly brought together key discourses around the national in terms of representation, profile, location and prestige. More negatively, framed in respect of the festival's heritage, the production was denuded of an immediately relevant politics. The production – and perhaps even more so its 1985 revival and 1986 revival and tour to Warsaw – sought to activate the cultural capital invested in the production in favour of the STC's goal of winning national company status. This was a very contemporary 'use' or deployment of what little there was of Scotland's theatrical heritage while overlooking the strength in diversity that was growing in Scotland's modern theatre culture in Edinburgh and beyond.

But now the production – even more than the play which was little discussed or recognized in reviews – seemed to show its age: 'we had', as the critic Peter Easton put it, 'passed this way before'.[35] Irving Wardle described a show with 'the quality of a well-rehearsed civic pageant'. John Berber of *The Daily Telegraph* witnessed 'a ponderous occasion' with ugly broad comedy suggesting 'the excesses of a feeble provincial pantomime'. In *The Guardian* Joyce McMillan described 'a sequence of couthy comic turns' constituting 'a garish and expensive summer pantomime'.[36] What none of the reviewers identify is a *play*: all the references are to performance practices – the pageant, a pantomime, a series of turns, an occasion or event – in which the literary text is of limited significance and other markers and qualities become more highly valued. In one way this links into previous points about the acting styles valued in the original EIF production but it might also signal a lack of dramaturgical awareness in the production, a lack of textual cohesion, robustness and relevance.

Against a generally negative critical backdrop it is, perhaps, surprising that Dunlop programmed the same team, and the same production, for his second festival in 1985. At that festival, too, critics were not overly enthusiastic, at least to begin: 'it is disappointing to have to report that Frank Dunlop's first major dramatic offering [of the 1985 festival] is yet another revival of Sir David Lindsay's now seven times revived 16th-century satire'. The appeal of a company of dozens of Scottish actors on

---

[35] Easton, 'The Thrie Estaitis', p. 5.

[36] John Barber, 'Ponderous revival of The Thrie Estaites', *The Daily Telegraph*, 14 August 1984, unpaginated press cutting (STA Cm Box 11/11); and, Joyce McMillan, 'Triumph of Scottish virtues', *The Guardian*, 14 August 1985, unpaginated press cutting (STA Cn Box 10/10).

stage in Edinburgh in an increasingly tepid production was beginning to wane. As Easton asked:

> Is the problem perhaps that it is impossible to recreate the spirit of 1948, now that the innovation of the thrust stage is a commonplace, and with the sound of Scots actors speaking the Scots tongue no longer a novelty? [...] In short, the text is revealed, for all its power as a piece of history. The way to bring that alive might be to strip away the pomp of a big spectacular production, that barrier between players and audience. The line between a Satyre and an escapist bourgeois pageant is a very fine stand of gold.[37]

Despite these naysayers the production was a critical and popular success. Barber's review went on to recognize that 'Tom Fleming's production [was] in far better shape than it was last year. More weight is properly given to the play's savage attacks on the church, and the comedians have now learned to control their pantomime excess and are often genuinely amusing.'[38] And yet for all its quality the production remained abstracted from its roots as political theatre and Easton's criticism of 1984 that 'It hardly helps illuminate our present political fortunes' held true.[39] Instead the production had transmogrified into an event, a spectacle, celebratory but narrowly and unquestioningly nationalist, and fatally removed from a role in the increasingly complex and culture-focused debates around 'nation' and 'national' in Scotland at the time.[40] Elsewhere in the culture critics found new modes and models with which to debate Scotland and its social, political and cultural organizations. Scotland's contemporary poets were busy articulating Scotland's national identities as both nostalgic and radical. Filmmakers presented Scotland as quirky and as beautiful. Singers told of Scotland's industrial devastation at the hands of an uncaring Westminster government. Fine artists demanded a reflexive and questioning look at the individual and at place. But this was not the tone of Fleming's production of *Ane Satyre*. This was not a questioning theatre but, instead, one stripped of political bite in favour of a curtailed, neutered existence as an historical, if essentially 'Scottish', oddity. Mapped against developments in the contemporary theatre culture – including a

---

37 Easton, 'The Thrie Estaitis', p. 7.
38 Barber, 'Ponderous revival of The Thrie Estaitis'.
39 Easton, 'The Thrie Estaitis', p. 7.
40 See, for example, Craig Beveridge and Ronald Turnbull, *The Eclipse of Scottish Culture: inferiorism and the intellectuals* (Edinburgh: Polygon, 1989); and David McCrone, Stephen Kendrick and Pat Straw (eds), *The Making of Scotland: Nation, Culture and Social Change* (Edinburgh: Edinburgh University Press, 1989).

new generation of Scottish-based and internationally-facing playwrights at the Traverse, for example – this seemed a poor excuse to raid the dressing up box.

But such a cultural product – for all its old values and conservative modes – had a general appeal and a cultural value, not least to what, in respect of other media, was identified as 'the culturally respectable, quality end of the market'[41] to which the STC was alert. Despite financial problems, and with an inconsistent relationship with the critics, the STC was still intent on securing 'national' status. In this respect one of the company's final hurrahs was a British Council-sponsored tour to Warsaw when it literally 'represented' Scotland in and to another country and did so with a revival of this production of *Ane Satyre*.

Two warm-up performances in Glasgow set a festive, even jingoistic, tone, that compared events to an earlier send-off for World Cup footballers: 'Never since Ally's ill-fated army left Hampden for Argentina in 1978 can a Scottish team, heading abroad, have received such a rapturous send-off.'[42] This was Scottish theatre in its heritage colours away kit. The associations for the European fixture were a combination of literary cachet and theatrical prestige: what was again underplayed to the point of invisibility was the play's potential politics – either in respect of its historical genesis or its place within a modern, contemporary society. This was a play and production accepted as a 'classic' but simultaneously condemned as a 'curiosity'. It might well put some of Scotland's acting talent through their paces in a well-appointed production but it was a production that was hopelessly out of touch with the quotidian reality of Scottish theatre culture and Scottish politics each of which was increasing oppositional to Thatcher's Westminster government and increasingly focused on stories and experiences of modern Scotland.

Two final examples

In the final stages of the push towards devotion – in fact in the last summer of a Conservative government in the UK before Blair's election in May 1997 – two very difference versions of Lindsay's satire were performed in Scotland. One worked hard to recover a relevant politics, the other collapsed into uncritical romp.

---

[41]   Andrew Higson, *English Heritage, English Cinema: Costume Drama since 1980* (Oxford: Oxford University Press, 2003), p. 5.

[42]   Joyce McMillan, 'Thrie Estaitis', *The Guardian*, 17 November 1986, unpaginated press cutting (STA Ct Box 6/12).

Scottish Youth Theatre (SYT) – the one 'national' theatre company at the time – presented *A Satire of the Three Estates* as part of its annual summer production. In a new adaptation by Fiona McGarry and directed by SYT artistic director Mary McCluskey the emphasis was on comedy and explicit parallels were drawn to the popular sit-com figure of 'Rab C Nesbitt':

> Just because its [sic] as auld as the hills disnea mane its [sic] load of boring auld rubbish. Picture Rac C meets a Carry On Film and ye'll no be far wrang. [...] SYT have [sic] got the thing put intae the sort o' Scottish that anybody can understand – well unless they're frae Morningside perhaps – so dinnae worry about missing any of the jokes – or any of the smutty bits either.[43]

In contrast to this essentially apolitical comedy romp – enlivened with some topical references to popular culture – was John McGrath's *A Satire Of The Four Estates* which was produced by Wildcat Theatre Company for the 1996 EIF and played at the then-new Edinburgh International Conference Centre: as in earlier productions far from a traditional theatre space but also inculcated as in the production as 'a shrine to the demonic forces [of international capital] against which McGrath rails'.[44] McGrath's adaptation deliberately sought to reinvent the politics of Lindsay's original play and make them relevant for a modern audience: 'I tried to emulate the original's excoriation of the venality and corruption and abuse of power with characters based on medieval stereotypes: Lord Merde, Sir Righteous Indignation, Ersatz Sensualitie, King Humanity et al.'[45] Lindsay's three estates of the Church, the aristocracy and the merchants become: firstly, the politicians – Thatcher, Major and 'Saviour Blair' are singled out; secondly, the political apparatchiks and the non-elected powers – the eurocrat, the NATO general and the multi-national corporation, NATO; and, thirdly, aspects of British industry – including Cheap Labour, Privatized Industry, Low Taxes. The new fourth estate was the media – Sal Sitcom, Slavering Drool the newspaper hack and, the main focus of the play's vitriolic ire, Lord Merde, an Australian media mogul.

The play was written on the cusp of devolution and in the wider context of the rise of the new nations of Europe and the immense and growing power of global capital: McGrath asks if a small independent

---

[43] Flyer for SYT production *A Satire of the Three Estates* (1996), STA 200/10/1.

[44] Ian Shuttleworth, ' A Satire bursting with vitality' *The Financial Times*, 20 August 1996, p. 11.

[45] John McGrath, *Naked Thoughts that Roam About: reflections on theatre*, ed. Nadine Holdsworth (London: Nick Hern Books, 2002), p. 221.

country – and, in particular, Scotland – could maintain its autonomy or its identity in the face of globalization. Typical of McGrath's vision for political theatre, the production used a raft of popular performance styles: drawing on traditions of the pantomime in terms of sing-alongs; the music hall in comedic tone, stereotype and identities; and even carnivalesque traditions as grotesque masks represented many of the archetypes of his satirical state of the nation debate.

There are competing – not to say contradictory – accounts of the production, which even McGrath himself described as 'a massive sprawling piece'.[46] It certainly seems clear that the production did excellent box office throughout the Festival. What is less clear is the production's critical meanings and reception. In some press accounts – in the reactions of the English press, according to McGrath, the pageant was derided – 'full of noise and shallow clichés', 'crude, predictable and awesomely un funny', 'a silly, coarse and imaginatively monotonous spin-off'.[47] In contrast McGrath identifies *The Scotsman*'s view that it was a 'triumph', and even *The Financial Times* found that while the verse 'sometimes veers into doggerel' the production overall had 'a fearsome energy'.[48] What is, perhaps, more compelling is whether the production was able to reinstate the politics into *Ane Satyre*? The leading Scottish critic Joyce McMillan struggled to reconcile the play's political vision and ambition with its actual form and content: 'Too much of the politics is unargued, as if the assent of the audience to both socialism and nationalism could be taken for granted [...] and the whole spectacle is far too widely focussed to hit any of its satirical targets very hard.'[49] Reflecting on this view the critic Edwin Morgan suggests that McGrath's version of the play is not successful in developing a strong political critique or analysis but, instead, that its politics – or rather its political philosophy – 'has a soft core, and that this appeals to a soft core in the audience'.[50] It is arguably the case that, despite the radical surgery of McGrath's new version, the hard politics of *Ane Satyre* are inevitably lost to a modern audience. Nevertheless, the McGrath/Wildcat adaptation, unlike earlier revivals, did aspire to see – and to use – the play as a political play. For McGrath: 'It was a play

---

[46]   McGrath, *Naked Thoughts that Roam About*, p. 221.

[47]   Edwin Morgan quotes from *The Sunday Times*, *The Daily Telegraph*, and *The Times* in 'Scottish drama; an overview', *ScotLit* 20 (spring, 1999), http://www.arts.gla.ac.uk/ScotLit/ASLS/Scottishdrama.html [web link checked, 18 April 2006].

[48]   Shuttleworth, 'A Satire bursting with vitality', p. 11.

[49]   Morgan, 'Scottish drama; an overview', quotes from Joyce McMillan in *Scotland on Sunday* in 'Scottish drama; an overview'.

[50]   Morgan, 'Scottish drama; an overview'.

about Scottish Devolution, independence and how independent Scotland could be as part of a global economy. It made a kind of symbolic figure of Scotland being born again.'

In fact, the impact and meanings of McGrath's version of Lindsay's satire as a political play became constrained by the wider 'story' of Scottish theatre and cultural politics. This pulled focus from the question of adaptation, cultural relevance and political potency towards funding decisions, political prejudice and cultural policy not least as the production was followed by – or precipitated, depending on one's point of view – a decision by key agency the Scottish Arts Council to cut core funding to the production company Wildcat, a spin-off of 7:84 (Scotland).[51]

Conclusion

Lindsay's plea to 'Mak reformatioun' claims political contemporaneity for *Ane Satyre* despite the passing of the centuries. Concluding his rather vitriolic review of the 1973 production of the play, the Scottish critic Christopher Small reflects that 'even while taking most of the real life out of Lindsay' the play remains tantalisingly close to rediscovery. Indeed, he suggests that Bryden's perceived failure 'puts an end, perhaps, to revivals of his masterpiece as a fancy-dress affair, a parade of historical finery'.[52] Small even proposes that 'Maybe the next [revival] will be in modern dress.'

Ironically the next productions of *Ane Satyre...* were, arguably, even more of the pageant than Bryden's and it was 23 years until McGrath at least attempted to revisit the play with a more contemporary eye and counter-culture ideology. While that re-visioning of the play may not have been the political theatre necessary at the cusp of devolution, Small hints that a contemporary production of Lindsay's reformist text still beckons. It seems an interesting proposition that a 'bare boards' production – or a wholly new dramaturgical take – might reinstate the political into a text that 60 years of modern production has all but reduced to a tired and toothless parody Scottish theatre.

---

[51] McGrath, *Naked Thoughts that Roam About*, pp. 221–5.

[52] Christopher Small, 'Two Cheers for The Thrie Estaites', *Glasgow Herald*, 22 August 1973, p. 11.

CHAPTER 12

A book for Lollards and Protestants: Murdoch Nisbet's New Testament

Martin Holt Dotterweich

I recall a colleague who, upon receiving the new edition of a textbook, would ask his teaching assistant to underline all the same passages in the new copy that he had underlined in the older version. To him, the older version sufficed, and what changes had been wrought to the newer edition could safely be ignored. I have known others who will accept only the newest edition of a book, discounting (and perhaps discarding) all previous editions. Readers occasionally devote themselves to a particular edition, such as the 1611 translation of the Bible, to the exclusion of either older or newer versions. In the case of Scripture, this competition between versions can become fierce, as the quest is not for the *best* version so much as for the *right* one.

In the sixteenth century, the Bible was translated into many languages, in many different versions, and debates about the right version raged across and within confessional boundaries. Erasmus was challenged for his translation into Latin that did not follow the Vulgate; English translator William Tyndale was attacked by Catholic critics for his choice of theological terms; Tyndale in turn attacked George Joye's New Testament for its apparent support of soul-sleep; the Elizabethan Bishops' Bible of 1568 was meant to challenge the popularity of the heavily-annotated Geneva edition of 1560; Miles Coverdale attacked an edition of his own diglot Latin-English New Testament for inaccuracies in printing. Where Bibles were concerned, the question of edition was not taken lightly.

Such debates occasionally affected lay readers, such as when a version was outlawed, or reading rights were restricted to certain estates, as in the latter years of the reign of Henry VIII. But in other cases, lay readers had to negotiate between different editions of the Bible without legal restraint or other compulsion, and such negotiations, if documented, can reveal a great deal about attitudes toward Scripture, theological divisions, and reading habits. Just such an encounter appears in a manuscript New Testament produced in Ayrshire in the late fifteenth or early sixteenth century by the notary public Murdoch Nisbet. Sometime after 1538, Nisbet or one of his circle made a careful comparison between this manuscript and a printed English New Testament, and the result offers insight into the mind of a lay Scot faced with two different versions of Scripture.

Murdoch Nisbet of Hardhill

Murdoch Nisbet (or Nesbit) acted as a notary public in Ayr in the 1530s, and among those for whom he drew up charters were the Campbells of Cessnock and Lockharts of Bar, both families known to have held evangelical beliefs around this time.[1] Through these personal contacts and his location in the parish of Loudoun, Nisbet may have some relationship to the 'Lollards of Kyle', against whom charges were brought in 1494.[2] The 'inexplicable reappearance' of Lollard belief at this stage suggests that Kyle had either seen a recent group of converts or had served as an incubator of Lollard sentiment since the preaching tours of Quintin Folkhyrde in the first decades of the fifteenth century.[3] In either case, Nisbet's physical location and personal contacts associate him generally with both Lollardy and early evangelicalism.

Nisbet's own Lollard attachment was attested long after his death by his descendent James Nisbet (d. 1728). In a pamphlet about his father, the Covenanting martyr John Nisbet, who had been executed on 4 Dec. 1685, James Nisbet opened with an account of his more distant forbear, who '[i]n the Reign of King *James* the IV. sometime before the year 1500' was enlightened by God

> for attaining to the true and saving Principles of Christian Knowledge. His Eyes were opened to see the Vanity and Evil of *Popery*; which, through Grace, instantly inclin'd his Heart to loath it: So he deliberately resolved against it, turn'd from it; and join'd himself with these called *Lollards*, the first Name given to *British* Protestants, whom *Papists* called *Hereticks* ...

Later, in the reign of James V, Murdoch Nisbet encountered persecution and fled 'over Seas, and took a Copy of the New Testament in Writ', returning

---

[1]   See John Anderson (ed.), *Calendar of the Laing Charters A.D. 854–1837* (Edinburgh: James Thin, 1899), p. 102 (no. 390, dated 16 June 1533); George S. Pryde (ed.), *Ayr Burgh Accounts 1534–1624* (Edinburgh: Scottish History Society, 1937), p. 74 (from 1535–36, 'for services to the town, 14s'); National Archives of Scotland MS GD 163 (Portland Muniments) 10/2, sasine for John Lockhart of Bar, 6 Nov. 1531 (for which I am indebted to Margaret Sanderson). On the families, see Margaret H.B. Sanderson, *Ayrshire and the Reformation: People and Change, 1490–1600* (East Linton: Tuckwell, 1997), pp. 42–7.

[2]   *The Works of John Knox*, 6 vols, ed. David Laing (Edinburgh: Wodrow Society, 1846–54): 1.7–11.

[3]   Ian B. Cowan, *The Scottish Reformation: Church and Society in sixteenth-century Scotland* (London: Weidenfeld and Nicolson, 1982), p. 89 (quotation); on Folkhyrde (or Fockhart), Sanderson, pp. 37–8.

with other exiles who would be executed in 1539, Jerome Russell and one Kennedy. Murdoch Nisbet remained safe, however, as he

> digged and built a Vault in the Bottom of his own House, to which he retired himself, serving GOD, and reading his new Book. Thus he continued, instructing some few that had Access to him, until the Death of King *James* the V.

Later, in the regency of Marie de Guise, Murdoch emerged to take part in iconoclastic activity.[4]

Internally, James Nisbet's account presents some difficulties. If it is correct in its dates, Murdoch was old enough in 1500 to profess Lollard belief, but survived until the regency of Marie (1554–60); that he should live so long is believable, but one wonders how much damage the octogenarian iconoclast could inflict. Nisbet's exile is also difficult to assess. The memoir places his flight during the reign of James V, but there is no evidence for religious persecution in Scotland from 1513–25, the first part of the reign, and comparatively little until the mid-1530s. There were episcopal complaints about Bible reading in the diocese of Glasgow sometime during 1524–31, and a flight in the 1520s is possible. The Russell and Kennedy with whom Nisbet returned were apprehended by 7 November 1538 (and burned 1 March 1538/9), offering a *terminus ad quem*.[5] Since Nisbet was working in Ayr from 1531–36, this would leave the possibility for an exile in 1537–38. However, he would surely not have bothered to transcribe a Lollard New Testament at this date, when so many printed editions in English were circulating. The Nisbet family tradition is vague; perhaps Murdoch Nisbet fled in the reign of James IV, or before 1531, when neither persecution nor printed New Testaments were plentiful.

What is certain is that he 'took a Copy of the New Testament in Writ', since the manuscript survives, a Scots translation of the latter version of the Lollard New Testament.[6] Although unsigned by Murdoch Nisbet himself, descendents of his inscribed their names in 1624 and perhaps 1596, and the manuscript was known to some outside the Nisbet family.[7] Moreover,

---

[4] James Nisbet, *A True Relation of the Life and Sufferings of John Nisbet in Hardhill*, 2nd edn (Edinburgh: Robert Brown, 1719), p. 3.

[5] *St Andrews Formulare, 1514–1546*, 2 vols, eds Gordon Donaldson and C. Macrae (Edinburgh: Stair Society, 1942–4), 1.192 (no. 185) (complaints); Knox, *Works*, i.63–6 and notes 6, 8 (Russell and Kennedy).

[6] On the revised Lollard version, see Ann Hudson, *The Premature Reformation: Wycliffite Texts and Lollard History* (Oxford: Oxford University Press, 1988), pp. 238–47.

[7] *The New Testament in Scots*, ed. Thomas Graves Law [and Joseph Hall], 3 vols (Edinburgh: William Blackwood and Sons, 1901–5), 1.viii–ix, 3.314 n. a for the signatures (BL MS Egerton 2880 fol. 234v). Hereafter *NT Scots*. In the

Nisbet's notarial sign manual – a mark unique to each notary public – closely resembles a mark on several verso leaves in the manuscript.[8] Nisbet made his manuscript with some leisure: the English of the later version of the Lollard New Testament is translated into Scots, large initial letters are drawn in three different colours at the beginnings of chapters, running titles run atop the verso leaves and chapter numbers on the rectos. The copying ended rather abruptly in the midst of one of several Old Testament 'epistles' – lectionary readings appended to the manuscript – but the entire New Testament had already been completed.[9]

It is Nisbet's translation of Middle English into Scots that has most interested scholars, and in general this has borne out a 1530 assessment that the language of the Lollards Thorpe and Oldcastle needed updating 'in the english that now is vsed in Engla[n]de / for ower sothern men', but that in 'his owne olde english' it would serve 'bothe for the northern men a[n]d the faythfull brothern of scotla[n]de'.[10] Nisbet's translation demonstrates this affinity between Middle English and Scots, as he left a great deal of the vocabulary unchanged. Other terms are changed regularly, such as *gang* for 'walk', *clepid* for 'called', and *leirit* for 'learned'.[11] It would appear that

---

seventeenth century Wodrow was aware of 'an old Wickliffe's Neu Testament, which had been in the family of Hardhill since the Reformation': Robert Wodrow, *Analecta: Or Materials for a History of Remarkable Providences*, ed. Matthew Leishman, 4 vols (Edinburgh: Maitland Club, 1842–3), 3.518.

[8]   BL MS Egerton 2880, fols 24v, 36v, 107v, 131v, 155v, 191v, 215v, 227v. The foliation cited here is that most recently added to the MS; to arrive at the folio reference in *NT Scots*, subtract three from the MS folio number given here. On the sign manual, see John Durkan, 'The early Scottish Notary', in *The Renaissance and Reformation in Scotland: Essays in honour of Gordon Donaldson*, eds Ian B. Cowan and Duncan Shaw (Edinburgh: Scottish Academic Press, 1983), pp. 22–40 (pp. 27–8). Durkan notes that notaries public by imperial and apostolic authority had to take vows of loyalty to the Pope and the Church.

[9]   The abrupt end of the manuscript is not due to damage; on the verso of this leaf are the signatures of the later Nisbet owners of the manuscript: BL MS Egerton 2880, fol. 234r; *NT Scots* 3.314. The OT epistle which is left incomplete is Gen. 27.6–39.

[10]   [William Tyndale?], *Examinacion of Master William Thorpe*, facsmilie reprint of 1530 edn (Amsterdam: Theatrum Orbis Terrarum, 1975), fol. Aii.v.

[11]   T.M.A. Macnab, 'The New Testament in Scots', *Records of the Scottish Church History Society* 11 (1951): 82–103 (pp. 85–8); Graham Tulloch, *A History of the Scots Bible* (Aberdeen: Aberdeen University Press, 1989), p. 8; David F. Wright, '"The Commoun Buke of the Kirke": The Bible in the Scottish Reformation', in David F. Wright (ed.), *The Bible in Scottish Life and Literature* (Edinburgh: St Andrew Press, 1988), pp. 155–78 (pp. 156–60). These and other assessments have dealt with the linguistic issues: see also W.I.P. Hazlett, 'Nisbet, Murdoch', in David F. Wright *et al.* (eds), *Dictionary of Scottish Church History and Theology* (Edinburgh: T&T Clark, 1993); T.G. Law's introduction to *NT Scots*, 1.xiv–xvi; Sanderson, *Ayrshire*, pp. 42–3; Paul Wiechert, 'Über die Sprache der einzigen schottischen Bibelübersetzung von Murdoch Nisbet' (unpublished

Nisbet, perhaps while abroad, had access to a Lollard New Testament, and time to copy and translate it, surely having in mind its use back in Scotland.

Two New Testaments

At some later date, Nisbet's manuscript was augmented with an adaptation of Luther's prologue to the New Testament and preface to the book of Romans, 203 marginal glosses, many marginal references, a 'Summe' of each book, and liturgical reading markers. Like the text of the Bible, all this material is translated into Scots. Whether Nisbet made these additions is uncertain; the handwriting is less careful and does not feature the flourishes of the original transcription, though at the bottom of the penultimate leaf (part of the 'Summe'), upside down, the name 'Hew Campbell of lowdoun' appears with a mark to its left.[12] As Sheriff of Ayr, Campbell might well have used Nisbet's professional services; this could be an old notarial minute-sheet being re-used. If so, it would suggest more strongly that the same Nisbet who translated the New Testament made these additions to the text. For the sake of simplicity, it will be assumed that the copyist of these additional materials was a Nisbet.

All the additional material has a single source, a New Testament of Miles Coverdale, printed sometime in late 1537 or early 1538 in Southwark by James Nicolson, a glazier from the Low Countries who undertook several commissions for Coverdale at the time.[13] This was one of many editions

---

doctoral thesis, Albertus University, Königsberg, 1908); less directly, Thomas M. Lindsay, 'A Literary Relic of Scottish Lollardy', *Scottish Historical Review* 1 (1904): 260–73.

[12] BL MS Egerton 2880, fol. 253v; *NT Scots* 3.355n.

[13] STC 2838 (other edns 2838.3 and 2839). The reason that this was not identified in previous assessments of Nisbet is largely because the Scottish Text Society's chosen editor, Thomas Graves Law, became ill and died during the production of the second of three volumes (this is mentioned in the 'Prefatory Note' to vol. 3). Law's primary focus in editing was comparison to the text of the Vulgate (see *NT Scots* 1.xxix–xxx), and he did not even mention the marginal material in his preface to vol. 1. Law's successor, Joseph Hall, completed the edition primarily in accordance with this policy. However, Hall also compared the text of the preface to Romans with English editions, and came into contact with three printings of the Coverdale New Testament – hampered, however, by the lack of a title-page for any surviving copy. Thus he knew that the preface to Romans was directly translated from this single source, but he only alludes to this in a footnote by referring to 'N., the book from which the transcript was copied': *NT Scots* 3.314 n.b. Hall was not aware that the prologue, the Summe, and all marginalia also came from this edition. The source was first identified in the entry on Murdoch Nisbet in the ODNB.

of the New Testament in English available from 1534 on, and there is no reason to believe that it was particularly singled out by Nisbet among others; it was probably simply what he had available. These, then, are the New Testaments between which Nisbet had to negotiate: his Lollard New Testament, translated into Scots some time earlier, and a printed New Testament with additional material meant to explain hard passages and provide a theological framework for reading.

The late date of the additional material raises some difficult questions. Was Nisbet's conventicle still using his Lollard manuscript in the late 1530s? His decision to translate and transcribe this material to his manuscript suggests that he thought this would be useful for group reading; although readers of Scots could read books in English, the translation would simplify reading aloud. Perhaps, with this in view, he would even have chosen to use a Scots manuscript over a printed English New Testament; this would be clearer if it were known whether he owned the Coverdale edition. And did Nisbet intend his augmented manuscript to be used only by his own conventicle, or did he have publication in mind? It is surely not unreasonable to suggest that a printed version of the New Testament in Scots was in view for the transcriber. As Parliament had permitted the use of vernacular versions of the Bible in Scotland from 1543, the obstacles would have been practical rather than legal. However, no steps appear to have been taken in this direction.

In spite of the uncertainties, the manuscript yields up Nisbet's primary concern in textual negotiation: the clarity of his book. He clearly admired the aids to the reader in the printed Coverdale New Testament, but did not in general regard its text as superior to that of his manuscript. In the course of his transcription of marginal glosses and references, Nisbet went through the text of most of the New Testament with both manuscript and printed copy in front of him, and despite differences between the two he made few changes to his original. An exception is the word *sacrament*, which Lollard translators had used for the Vulgate's *sacramentum*. Following Erasmus's 1516 translation of the Greek *musterion* into the Latin *mysterium* or *arcanum*, Miles Coverdale (like Tyndale) used the English words *mystery* or *secret*, and Nisbet therefore changed some nine instances of *sacrament* to *sacrait* in his Scots manuscript.[14] This change had theological implications,

---

[14] Changes at Eph. 1.9 (2X, though the second instance was based on a mistranslated pronominal referent in the Lollard original: *NT Scots* 2.228 n. 9), 3.3, 3.9, 5.32; Col. 1.27; 1 Tim. 3.16; Rev. 1.20, 17.7. In referring to passages by book and chapter for the *NT Scots*, it should be noted that the books do not follow the modern order, and occasionally the versification differs slightly. For Erasmus's translation, *Novvm instrumentu[m] omne, diligenter ab Erasmo Roterdamo recognitum & emendatum* (Paris: Johannes Froben, 1516), at references and

since it challenged the sacramental understanding of marriage based on Eph. 5.32.

A more famous difference between the Vulgate and Erasmian translations concerned the Greek word *metanoeite*: the Vulgate's *paenitentiam agite* suggested penance to sixteenth-century readers, so Erasmus opted for *resipiscite*, which more accurately conveyed the sense of repentance.[15] Again, this was theologically charged, and the use of *repent* instead of 'do penance' could be seen as an attack on the practice of penance. To make his translation seem less controversial, therefore, Coverdale had translated some ten instances of the word with '[do] penance', noting in his 1535 Bible that 'we abhorte not this worde penaunce', but that it meant 'a very repe[n]taunce, ame[n]dment, or conuersyon vnto God'.[16] In the *loci classici* for the word, Mt. 3.2 and 4.17, however, he had used 'Ame[n]de your selues' and 'Repente', respectively. It is indicative of Nisbet's preference for his original text that he did not in fact change any instances of 'do penance' in spite of Coverdale's usage.[17]

Not only did Nisbet keep the text of his manuscript almost unchanged, he also omitted four of Coverdale's marginal glosses which did not apply to it. In Coverdale's New Testament, Mt. 10.3 refers to the disciple Lebbeus, and a gloss explains that this is Jude; since the Lollard text referred to 'Thadee', Nisbet simply omitted the note rather than change his text to suit it. In two instances, the Lollard translation already explained a word which required explanation by Coverdale: for 'mammon' in Lk. 16.9, Nisbet's text offered 'the richesse of wickitnes', and for 'syrtes' in Acts 27.17 it provided 'sandy places'. So Nisbet did not translate these notes. At 1 Cor. 14.2, Coverdale's gloss explained that speaking in the Spirit was speaking by oneself, but the Lollard translation had the Spirit as the subject of the sentence, and the note was unnecessary.[18] In several other cases, when the

---

pp. 523, 533 (on marriage). Erasmus did use *sacramentum* for *musterion* at Rev. 1.20 and 17.7, though in his third edition he changed the latter.

[15] Erasmus actually used 'poeniteat vos' at Mt. 3.2 and 4.17 in his first edition, but he notes, 'Meo iudicio commode uerti poterat, Respiscite, siue ad mentem redite': Erasmus, *Novum instrumentum*, p. 241.

[16] *The Coverdale Bible 1535*, intro. by S.L. Greenslade (Folkestone: Dawson, 1975), pp. 15–16, 42. See also J.F. Mozley, *Coverdale and his Bibles* (London: Lutterworth, 1953), pp. 105–6.

[17] One other change to the manuscript based on Coverdale, not controversial, was the addition of 'bot deliuer vs fra ewill' to the paternoster at Lk. 11.4.

[18] In one case, Nisbet modified Coverdale's gloss on 'body of this death' at Rom. 7.24 to make it fit with his text, 'body of this syn'.

foreign terms were in his translation as well, Nisbet used Coverdale's gloss, such as *proselytes* in Acts 2.10 or *legions* in Mt. 26.53.[19]

Confronted with different translations, Nisbet seems on the whole to have been unconcerned. Particular words differed consistently, but he only opted to change one of them throughout his text, showing that he did not assume the printed Coverdale version rendered his own obsolete or even deficient. Nor did Nisbet make changes to accommodate the exotic terms in Coverdale which did not appear in the Lollard version; since his text made these clear, the notes could be left out.

Marginal notes and the negotiation between versions

However, when it came to explanation of the text, Nisbet made a careful translation of Coverdale's glosses and marginal references, and clearly found them useful. In the Nicolson printings of Coverdale's New Testament, pointing hands in the margin indicate that a gloss will appear at the end of the chapter, where the comment follows a short phrase from the text. Nisbet transcribed the annotations in red in the margins of his manuscript.[20] A great many of these notes, with their ultimate provenance in Luther's 1536 Bible or the Matthew Bible of 1537, provide a guide to passages that would confuse someone new to the reading or hearing of Scripture.[21]

For example, readers might wonder why the genealogy of Jesus Christ in Mt. 1 begins with Abraham and David, rather than Adam. This, the gloss explains, is 'because that Christe was specially promised vnto them to be of their sede'. Why had Jesus told Mary Magdalene not to touch him in the garden in Jn 20.17? 'Jt apperis that Mary Magdalene belewed nocht yit steadfastly that Christ was rysin weray God, and tharfor forbad he hir to tuiche him', explains Coverdale, whereas 'other wemmen that wer

---

[19]   On the legion, Coverdale's gloss suggested that this was around 6000 men, but Nisbet adjusted this to the more apocalyptically suggestive 'sex thousand sex hundreth lxvi'.

[20]   Many of the marginal additions to Nisbet's manuscript have been damaged, but in all cases they may be completed neatly with reference to Coverdale's notes. Thus many notes are incomplete in *NT Scots*. Coverdale's marginal glosses were distributed unevenly across the New Testament: fully a fourth appear in Matthew, and none for several books. This was a work in progress for Coverdale, and it was slightly modified in later editions printed in Antwerp.

[21]   There is virtually no scholarly mention of the Coverdale New Testament editions of 1537/8; I am preparing an article on them based on ch. 2 and app. 1 of my dissertation, 'The emergence of evangelical theology in Scotland to 1550' (unpublished PhD dissertation, Edinburgh University, 2002).

nocht carnell myndit onn him, he sufferit them to twych him'. Why was Satan called the god of this world in 1 Cor. 4.4? 'Satann is Godis minister, and can do na mair nor he appoynttis him ado. Neuirtheless, … heir the apostil callis him the God of this warld … for vnto quhomm sa euir we obey, we mak him our God.' Examples of this sort of explanation abound, and Nisbet copied them studiously.

Some glosses address questions which seem rather quaint, and these were surely aimed at first-time readers. Nisbet includes these, even though his reading circle had been reading the New Testament for some time. When Paul instructs the Romans to make no provision for the flesh in Rom. 13.14, a reassuring gloss states, 'Euiry man may mak honest prouisiounn for his body and vse the creaturis of Gode, for tha ar all gude … as lang as tha vse thame for necessite, ande nocht for the lustis of the fleische.' Likewise, prayer without ceasing, commanded in 1 Thes. 5.17, was explained in the gloss as being like the wish of a prisoner for release, or an invalid for health: the Christian always had a 'vehement desire of the hart towarttis Gode', not 'mony wordis'. In Mt. 20.15, the lord of the vineyard asks 'Quhethir thin ee is wickit, fore I am gude?', which is glossed as 'sum strange maner of speiking, and is alss mekill as to saye, Lukkis thow frawart of ewill becauss I am gud[?]' It was not, in any case, a reference to the evil eye.

Nisbet's negotiation between New Testaments shows his fundamental satisfaction with the text of his Lollard manuscript, but also his sense that the addition of Coverdale's glosses would be helpful to his conventicle or perhaps even other Scots. How might his reading circle have reacted to this new apparatus? The notes provide a comforting pastoral authority, and show Coverdale's sensitivity toward simple lay study of the Bible, but how would a group so long engaged with Scripture have accepted this? The fact that Nisbet transcribed the notes as carefully as he did suggests that they would welcome this addition, which helps illustrate a second negotiation the translator faced.[22]

---

[22] Nisbet did make mistakes, though they are the exception that proves the rule of his care in copying. At 1 Cor. 7.21, he inserted an extra negative ('gif a seruande cann *nocht* agre with his maistir', italics mine); at Heb. 6.4 he mistranscribed 'denyeth no possibilite' as 'denyis na impossibilite'. Most dangerously, at 1 Cor. 7.23 Paul enjoins the Corinthians not to be the servants of men, and Coverdale clarifies that all should give due obedience, including subjects to princes, but Nisbet omitted this phrase, having skipped from *subject* ahead to *servant* as he copied the text. Hence Nisbet reads 'euiry subiect [obe]ye his maister' and makes no mention of princes. However, other notes on obedience are transcribed, and the omission was not deliberate. The MS is damaged, but it is clear that the phrase was omitted: BL MS Egerton 2880, fol. 122v.

Two theologies

As Nisbet augmented his manuscript with Coverdale's glosses and prefaces, he also negotiated between theologies. Similar in many respects, Lollardy and Protestantism were not identical, and their differences of emphasis as well as their disagreements faced Nisbet in his editorial task. By the time he began his work, not earlier than late 1537, Nisbet was surely aware of the new theology of salvation being disseminated in Scotland by books and dissident clergy, so this was probably not his first encounter with justification by faith alone and the implications for Christian life that flowed from it. Still, there was a negotiation to be made, since Lollard belief did not include (nor did it preclude) this position.

Nisbet translated the prologue and preface to Romans, both of which had their ultimate provenance in Luther but had been modified by Coverdale and Tyndale, respectively. The prologue immediately offers a pithy summary of justification: the gospel is the joyous news that Christ has 'deliuerit, iustifiit and savit thaim that beleve in Him w[ithout] ony of thaire deseruyng'.[23] The Romans preface, perhaps the most widely disseminated Protestant tract in English, defines faith as 'lyffly ande steadfast traist in the fauour of Gode' rather than 'mannis opinion ande dramme'. Such faith cannot fail to 'wyrk all wayis gude werkis without ceassing'.[24] The Romans preface distinguishes in detail the difference between law and gospel, following Luther.[25] Nisbet copied all this material as well as many marginal glosses which reinforce their central theological thrust, showing his thorough reception of the evangelical doctrine of salvation.

While Nisbet found justification by faith alone congenial if rather new, other glosses in the printed Coverdale New Testament would have been comfortably familiar. The reading of Scripture, for which Nisbet himself had gone to such lengths, is reinforced by the gloss at Jn 5.39 that the faithful ought 'always to excerse them selfis in the scripture, ethyr be redyng, be

---

[23]   *NT Scots* 1.2.

[24]   *NT Scots* 3.325–7.

[25]   Tyndale made some changes to the Romans Preface which modify Luther's radical distinction of law and gospel by suggesting something like the Reformed 'third use of the law' as a guide for Christian life: L.J. Trinterud, 'A Reappraisal of William Tyndale's Debt to Martin Luther', *Church History*, xxxi (1962), 24–45. However, 'the differences between the Lutheran and the Reformed doctrine of the uses of the law is not as easy for historical research to define as it was for confessional polemics': Jaroslav Pelikan, *The Christian Tradition*, 5 vols (Chicago: University of Chicago Press, 1971–89), 4.215. The distinction here is fine, and if any of Nisbet's circle had discerned differences regarding the *tertius usus legis*, these would have given them no more trouble than the tensions between the books of Romans and James which they had encountered for years.

exhorting, or teaching other'. The prologue likewise commended Bible-reading: 'quha saeuire dois sa rede or heir Goddis [wor]d that the hale lust and desyre of his hert is to leve thareftir, [the] same vndirstandis quhat is red, and is na vayne herar'.[26]

Another central issue for Lollards was the denial of transubstantiation, and if less emphatic on that point, Coverdale's glosses were nevertheless in accord. When in Jn 6.53 Jesus states that no one had life without eating his flesh and drinking his blood, the note states that '[t]his chaptur speikis not of the sacrament of the body and blude of Crist, bot of the spiritual eating namely, of faith'. This was not least because 'els wer our chyldren dampned that ar nocht abile to receaue the sacrament'.

Polemical attacks on the hierarchy of the church were common amongst Lollards, and mild reinforcement could be found in Coverdale's glosses. For his part, Coverdale was hoping for royal license, and did not want to alienate Henry VIII, but in 1537–38 this left the regular clergy fair game. Hence 'the strayte lyues of monkes and frerers' are false mourning at Mt. 9.15, clerical celibacy was 'aganiss the manifest worde of Gode' at 1 Cor. 7.35, and monastic obedience is a violation of Christian freedom at 1 Cor. 7.23. More importantly for Lollards, the 'pape and his cumpanye' were the abomination of desolation at Mt. 24.15. Here, Nisbet's negotiation between texts presented no difficulty.

The majority of the material that Nisbet transcribed from the Coverdale New Testament had to do with salvation, which he clearly found congenial; on points which were less fully covered, there were strong affinities with Lollard belief and practice. The theological negotiation seems primarily a matter of emphasis rather than of content. Nisbet thus resembles other Lollards who adopted evangelical positions on salvation, who 'do not seem to have seen themselves as undergoing any kind of conversion, but simply to have incorporated some new ideas into their existing framework'.[27]

But on one point Nisbet refused to negotiate. At Mt. 5.34, Jesus forbade swearing, and Coverdale's gloss softens the prohibition: swearing by one's self was forbidden, but 'whan ye honoure of God, loue, necessite or wealth of a mans neghboure requyreth, it is well done'. Uniquely, Nisbet simply omits this note. This cannot have been an oversight for the careful copyist; it was a refusal to give up the general prohibition on

---

[26] *NT Scots* 1.5.

[27] Alec Ryrie, *The Gospel and Henry VIII* (Cambridge: Cambridge University Press, 2003), p. 234. Evangelicals could use Lollard texts as well, adding in solafideist elements: see D.S. Dunnan, 'A Note on John Gough's *The Dore of Holy Scripture*', *Notes and Queries* 36 (1989), 309–10.

swearing which Lollards tended to espouse.[28] In this case the negotiation between theological positions was equivocal; however enthusiastically Nisbet copied Coverdale's prefaces and annotations, he did not feel himself obliged to deny the Lollard position on swearing simply because the printed New Testament's note suggested that there were cases in which it was acceptable. On the other hand, this impasse in textual negotiation did not affect the whole in any way, nor did Nisbet feel it necessary to gloss Mt. 5.34 differently. In the end, Nisbet appears to have embraced evangelical theology without compromising his Lollard distinctives.

Reading habits

In England, most Lollards became evangelicals; in Scotland, where evidence for Lollardy is scarce, Murdoch Nisbet's experience shows the same pattern. In his negotiation between a Lollard manuscript and a printed New Testament, he offers some clues about how he read Scripture. First, Nisbet did not assume that the newer, printed New Testament was necessarily superior to his older manuscript. Nor did he give absolute preference to the Lollard translation, as he changed the word *sacrament* on the basis of his textual comparison. It would appear that he did not see any competition between the two books in front of him. However, certain negotiations had to be made; while he copied numerous explanatory annotations, he did not bother to do so if they were unnecessary in light of the translation he had already made. Likewise, the single instance of a disagreement between the evangelical notes and Nisbet's Lollard belief could simply be ignored; it did not discredit the rest of the annotations or the theology that lay behind them.

Faced with two New Testaments, Murdoch Nisbet's primary interest was intelligibility, whether in his concern to translate the text into Scots or his painstaking addition of Coverdale's helpful explanatory material. This to him was the most important aspect of reading – which was after all a group activity – and it also demonstrates how firm the bridge from Lollardy to evangelicalism was. In addition to their theological affinities, Nisbet the Lollard shared a concern for clarity with Coverdale the evangelical, and this laid a sure path for the two theological positions to merge in Kyle in the 1530s and 1540s. The *right* version of Scripture was the one that was clearest to its readers.

We may imagine Murdoch Nisbet, or one of his relations or friends, seated at a table, carefully transcribing from the octavo Coverdale New

---

[28]   Ryrie, *Gospel and Henry VIII*, pp. 76–9; Hudson, *Premature Reformation*, pp. 158, 371–4.

Testament into his own well-worn manuscript, an act which shows not only his concern for clarity but also his general attitude to Scripture. Bible-reading lay at the heart of both Lollard and evangelical practice, and the copyist was working to ensure that it would continue in his own conventicle; perhaps he had a much larger distribution in mind. As it happened, a great increase in the printing of New Testaments and complete Bibles took place in the latter 1530s, and the Nisbet New Testament would fade into obscurity as these English editions made their way into Scotland. But Nisbet's work stands as a testament to the close affinities between Lollard and evangelical Bible-reading, the enthusiasm with which a Scottish Lollard embraced justification by faith alone, and his lingering adherence to Lollard distinctives when a theological disagreement with an evangelical arose.

Whether later Lollard belief existed in Scotland outside the circle of Campbells, Lockharts, and Nisbets of Ayrshire is doubtful.[29] But the influence of these Lollards-cum-evangelicals would affect the entire nation. With them George Wishart would find a safe haven during his preaching tours of the 1540s; among them John Knox would be active in the 1550s. Their reading habits and theological priorities led them to welcome the Protestant preachers, and shaped Scottish Protestantism as a whole.[30]

---

[29] The lone reference to later Lollard practice outside the southwest is to one John Andrew Duncan in Fife, but the account is from the 1640s and presents considerable internal inconsistencies. It is described in note to the entry on Daniel Duncan in Andrew Kippis et al., *Biographia Britannica*, 5 vols, 2nd edn (London: John Nichols, 1778–93), 5.492–6, n. A.

[30] I am grateful to John Craig McDonald and Alec Ryrie for their helpful input on this article. Most particularly, I am grateful to the late David Wright, who cheerfully read and commented on this while very ill, and whose gracious supervision of my doctoral work was one of the greatest gifts I will ever be given.

A few concluding observations

David George Mullan

So we come to the end of a book, and it behoves us to ask ourselves, both essayists and readers, to what useful purpose can this enterprise direct us? It is obvious that, frequently, literature specialists and historians are mining the same ore. The effective study of literature cannot be other than historical, while historians read writings of diverse genres, leading to both contrasting and complementary kinds of scholarship and interpretation. In fact, at some times it is difficult to tell scholars of history and literature apart, but at other times the two species seem to speak different languages. If Gribben's introductory essay is built on ground familiar to the historian, some of the other literary scholars have supplied essays which require a close reading for the traditional historian to penetrate a technical language which may be quite foreign.

Christianity is a logocentric religion, meaning that the *Logos*, Word – comprehending Christ, Bible, sermon – is central, and that doctrinal expression is a natural outcome of reflection upon the substance of language. Thus it is inevitable that Church – and related political – reform is to a great extent a question of language – rethinking the meaning of the Bible, establishing new hermeneutical methods, re-evaluating the nature of pastoral ministry and of kingship (Stilma), and redefining the very tongue of expression. To medieval Catholics that language was Latin for liturgy and (generally) for Bible. In the late medieval period, especially after Wyclif and Hus, vernacular Bibles generated a good deal of suspicion and were frequently identified with heresy. From the very beginning Protestants insisted upon putting the Bible into the language and the hands of the common folk. In Scotland, however, that still represented a difficulty, and not just because of the Gaelic culture of the Highlands and the Isles. Indeed little attention was given by the early reformers to this cultural zone, not least because only one of the first generation of leaders could speak the language. John Carswell, superintendent of Argyll and then Marian, but nonetheless Protestant, bishop of the Isles, translated the Book of Common Order in 1567. Well into the next century this relative neglect remained, with 'Irish' speakers in continued short supply for ecclesiastical work. More to the point is that in the Lowlands there was dispute about the use of English by some Protestants, notoriously John Knox, in place of Scots, a cognate language and not unlike the spoken language of Northumberland, but in some respects significantly divergent from the queen's English. Of course learnèd Scots could speak both, and ministers might indeed preach in Scots and write in English, the latter perhaps determined by the greater marketplace for published divinity south of the Borders. Knox, notoriously, spoke Southron (Dossena), and also sent his sons to be educated in the south. Thus was his patriotism suspect in the ears of his Catholic critics, but this was not a time for Protestants to be shy of English support or to question the value of a ready-made Bible in a known tongue and it was the Geneva Bible (1560) which was crucial to Protestantism's advance in Scotland. It was first published in Scotland in 1579 (the Bassandyne Bible), followed by a revision in 1610. These were both folios, and it was only in 1633 that an octavo edition of the Authorized Version was published, and a pocket Bible in 1638. An 'Irish' or classical literary Gaelic New Testament was published in 1602, and the Old Testament followed in 1685. The language was accessible to the literati, though the script might have proven a challenge. A Scots Gaelic New Testament appeared in 1767 and the complete Bible in 1801. A complete Scots edition appeared only in 1901, the same year that Nisbet's 1520s version (Dotterweich) was published.[1]

The essays in this collection manifest the liveliness and diversity of Scotland's reformation culture. Written by a disparate group of early-modern scholars in two disciplines, these essays do not construct a one-track narrative of religion, language, and culture. A convincing narrative depicting the literary culture of the time must deal with a number of complexities of not only language in a general sense, but also form, argument, vocabulary. Such a narrative must address a plethora of competing trajectories with a variety of meanings for the formation of both personal and national identities, questions which remained unanswered at least until the end of the direct Stewart line in 1714, and even then there remained three Christian trajectories, Catholic, Episcopalian, and Presbyterian, and at least the latter two suffered from deep internal divisions, with Presbyterians on the cusp of further fragmentation. The literature of the reformation period, while not covering such a broad spectrum as the contemporary literature of England, continues to exercise an influence and to stimulate the imagination four hundred years and more after the fact.

If nothing else, lamentations about the reformation having killed off literature are clearly *passé*. Religious polemic may not be to everyone's taste any more than some other genre, but a subjective judgement does not

---

[1]   For an important collection of essays relevant to this theme, David F. Wright (ed.), *The Bible in Scottish Life and Literature* (Edinburgh: Saint Andrew Press, 1988), and especially the essays by Donald Meek and David Wright; and Graham Tulloch, *A History of the Scots Bible* (Aberdeen: Aberdeen University Press, 1989).

deprive this literature of its quality, its enduring value, and even its charm. In any event, polemic does not encompass the entirety of the Scottish reformation's canon, even if the ambiguities of theology may be felt nearly throughout. By means of its symbolism and metaphor, religion plumbs the depths of human experience and provides an intellectual structure and vocabulary for treating the greatest questions confronting humanity. Religion in the sixteenth century did not stifle and constrict human imagination, but rather enabled it, though not always without some dire results for this literature is the product of conflict and the quest to achieve something better, if not an ideal form.

Our essays deal with several over-arching questions. These include: thinking about the nature of the church, the position of the country, and, of course, the self. Ambiguity abounds, as manifested in the life and work of Alexander Montgomerie (Sweetnam). Likewise one may view here the extent of the reformation's impact across time. Through all these complexities the impact of the Bible remains a constant. It was the fundamental means of communication in the time of reformation, and the Reformed interpretation of it remained a potent feature of Scottish life and literature as one may see, however negatively, in James Hogg and George Douglas Brown.

There is an ambiguity in the sum of this book. It shows us a number of divergent trajectories beginning from the Bible – no mean source for the literary-minded in any time or place, and every artful use of the Bible is bound to lead to a level of sophistication given the multi-layered and multi-valenced nature of that ancient library. Even if it were the sole source of metaphor, writers would still have in their hands a rich and vast source of literary material. But there lies here also the potential for a new unity of focus upon two remarkable craftsmen, namely Sir David Lindsay of the Mount (Piesse, Scullion) and John Knox (Almasy, Farrow). These men produced the two most enduring pieces of native literature of the Scottish reformation, namely *Ane Satyre of the Thrie Estaitis* and the *History of the Reformation in Scotland*. Not that they did not write other works – the nineteenth-century edition of Knox's writings runs to six volumes, Lindsay's *oeuvre* contains a number of skilful productions, and we must not be oblivious of the continental prominence both for form and content of Buchanan's works (Allan). However, in terms of reach, the pre-eminence of these two particular literary items can hardly be gainsaid. Lindsay really had no vernacular competitor – being in the royal retinue did his career no harm – and while Knox's *History* has awarded him a centrality in the early reform movement which historians sometimes remind us is artificial, the very fact of his productivity combined with no mean skill in presenting his case succeeds in returning him once again to a justly ascribed place of prominence on the sixteenth-century horizon and in the literary canon. He is not the sum total of the Scottish Reformation, but one can hardly conceive of that event without him standing tall as he does in the quadrangle at New College.

However, even if one were, imprudently, to reduce the horizon to a couple of individuals, one still does not do away with complexity. When Knox identifies himself as a biblical trumpeter, there are four different metaphorical uses of the instrument in scripture, and Knox does not restrict himself to a single biblical trope in any event. His effective argumentation can be construed according to the classical traditions of oratory, and so one may regard him as a mirror of the cultural complexities of the sixteenth century. The same might be said of the employment of rhetorical arts by Hume of Godscroft (Reid).

And so in the modern world Lindsay continues to find directors and players and audiences, and the literati continue to disport themselves with Knox, though too frequently without the kind of insights represented in these essays where authors demonstrate the capacity for more sympathetic analysis in the place of personalized diatribe.

As a linguistic phenomenon, the reformation in Scotland was, as elsewhere, a pluralistic movement both drawing from varied sources and pointing to divergent destinations (Mullan). Protestant writers drew on more than one theological and ecclesiastical tradition, and the relative value they placed upon Christian Antiquity did much to prescribe their places in the emerging Protestant schism.[2] These essays join with a growing spate of revaluation of the Scottish Reformation from varied perspectives over the past half-century, and their liveliness will ensure that that stimulating enterprise will be nourished for years to come.

Scotland was, as noted, an importer of religious culture, but also functioned as an exporter. Buchanan and later contributors wrote neo-Latin poetry of a high calibre, contributing to that literary stream in western Europe, while Henry Lok returned to his native England having been influenced by poetic forms of the Scottish court, and thereby exercising a seminal role in the further development of English religious poetry (Serjeantson).

And so we come to the end of a book, and nearer the beginning of a re-assessment of the Scottish reformation from a variety of angles, but, at least in intent, avoiding the denominational. Not that the story and its literature ought to be excluded from both nurturing and challenging the beliefs and practices of modern communities of faith. That narrative, however, belongs to no single group, and so may, like Lindsay, challenge an entire society in its moral and intellectual self-satisfaction.

---

[2]   David George Mullan, *Scottish Puritanism, 1590–1638* (Oxford: Oxford University Press, 2000), 234–40.

Index

St Andrews Studies in Reformation History

Editorial Board: Bruce Gordon, Andrew Pettegree and Roger Mason,
St Andrews Reformation Studies Institute,
Amy Nelson Burnett, University of Nebraska at Lincoln,
Euan Cameron, Union Theological Seminary, New York and
Kaspar von Greyerz, University of Basel

*The Shaping of a Community: The Rise and Reformation of the English
Parish c. 1400–1560*
Beat Kümin

*Seminary or University? The Genevan Academy and Reformed Higher
Education, 1560–1620*
Karin Maag

Marian Protestantism: Six Studies
Andrew Pettegree

Protestant History and Identity in Sixteenth-Century Europe
(2 volumes) edited by Bruce Gordon

*Antifraternalism and Anticlericalism in the German Reformation:
Johann Eberlin von Günzburg and the Campaign against the Friars*
Geoffrey Dipple

*Reformations Old and New: Essays on the Socio-Economic
Impact of Religious Change c. 1470–1630*
edited by Beat Kümin

Piety and the People: Religious Printing in French, 1511–1551
Francis M. Higman

The Reformation in Eastern and Central Europe
edited by Karin Maag

John Foxe and the English Reformation
edited by David Loades

The Reformation and the Book
Jean-François Gilmont, edited and translated by Karin Maag

The Magnificent Ride: The First Reformation in Hussite Bohemia
Thomas A. Fudge

Heinrich Heshusius and the Polemics of Early Lutheran Orthodoxy
Confessional Conflict and Jewish-Christian Relations in
North Germany, 1556–1597
Michael J. Halvorson